Excel® Advanced Report Development

Excel® Advanced Report Development

Timothy Zapawa

Wiley Publishing, Inc.

Excel® Advanced Report Development

Published by
Wiley Publishing, Inc.
10475 Crosspoint Boulevard
Indianapolis, IN 46256
www.wiley.com

Copyright © 2005 by Wiley Publishing, Inc., Indianapolis, Indiana

Published simultaneously in Canada

ISBN: 0-7645-8811-7

Manufactured in the United States of America

10 9 8 7 6 5 4 3 2 1

1MA/RR/QX/QV/IN

Library of Congress Cataloging-in-Publication Data: Available from the Publisher

For Lisa

About the Author

Timothy Zapawa (Darnestown, Maryland) obtained a baccalaureate in Accounting and Arabic from the University of Michigan in Ann Arbor in 1997. Prior to that, he served four years in the United States Navy, specializing in electronic communications. He has completed several certifications and professional examinations in a variety of financial and technical fields, including Certified Public Accountant (CPA), Certified Management Accountant (CMA), Certified Financial Manager (CFM), Project Manager Professional (PMP), Microsoft Certified Systems Engineer (MCSE), and Microsoft Certified Database Administrator (MCDBA). Tim is currently a project director at Advantage Computing Systems, Inc. (www.advantagecs.com), a company that produces enterprise software for publishing companies and service bureaus. He leads teams of engineers, developers, and managers through software implementation projects. He has also developed several technical training courses for his company's clients, including modules on Crystal Reports, SQL query development for Oracle and SQL Server, and Excel PivotTable Reporting.Credits

Acquisitions Editor
Katie Mohr

Senior Development Editor
Jodi Jensen

Technical Editor
Brian Patterson

Production Editor
Pamela Hanley

Copy Editor
Kathryn Duggan

Editorial Manager
Mary Beth Wakefield

Vice President & Executive Group Publisher
Richard Swadley

Vice President and Publisher
Joseph B. Wikert

Project Coordinator
Michaek Kruzil

Graphics and Production Specialists
Denny Hager, Stephanie D. Jumper

Quality Control Technicians
John Greenough, Leeann Harney

Proofreading and Indexing
TECHBOOKS Production Services

Contents

Acknowledgments

The first-rate business culture at Advantage Computing Systems has been instrumental in shaping my personal and professional development, while the outstanding senior management and supportive environment at ACS have enabled me to meet and often exceed my expectations for seeking new challenges. Over the years, I've had the good fortune to work with many very talented colleagues and clients who have contributed to the knowledge and experience that supported the writing of this book. I'd like to especially thank the following individuals for their time and consideration:

Karl Davis, for his always wise and encouraging counsel;

Tom Burbeck, for his valuable mentoring and investment in my professional development; and

Mark Fung-A-Fat, for his assistance in getting me started with PivotTable reports and teaching me the basics of SQL.

Additionally, I've had the benefit of working with the wonderful staff at Wiley Publishing, Inc. I would like to thank everyone who helped with the writing, development, editing, and publishing of this book. In particular, I'd like to express my profound appreciation to:

Katie Mohr, an outstanding acquisitions editor who helped get this project off the ground and ensured that it remained grounded, and

Jodi Jensen, a brilliant development editor who helped me express myself far better than I could have managed on my own.

And last, but certainly not least, I'd like to thank my wife, Lisa, who helped me whenever an all-nighter was needed and always made sure that I kept my focus.

Introduction

If you are a SQL programmer, report developer, or sophisticated Excel user and want to learn more about Excel's reporting capabilities, this book is for you. In the pages that follow, I provide comprehensive information on both the technical and strategic areas of Excel report development—paying special attention to *online transactional processing* (OLTP) databases.

By reading this book and following the practice exercises scattered liberally throughout the chapters, you can learn to develop powerful and innovative reporting solutions using Microsoft Excel 2003. This book's step-by-step approach can help you steadily gain confidence in your ability to use Excel's reporting functions as you enhance your skills by working through the hands-on examples. Many of the examples offer an accompanying video on the book's companion web site that you can watch to ensure that you fully understand every step (see the section "On the Web Site" later in this Introduction).

Highlights

This book covers a broad range of topics having to do with report development with Excel. Here are some of the highlights:

- Single-source coverage of Excel's report development features with notes, tips, warnings, and real-world examples at the end of each chapter
- Extensive and in-depth information on PivotTable and Spreadsheet report features, functions, and capabilities
- Thorough documentation of the Microsoft Query program included with Excel

- Comprehensive information on Excel's client-based OLAP cube tools for processing very large data sets from OLTP data sources

- Detailed information on creating and working with web-enabled Excel reports

In addition, this book helps you thoroughly understand these main features of Excel's reporting technology:

- **PivotTable reports:** A powerful and dynamic reporting tool that allows users to analyze data sets by dragging-and-dropping fields into various report sections. Numerical data can be aggregated and summarized into a myriad of products and forms. Using this technology, you can rapidly move fields in and out of the report, change aggregations, and customize filters. Drill down on any subtotal or total cell to reveal the underlying data—and simply click the mouse button to refresh your report with the most up-to-date information from OLTP databases and other external data sources.

- **Spreadsheet reports:** A reporting tool that allows users to import data into a more traditional columnar-type format. After the data is in the Spreadsheet report, users have numerous options and powerful functions at their fingertips, such as filters, advanced sorts, conditional formatting, lists, and fill-down formulas. As is the case with PivotTables, Spreadsheet report data can be immediately refreshed with a click of a button.

- **Parameter queries:** One of the most powerful, overlooked, and undocumented areas of Excel reporting, parameter queries allow users to dynamically specify filters each time a Spreadsheet report or PivotTable list is updated. Using this feature, you can restrict the number of records returned from a data source *before* the data is even imported into Excel. This results in faster report run-times and more concentrated focus of report information. Parameter queries are frequently used in conjunction with SQL stored procedures, views, and queries to target a specific range of data such as a date range, product line, region, or division.

- **Web components:** Reports can easily retrieve information from an intranet or Internet web site. And just as easily, PivotTable and Spreadsheet reports can be published to intranet and Internet web sites using native Microsoft FrontPage functionality. An exceptionally powerful and feature-rich technology, it is also easy to use. This book provides comprehensive and detailed information on using web queries and web-enabled Excel reports.

What You Need to Know

You don't have to know Structured Query Language (SQL) to get real value from this book. However, readers who are familiar with SQL programming will probably get the most out of it. Indeed, many SQL programmers find that Excel report development is the next logical progression in their technology education. Still, even if you are only an experienced user of Excel, you will learn a substantial amount about Excel reporting, especially in the earlier chapters where the graphical Excel tools are used to build SQL queries that run against external data sources such as delimited files, spreadsheets, databases, and data cubes.

What You Need to Have

To make the best use of this book, you need the following software installed on your computer:

- **Excel 2003:** Microsoft has made several enhancements to both the graphical display and report development features in this latest Excel release. Excel 2003 is preferable; however, Excel 2002 (also known as Excel XP) and Excel 2000 can be used for most of the material and exercises. If you do decide to use an earlier version, keep in mind that the screen captures found in this book will frequently vary from what you see with Excel 2002 or Excel 2000. There are also a few instances where functions and features are available only in Excel 2003.

- **Microsoft SQL Server 2000:** Much of the material in this book is focused on report development using OLTP databases. Many exercises require access to the SQL Server Northwind database that is included as part of a default installation of SQL Server 2000 or can be created from Microsoft Access (explained in Appendix A). Any type of SQL Server installation (Desktop, Regular, or Enterprise) is suitable.

- **Microsoft Analysis Services:** This program is included on the Microsoft SQL Server 2000 CD-ROM. It should be installed so that you can complete some of the exercises on *offline analytical processing* (OLAP) data cubes.

- **Microsoft Access 2003:** This application is necessary to create the NorthwindCS database on your SQL Server, although you can simply use the Northwind database included as part of a default installation of SQL Server 2000 if you prefer. I use the NorthwindCS database because it enables beginner-level SQL users to modify data from a graphical user interface (GUI) program for report testing. It can also be readily restored to its original state.

- **Microsoft FrontPage 2003:** Chapter 12 of the book includes information on retrieving or publishing Excel reports to the web. If you have this latest version of Microsoft FrontPage, you can customize the reports.

How This Book Is Organized

Because there are so many enterprise software systems in the marketplace, it's impractical to include report examples for each one of them. Instead, for most of the exercises and examples I've used Microsoft SQL Server's NorthwindCS database, which you can create from Microsoft Access. (Alternatively, as mentioned earlier, you can use the Northwind database that is included as part of a default installation of SQL Server 2000.) NorthwindCS performs several functions that are similar to what many enterprise software applications might handle, but on a much larger scale. Using this database program, I think you can obtain a useful and informed perspective on how you might go about developing comparable reports for your enterprise systems.

I've organized this book to help readers of all skill levels. If you're new to Excel reports, you should start with Part I of the book. Advanced users who are already familiar with Excel's reporting features and with external data sources can skip to Part II, where the core features, functions, and components of Excel reports are covered. The appendixes in Part III provide references for installing the NorthwindCS database, configuring your Windows operating system to display extensions for known file types, and using basic SQL.

Part I – Excel Report Initiation and Source Data

This part consists of six chapters. Chapter 1 provides an introduction and orientation to the major types of Excel reports and reporting components. The next two chapters include step-by-step examples for helping you create your first PivotTable and Spreadsheet reports from an external data source. Chapter 4 walks you through using the Query Wizard. Chapters 5 and 6 provide comprehensive information on the Microsoft Query program, the principal tool for creating SQL queries to import data from external files and databases. In these chapters, you learn how to use Microsoft Query to develop complex queries, build offline OLAP cubes, and create parameter fields that can be passed to SQL queries and stored procedures.

Part II – Advanced Reporting Features

The principal topics of Excel reports are included in the final six chapters that comprise Part II. Chapters 7 through 9 focus on PivotTable and PivotChart reports. In these chapters, you learn about advanced topics related to PivotTable and PivotChart report design, including the formatting and sorting features, data retrieval options, data summarization methods, and calculated fields. Chapter 10 introduces you to OLAP cubes, while spreadsheet reports and parameter queries are covered in Chapter 11. Here, you learn how to work with parameter and web queries, filters, subtotaling functions, conditional formatting, and report automation features. Chapter 12 includes comprehensive information on publishing Excel reports to the web, including a detailed review of PivotTable list features and functions.

Part III – Appendixes

Appendix A includes information for configuring your Windows operating system to display file extensions for known file types and for installing the NorthwindCS database on an SQL Server from Microsoft Access. An SQL reference is included in Appendix B. Here, basic and sophisticated query structures are dissected and reviewed in detailed. This appendix includes a review of string and mathematical operators, aggregate functions, and Case logic.

Conventions

To help you get the most from the text of this book and keep track of what's happening, I've used a number of conventions throughout the book.

NOTE In text formatted like this you will find important "extra" information that is directly relevant to the surrounding text. By reading these Notes, Tips, Warnings, Cross-References, On the Web, and Watch the Video text boxes, you can get additional help and learn some special tips.

These special styles are used in the text throughout the book:

- Important words are highlighted in *italics* when they are first introduced.
- Text you are being asked to type is shown in **bold**.
- URLs and portions of SQL queries or statements shown within the text are shown in a special `monofont` typeface.

On the Web Site

As you work through the examples in this book, you will run into special text boxes that remind you go to the book's companion web site to download example files. These boxes look like this:

ON THE WEB You can download the Expense Data.csv document to your computer from this book's companion web site at www.wiley.com/go/excelreporting. **Look for this document in either the Chap03.zip file or the Chap03 directory.**

Be sure to take advantage of the provided files so that you can follow along seamlessly with the step-by-step examples used in the chapters.

All the files you need are available for download at www.wiley.com/go/excelreporting. When you get to that page, you can choose to

- Download all the files for a single chapter (Chap01.zip, for example)
- Download one large zip file that includes the files for all chapters (Excel Reporting.zip) and which will create a folder structure on your hard drive with directories for each chapter
- Click one of the listed .avi files to watch a video of a particular exercise

When you see a box like the following after an exercise, it's telling you that an accompanying video is available on the web site:

WATCH THE VIDEO To see how to convert a PivotTable report to a PivotTable list, click the ch1201_video.avi file at www.wiley.com/go/excelreporting **to watch the video.**

So watch for these notes in the text that steer you to a plethora of available—and helpful—files on the web site.

Why I Wrote This Book

For the last 8 years, I have helped lead several prominent organizations through implementations of our proprietary enterprise software. Like many enterprise systems, our software affects many departments within a particular company. In order to implement our system, department managers assign staff to ensure that their particular needs are properly handled. One of the many needs usually involves replacing reports that managers and personnel rely on to identify problems, track productivity, show profitability, and summarize results.

Replacing reports that may have been used for several years can be difficult. Depending on the number of reports and the size of the organization, this activity can become both expensive and time-consuming. Just picture interviewing numerous users of hundreds, or even thousands, of reports across various departments in hopes of trying to understand what data is being summarized. Not only are the two systems much different, but report-users may also use terminology that only their peers who are familiar with the system being replaced can understand. Trying to decipher field meanings, determine what data needs to be summarized—and when—is only the beginning. Breaks, sorts, totals, and filters also need to be identified, documented, and programmed. After that, the report still needs to undergo rigorous testing to ensure that the data is accurate and properly formatted. This process may be repeated several times before the new report is fully approved as an acceptable replacement.

As a project manager, I found that reports were consuming more money, time, and resources than the project had been allocated. Beyond just eliminating some of the reports, I had to find a faster, cheaper, and more effective method of replacing them. First, I started using Crystal Reports (now Business Objects). I liked Crystal's reporting features, graphical tools, and tight integration with Microsoft SQL Server's stored procedures. Getting the report to look just right, however, took substantially more time than simply using our native application report development utilities. Sure, the report looked a lot better than a traditional columnar report, but I didn't get any closer to achieving my goals of developing reports faster and cheaper.

Around the same time, I also started using Excel reports. Being new to this technology, I didn't immediately grasp its full potential and capabilities. Eventually, things clicked. With some experience, I learned how a single PivotTable could replace dozens of existing reports. I also discovered that most report users could easily be trained to run, maintain, and modify the report once the underlying data was extracted for them. I no longer had to spend unnecessary time trying to understand sorts, breaks, totals, and filters. Instead, I simply had to focus on the main purpose of the report, and then simply develop an SQL query that extracted the data. Once a basic report shell was created with the fields from the SQL query, report users could shape and format the report as they saw fit. Often, a single Excel report replaced numerous existing reports. On many implementation projects, we not only reduced the time and expense involved in replacing the reports, we also provided the report users with increased data analysis capabilities. In finding a better reporting tool that also reduced project costs, you can probably see why it didn't take long for this technology to quickly take hold at our company, and throughout our user community. PivotTable reporting became—and still is—a real buzzword among our clients.

Before writing this book, I developed a two-day course on advanced Excel reporting techniques that I presented at our company's annual user training. This was in response to many of our clients who requested more information on Excel's reporting features. When I first embarked on this task, I was amazed to find that there were no books on Excel's reporting features. As I researched numerous news and Usenet groups and various web sites, I found that many people were seeking answers to the same questions I had finally answered for myself after years of experience. I decided it might be worthwhile to write a book to help answer these questions for a wider audience than our company's user community.

The book you hold in your hand is the result of this endeavor. If your goal is to become proficient in Excel report development, I hope you find information here that can help speed you along on the journey.

Excel® Advanced
Report Development

PART

I

Report Initiation and Source Data

Taking a First Look at Excel's Reporting Tools

This chapter provides you with an overview of Excel's reporting features. It shows you the principal types of Excel reports and how you can use them to satisfy many of the business requirements you may face. It covers some of the benefits of using Excel reports, including real-time access, simplified report updates, and reduced cost of ownership. It also highlights the various types of reporting tools included in Excel and the related components in other Microsoft applications.

In this first chapter, I try to give you a snapshot overview of PivotTable and PivotChart reports, Spreadsheet reports, parameter queries (how you can map parameters to stored procedure variables), and web queries, along with a quick look at some of the related Microsoft Office components, such as Front-Page, Access, and MapPoint.

Keep in mind that this chapter just helps you get started with the basics. As you work your way through the other chapters, you have the opportunity to dive into these topics in a lot more detail. So let's begin!

Why Use Excel for Reports?

Companies produce reports from enterprise software systems using numerous methods. A report might be generated from the native enterprise software program or from a standalone report development software program such as

Business Objects (formerly Crystal Reports). In other scenarios, the report data may be extracted to a delimited file that is loaded into a program such as Excel or Access. The number of enterprise software applications, the amount and level of internal expertise, and the degree of organizational leadership are just a few factors that can determine how reports are managed within a company.

> **NOTE** You might be asking yourself, "What is an enterprise software system, anyway?" Some popular enterprise software systems include SAP, PeopleSoft, Siebel, and Baan. These systems are used in all types of organizations to run the business more efficiently and effectively. Hospitals use medical information systems to track a patient's vital data and health care history. Companies such as Amazon.com or Barnes & Noble use warehouse management systems to reduce the time and labor expenses for shipping products to customers. The company I work for produces enterprise software for magazine and book publishers. More than 30 modules are available to perform business functions from advertising, billing, inventory, circulation, and payroll to conference management, web access, and customer relationship management.

Although report development tools are often bundled with enterprise software applications, many organizations use a separate report development software application for creating and running reports. So why would an organization spend additional funds to purchase reporting software if it is already included as part of its enterprise software system? Learning and supporting the report development tools included with an enterprise software application can be both difficult and expensive. Furthermore, many organizations have numerous enterprise applications, so that work and cost can be magnified several times. Enhanced performance and standardization to a single system are major benefits for organizations seeking to reduce costs and maintain their report development skills. Instead of paying six employees to develop and manage reports using the report development tools in a few enterprise software applications, it may take only two employees to develop and manage equivalent reports for the same enterprise systems using a single report development software program.

Initially, information technology (IT) professionals and business managers unfamiliar with Excel's reporting capabilities are often skeptical about using Excel to produce reports from an enterprise system. However, even the most skeptical of IT decision-makers are generally convinced once they

- See Excel's powerful reporting tools
- Receive superb feedback from report users
- Witness the reduced software licensing feeds and support costs

Here are some of the top considerations for using Excel reports over competing report development software programs:

- **Excel reports can retrieve data from an Enterprise software application's OLTP database in real-time.** Many systems require reports to be run by first launching the application and then requesting it. If the report is exported to Excel, a second step is likely involved for actually importing and formatting the data. (Many software systems build interfaces to Excel.) In comparison, by using native Excel reporting functionality, you can accomplish all of this in a fraction of the time. With hardly more than a mouse click, data can be fetched directly from one or more databases to update an Excel report with the most up-to-date information.

- **Sorts, breaks, and totals can easily be applied, modified, and removed.** With only limited training, even a novice Excel user can add or remove subtotals, apply complex sorts, and insert page breaks or lines between various report groups. It can take days or weeks of training to be able to understand and perform this same type of task with competing report development software programs and enterprise reporting tools.

- **Some Excel report types, such as PivotTable reports, are very dynamic and powerful.** One report can replace dozens of traditional columnar reports. A PivotTable report can contain many more fields than what is actually displayed in a single view of the report. Inserting and removing fields, changing field locations, and applying filters are easily and readily performed.

- **Excel reports are cost effective.** Running and modifying reports from an enterprise software application or report development software program usually requires that the application be installed. This can add a considerable burden to support, training, and software licensing costs. In contrast, most computers already have Excel installed and users are often familiar with the basics of how this program works.

- **Report development time is often much faster than with competing reporting software applications.** Enterprise reporting tools and report development software programs can be very intricate and complex. Organizations regularly hire report programmers or consultants to help develop many of their reports. In contrast, learning and using Excel report development tools is simple. Reports can frequently be developed more quickly, and at a lesser cost, than competing report development software programs and enterprise reporting tools.

- **Excel reports are integrated with related Microsoft products, such as FrontPage, MapPoint, Access, Data Analyzer, and SQL Server.** The integration among the various Office programs becomes more seamless and feature-rich with each new release of Microsoft Office, allowing you to develop ever more powerful and innovative reporting solutions.

PivotTable Reports

With PivotTable reports, you can interactively create and build cross-tabular reports from a list of available fields. These fields can be derived from another worksheet tab, a SQL or Oracle database, a text file, an OLAP cube, or some other external data source. After the PivotTable shape is created, users can move fields to different locations in the report, change the type of aggregation (for example, calculate an average amount instead of a total amount), apply filters to determine which items in a report field are displayed, and apply complex sorts based on aggregated values or other fields in the report.

Using PivotTable technology, report users can do the following:

- Produce a number of different views and reports
- Move fields to various locations in the report
- Determine which fields should be displayed
- Aggregate numerical fields in a variety of ways
- Use filters to control which values in a field are displayed
- Drill-down on numerical data to reveal the underlying data set
- Create multiple reports from a single PivotTable

The PivotTable in Figure 1.1 shows Total Revenue by Payment Method and Type of Service. Notice that State is another field in the PivotTable Field List window that is not shown in the report. With a few clicks of the mouse, the report can instantly be changed to instead show Average Revenue by Month and State (see Figure 1.2).

Do you want to display data for the first quarter only? Just click the drop-down arrow on Month to deselect the values Apr and May, as shown in Figure 1.3.

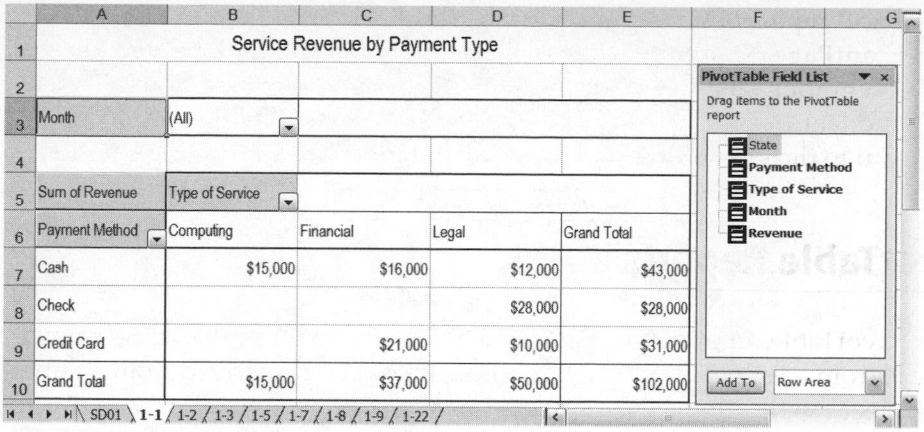

	A	B	C	D	E	F	G
1			Service Revenue by Payment Type				
2							
3	Month	(All)					
4							
5	Sum of Revenue	Type of Service					
6	Payment Method	Computing	Financial	Legal	Grand Total		
7	Cash	$15,000	$16,000	$12,000	$43,000		
8	Check			$28,000	$28,000		
9	Credit Card		$21,000	$10,000	$31,000		
10	Grand Total	$15,000	$37,000	$50,000	$102,000		

PivotTable Field List — Drag items to the PivotTable report: State, Payment Method, Type of Service, Month, Revenue. Add To | Row Area

Sheet tabs: SD01 / 1-1 / 1-2 / 1-3 / 1-5 / 1-7 / 1-8 / 1-9 / 1-22 /

Figure 1.1 A first view of the PivotTable.

After the filter is applied, the report is automatically resized to show only the first three months, as shown in Figure 1.4.

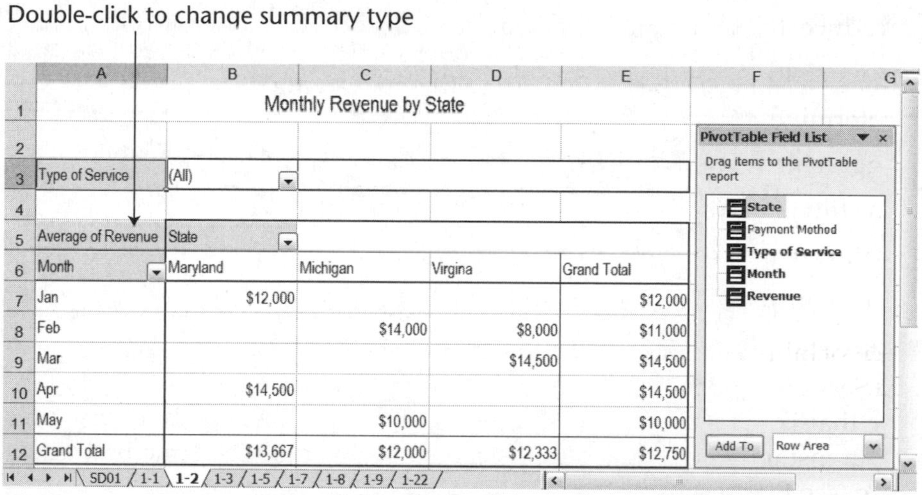

Double-click to change summary type

	A	B	C	D	E	F	G
1			Monthly Revenue by State				
2							
3	Type of Service	(All)					
4							
5	Average of Revenue	State					
6	Month	Maryland	Michigan	Virgina	Grand Total		
7	Jan	$12,000			$12,000		
8	Feb		$14,000	$8,000	$11,000		
9	Mar			$14,500	$14,500		
10	Apr	$14,500			$14,500		
11	May		$10,000		$10,000		
12	Grand Total	$13,667	$12,000	$12,333	$12,750		

PivotTable Field List — Drag items to the PivotTable report: State, Payment Method, Type of Service, Month, Revenue. Add To | Row Area

Sheet tabs: SD01 / 1-1 / 1-2 / 1-3 / 1-5 / 1-7 / 1-8 / 1-9 / 1-22 /

Figure 1.2 A second view of the PivotTable showing Average Revenue by State and Month.

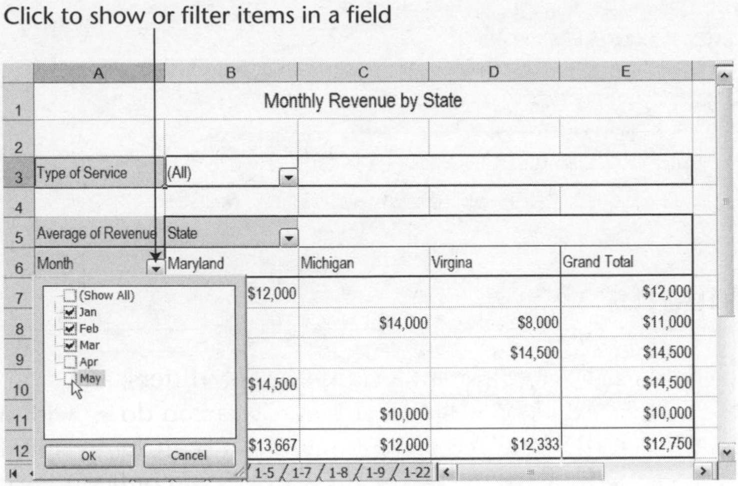

Click to show or filter items in a field

Figure 1.3 Clicking a drop-down arrow for a field shows a list of valid items that can be filtered.

One of the most powerful utilities of PivotTable Reports is the capability to drill down on the summarized report data. In Figure 1.4, double-clicking any cell value in the range B7:E10 creates a new worksheet with the full data set that makes up that cell. Figure 1.5 shows the underlying data for cell D9.

CROSS-REFERENCE Be sure to read Chapter 2 to learn more about the basics of PivotTable reports, and then turn to Chapter 7 for a more complete analysis of PivotTable functionality.

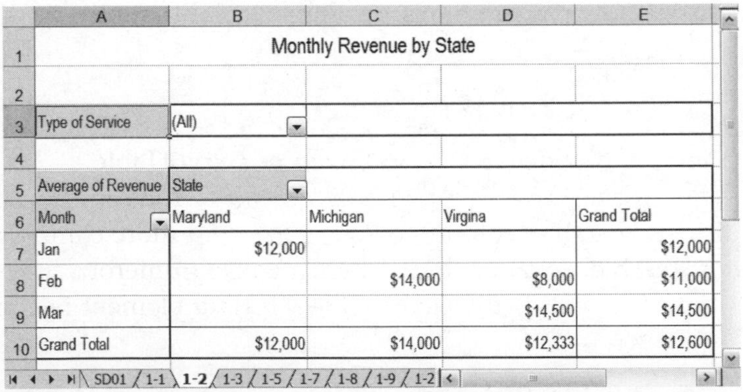

Figure 1.4 PivotTable reports are automatically resized once a filter is applied.

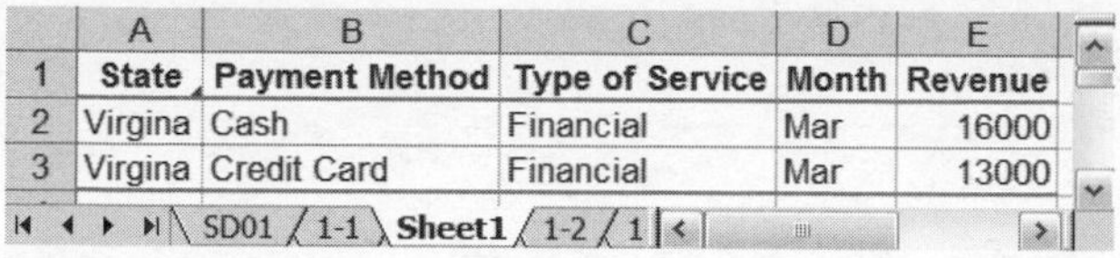

	A	B	C	D	E
1	State	Payment Method	Type of Service	Month	Revenue
2	Virgina	Cash	Financial	Mar	16000
3	Virgina	Credit Card	Financial	Mar	13000

SD01 / 1-1 \ **Sheet1** / 1-2 / 1

Figure 1.5   The supporting data set that makes up cell D9 in Figure 1.4.

PivotChart Reports

If you want to move fields easily to different locations, apply filters, and summarize numerical fields in a number of different ways, you can do so with a PivotChart. The main difference between PivotTables and PivotCharts is that with a PivotChart you can display data graphically, rather than only numerically, as is the case with a PivotTables.

Being able to visually view and analyze trends in data can be a big benefit of PivotCharts. Some users can see and appreciate the data better when analyzing it graphically than when viewing only the numerical data. I have found, however, that report developers typically use PivotCharts to complement, rather than replace, PivotTable reports. This makes linking your data to a PivotTable very valuable.

PivotCharts have much the same functionality as PivotTables. PivotCharts enable you to

- Produce a variety of chart types
- Move fields to various locations in the chart
- Determine which fields are included in the chart
- Graphically represent numerical aggregations in many different ways
- Use filters to control which values are charted
- Optionally link to a PivotTable Report

Figure 1.6 shows a sample PivotChart Report linked to a PivotTable.

There are several types of charts available with PivotCharts. You can choose from a simple two-dimensional bar, column, or pie chart, to a more complex three-dimensional area, bubble, or radar chart. There are also numerous functions for controlling how the data is displayed for each data element in the series.

CROSS-REFERENCE To find out the details of creating and using PivotCharts, see Chapter 9.

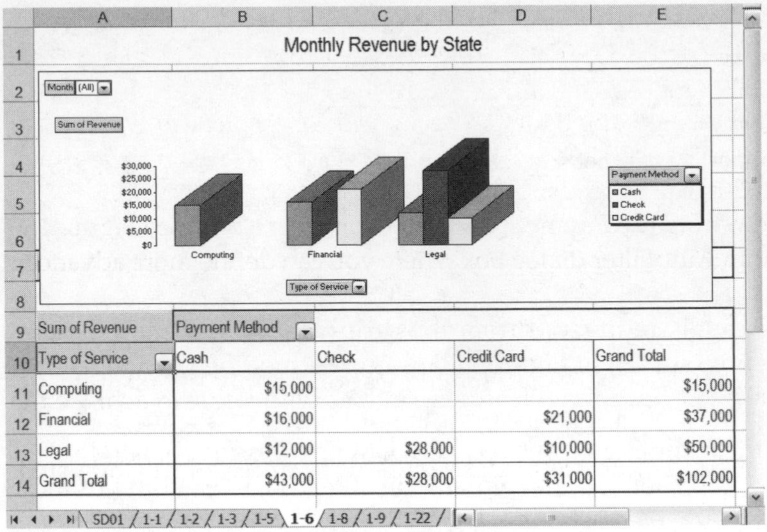

Figure 1.6   A PivotChart linked to a PivotTable.

Spreadsheet Reports

Despite the powerful and dynamic features of PivotTables, sometimes you want to generate a more traditional type of report. Spreadsheet reports are designed to display data in a traditional columnar report format. This report type is particularly suited to display non-aggregated data in multiple columns. And, like most traditional columnar reports, you can apply sorts, filters, breaks, and totals. Unlike other traditional report development software, however, Spreadsheet reports enable you to use all the powerful tools and functions included with Excel. In addition, Spreadsheet reports

- Give you clear-cut functions for applying sorts, breaks, and totals

- Permit numerical fields to be aggregated many different ways

- Give you easy-to-use filters to control whether particular values are displayed

- Include features for applying conditional formatting.

- Update report data automatically at predefined intervals or when the report is opened

Figure 1.7 shows how a Spreadsheet report might extract and format data from an external database system. Notice that this report contains the same data as the PivotTable reports in the previous section of this chapter. It is, however, in a more traditional type of format. Don't be fooled by the simplicity of the report layout. It offers many powerful features for creating subtotals or calculated fields, applying conditional field formats, or refreshing data at predefined intervals.

What if you want to show the data for checks and credit cards only? It's easy to apply a filter; just choose Data ➪ Filter ➪ Auto Filter to create drop-down boxes for each field in the Spreadsheet report, as shown in Figure 1.8.

Selecting Custom from the Payment Method drop-down box (see Figure 1.9) launches the Custom AutoFilter dialog box where you can define more advanced filters.

Selecting Check and Credit Card from the drop-down lists in the Custom AutoFilter dialog box, shown in Figure 1.10, is one method of applying a constraint. You can also use additional features, such as wildcards, to achieve the same result.

After the filter is applied, the Spreadsheet report is automatically adjusted, as shown in Figure 1.11.

CROSS-REFERENCE To find out the details of creating and using Spreadsheet reports, see Chapter 11.

1 2 3		A	B	C	D	E
	1			Monthly Revenue by State		
	2					
	3	State	Month	Type of Service	Payment Method	Revenue
	4	Maryland	Apr	Computing	Cash	$15,000
	5	Maryland	Apr	Legal	Check	$14,000
	6	Maryland	Jan	Legal	Cash	$12,000
	7	**Maryland Total**				$41,000
	8	Michigan	Feb	Legal	Check	$14,000
	9	Michigan	May	Legal	Credit Card	$10,000
	10	**Michigan Total**				$24,000
	11	Virgina	Feb	Financial	Credit Card	$8,000
	12	Virgina	Mar	Financial	Credit Card	$13,000
	13	Virgina	Mar	Financial	Cash	$16,000
	14	**Virgina Total**				$37,000
	15	**Grand Total**				$102,000

SD01 / 1-1 / 1-2 / 1-3 / 1-5 / 1-6 \ **1-7** / 1-9 / 1-22 /

Figure 1.7 A Spreadsheet report displays data in a traditional columnar format.

1 2 3		A	B	C	D	E
	1			Monthly Revenue by State		
	2					
	3	State	Month	Type of Service	Payment Method	Revenue
	4	Maryland	Apr	Computing	Cash	$15,000
	5	Maryland	Apr	Legal	Check	$14,000
	6	Maryland	Jan	Legal	Cash	$12,000

SD01 / 1-1 / 1-2 / 1-3 / 1-5 / 1-6 \ **1-7** / 1-9 / 1-

Figure 1.8 The Auto Filter function automatically creates drop-down filters for each field in the Spreadsheet report.

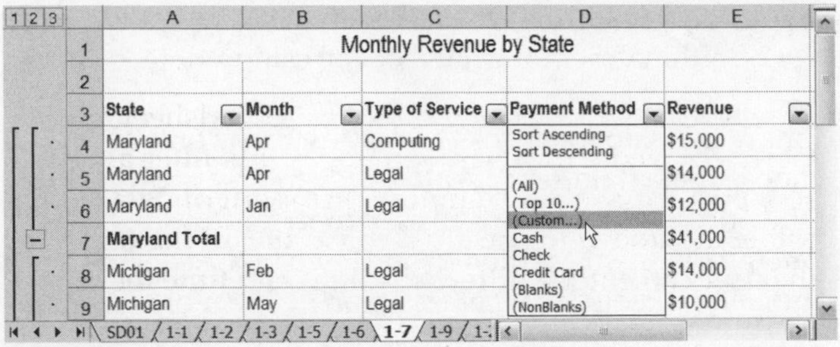

Figure 1.9   Several standard filters are available from the filter drop-down box. Selecting Custom lets you define a more advanced filter.

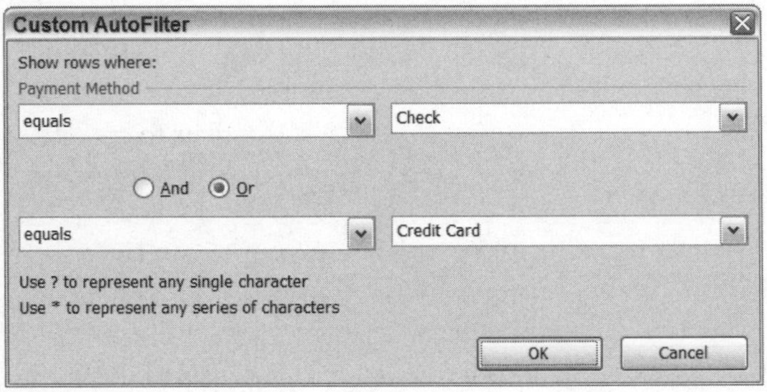

Figure 1.10   You can enter advanced filter conditions in the Custom AutoFilter dialog box.

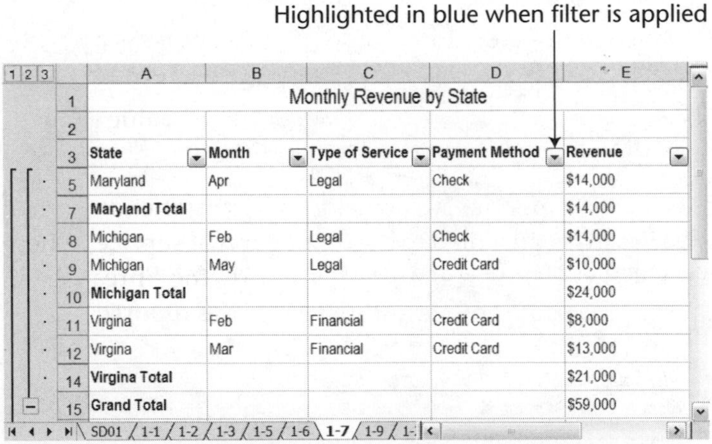

Figure 1.11   The Spreadsheet report filtered on payment types of Check and Credit Card.

Parameter Queries

In the previous section, you learned about using filters in Spreadsheet reports to restrict the type of data displayed. However, you apply this filter after the data is imported into the report. How can you limit the amount of data before it is imported? One possible method is to specify a constraint in the underlying SQL query. Unless the user can enter a different value each time the report is run, however, that constraint is static.

Static constraints might filter data to a particular product line, region, company division, or period of time (for example, the last 30 days). However, if the report user has to define the product line, region, company division, or period of time before the report is run, the underlying SQL query must be modified or a parameter query must be used. Most report users are not versed in SQL programming or databases, so parameter queries are the best way to satisfy this requirement.

Parameter queries act as dynamic constraints, allowing the user to specify a value (or values) each time the report is run. Instead of importing a huge data set into Excel, Parameter Queries apply a filter to return only a subset of the records from the data source. With a smaller data set, the report can run much quicker because it uses fewer server resources. It also consumes less memory and disk space on the computer running the report, enhancing report manipulation performance and computer processing speed. Using parameter queries, you can

- Limit the amount of data that is displayed in a report before the data is imported into the report
- Integrate the parameters with SQL stored procedure arguments and/or SQL queries to restrict the type and amount of data that is returned
- Automatically re-query the data source when a parameter value is changed

Figure 1.12 shows how a parameter query can be used in conjunction with a Spreadsheet report to restrict the report data to a specific type of service. When the value is changed in this field from the drop-down box, the Spreadsheet report automatically queries that data source and refreshes the report.

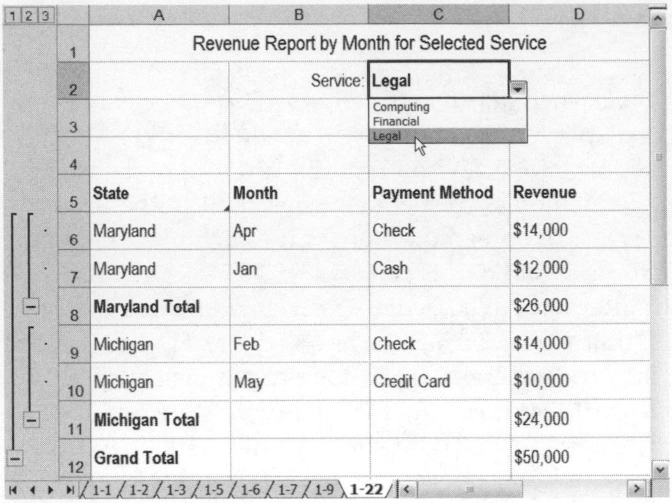

Figure 1.12　Parameter queries can automatically refresh the report as different values are selected.

> **CROSS-REFERENCE** To find out the details of creating and using Parameter Queries, see Chapter 11.

Web Queries

The web query feature is another exciting and novel reporting tool included as part of Microsoft Excel. Imagine getting the latest currency exchange rates or mortgage interest rates imported directly from the web into your Spreadsheet report. It's as easy as navigating to the web page within Excel and selecting the table (or tables) that you want to import. By simply clicking on the report and selecting the Refresh Data function, you can automatically refresh the report at predefined intervals.

Using this technology, you can

- Import data from the Internet and intranet web sites
- Update report data automatically at predefined intervals or when the report is opened

Figure 1.13 shows how a Historical Mortgage Rate Report might look. This report uses the `http://www.freddiemac.com/pmms/pmms30.htm` link at the Freddie Mac web site.

	A	B	C	D	E	F	G	H	I	J	K	L	M	N	O
1															
2															
3					Historical Mortgage Rate Report										
4					1990 - 1994										
5					http://www.freddiemac.com/pmms/pmms30.htm										
6															
7		1994			1993			1992			1991			1990	
8		Rate	Pts		Rate	Pts		Rate	Pts		Rate	Pts		Rate	Pts
9	January	7.1	1.7		8.0	1.6		8.4	1.8		9.6	2.1		9.9	2.1
10	February	7.2	1.8		7.7	1.5		8.8	1.8		9.4	2.0		10.2	2.1
11	March	7.7	1.7		7.5	1.6		8.9	1.9		9.5	2.1		10.3	2.1
12	April	8.3	1.8		7.5	1.7		8.9	1.7		9.5	2.0		10.4	2.1
13	May	8.6	1.8		7.5	1.8		8.7	1.7		9.5	2.0		10.5	2.0
14	June	8.4	1.8		7.4	1.6		8.5	1.7		9.6	2.1		10.2	2.0
15	July	8.6	1.8		7.2	1.6		8.1	1.6		9.6	2.0		10.0	2.0
16	August	8.5	1.8		7.1	1.5		8.0	1.7		9.2	1.9		10.1	2.0
17	September	8.6	1.8		6.9	1.5		7.9	1.7		9.0	1.9		10.2	2.1
18	October	8.9	1.8		6.8	1.5		8.1	1.8		8.9	1.9		10.2	2.2
19	November	9.2	1.8		7.2	1.6		8.3	1.9		8.7	1.8		10.0	2.1
20	December	9.2	1.8		7.2	1.7		8.2	1.6		8.5	1.8		9.7	1.9
21															
22	Annual Average	8.4	1.8		7.3	1.6		8.4	1.7		9.3	2.0		10.1	2.1

D01 / D02 / 1-1 / 1-2 / 1-4 / 1-5 / 1-6 / 1-7 / 1-8 / 1-9 / 1-10 / 1-11 \ **1-13** / 1-14 /

Figure 1.13 A Spreadsheet report that uses a table from an intranet or Internet web page as its data source.

Related Office Components

Some Microsoft Office programs include tools and components that can be interfaced with your Excel reports. The integration among the Microsoft Office programs seems to become more feature-rich and seamless with each new release of Office. Some of the Office programs and components that work with Excel include the following:

- Microsoft MapPoint
- Microsoft FrontPage
- Microsoft Access

I've included the following sections to familiarize you with some of the capabilities and features available in these related Microsoft Office software programs. Additionally, in Chapter 12, I cover how you can embed Excel reports in a web page and edit them with Microsoft FrontPage. This editing simply uses an OLE DB, so the interface with Microsoft Access is the same. I include this peripheral information here so that you know it exists.

Microsoft MapPoint

Microsoft MapPoint allows you to graphically represent your data on a map. You can choose from many types of plotting options to display data. In Figure 1.14, you can see how a corporate profitability report might use a Pivot Table, a PivotChart, and a Map object created from the MapPoint program to analyze revenue, expenses, and profits across its various sales offices. The pie charts in the MapPoint object graphically display Revenue, Expenses, and Net Profit for each sales office across the country.

MapPoint automatically converts and reads any geographical data such as city, county, and country names, postal codes, and longitudinal/latitudinal coordinates. With this program, you can zoom in on various locations and plot data elements individually by using unique graphical indicators such as pushpins, charts, and shaded circles. You can even create driving directions and calculate the distance and time it takes to travel from one location to the next. Several other features useful for reporting and analysis are also included in this program and are covered in the program's user manual. If this program in installed on your computer, you can insert the MapPoint object into Excel using OLE DB.

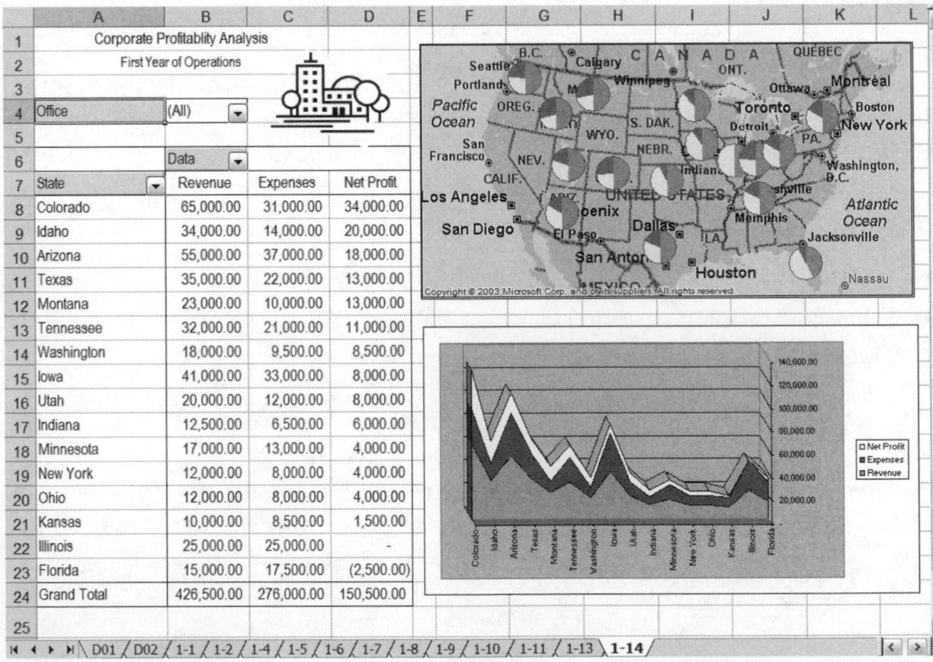

Corporate Profitablity Analysis

First Year of Operations

Office	(All)		
	Data		
State	Revenue	Expenses	Net Profit
Colorado	65,000.00	31,000.00	34,000.00
Idaho	34,000.00	14,000.00	20,000.00
Arizona	55,000.00	37,000.00	18,000.00
Texas	35,000.00	22,000.00	13,000.00
Montana	23,000.00	10,000.00	13,000.00
Tennessee	32,000.00	21,000.00	11,000.00
Washington	18,000.00	9,500.00	8,500.00
Iowa	41,000.00	33,000.00	8,000.00
Utah	20,000.00	12,000.00	8,000.00
Indiana	12,500.00	6,500.00	6,000.00
Minnesota	17,000.00	13,000.00	4,000.00
New York	12,000.00	8,000.00	4,000.00
Ohio	12,000.00	8,000.00	4,000.00
Kansas	10,000.00	8,500.00	1,500.00
Illinois	25,000.00	25,000.00	-
Florida	15,000.00	17,500.00	(2,500.00)
Grand Total	426,500.00	276,000.00	150,500.00

Figure 1.14 A PivotTable report linked with a PivotChart and a Microsoft MapPoint object.

Microsoft FrontPage

Microsoft FrontPage includes tools for publishing your PivotTable reports to an intranet or Internet web site. Thus, many of the features included with Excel PivotTables are still available through an Internet Explorer browser window. You can also configure options to allow users to download the report to their local machine running Excel. Instead of complicated and expensive report and distribution processes, users can simply traverse their company's intranet to access and manage their reports.

NOTE Publishing PivotTable reports to a centrally located corporate intranet server can also reduce the problems associated with configuration management. The master report version can be stored on this server, so changes do not have to be made to multiple files.

The Corporate Profitability Report from Figure 1.14 is represented as an Internet report in Figure 1.15. Notice that the report and the PivotTable Field List are still available, even though the report is accessed through a browser program.

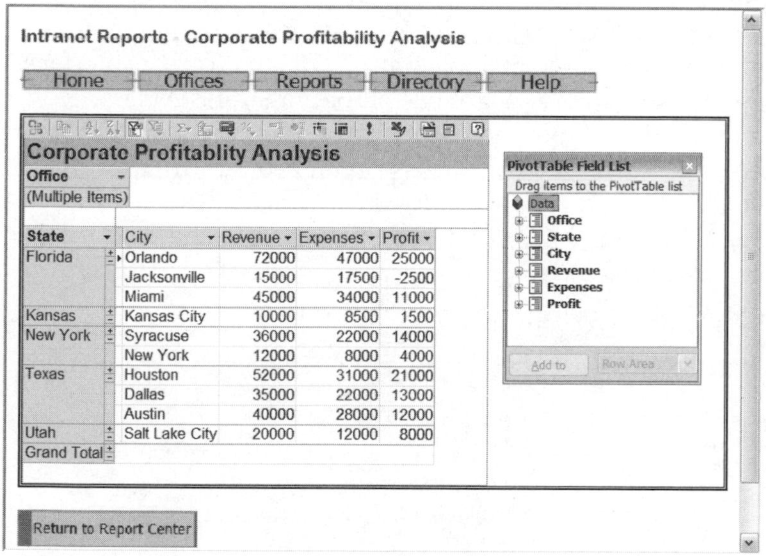

Figure 1.15   PivotTable reports can be accessed from intranet and Internet web sites.

Microsoft Access

With Microsoft Access, you can create reporting systems that automatically control how and what data is displayed in a PivotTable. Instead of manually dragging fields or customizing the PivotTable, users can click buttons to change report views, apply filters, or change the report layout. A sample Access Reports Management System for the Corporate Profitability example is shown in Figure 1.16.

You can program Access buttons to control how data is displayed in the PivotTable. In this example, the buttons are customized to apply filters and produce different types of report views. Instead of using the typical static reports in Access, you can enhance your current database programs with this interactive and dynamic reporting capability.

Chapter Review

This chapter provided an introduction to some of the principal types of Excel reports and highlighted some of the innovative tools and features included with each report type. It highlighted some of the features available in the numerous types of Excel reporting tools, including PivotTable reports, PivotChart reports, Spreadsheet reports, parameter queries, and web queries. It also introduced you to a few of the related components that can be interfaced with Excel's reporting tools, such as MapPoint, FrontPage, and Access.

The next chapter provides a more comprehensive look at PivotTable reports. Chapter 2 is where you learn how the data is organized and the purpose of each area in a PivotTable.

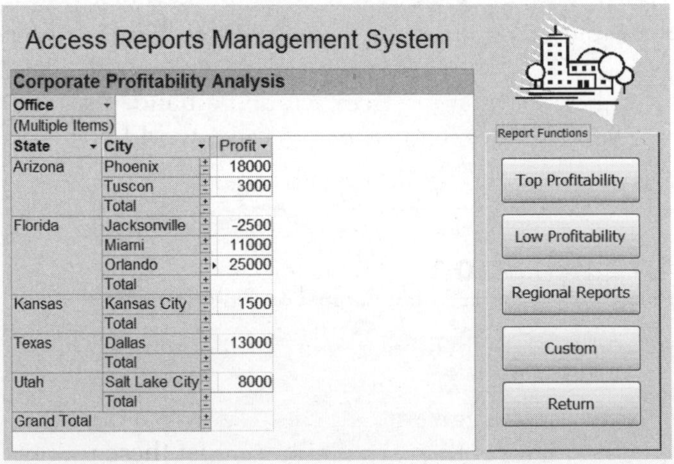

Figure 1.16 A PivotTable inserted into a Microsoft Access form.

Getting Started with PivotTables

If you are not familiar with PivotTables and how they work, it is important to read this chapter. Here, I cover the concepts, terminology, and core functions of PivotTables. Even if you are experienced with this technology, I recommend at least skimming this chapter, as you may learn something new — especially with all of the new features in Excel 2003.

I start by providing you with a basic framework of how data is summarized in a PivotTable report and how you can change the report shape by moving fields to different areas in the PivotTable. Here, you create your first PivotTable and learn about the purpose and use of each area in the report. I also review the essential components of a PivotTable report and familiarize you with some of the terminology. At the end of this chapter, I've included a hands-on exercise where you can practice what you've learned using a real-world business example.

PivotTable Data Organization

It's important for you to know that a PivotTable displays only the unique values in a dataset in a cross-tabular format. (See the note that follows if you are not familiar with the term *dataset*.) An aggregate function, such as a count, an average, or a total of some other field, is then calculated against these unique values. The next example illustrates how this works.

NOTE A *dataset* can also be referred to as a *recordset*. This term refers to the data included in a table or returned from an SQL query. In the Travel Expenses example used here, the dataset is simply the information in the rows and columns of Table 2.1.

Taking the sample list of travel expenses shown in Table 2.1, you can see that many of the transactions have a duplicate Category or Month.

Table 2.1   Sample List of Travel Expenses

MONTH	TYPE	CATEGORY	AMOUNT
Jan	Personal	Restaurant	35
Jan	Business	Taxi	42
Jan	Business	Restaurant	64
Jan	Personal	Restaurant	22
Jan	Business	Tips	12
Feb	Personal	Restaurant	32
Feb	Personal	Entertainment	24
Feb	Business	Entertainment	45
Feb	Business	Lodging	98
Mar	Business	Airfare	250
Mar	Personal	Restaurant	24
Mar	Business	Restaurant	45
Mar	Business	Lodging	160
Mar	Business	Tolls	8

Table 2.2 shows how this data is organized into a PivotTable report of Amount by Month. Note that only the unique values of Month are displayed. Jan, Feb, and Mar are listed only once, not multiple times, as they are in Table 2.1. In this example, Amount is summed for each value of Month.

Table 2.2   Total Amount by Month

MONTH	AMOUNT
Jan	175
Feb	199
Mar	487

If, instead, you want to display the Sum of Amount by Category, the Pivot Table calculates the total Amount for each unique value of Category, as shown in Table 2.3.

Table 2.3   Total Amount by Category

CATEGORY	AMOUNT
Airfare	250
Entertainment	69
Lodging	258
Restaurant	222
Taxi	42
Tips	12
Tolls	8

As you discovered in Chapter 1, PivotTables are a very flexible reporting tool. So you could also analyze the total Amount by Month and Category. In this case, the data would look like Table 2.4.

Table 2.4   Total Amount by Month and Category

	JAN	FEB	MAR
Airfare			250
Entertainment		69	
Lodging		98	160
Restaurant	121	32	69
Taxi	42		
Tips	12		
Tolls			8

You could just as easily count the number of records instead of summing Amount. In that case, the PivotTable report would display the data as shown in Table 2.5.

Table 2.5   Count of Expenses by Month and Category

	JAN	FEB	MAR
Airfare			1
Entertainment		2	
Lodging		1	1
Restaurant	3	1	2
Taxi	1		
Tips	1		
Tolls			1

And finally, instead of calculating a sum or a count of Amount, you could do both. Table 2.6 shows a count and a sum of Amount by Month and Category.

Table 2.6   Count and Total of Amount by Month and Category

	JAN		FEB		MAR	
	AMOUNT	COUNT	AMOUNT	COUNT	AMOUNT	COUNT
Airfare					1	250
Entertainment			2	69		
Lodging			1	98	1	160
Restaurant	3	121	1	32	2	69
Taxi	1	42				
Tips	1	12				
Tolls					1	8

PivotTable reports enable you to do much more than just count or sum data against unique values. You can also calculate averages, maximum or minimum values, standard deviations, and running totals, and perform many other mathematical and statistical functions. What data is displayed and how you display it is totally up to you. It's easy to turn the data around and around while performing different functions and calculations against it.

Creating Your First PivotTable

Now that you know the basics of how data is organized in a PivotTable, you're ready to create your first one.

WATCH THE VIDEO To see how to create a PivotTable, watch the ch1201_video.avi video file on this book's companion web site at `www.wiley.com/go/excelreporting`.

To create a PivotTable, follow these steps:

1. Type the field headings and values shown earlier in Table 2.1 into Excel (see Figure 2.1).

2. When you have finished entering the data, click cell A1 and choose Data ⇨ PivotTable And PivotChart Report, as shown in Figure 2.2.

	A	B	C	D
1	Month	Type	Category	Amount
2	Jan	Personal	Restaurant	35
3	Jan	Business	Taxi	42
4	Jan	Business	Restaurant	64
5	Jan	Personal	Restaurant	22
6	Jan	Business	Tips	12
7	Feb	Personal	Restaurant	32
8	Feb	Personal	Entertainment	24
9	Feb	Business	Entertainment	45
10	Feb	Business	Lodging	98
11	Mar	Business	Airfare	250
12	Mar	Personal	Restaurant	24
13	Mar	Business	Restaurant	45
14	Mar	Business	Lodging	160
15	Mar	Business	Tolls	8

Figure 2.1 Type the data from Table 2.1 into Excel.

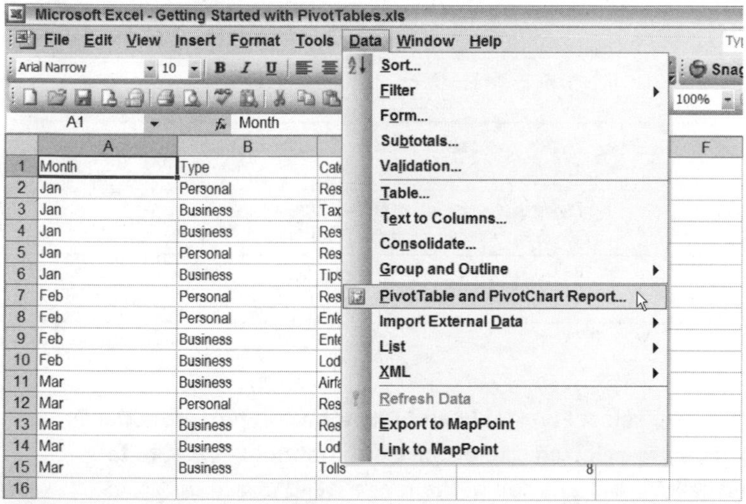

Figure 2.2 Select PivotTable And PivotChart Report from the Data menu to create a PivotTable report from the data you entered.

DRAGGING PIVOTTABLE FIELDS

Take careful note of how the PivotTable areas are outlined when you drag a field from the PivotTable Field List to the PivotTable area. Notice that the PivotTable area is highlighted when you drag a field over it. Don't worry if you accidentally drop a field in the wrong area, just click Undo from Excel's Standard toolbar.

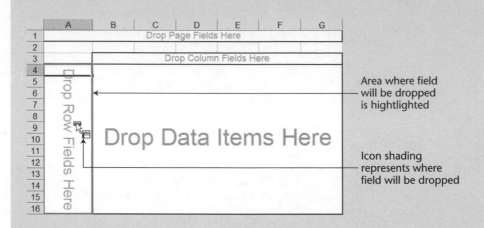

Notice that the location of the shading on the icon changes as you move a field over a particular area of the PivotTable. This icon can be particularly helpful when the PivotTable size is very small. The following table explains these various icons.

ICON	EXPLANATION
	Dragging field to the Page area
	Dragging field to the Row area
	Dragging field to the Column area
	Dragging field to the Data area
	Moving field off the report

WARNING Before you select PivotTable and PivotChart Report from the Data menu, make sure you have selected one of the cells containing data. In this example, I selected cell A1, but any cell in the range A1–D15 will do.

3. When the PivotTable And PivotChart Wizard – Step 1 Of 3 dialog box appears, as shown in Figure 2.3, click Finish.

4. Verify that a PivotTable layout area and PivotTable Field List dialog box are created, as shown in Figure 2.4.

5. Drag the Month field from the PivotTable Field List to the Drop Row Fields Here section of the PivotTable, as shown in Figure 2.5.

6. Instead of dragging, you can also move a field into the report by using the Add To button in the PivotTable Field List dialog box. Click Amount in the PivotTable Field List, change the field location from Row area to Data area in the drop-down box (see Figure 2.6), and then click the Add To button.

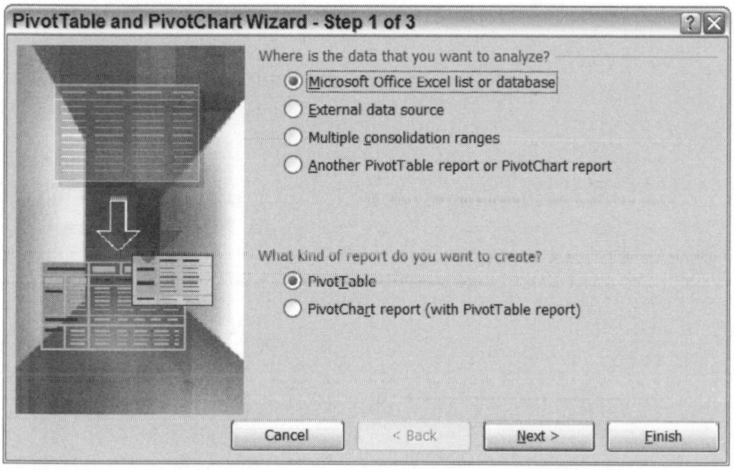

Figure 2.3   Click Finish to tell Excel to create a PivotTable.

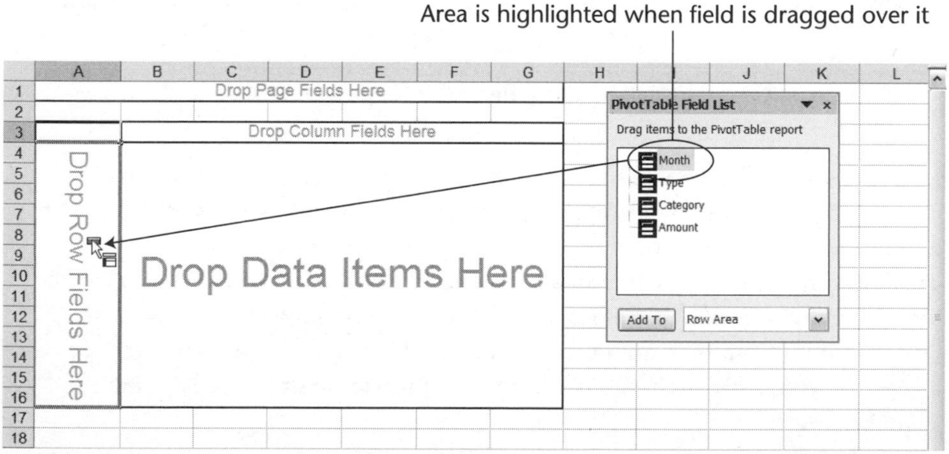

Area is highlighted when field is dragged over it

Figure 2.4   The circle and arrow show where you're going to drag the field in the next step.

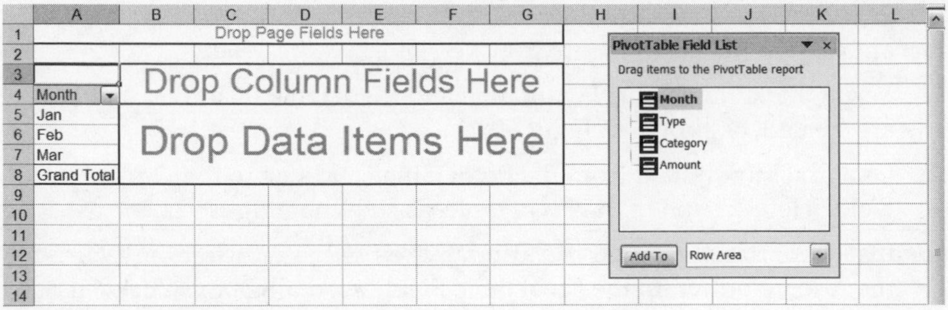

Figure 2.5   Notice that the PivotTable is automatically resized to show only the column header, unique values, and a Grand Total field once a field is dropped into this section.

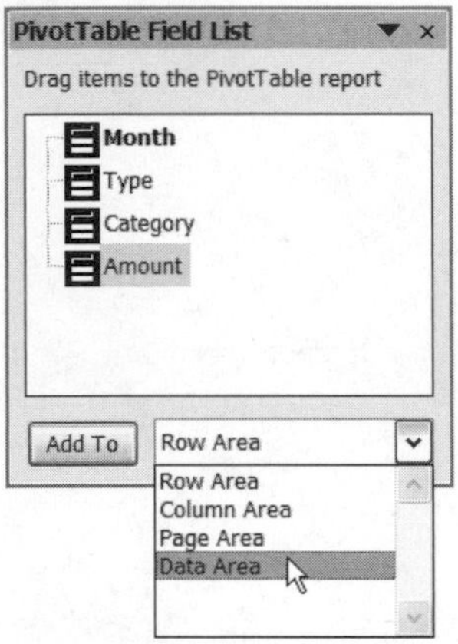

Figure 2.6   You can use the PivotTable Field List to move fields into the PivotTable report.

NOTE The PivotTable Field List window appears only when you have selected a cell in the PivotTable. Clicking off the PivotTable automatically hides the window.

The PivotTable now looks like Figure 2.7.

TIP If you use the mouse to drag fields into the report, drag fields into the Data section last. This keeps a larger drop area for dragging fields in and out of the report. When there is only one item in the PivotTable and it is in the Data section, the PivotTable is very small, making it difficult to tell which area is being highlighted when a field is dragged over it. Alternatively, you could drag the field out of the Data area first, making the PivotTable drop area much bigger. Or you could even add fields into the PivotTable from the PivotTable Field List window.

Figure 2.7 PivotTable of Expenses by Month that matches the information in Table 2.2.

Notice that the PivotTable has changed shape again. It also displays the same data that was shown in Table 2.2 (with the exception that a Grand Total is displayed by default in a PivotTable). You've now learned how to move data into the PivotTable report using two methods:

- By dragging a field from the PivotTable Field List to the PivotTable Report area

- By using the Add To button in the PivotTable Field List dialog box

CROSS-REFERENCE Read Chapter 7 to learn how to use the Layout Manager to move fields to the PivotTable report.

Modifying the PivotTable

You've successfully created your first PivotTable report, hopefully with ease. As you have learned so far, creating a PivotTable is simple. And, it's just as easy to modify one that's already created. This section covers some of the basic functions that you can use to customize or *shape* your PivotTable report.

NOTE Moving fields into and out of a PivotTable report results in the shape of the PivotTable being changed. Look at the difference between Figure 2.4 and Figure 2.5 if you forgot how that works. PivotTable experts often refer to the act of customizing a PivotTable as "shaping" the report.

Removing a Field from a PivotTable

What if you need to move a field *off* the PivotTable report? You shouldn't be surprised to learn it's just as easy as moving fields *into* the report. Simply click the field that you want to move and drag it off the PivotTable.

In the PivotTable you created in the preceding section, for example, select Month in Cell A4 (refer to Figure 2.7) and drag it off the report as shown in Figure 2.8. Notice the icon appearance as you "pick up" the field and drag it off the report.

Figure 2.9 shows the PivotTable report after the Month field has been moved out.

Changing the Summary Type

When you dragged Amount into the Data section of the PivotTable report, the data in this field was summed to derive the total Amount by Month (see step 6 and Figure 2.7 in the previous section if you forgot how this was done). How can you *count* the number of expenses instead of calculating a *sum* of the expense amount? You do that by changing how the data is aggregated.

NOTE By default, numerical fields are *summed* and alphanumeric fields are *counted* when they are dragged into the Data area of a PivotTable.

Note icon's appearance
as you drag Month field
off the PivotTable report

	A	B	C	D
1	Drop Page Fields Here			
2				
3	Sum of Amount			
4	Month ▾	Total		
5	Jan	175		
6	Feb	199		
7	Mar	487		
8	Grand Total	861		
9				
10				
11				

Figure 2.8   Removing a field from the PivotTable is easy: just click on it and drag it off the report.

	A	B
1	Drop Page Fields Here	
2		
3	Sum of Amount	Total
4	Total	861

Figure 2.9   PivotTable with only the Amount field remaining in the data section.

To *count* the number of expenses instead of *totaling* expenses, follow these steps:

1. Drag Category into the report. The PivotTable report should now look like Figure 2.10.

2. Modify the PivotTable to *count* the number of expenses instead of calculating the *sum* of expenses. To do this, double-click the Sum of Amount field in cell A3. The PivotTable Field dialog box appears, as shown in Figure 2.11.

3. Select Count in the Summarize By box (see Figure 2.12) and then click OK.

4. The PivotTable now counts the number of entries for each Category. Compare the total and number of entries by Category in Figure 2.13 to what is displayed in Figure 2.1. Notice that the Grand Total count of 14 records in cell B12 of Figure 2.13 is equal to the 14 records in Figure 2.1.

	A	B
1	Drop Page Fields Here	
2		
3	Sum of Amount	
4	Category ▼	Total
5	Airfare	250
6	Entertainment	69
7	Lodging	258
8	Restaurant	222
9	Taxi	42
10	Tips	12
11	Tolls	8
12	Grand Total	861

Figure 2.10   The PivotTable of total Amount by Category that matches the information from Table 2.3.

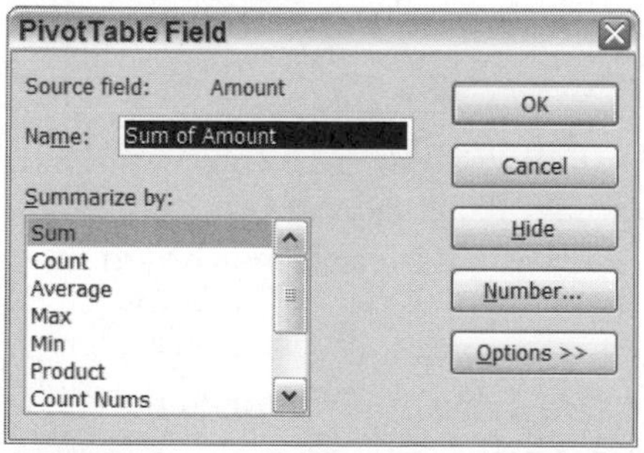

PivotTable Field   ✕

Source field: Amount
Name: Sum of Amount   OK

Summarize by: Cancel
Sum
Count   Hide
Average
Max   Number...
Min
Product   Options >>
Count Nums

Figure 2.11   The PivotTable Field dialog box opens when you double-click the Sum Of Amount field.

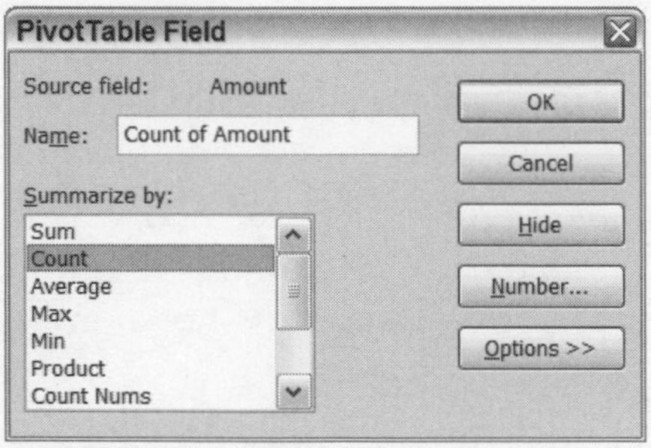

Figure 2.12   In this dialog box, you can change how a data field is summarized.

Figure 2.13   Count of Expenses by Expense Category.

NOTE Notice that Sum of Amount in cell A3 of Figure 2.10 was changed to Count of Amount in cell A3 of Figure 2.13 when the summary type was changed from Sum to Count.

5. Drag Month into the Column area of the PivotTable as shown in Figure 2.14.

   Your PivotTable should now look like Figure 2.15.

6. By now, you're probably getting quite adept with using a PivotTable report. Try dragging a field into the report for the second time. Drag Amount into the center — Data area — of the PivotTable, as shown in Figure 2.16.

   The PivotTable report should now look like Figure 2.17. Notice that Amount is now being *counted* and *summed* by Category and Month.

NOTE With the exception of the Data area, fields can appear in only one location of the PivotTable. Dragging a field from the PivotTable List window into another area of the PivotTable simply moves the field to that area of the report, even if it already exists in a different area. Try it and see.

	A	B	C	D	E	F
1	Drop Page Fields Here					
2						
3	Count of Amount					
4	Category ▼	Total				
5	Airfare	1				
6	Entertainment	2				
7	Lodging	2				
8	Restaurant	6				
9	Taxi	1				
10	Tips	1				
11	Tolls	1				
12	Grand Total	14				
13						

PivotTable Field List ▼ ×

Drag items to the PivotTable report

- Month
- Type
- Category
- Amount

Add To — Row Area ▼

Figure 2.14 Drag Month from the PivotTable List to the Column area of the PivotTable report.

	A	B	C	D	E
1	Drop Page Fields Here				
2					
3	Count of Amount	Month ▼			
4	Category ▼	Jan	Feb	Mar	Grand Total
5	Airfare			1	1
6	Entertainment		2		2
7	Lodging		1	1	2
8	Restaurant	3	1	2	6
9	Taxi	1			1
10	Tips	1			1
11	Tolls			1	1
12	Grand Total	5	4	5	14

Figure 2.15 Count of Expenses by Expenses Category and Month that matches the information from Table 2.4.

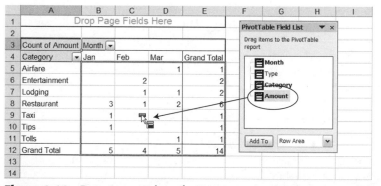

Figure 2.16 Drag Amount into the Data area section for a second time.

Refreshing Report Data

You might find that the underlying source data is changed or that you need to modify it. Don't worry if that happens. You don't need to recreate the entire PivotTable report from scratch. You just have to right-click the PivotTable and select Refresh Data from the pop-up menu to update the report with the new data.

To refresh the report data, follow these steps:

1. Click the worksheet tab you created in Figure 2.1, and then change the Amount for Lodging in cell D14 from 160 to **120**, as shown in Figure 2.18.

2. Refer to the PivotTable report on the preceding Excel worksheet (the one shown in Figure 2.17). Right-click the PivotTable and select Refresh Data from the pop-up menu, as shown in Figure 2.19.

   Excel examines the original data source, in this case the Excel worksheet in Figure 2.9, and refreshes the PivotTable report with the updated data. In this example, the only cell updated was the Amount for Lodging in Mar. If you did everything right, your report should now look like Figure 2.20.

	A	B	C	D	E	F
1		Drop Page Fields Here				
2						
3			Month ▾			
4	Category ▾	Data ▾	Jan	Feb	Mar	Grand Total
5	Airfare	Count of Amount			1	1
6		Sum of Amount			250	250
7	Entertainment	Count of Amount		2		2
8		Sum of Amount		69		69
9	Lodging	Count of Amount		1	1	2
10		Sum of Amount		98	160	258
11	Restaurant	Count of Amount	3	1	2	6
12		Sum of Amount	121	32	69	222
13	Taxi	Count of Amount	1			1
14		Sum of Amount	42			42
15	Tips	Count of Amount	1			1
16		Sum of Amount	12			12
17	Tolls	Count of Amount			1	1
18		Sum of Amount			8	8
19	Total Count of Amount		5	4	5	14
20	Total Sum of Amount		175	199	487	861

Figure 2.17 The Count Of Amount and Sum Of Amount by Category and Month that summarizes information similar to Table 2.6.

	A	B	C	D	E
1	Month	Type	Category	Amount	
2	Jan	Personal	Restaurant	35	
3	Jan	Business	Taxi	42	
4	Jan	Business	Restaurant	64	
5	Jan	Personal	Restaurant	22	
6	Jan	Business	Tips	12	
7	Feb	Personal	Restaurant	32	
8	Feb	Personal	Entertainment	24	
9	Feb	Business	Entertainment	45	
10	Feb	Business	Lodging	98	
11	Mar	Business	Airfare	250	
12	Mar	Personal	Restaurant	24	
13	Mar	Business	Restaurant	45	
14	Mar	Business	Lodging	120	
15	Mar	Business	Tolls	8	
16					

Figure 2.18 Change the amount for Lodging in Mar from 160 to 120.

	A	B	C	D	E	F
1			Drop Page Fields Here			
2						
3			Month ▾			
4	Category ▾	Data ▾	Jan	Feb	Mar	Grand Total
5	Airfare	Count of Amount			1	1
6		Sum of Amount			250	250
7	Entertainment	Count of Amount				2
8		Sum of Amount				69
9	Lodging	Count of Amount				2
10		Sum of Amount				258
11	Restaurant	Count of Amount				6
12		Sum of Amount				222
13	Taxi	Count of Amount				1
14		Sum of Amount				42
15	Tips	Count of Amount				1
16		Sum of Amount				12
17	Tolls	Count of Amount				1
18		Sum of Amount				8
19	Total Count of Amount					14
20	Total Sum of Amount		175	199	487	861

Context menu overlapping the PivotTable:
- Format Cells...
- PivotChart
- PivotTable Wizard
- Refresh Data
- Hide
- Select ▸
- Group and Show Detail ▸
- Order ▸
- Field Settings...
- Table Options...
- Hide PivotTable Toolbar
- Hide Field List

Figure 2.19 Use the Refresh Data command to update the PivotTable report data from the data entered into the Excel worksheet.

NOTE In this example, the data source is just another worksheet tab in the Excel workbook. The true power of the Excel PivotTable is the capability to fetch the source data from an external data source, such as an online transaction processing (OLTP) database. Imagine getting critical business data such as new orders, marketing responses, or financial information in near real-time with barely more than a simple click of a mouse button.

	A	B	C	D	E	F
1			Drop Page Fields Here			
2						
3			Month ▼			
4	Category ▼	Data ▼	Jan	Feb	Mar	Grand Total
5	Airfare	Count of Amount			1	1
6		Sum of Amount			250	250
7	Entertainment	Count of Amount		2		2
8		Sum of Amount		69		69
9	Lodging	Count of Amount		1	1	2
10		Sum of Amount		98	120	218
11	Restaurant	Count of Amount	3	1	2	6
12		Sum of Amount	121	32	69	222
13	Taxi	Count of Amount	1			1
14		Sum of Amount	42			42
15	Tips	Count of Amount	1			1
16		Sum of Amount	12			12
17	Tolls	Count of Amount			1	1
18		Sum of Amount			8	8
19	Total Count of Amount		5	4	5	14
20	Total Sum of Amount		175	199	447	821

Figure 2.20   The PivotTable report is updated with the new Lodging expense of $120 when the Refresh Data function is selected from the pop-up menu.

Drilling Down on Report Data

Did you ever look at a report and find that some of the figures are difficult to accept? I know from experience it can take a long time to determine whether it's an error or a legitimate figure. You might have to track down several people in an organization or run database queries to determine what actually happened. PivotTables can make this investigation process much easier. You can *drill down* (that, is bring up the underlying dataset that makes up the value in that cell as a new worksheet tab) on any numerical value in the Data area of the PivotTable report to reveal the underlying data that makes up a particular cell value.

To see how drilling down works, follow these steps:

1. Double-click any of the cells in the Data area (defined as the cell range C5–F20) to drill down on the full dataset that makes up a particular cell Sum or Count. In Figure 2.21, I've double-clicked cell C11.

   A new Excel worksheet is created with the underlying data (see Figure 2.22).

	A	B	C	D	E	F
1		Drop Page Fields Here				
2						
3			Month ▾			
4	Category ▾	Data ▾	Jan	Feb	Mar	Grand Total
5	Airfare	Count of Amount			1	1
6		Sum of Amount			250	250
7	Entertainment	Count of Amount		2		2
8		Sum of Amount		69		69
9	Lodging	Count of Amount		1	1	2
10		Sum of Amount		98	120	218
11	Restaurant	Count of Amount	3	1	2	6
12		Sum of Amount	121	32	69	222
13	Taxi	Count of Amount	1			1
14		Sum of Amount	42			42
15	Tips	Count of Amount	1			1
16		Sum of Amount	12			12
17	Tolls	Count of Amount			1	1
18		Sum of Amount			8	8
19	Total Count of Amount		5	4	5	14
20	Total Sum of Amount		175	199	447	821

Figure 2.21 Double-clicking cell C11 reveals the underlying table data that makes up the count of three expense entries for the Restaurant category.

	A	B	C	D
1	Month	Type	Category	Amount
2	Jan	Personal	Restaurant	35
3	Jan	Personal	Restaurant	22
4	Jan	Business	Restaurant	64

Figure 2.22 A new Excel worksheet with three restaurant expense entries.

NOTE The worksheet in Figure 2.22 is produced by double-clicking cell C11 or cell C12 in Figure 2.21. Why? Because, even though the data is being counted and summed in different cells of the PivotTable, it is still the same underlying data.

2. When you're finished looking at the data, choose Edit ⇨ Delete Sheet (or right-click the worksheet tab and choose Delete from the pop-up menu) to return to the PivotTable report shown in Figure 2.21.

The next section covers the basic components and terminology of PivotTable reports. But first, let's review what you've learned so far:

■ You can convert data entered into an Excel spreadsheet with field headings into a PivotTable by clicking any cell in the data range, choosing Data ⇨ PivotTable and PivotChart Report, and then clicking the Finish button.

- When source data changes, you can update a PivotTable by right-clicking anywhere in the report and selecting Refresh Data from the pop-up menu.

- You can drag fields into and out of the report.

- You can perform many types of functions on items in the Data area of a PivotTable report. A couple of the functions used here were Count and Sum.

- You can double-click a data cell to produce a new Excel worksheet that reveals the underlying data that composes a cell value.

Basic Components and Terminology

Now that you understand a little more about PivotTables, you're ready to learn some of the basic components and terminology. When a PivotTable is first created, as you saw in Figure 2.4, a PivotTable Drop area and a PivotTable Field List are created. The PivotTable Drop area is like an artist's blank canvas. This is where you create your magnificent works. The PivotTable Field List is like an artist's palette. This palette or PivotTable list stores all the different types of fields you can drag to the various locations on your canvas. Somewhere on your Excel worksheet, you should also see the PivotTable toolbar. Think of this as your assistant. You can control all the functions and features of PivotTables here. All of these components are shown in Figure 2.23.

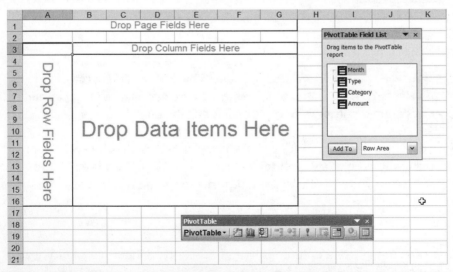

Figure 2.23 The primary components of a PivotTable include the PivotTable Drop area, the PivotTable Field List, and the PivotTable toolbar.

In the preceding section, you moved fields to different areas of the PivotTable without really knowing the purpose of each area. Let's review them here. First, organize your PivotTable to include Month in the Page area, Category in the Row area, Type in the Column area, and Amount in the Data area. Figure 2.24 shows what the report looks like after you drag the fields to these areas.

NOTE Don't forget to move Amount into the Data area last. This will make dragging fields into the PivotTable easier since the shape of the PivotTable will not change as dramatically as when a field is first dropped in the Data area.

PivotTable Areas

Now that you've set up a basic PivotTable, it's a good time to review the purpose of each of the four PivotTable areas.

Page Area

You can drag fields to the Page area to display data as if it were on separate pages. Use this area to see data for a single value or all values. As you can see in Figure 2.25, you can choose to display values for Jan, Feb, Mar, or All. You can also display multiple values in this area, but that is not an option in the drop-down list.

CROSS-REFERENCE Read Chapter 6 to learn how to select multiple values from a Page area field.

	A	B	C	D
1	Month	(All)		
2				
3	Sum of Amount	Type		
4	Category	Business	Personal	Grand Total
5	Airfare	250		250
6	Entertainment	45	24	69
7	Lodging	218		218
8	Restaurant	109	113	222
9	Taxi	42		42
10	Tips	12		12
11	Tolls	8		8
12	Grand Total	684	137	821

Figure 2.24 PivotTable report with Month in the Page area, Category in the Row area, Type in the Column area, and Amount in the Data area.

	A	B	C	D
1	Month	(All) ▾		
2		(All)		
3	Sum of Amount	Jan		
4	Category ▾	Feb		al
5	Airfare	Mar		0
6	Entertainment			9
7	Lodging			8
8	Restaurant	OK	Cancel	2
9	Taxi	42		42
10	Tips	12		12
11	Tolls	8		8
12	Grand Total	684	137	821

Figure 2.25 Choose to display either a single value, such as Jan, or all values from a Page area drop-down list.

Notice that only three values for Category are displayed when Jan is selected from the Month field in Figure 2.25 (see Figure 2.26). This is because other transaction categories such as Airfare and Entertainment were not incurred during that month. The expenses in Jan had a Type of both Business and Personal, so the Column area was not automatically resized. Had all the expenses in Jan had a Type of Business, the Column field would have been resized to display only Business.

Try selecting a few different months to see how different values in a Page area field affect the shape of the PivotTable. When you're finished, reset the PivotTable report to look like it does in Figure 2.24.

CROSS-REFERENCE Read Chapter 7 to learn how to always display all of the Column and Row values regardless of whether a Page area filter is applied.

	A	B	C	D
1	Month	Jan ▾		
2				
3	Sum of Amount	Type ▾		
4	Category ▾	Business	Personal	Grand Total
5	Restaurant	64	57	121
6	Taxi	42		42
7	Tips	12		12
8	Grand Total	118	57	175

Figure 2.26 Changing the Page area field — Month — to filter only those records that have a Month of Jan can result in the shape of the PivotTable being changed to display only the unique values of Category and Type incurred during Jan.

Row Area

You can drag fields to the Row area to vertically display unique fields, one item per row. As you can see in Figure 2.27, you can click the check boxes to choose to display a single value, multiple values, or all values. Use this section when there are several unique values.

Selecting only Airfare and Tolls resizes the Column area as shown in Figure 2.28. Why? These expense Categories all have a Type of Business, so Personal data is not displayed.

Try selecting a few different combinations of Category to see how different values in a Row area field affect the shape of the PivotTable. When you're finished, reset the PivotTable report to appear as shown in Figure 2.24.

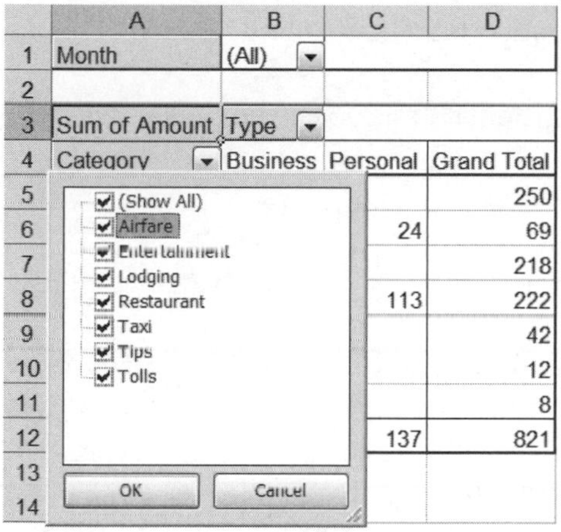

Figure 2.27 You can choose to display a single value, multiple values, or all values from the drop-down list for fields in the Row area of a PivotTable.

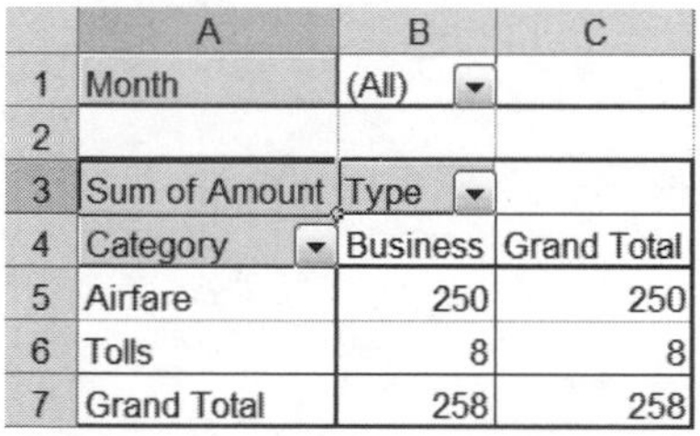

Figure 2.28 Selecting Airfare and Tolls results in the Column area being resized because all the expenses for Airfare and Tolls had a Type of Business.

Column Area

You can drag fields to the Column area to horizontally display unique fields, one item per column. As shown in Figure 2.29, you can choose to display a single value, multiple values, or all values in the dataset. Use this section when there are only a few unique values.

Selecting only Business resizes the Row area as shown in Figure 2.30. This works the same way as it did for Column area fields. Only the expense categories that have a Type of Business are displayed when this filter is applied.

> **NOTE** I recommend that you place fields with several unique values into the Row area for a few reasons. First, Excel can display only 256 columns compared to 65,536 rows. Second, it is usually easier to work with values that scroll down rather than those that scroll across. And third, most printed reports are better suited to display multiple values as rows, rather than as columns.

Before moving on, reset the PivotTable report so it looks like Figure 2.24.

Data Area

You can drag fields into this area to perform some type of aggregation. Here you can choose to count, sum, or average data against values that appear in Row and Column areas of the PivotTable. You can also use this area to find a minimum or maximum value for values in a Row, a Column, or a Row and Column combination.

When there is only value in the Data section of the PivotTable report, the field is preceded with a description of the aggregation type. In Figure 2.31, it's Sum Of Amount. If you change the summary type to Count, the field heading is displayed as Count Of Amount.

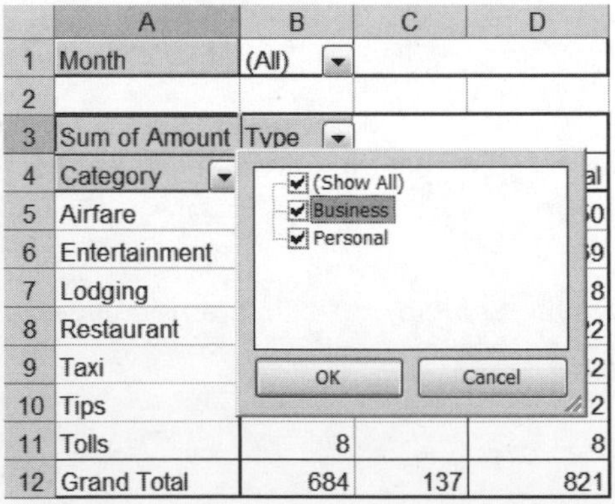

Figure 2.29   You can choose to display a single value, multiple values, or all values from the drop-down list of fields in the Column area of a PivotTable.

	A	B	C
1	Month	(All) ▼	
2			
3	Sum of Amount	Type ▼	
4	Category ▼	Business	Grand Total
5	Airfare	250	250
6	Entertainment	45	45
7	Lodging	258	258
8	Restaurant	109	109
9	Taxi	42	42
10	Tips	12	12
11	Tolls	8	8
12	Grand Total	724	724

Figure 2.30 You can choose to display a single value, multiple values, or all values from the drop-down list of fields in the Column area of a PivotTable.

If you drag Amount into the Data area of the report a second time, the heading is removed and replaced with the field heading Data and a drop-down box, as shown in Figure 2.32.

CROSS-REFERENCE Read Chapter 7 to learn how to change how the Data field heading is displayed when multiple fields are dragged into the Data area.

	A	B	C	D	E	F	G	H	I	J	K
1	Month	(All) ▼									
2								PivotTable Field List ▼ ×			
3	Sum of Amount	Type ▼						Drag items to the PivotTable report			
4	Category ▼	Business	Personal	Grand Total							
5	Airfare	250		250				Month			
6	Entertainment	45	24	69				Type			
7	Lodging	218		218		✛		Category			
8	Restaurant	109	113	222				Amount			
9	Taxi	42		42							
10	Tips	12		12							
11	Tolls	8		8							
12	Grand Total	684	137	821				Add To	Row Area ▼		
13											
14											
15											
16											

Figure 2.31 The aggregation type and field are shown where the Row and Column field heading meet when only a single value is being summarized.

	A	B	C	D	E
1	Month	(All)			
2					
3			Type		
4	Category	Data	Business	Personal	Grand Total
5	Airfare	☑ (Show All)			250
6		☑ Sum of Amount			250
7	Entertainment	☑ Sum of Amount2		24	69
8				24	69
9	Lodging				218
10					218
11	Restaurant			113	222
12				113	222
13	Taxi				42
14		OK	Cancel		42
15	Tips	Sum of Amount	12		12
16		Sum of Amount2	12		12
17	Tolls	Sum of Amount	8		8
18		Sum of Amount2	8		8
19	Total Sum of Amount		684	137	821
20	Total Sum of Amount2		684	137	821

Figure 2.32 By default, the Data field heading is created when multiple fields are dragged into the Data area of the PivotTable. You can remove fields by unchecking them in the drop-down box.

PivotTable Toolbar

All of the functions of a PivotTable are accessible from the PivotTable toolbar shown in Figure 2.33. This toolbar provides you with a handy means of managing the PivotTable. Buttons are included for refreshing data, generating a PivotChart, toggling the display of the PivotTable Field List, and changing the report format. A button for exporting data to Microsoft MapPoint is also displayed on this toolbar if that software program is installed on your computer.

Clicking the PivotTable drop-down button (the left-most button on the PivotTable toolbar) generates a menu that displays all the PivotTable functions. Most, but not all, of these functions are also available from the pop-up menu that is displayed when you right-click the PivotTable report. These menus are similar in appearance and are shown in Figure 2.34.

Figure 2.33 Use the PivotTable toolbar to manage, format, and refresh data in the PivotTable.

Figure 2.34 The PivotTable menu (left) is displayed when you click the PivotTable drop-down arrow on the PivotTable toolbar; the pop-up menu (right) is displayed when you right-click the PivotTable report.

TIP The most commonly used functions are available from the pop-up menu that is displayed when you right-click the report. Be sure that you have selected a cell on the PivotTable if you plan to use the menu from the PivotTable toolbar; otherwise, many of the functions are inaccessible (displayed as dimmed items in the menu).

Chapter 7 provides much more information about the functions displayed in these menus. For now, it's only important that you know that they exist and that you can manage and control the PivotTable from here.

PivotTable Field List

The last basic component of a PivotTable is the PivotTable Field List. All the available fields that can be displayed on a PivotTable are located here. Fields displayed in the PivotTable are bolded in the PivotTable Field List, as shown in Figure 2.35.

As you learned earlier in this chapter, you can also move fields to various locations on the PivotTable report from the PivotTable Field List. Clicking the drop-down box next to Add To shows the various areas where fields can be moved.

The PivotTable Field List can be docked on the right or left side of your worksheet, undocked (as shown in Figure 2.35) or hidden. Figure 2.36 shows how the PivotTable Field List can be left-docked on a worksheet.

	A	B	C	D	E	F	G	H	I	J	K
1			Drop Page Fields Here								
2											
3	Sum of Amount	Month ▾									
4	Category ▾	Jan	Feb	Mar	Grand Total						
5	Airfare			250	250						
6	Entertainment		69		69						
7	Lodging		98	120	218						
8	Restaurant	121	32	69	222						
9	Taxi	42			42						
10	Tips	12			12						
11	Tolls			8	8						
12	Grand Total	175	199	447	821						
13											
14											
15											
16											
17											
18											
19											
20											
21											
22											

PivotTable Field List
Drag items to the PivotTable report
- Month
- Type
- Category
- Amount

Add To   Row Area

Figure 2.35   Type is not a field displayed on the PivotTable report and therefore is not bold.

By default, the PivotTable Field List it right-docked. I prefer to undock it and move it closer to the PivotTable report because I'm generally too lazy to move my mouse that far over the worksheet. I often hide the PivotTable Field List when I'm not using it by clicking the Close box (X) in the top-right corner. The PivotTable Field List display can be toggled from the PivotTable toolbar and right-click pop-up menus shown in Figure 2.34. Also notice that the PivotTable Field List, regardless of whether it is docked or undocked, is automatically hidden when the PivotTable report is not selected.

Microsoft Excel - Book1.xls
File   Edit   View   Insert   Format   Tools   Data   Window   Help

PivotTable Field List ▾ ×
Drag items to the PivotTable report
- Month
- Type
- Category
- Amount

Add To   Row Area

	A	B	C	D	E
1		Drop Page Fields Here			
2					
3	Sum of Amount	Month ▾			
4	Category ▾	Jan	Feb	Mar	Grand Total
5	Airfare			250	250
6	Entertainment		69		69
7	Lodging		98	160	258
8	Restaurant	121	32	69	222
9	Taxi	42			42
10	Tips	12			12
11	Tolls			8	8
12	Grand Total	175	199	487	861

Figure 2.36   PivotTable Field List left-docked on the Excel worksheet.

Terminology

By this point, I hope you are finding that PivotTable reports are understandable and easy to use. As you can probably tell, these reports can be a powerful reporting solution. You can dynamically drag fields on or off the report, apply filters in the Row, Column, or Page areas, and change the type of aggregation using easy-to-learn functions that you can control from your mouse. These tremendous capabilities make this technology very popular with several Microsoft programs. When used within these different applications, the terminology and icons are sometimes different. I cover these differences in more detail as these new topics are introduced. For now, here's a brief review of a few of the terms you've learned so far in this chapter:

- **Dataset:** Also called a *recordset*. This term refers to the rows and columns in a data source.

- **Data source:** The location of the source data. It could be an Excel worksheet, a delimited file, or an SQL query extract. In this chapter, the data source for the PivotTable was simply an Excel worksheet.

- **Drilling down:** The act of double-clicking on cell values in the Data area of a PivotTable report to create a new worksheet that shows the underlying data.

- **Drop area:** The PivotTable area where fields are dropped. It includes the Page, Row, Column, and Data areas.

- **Shaping the report:** The act of customizing the PivotTable report. This includes moving fields into or out of the PivotTable, changing the area where fields are located, or applying a filter against a field in the report.

- **Summary type:** Also called an *aggregation type,* this is the kind of function applied to a group of data in the Data area. The functions covered in this chapter include Sum and Count.

You're now ready to try a real-world example that demonstrates how you can import data from an external software application into Excel to create a PivotTable report.

Trying It Out in the Real World

You've just been hired as a new financial analyst at Northwind Traders. Your first assignment is to create a PivotTable report for Andrew Fuller, the Vice President of Sales. Andrew has asked that the PivotTable report provide the total Sales Amount by Salesperson and City. He would also like the report to include filters for State and Product. The information technology manager has created a comma-delimited extract file for you.

ON THE WEB You can download the Invoices.nwxpt file to your computer from this book's companion web site at `www.wiley.com/go/excelreporting`. Look for this file in the Chap02.zip file or the Chap02 directory.

Getting Down to Business

After you download the Invoices file to your computer, complete these steps to import the file into Excel and create the PivotTable report:

1. Open Excel, choose File ⇨ Open, and locate the folder where you saved the file. Change the Files Of Type field drop-down to All Files (*.*) at the bottom of the Open dialog box, as shown in Figure 2.37.

NOTE I made up the file extension .nwxpt (Northwind Export) instead of using the extension .csv (comma separated value). Excel does not start the Text Import Wizard for .csv file extensions.

2. Select the file and click Open. The Text Import Wizard – Step 1 Of 3 dialog box should appear, as shown in Figure 2.38.

3. Verify that the Delimited radio button is selected and click Next. The next view of the Text Import Wizard dialog box, Step 2 Of 3, should look like Figure 2.39.

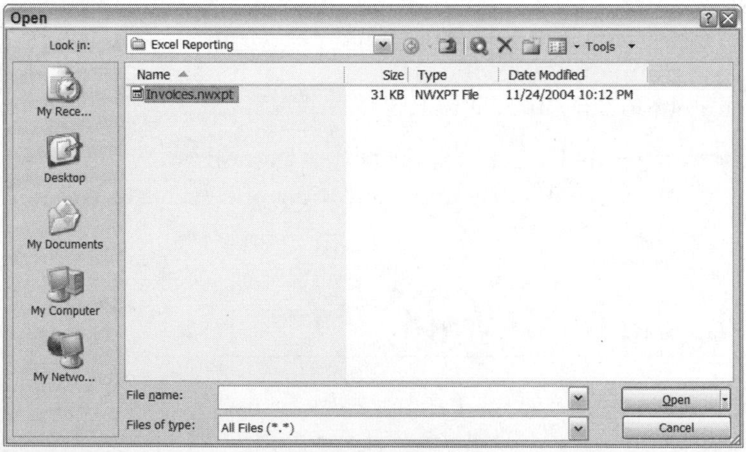

Figure 2.37   Open the Northwind Invoice file by locating the folder where it is saved and changing the Files Of Type to All Files (*.*).

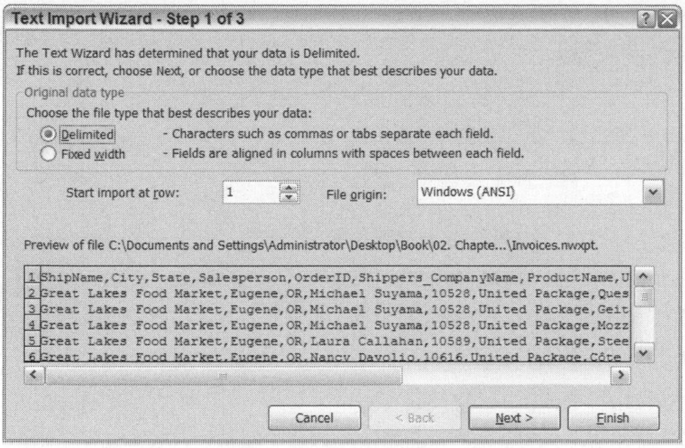

Figure 2.38 The Text Import Wizard – Step 1 Of 3 dialog box is displayed when a file with an unknown file extension is opened from Excel.

4. Uncheck the Tab delimiter and check the Comma delimiter because each field in the Northwind export file is delimited by a comma and not by a tab. Click Finish to import the data into Excel. Verify that the data is imported, as shown in Figure 2.40.

   Now you're back to the starting point of creating a PivotTable. Instead of manually entering the data, you've simply imported the data from a file. All you have to do now is repeat the process of creating a Pivot-Table report.

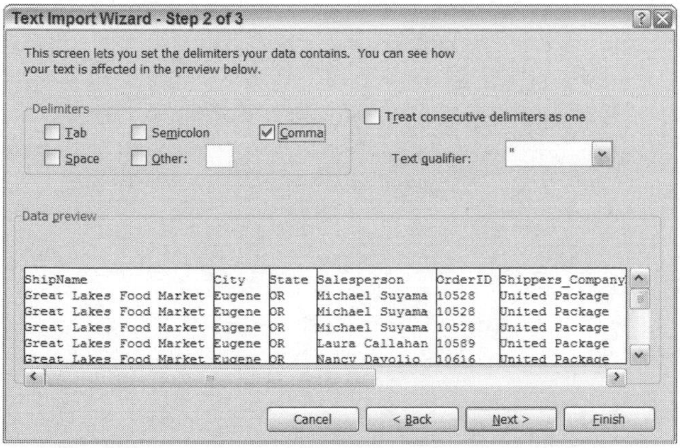

Figure 2.39 Uncheck the Tab delimiter and check the Comma delimiter.

	A	B	C	D	E	F	G	H	I	J	K	L
1	ShipName	City	State	Salespers	OrderID	Shippers_	ProductNa	UnitPrice	Quantity	SaleAmount		
2	Great Lak	Eugene	OR	Michael S	10528	United Pa	Queso Cal	$21.00	3	$63.00		
3	Great Lak	Eugene	OR	Michael S	10528	United Pa	Geitost	$2.50	8	$20.00		
4	Great Lak	Eugene	OR	Michael S	10528	United Pa	Mozzarella	$34.80	9	$313.20		
5	Great Lak	Eugene	OR	Laura Call	10589	United Pa	Steeleye S	$18.00	4	$72.00		
6	Great Lak	Eugene	OR	Nancy Dav	10616	United Pa	Côte de Bl	$263.50	15	########		
7	Great Lak	Eugene	OR	Nancy Dav	10616	United Pa	Gnocchi d	$38.00	14	$532.00		
8	Great Lak	Eugene	OR	Nancy Dav	10616	United Pa	Outback L	$15.00	15	$225.00		
9	Great Lak	Eugene	OR	Nancy Dav	10616	United Pa	Fløtemyso	$21.50	15	$322.50		
10	Great Lak	Eugene	OR	Margaret F	10617	United Pa	Raclette C	$55.00	30	########		
11	Great Lak	Eugene	OR	Michael S	10656	Speedy E	Tofu	$23.25	3	$69.75		
12	Great Lak	Eugene	OR	Michael S	10656	Speedy E	Gula Mala	$19.45	28	$544.60		
13	Great Lak	Eugene	OR	Michael S	10656	Speedy E	Zaanse ko	$9.50	6	$57.00		
14	Great Lak	Eugene	OR	Janet Leve	10681	Federal Sl	Teatime C	$9.20	30	$276.00		
15	Great Lak	Eugene	OR	Janet Leve	10681	Federal Sl	Sir Rodne	$10.00	12	$120.00		
16	Great Lak	Eugene	OR	Janet Leve	10681	Federal Sl	Wimmers	$33.25	28	$931.00		
17	Great Lak	Eugene	OR	Margaret F	10816	United Pa	Côte de Bl	$263.50	30	########		
18	Great Lak	Eugene	OR	Margaret F	10816	United Pa	Tarte au s	$49.30	20	$986.00		
19	Great Lak	Eugene	OR	Janet Leve	10936	United Pa	Inlagd Sill	$19.00	30	$570.00		
20	Great Lak	Eugene	OR	Janet Leve	11006	United Pa	Chai	$18.00	8	$144.00		
21	Great Lak	Eugene	OR	Janet Leve	11006	United Pa	Thüringer	$123.79	2	$247.58		
22	Great Lak	Eugene	OR	Margaret F	11040	Federal Sl	Sir Rodne	$10.00	20	$200.00		
23	Great Lak	Eugene	OR	Margaret F	11061	Federal Sl	Camembe	$34.00	15	$510.00		
24	Lonesome	Portland	OR	Andrew Fu	10307	United Pa	Tarte au s	$39.40	10	$394.00		
25	Lonesome	Portland	OR	Andrew Fu	10307	United Pa	Scottish Lo	$10.00	3	$30.00		

H ◄ ► H \ Invoices /

Figure 2.40   The Text Import Wizard imports the data from the Invoices.nwxpt file into Excel.

5. Verify that you selected one of the cells in the dataset and choose Data ➪ PivotTable and PivotChart report.

6. When the PivotTable And PivotChart dialog box appears, click Finish.

7. Drag Salesperson to the Row area, City to the Column area, and SaleAmount to the Data area.

8. Drag State and ProductName to the Page area.

9. Verify that your PivotTable report looks like Figure 2.41.

	A	B	C	D	E	F	G	H	I	J
1										
2	Region	(All) ▼								
3										
4	Sum of SaleAmount	City ▼								
5	Salesperson ▼	Albuquerque	Anchorage	Boise	Butte	Eugene	Kirkland	Lander	Portland	Grand Total
6	Andrew Fuller	1075		7944.1					424	9443.1
7	Anne Dodsworth	11380		6155.9			569			18104.9
8	Janet Leverling	17138.8	4595.75	4244	326	2288.58		924	125	29642.13
9	Laura Callahan	3608.8	6604.4	6438.5		72		5014.7	36	21774.4
10	Margaret Peacock	3186.6	934.5	14848.4	1393.24	11251	764.3	4819.4	1992.2	39189.64
11	Michael Suyama	1456	848	13891.44		1067.55	237.9	48	386.4	17935.29
12	Nancy Davolio	12793.7	1682.5	21935.55		5032		1542	1295	44280.75
13	Robert King			26347.4	228			141.6		26717
14	Steven Buchanan	1607		13868.1						15475.1
15	Grand Total	52245.9	14665.15	115673.39	1947.24	19711.13	1571.2	12489.7	4258.6	222562.31

H ◄ ► H \ Sheet1 / Invoices /

Figure 2.41   If you did everything right, the PivotTable report should look like this.

WATCH THE VIDEO To see how to do this exercise, watch the
ch1202_video.avi video on the companion web site at www.wiley.com/go/
excelreporting.

Due to space constraints, I don't show a screen shot for every step in this
exercise, or for the exercises in other chapters. I'm confident that you can complete most of the steps without a visual aid. If you do get stuck on a step, however, don't forget that you can reference this book's companion web site at
www.wiley.com/go/excelreporting and watch a video showing how
many of the tasks are done.

Reviewing What You Did

This example demonstrates how you can create PivotTable reports by importing delimited files that are created by various types of software programs and
enterprise systems. In the real world, this technology is useful for analyzing
important business data that is derived from mainframe systems and software
programs that have outdated or minimal report development tools.

Chapter Review

In this chapter, you learned about the basic components and functions of a
PivotTable report. It showed you how data is summarized in a PivotTable
report and how you can move fields to different locations of the report by
dragging fields or using the PivotTable Field List. It illustrated how columnar
formatted data can be aggregated into the cross-tabular format of a PivotTable,
and it demonstrated how you can interactively change the PivotTable report
view to design several different types of reports from a list of available fields.

CHAPTER 3

Understanding and Accessing Source Data

In Chapter 2, you learned how to create a PivotTable report from data that was manually input into a different tab — or worksheet — of that same Excel workbook. The data used to create the PivotTable report is called the report's source data, and it was input into Excel using the simplest, least-efficient, and most error-prone method: manually typing the information into the worksheet. In this chapter, you learn how to access and import data from external data sources that enable you to use more automated methods.

I start this chapter by describing the essential components required to access a data source. After that, I demonstrate how to create reports by importing data from delimited and fixed-width files. You then learn how to create Data Source Name (DSN) files that can link an Excel report to its data source. Creating this link enables an Excel report to instantly retrieve data from sources such as text files, databases, web sites, and Online Analytical Processing (OLAP) cubes.

CROSS-REFERENCE Read Chapter's 7 and 8 for more information on developing reports against OLTP databases, Chapter 10 for developing reports against OLAP cubes, and Chapter 11 for developing reports against web site tables.

This chapter focuses only on how to import and connect to external data sources. Learning and understanding this material is essential to developing

Excel reports that retrieve important business data from your enterprise databases, data warehouse OLAP cubes, and from intranet and internet web tables.

Characteristics of a Data Source

In order to connect a data source, you need to specify the type of data source you want to access and where it is located. If you are accessing a database or OLAP cube, a user login and password may also be required. The following sections describe these elements in more detail.

Types of Data Sources

In order to set up a connection to an external source, Microsoft Excel requires that you first specify the type of data you want to access by choosing a data driver. Once the data driver is specified, you can enter the location, user id, and password to connect to the data source. (The user id and password only apply when required by the data source.)

You choose the type of data to be accessed by selecting a *data source driver*, which is simply a program designed to connect to a specific type of source data and extract data from it. For example, if the data source is a text file, the data driver instructs Excel to prompt for elements such as the file directory and file format. If instead, the data source is a SQL database, the data driver instructs Excel to prompt for elements such as the database server and database name.

A default installation of Microsoft Excel includes drivers for the following types of data sources:

- Microsoft SQL Server database
- Microsoft OLAP cube
- Microsoft Access database
- dBASE database
- Microsoft FoxPro database
- Microsoft Excel worksheet
- Oracle database
- Paradox database
- Delimited file or a text file database

You can also access other types of applications and database systems if you have the appropriate drivers installed on your computer.

TIP If the source system you want to access is not supported by one of these drivers, you can try using Microsoft's generic ODBC driver or contact the software program's manufacturer to see if one is available.

Data Source Locations

The location identifies where the data source resides. Depending on the type of data you are accessing, the location could be a database server, a web site, a file directory, or even an Analysis Server. Locations can be local to the computer you are working on, a server in your organization, a remote server in another state or country, or even an FTP site.

Authenticating to a Data Source

Some types of data sources require a user login and password for access. There are a couple of ways of authenticating to data sources, and I cover these methods individually, in the following sections.

Importing Text Files

Many software programs include tools to export data to a text file that can in turn, be imported into Microsoft Excel for further analysis or reporting. Some examples of personal software programs include Quicken, Microsoft Money, and Access. There are also many middle-tier and enterprise-level software packages in the marketplace that provide similar functionality. And if you are stuck on a mainframe system, it's usually not too difficult to create an extract file that can be imported into Excel. Figure 3.1 shows how a mainframe application produces a text file that can be imported into Excel to produce a report.

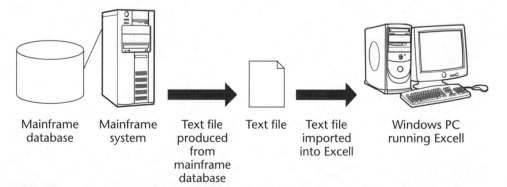

| Mainframe database | Mainframe system | Text file produced from mainframe database | Text file | Text file imported into Excell | Windows PC running Excell |

Figure 3.1 Data exported to a text file from a mainframe system can be imported into Excel to produce a report.

Typically, a mainframe's database is not accessible from Excel, so a text file of the data is produced instead. This text file can then be imported into Excel to produce some type of report. Keep in mind that this situation is not exclusive to mainframe systems. Many other types of software applications and web sites produce text files that are specifically designed to be imported into programs such as Excel. The data is exported to the text file in one of two ways:

- **Delimited:** Each field in the file is delimited by a special character, such as a comma, tab, or pipe symbol (|).

- **Fixed-width:** Each field is delimited by its relative column position in the file.

This section shows you how to import both types of files into Excel and circumvent potential conversion problems with text fields that have numeric data. You should use this method when the file is not regularly being imported into Excel. If, however, that file is being regularly produced from an external system (a weekly revenue report from a sales tracking program, for example), you should consider setting up a connection to a filename and/or file directory. (To learn more about creating filename and file directory connections, see "Creating Data Source Name Files" later in this chapter.)

Delimited Files

In order to distinguish each column or field in a file, fields are delimited with a special character, usually a comma or a tab. This allows programs such as Excel to identify and separate the data into individual fields as the data is being imported.

In this next example, I modified the file used in the "Trying It Out in the Real World" section at the end of Chapter 2 by adding a new column, AuthCode. This column comprises a two-position month followed by a decimal point and a code of 100 for Business expenses or 200 for Personal expenses. So, in the first line, Jan = 01 and Personal = 200 for an AuthCode of 01.200. This kind of coding scheme is frequently used in marketing and financial systems to analyze data. Don't worry about trying to understand the coding scheme; it isn't important. I've simply included it here so that you can see how Excel handles text fields that have numerical values.

To import a delimited file into Excel, follow these steps:

1. Download the Expense Data.csv file from the web site or type the data in manually and save it as **Expense Data.csv**.

ON THE WEB You can download the Expense Data.csv file to your
computer from this book's companion web site at www.wiley.com/go/
excelreporting. **Look for the file in the Chap03.zip file or Chap03 directory
(depending on which file you choose to download from the site).**

```
Month,Type,Category,Amount,AuthCode
Jan,Personal,Restaurant,35,01.200
Jan,Business,Taxi,42,01.100
Jan,Business,Restaurant,64,01.100
Jan,Personal,Restaurant,22,01.100
Jan,Business,Tips,12,01.100
Feb,Personal,Restaurant,32,02.200
Feb,Personal,Entertainment,24,02.200
Feb,Business,Entertainment,45,02.100
Feb,Business,Lodging,98,02.100
Mar,Business,Airfare,250,03.100
Mar,Personal,Restaurant,24,03.100
Mar,Business,Restaurant,45,03.100
Mar,Business,Lodging,160,03.100
Mar,Business,Tolls,8,03.100
```

2. From Excel, choose File ➪ Open.

3. When the Open dialog box appears, locate the directory where you
   saved the file and change the value in the Files Of Type drop-down box
   to Text Files (*.prn; *.txt; *.csv) as shown in Figure 3.2.

4. Select the file and click Open. The data should be imported into Excel
   as shown in Figure 3.3.

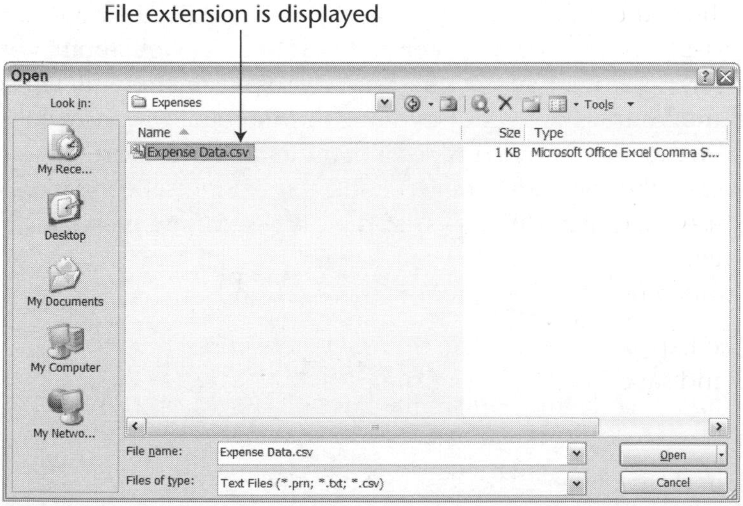

File extension is displayed

Figure 3.2 Select Text Files (*.prn, *.txt, *.csv) in Files Of Type to open the Expense
Data.csv file.

AuthCode is automatically converted
to a data type of General

	A	B	C	D	E	F	G	H	I	J	K	L
1	Month	Type	Category	Amount	AuthCode							
2	Jan	Personal	Restaurant	35	1.2							
3	Jan	Business	Taxi	42	1.1							
4	Jan	Business	Restaurant	64	1.1							
5	Jan	Personal	Restaurant	22	1.1							
6	Jan	Business	Tips	12	1.1							
7	Feb	Personal	Restaurant	32	2.2							
8	Feb	Personal	Entertainm	24	2.2							
9	Feb	Business	Entertainm	45	2.1							
10	Feb	Business	Lodging	98	2.1							
11	Mar	Business	Airfare	250	3.1							
12	Mar	Personal	Restaurant	24	3.1							
13	Mar	Business	Restaurant	45	3.1							
14	Mar	Business	Lodging	160	3.1							
15	Mar	Business	Tolls	8	3.1							
16												
17												
18												
19												
20												
21												

Expense Data

Figure 3.3 Excel automatically assigns a data type to each field for imported files that have a .csv extension. This can result in data corruption of text fields that have numeric data.

WARNING If you don't see the file extension, your computer is configured to automatically hide file extensions for known file types. Read the section "Displaying File Extensions" in Appendix A to properly configure Windows to show .csv file extensions.

The authorization code is actually a text field, but Excel interpreted it to be numeric and thus assigned the field a data type of General. That's a nice feature if the data was actually numeric; but in this case, it isn't. Cell E2 should have been imported as 01.200, but Excel converted it to 1.2. Well, then how do you define the data type? Even editing the text file to put the field heading and field values in quotes does not result in that column being properly converted. If you want to specify field data types when the data is imported, you first need to change the file extension.

To change the file extension and specify field data types, follow these steps:

1. Rename the file Expense Data.csv to **Expense Data.xpt**.

2. From Excel, choose File ➪ Open.

3. When the Open dialog box appears, locate the directory where you saved the file and change the value in the Files of Type drop-down box to All Files (*.*).

4. Select the file and click Open. The Text Import Wizard – Step 1 Of 3 appears as shown in Figure 3.4.

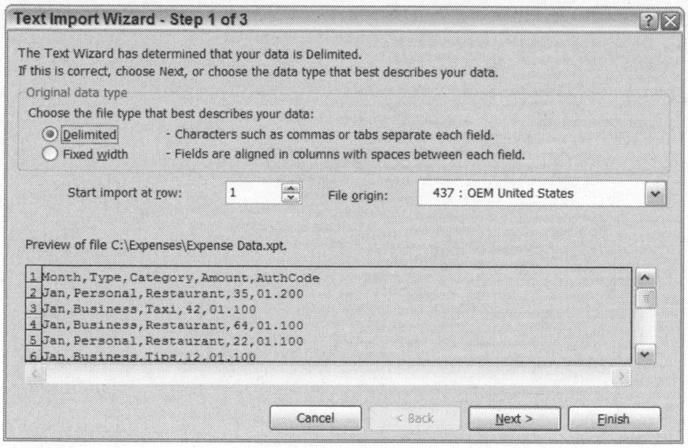

Figure 3.4 To import a comma-delimited file, the Delimited file type button must be selected.

5. Verify that the Delimited button is selected and click Next to continue. You should now see the next view of the Text Import Wizard, Step 2 Of 3, shown in Figure 3.5.

6. Uncheck the Tab delimiter and check the Comma delimiter as shown in Figure 3.6. Notice how the text in the Data Preview window changes when the Comma delimiter is selected. Click Next to continue.

7. In the final Text Import Wizard box (Step 3 Of 3, as shown in Figure 3.7), you assign a data format to each field. Set the column data format to Text for the fields Month, Type, Category, and AuthCode by selecting each column and clicking the Text button. Leave the Amount column with a data format of General.

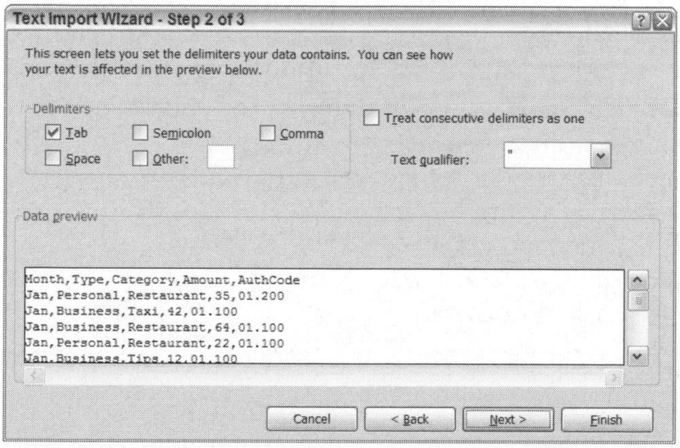

Figure 3.5 Tab is the default delimiter used when files are imported into Excel.

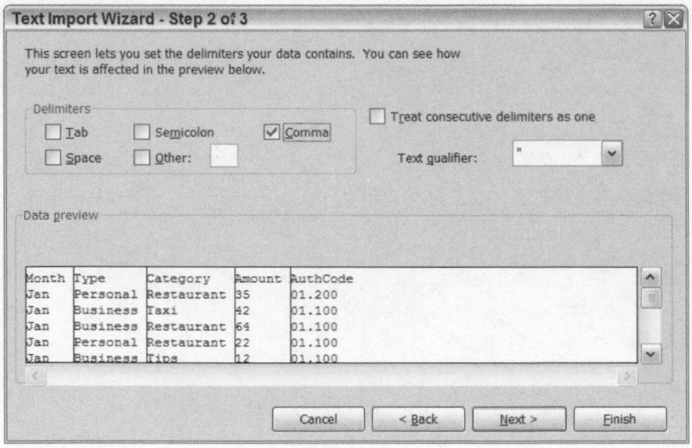

Figure 3.6 The text in the Data Preview pane displays a new column for each field previously separated by a comma.

TIP If you do not want to import a column into Excel, select the column and click the Do Not Import Column (Skip) button.

TIP From a practical perspective, the column data format has to be set only for fields in which the data might be misinterpreted or require a certain date format. In this example, setting only AuthCode to text is sufficient.

8. Verify that your dialog box looks like Figure 3.7, and then click Finish. The data should now be imported as shown in Figure 3.8.

The data in AuthCode has now been loaded into Excel with a Text data type; the preceding zeros to the left and right of the decimal point remain intact.

CREATING NEW FILE EXTENSIONS

I created a new file extension of .xpt, although I could have used an existing one, such as .txt. By creating a new file extension, you can associate it to a program, icon, and description. This results in enhanced searching, presentation, and identification. For example, comma-delimited files that are exported from a contact management program might have an extension of .cmp. That extension could display the file with a telephone icon and be associated with a program file such as Microsoft Wordpad.

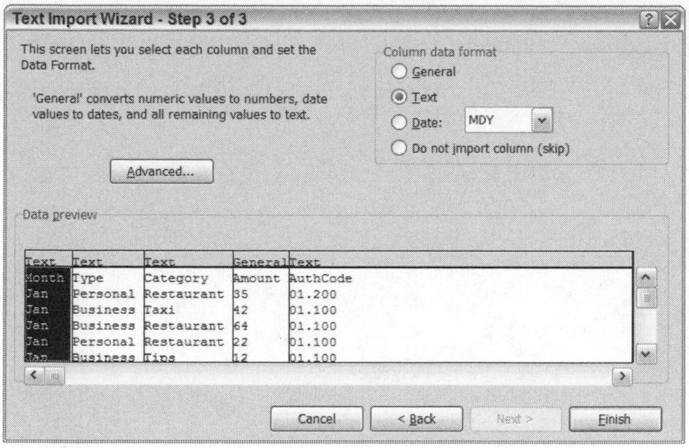

Figure 3.7 Each column is assigned a column data format of Text except for the Amount column, which remains as General.

NOTE Notice that each cell under the AuthCode column heading has a green triangle in the upper-left corner. This is Excel's way of communicating that although the field appears to be numeric, it is being stored as text.

Fixed-Width Files

Fixed-width files are not delimited with any type of special character, such as a comma or a tab. Instead, the position of the data represents a particular field. Here's how the Expense Data file looks in a fixed-width format:

	A	B	C	D	E
1	Month	Type	Category	Amount	AuthCode
2	Jan	Personal	Restaurant	35	01.200
3	Jan	Business	Taxi	42	01.100
4	Jan	Business	Restaurant	64	01.100
5	Jan	Personal	Restaurant	22	01.100
6	Jan	Business	Tips	12	01.100
7	Feb	Personal	Restaurant	32	02.200
8	Feb	Personal	Entertainm	24	02.200
9	Feb	Business	Entertainm	45	02.100
10	Feb	Business	Lodging	98	02.100
11	Mar	Business	Airfare	250	03.100
12	Mar	Personal	Restaurant	24	03.100
13	Mar	Business	Restaurant	45	03.100
14	Mar	Business	Lodging	160	03.100
15	Mar	Business	Tolls	8	03.100

Figure 3.8 AuthCode is converted as a Text data type, maintaining the data's integrity.

```
MonthType     Category       AmountAuthCode
Jan   PersonalRestaurant    35    01.200
Jan   BusinessTaxi          42    01.100
Jan   BusinessRestaurant    64    01.100
Jan   PersonalRestaurant    22    01.100
Jan   BusinessTips          12    01.100
Feb   PersonalRestaurant    32    02.200
Feb   PersonalEntertainment24    02.200
Feb   BusinessEntertainment45    02.100
Feb   BusinessLodging       98    02.100
Mar   BusinessAirfare       250   03.100
Mar   PersonalRestaurant    24    03.100
Mar   BusinessRestaurant    45    03.100
Mar   BusinessLodging       160   03.100
Mar   BusinessTolls         8     03.100
```

The fields are position-delimited as shown in Table 3.1.

Table 3.1 Field Positions for Expense Data.txt

FIELD	START POSITION	NUMBER OF POSITIONS	END POSITION
Month	1	5	5
Type	6	8	13
Category	14	13	26
Amount	27	6	32
AuthCode	33	6	38

ON THE WEB You can download the Expense Data.txt file to your computer from the companion web site at www.wiley.com/go/excelreporting.

Follow these steps to import a fixed-width file into Excel:

1. Download the file from the web site or type the data in manually and save it as Expense Data.txt.

2. From Excel, choose File ⇨ Open.

3. When the Open dialog box appears, locate the directory where you saved the file and change the value in the Files of Type drop-down box to Text Files (*.prn; *.txt; *.csv).

4. Select the file and click Open. You should see the Text Import Wizard – Step 1 Of 3 dialog box shown in Figure 3.9.

Text Import Wizard - Step 1 of 3

The Text Wizard has determined that your data is Fixed Width.
If this is correct, choose Next, or choose the data type that best describes your data.

Original data type

Choose the file type that best describes your data:

○ Delimited — Characters such as commas or tabs separate each field.
◉ Fixed width — Fields are aligned in columns with spaces between each field.

Start import at row: 1   File origin: 437 : OEM United States

Preview of file C:\Expenses\Expense data.txt.

```
1 MonthType   Category    AmountAuthCode
2 Jan  PersonalRestaurant  35   01.200
3 Jan  BusinessTaxi        42   01.100
4 Jan  BusinessRestaurant  64   01.100
5 Jan  PersonalRestaurant  22   01.100
6 Jan  BusinessTips        12   01.100
```

Cancel   < Back   Next >   Finish

Figure 3.9 To import a fixed-width file, you must select the Fixed-Width file type button.

5. Verify that the Fixed-Width button is selected, and then click Next to continue. You should see the next view of the Text Import Wizard, as shown in Figure 3.10.

   Notice that Excel has automatically created break lines for the data. These break lines define the various columns — or fields — that will be created as the data is imported into Excel. Often, the break lines are incorrect and require adjustment, as is the case for this example. Figure 3.10 shows that Month is cut off (*Mon* instead of *Month*) and Type and Category are being interpreted as one field instead of two fields.

6. Select the first break line for Month and drag it over 2 positions to the right. Notice that the solid arrow changes to a dotted line as you move it (see Figure 3.11).

Text Import Wizard - Step 2 of 3

This screen lets you set field widths (column breaks).

Lines with arrows signify a column break.

To CREATE a break line, click at the desired position.
To DELETE a break line, double click on the line.
To MOVE a break line, click and drag it.

Data preview

```
MonthType   Category    AmountAuthCode
Jan  PersonalRestaurant  35   01.200
Jan  BusinessTaxi        42   01.100
Jan  BusinessRestaurant  64   01.100
Jan  PersonalRestaurant  22   01.100
Jan  BusinessTips        12   01.100
```

Cancel   < Back   Next >   Finish

Figure 3.10 Excel automatically generates break lines that define the fields created when a file is imported.

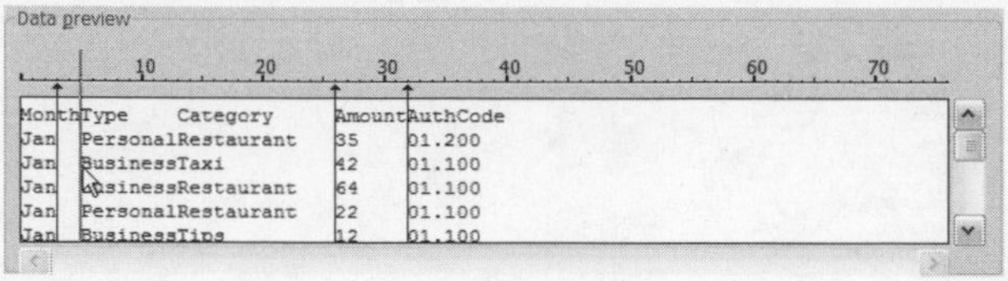

Figure 3.11   Click the first Break Line and drag it over two positions to the right.

7. Verify that the Data Preview window looks like Figure 3.12.

8. Aim the mouse pointer at about the 13 mark on the ruler and click once to create a break line between the Type and Category fields, as shown in Figure 3.13.

TIP Don't worry if you accidentally create a break line in the wrong position or one too many break lines. Just drag the line to the correct position if it's not properly aligned, or double-click the break line to remove it.

9. Verify that the Data Preview window looks like Figure 3.13, and then click Next to continue.

10. Set the column data format to Text for the fields Month, Type, Category, and AuthCode by selecting each column and choosing Text. Leave Amount with a data format of General.

11. Verify that your dialog box looks like Figure 3.14 and click Finish.

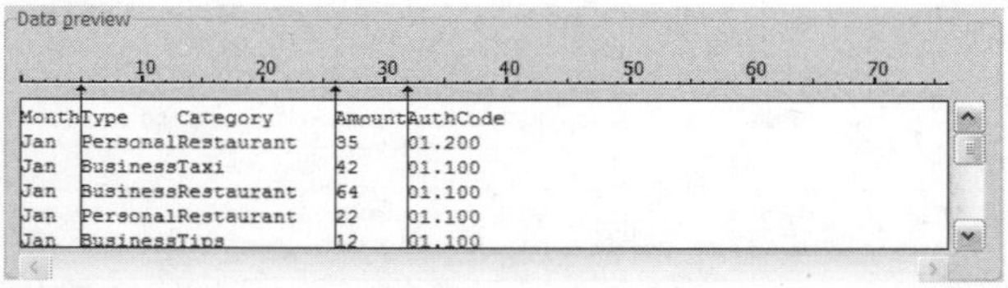

Figure 3.12   The dotted line reverts back to a solid arrow when you drop it in place.

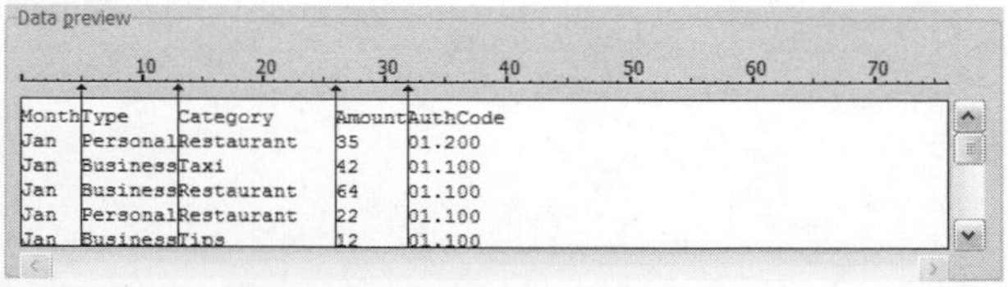

Figure 3.13   With the break lines added and properly positioned, you're ready to proceed to the next step of defining the data types for each column.

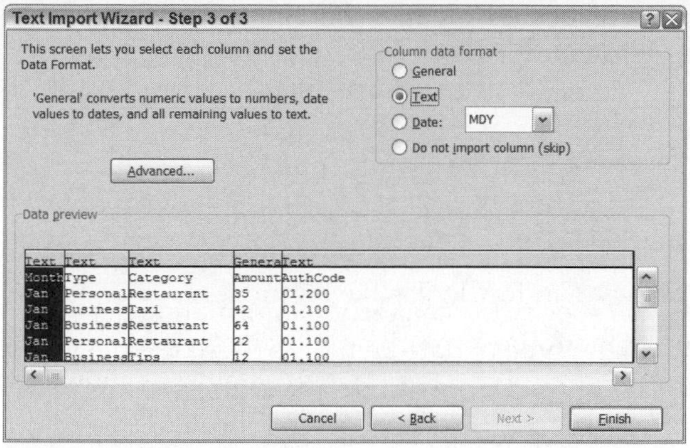

Figure 3.14 Set the Column data format to Text for all columns except Amount.

The data should now be imported as shown in Figure 3.15.

WATCH THE VIDEO You can see how the Expense Data.txt **fixed-width file is imported into Excel by watching the video named ch0301_video.avi on the companion web site at** www.wiley.com/go/excelreporting.

Use these methods to import delimited and fixed-width files into Excel. Keep in mind that while this process is more efficient and less error-prone than manual data entry, it is not without its faults. You need to repeat these steps each time a file is imported. This can take awhile, especially if the file has several columns. It's also easy to make mistakes by assigning an incorrect data type or width to a field.

	A	B	C	D	E
1	Month	Type	Category	Amount	AuthCode
2	Jan	Personal	Restaurant	35	01.200
3	Jan	Business	Taxi	42	01.100
4	Jan	Business	Restaurant	64	01.100
5	Jan	Personal	Restaurant	22	01.100
6	Jan	Business	Tips	12	01.100
7	Feb	Personal	Restaurant	32	02.200
8	Feb	Personal	Entertainm	24	02.200
9	Feb	Business	Entertainm	45	02.100
10	Feb	Business	Lodging	98	02.100
11	Mar	Business	Airfare	250	03.100
12	Mar	Personal	Restaurant	24	03.100
13	Mar	Business	Restaurant	45	03.100
14	Mar	Business	Lodging	160	03.100
15	Mar	Business	Tolls	8	03.100

Figure 3.15 AuthCode is converted as a data type of Text, maintaining the data integrity of the values in that field.

The next section covers how to create DSN files that link an Excel report to its source data. This enables you to import the data from text files, databases, and OLAP cubes without having to repeat all the steps each time the source data is modified.

Creating Data Source Name Files

When you create a DSN file, you specify the connection information needed to access that data. Depending on the type of data being accessed, the file might include a directory and file, a database server and database, or even an Analysis Server and OLAP cube.

This section showed you how to create DSN files in Excel and import data for the following types of data sources:

- Text files
- SQL databases
- OLAP cubes

When you create an Excel report that accesses an external data source, the connection information is stored in the Excel report. This enables any user who has connectivity to the data source and sufficient security privileges to refresh that report data.

In addition to storing the connection information in the Excel report, a copy of the connection information is also saved to a DSN file. This DSN appears each time you create an Excel report that uses an external data source. For example, if you are regularly writing reports against the Northwind database, you only have to specify the connection information once. You do not have to re-create the connection information each time a report is created from that data source.

WARNING Creating numerous external data sources can lead to confusion, especially if you have multiple environments for testing, development, and production that all use the same type of data source. Be sure to develop a smart naming convention that considers all these potential variables.

CREATING NEW FILE EXTENSIONS

When the connection information is stored in the file, as it is for Excel, it is referred to as a File DSN. Other types of DSN's include Machine, User, and Connection. Machine data sources permit only a specific computer to access the data source; User data sources permit only a specific user to access the data source; and Connection data sources permit only a particular application or report to connect to a data source using a programmatic connection object.

The connection information in the DSN files is easy to interpret and can be modified through a simple text editor such as Notepad. The DSN files are covered individually, under each data source.

Creating a Data Source for a Text File

If you are regularly accessing a file that is created from an enterprise software program or some other type of software application, you do not have to manually import it each time. In this situation, the connection information (filenames and location) is stored in the Excel report. You do not have to go through all the steps of importing the new data each time the file is updated or replaced. Instead, the data can be automatically imported *on-demand*, using a simple click of the mouse button, or *scheduled*, using a refresh interval that you define. I've included a detailed, step-by-step example using the file from the previous section to show you how this works.

ON THE WEB You can download the Expense Data.csv file to your computer from www.wiley.com/go/excelreporting.

To create a DSN file for Expense Data.csv, follow these steps:

1. Create a folder called Expenses in the root directory of your C drive.

2. Download and save the Expense Data.csv file to the Expenses directory you created in step 1.

3. Starting with a new workbook in Excel, choose Data ➪ PivotTable and PivotChart Report to bring up the PivotTable and PivotChart Wizard — Step 1 of 3 dialog box.

4. Select the External Data Source button and click Next.

5. When the Wizard's second dialog box appears, click the Get Data button.

WARNING The Typical installation of Excel does not include this feature for accessing external data. If it is not already installed, you will need access to the original Excel CD to complete the installation.

6. When the Choose Data Source dialog box shown in Figure 3.16 appears, select <New Data Source> and click OK.

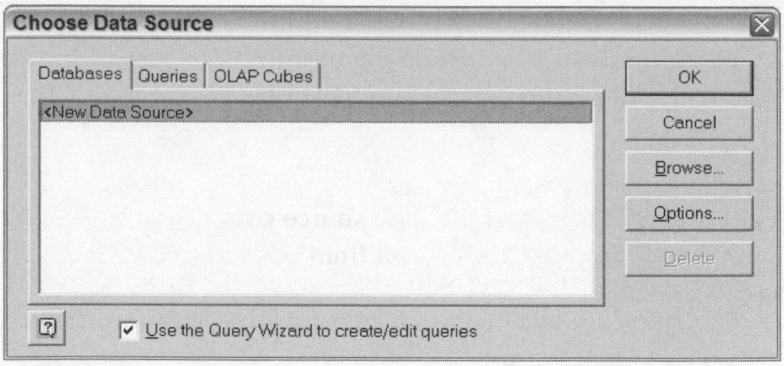

Figure 3.16   Selecting <New Data Source> creates a new DSN file that uses a Text File as its external data source.

> **NOTE**   You might see about six to eight additional data sources beneath <New Data Source> in your view of the Choose Data Source dialog box. These data sources are created when this feature is installed. You can just ignore them for this exercise.

7. Type **Weekly Expense Extract** into the data source description field, select Microsoft Text Driver (*.txt, *.csv) as the driver for the type of database you are accessing, and then click the Connect button (see Figure 3.17).

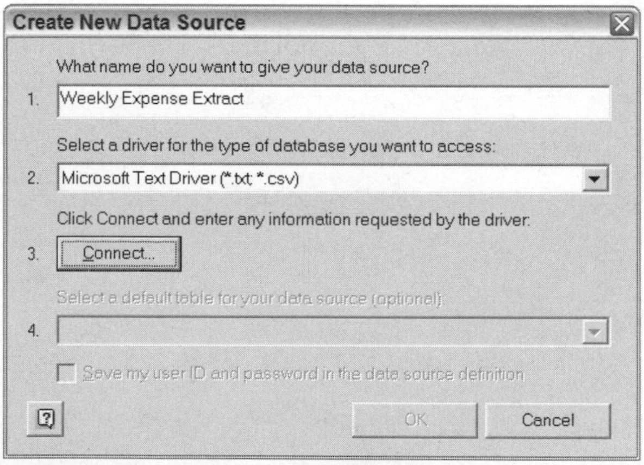

Figure 3.17   Select the Microsoft Text data driver and enter a meaningful description for the type of text file data being accessed.

Make sure that the name you choose for the DSN in the Create New Data Source dialog box is meaningful; it will appear in the Choose Data Source dialog box each time a new Excel report is created from an external data source.

WATCH THE VIDEO Watch how a text file data source connection is created by watching the video file ch0302_video.avi from www.wiley.com/ go/excelreporting.

Setting the Directory

When you click the Connect button in the Create New Data Source dialog box, the ODBC Text Setup dialog box appears, as shown in Figure 3.18. Here, you can opt to use the My Documents default directory or choose a specific location that should be searched for importing one or more files into Excel. The location can be a local directory, a network share, or even an FTP site.

When determining the directory to use, keep in mind that you can configure the DSN to import a single file from that location or prompt for a choice of files. Various types of text file types (fixed-width, comma-delimited, tab-delimited, and so on) can be stored in a single directory along with the file format definitions. (To understand how to set file formats for one or more text files in a specific directory, read "Viewing the DSN File" a little later in this chapter.)

After you select the file directory and create the DSN, it cannot be modified from Excel. If you want to change this location later, you must either create a new DSN or edit the DSN file from Windows using Notepad. (To find out more about changing DSN file information, see "Supporting Files of Text File DSNs" later in this chapter.)

Figure 3.18 Leave the Use Current Directory option checked to use the default My Documents directory. If you uncheck it, the Select Directory button is enabled, and you can click it to define a specific location.

To set the file directory for Expense Data.csv to C:\Expenses, follow these steps:

1. In the ODBC Text Setup dialog box, uncheck Use Current Directory and click the Select Directory button to choose a specific location where you want to import the file.

2. Change the directory to C:\Expenses and click OK when the Select Directory dialog box shown in Figure 3.19 appears.

> **TIP** You can also specify a Universal Naming Convention (UNC) share by clicking the Network button in the Select Directory dialog box.

3. In the ODBC Text Setup dialog box, click the Options button and then click the Define Format button (see Figure 3.20).

Defining the File Format

You configure file formats in the Define Text Format dialog box shown in Figure 3.21. The Tables pane shows all the valid files in this directory for which a format file can be defined. If multiple files are saved in this directory, you can define formats for all of them from this dialog box. The file formats are saved to a single Schema.ini file that is created in that same directory. The next section, "Supporting Files of Text File DSNs," shows you what's stored in that file.

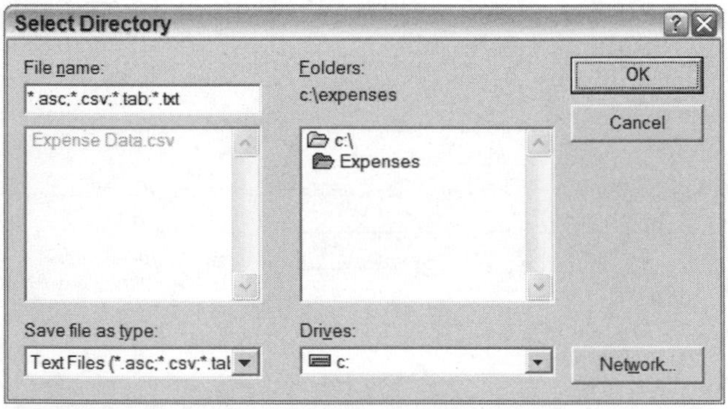

Figure 3.19   Locate the folder where the Expense Data.csv is stored and click OK.

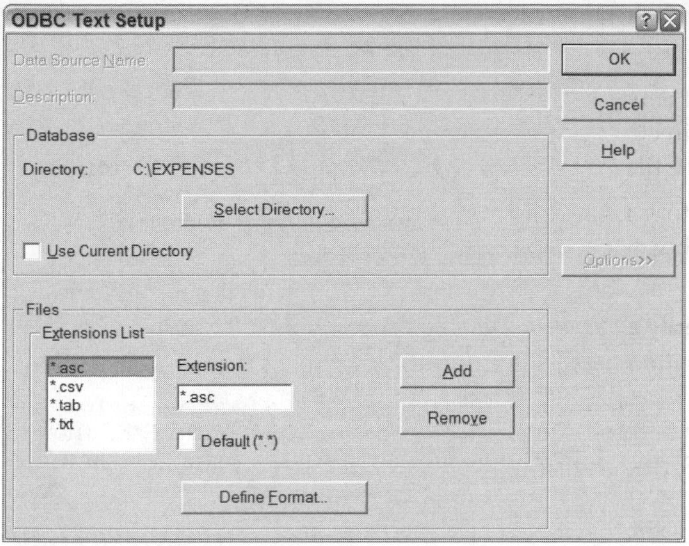

Figure 3.20 Clicking the Options button reveals the bottom part of this dialog box.

TIP Only files that have extensions displayed in the Extensions List pane in the ODBC Text Setup dialog box (refer to Figure 3.20) appear in the left Tables pane of Figure 3.21. You can remove these file extensions or create custom extensions using the Add and Remove buttons in the ODBC Text Setup dialog box. (Note that custom extensions cannot be more than three positions in length.) For example, in order to import the Expense Data.xpt file, you would add .xpt as a valid file extension.

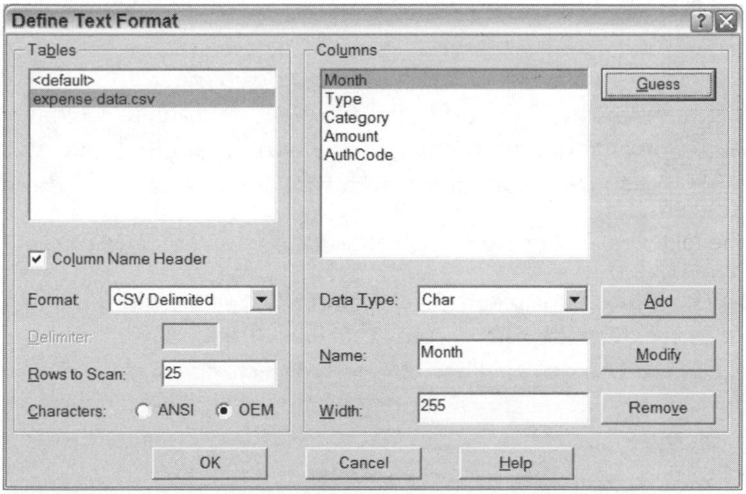

Figure 3.21 You configure file formats in this dialog box.

The Column Name Header option box is checked when the field headings are included in the first row of the data. Use the Format field to select a file format for each file in the directory. You can choose from four types of formats from the Format drop-down list:

- **CSV Delimited:** Select this option when the data is comma-delimited.

- **Tab Delimited:** Select this option when the data is tab-delimited.

- **Custom Delimited:** Select this option when the data is delimited by something other than a Tab or Comma. If this option is selected, the Delimiter Character field is enabled, allowing you to enter a 1–5 position delimiter.

- **Fixed Length:** Select this option when the field is a fixed-width file.

The Rows to Scan field controls the number of fields scanned when previewing the data. I suggest leaving it set to the default of 25. ANSI and OEM determine the character set that is used for reading the data. In most cases, this shouldn't matter and you can ignore it.

The Guess function is similar to the Import Wizard you saw in the last section. Basically, it guesses at field information, including the data type of each field. You learned that Excel's guessing can be problematic, especially when text fields appear to be numeric, so carefully review every field for accuracy each time you use this function.

NOTE Guess can be used only for delimited files. Fixed-width files require that you define the data type, field width, and field name for each field in the file.

To define a field format for Expense Data.csv, follow these steps:

1. Select Expense Data.csv, check the Column Name Header, and then click the Guess button. Your dialog box should look like the one shown earlier in Figure 3.21.

2. Every column that has a Data Type of Char must be changed to LongChar. Additionally, the AuthCode field (which defaults to a Float data type) should be changed to LongChar to ensure that the data is not corrupted. For this example, change the data type to LongChar for the fields Month, Type, Category, and AuthCode, as shown in Figure 3.22.

WARNING A software bug in Microsoft Excel requires that fields with a data type of Char be set to LongChar. Be sure to verify that you click Modify after each field is changed from Char to LongChar, otherwise the change is not processed. For this example, you must click Modify *five* times, not just once. You can verify the change is completed by checking that the Width field is blank and disabled, as shown in Figure 3.22 for the Month field.

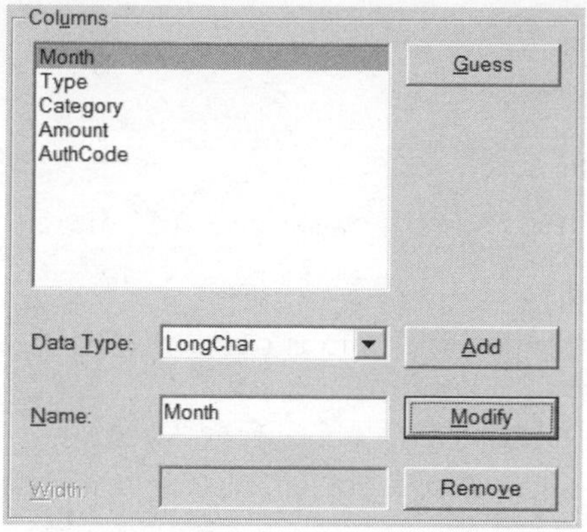

Figure 3.22 Ensure that the file format is accepted by changing the data type of the fields Month, Type, Category, and AuthCode from Char to LongChar.

NOTE Setting AuthCode as LongChar ensures that the text data remains intact. The default data type of General would have corrupted the data.

3. After the fields have been updated, click OK in this dialog box and OK again when you are returned to the ODBC Text Setup dialog box.

TIP To ensure that the source data has been properly configured, click Define Format again and verify that the field formatting settings are still present. If you see an error message, you did something wrong and you'll need to repeat steps 1–3.

4. The Create New Data Source dialog box appears as shown in Figure 3.23. Notice that the file directory of C:\Expenses is shown next to Connect. Select Expense Data.csv as the default table and click OK to continue.

TIP If you do not select a filename as a default table in Figure 3.23, Microsoft Query and the Query Wizard display a dialog box that shows a list of all the files in that directory with valid extension types listed in the ODBC Text Setup dialog box. This can be useful if you have several types of files you want to associate with a data source.

You have now created a DSN for the text file, Expense Data.csv. The DSN appears in the Choose Data Source dialog box shown in Figure 3.24 whenever you create an Excel report that has an external data source. When you no longer plan to use this data source, you can click the Delete button to remove it from the list of valid data sources.

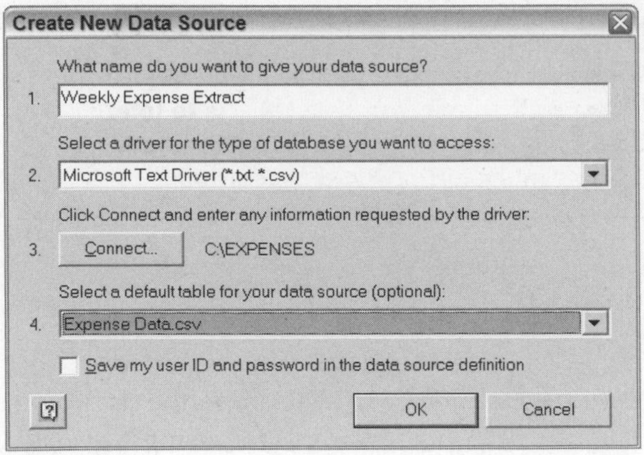

Figure 3.23   Select Expense Data.csv from the drop-down box and click OK if you want this data source to be associated with a specific file, rather than a directory.

Supporting Files of Text File DSNs

A Schema.ini file and a DSN file are created for text files. This is unlike most other data sources where only a DSN file is created. The Schema.ini file is necessary, because text files cannot store field information such as field data type and field width.

This section shows you what these files contain and provide a brief description of their contents.

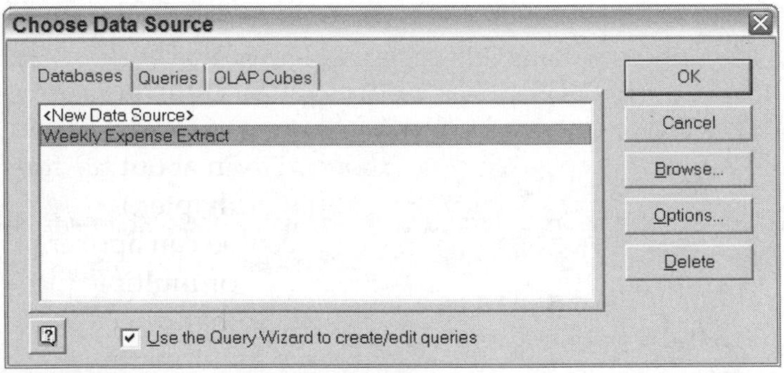

Figure 3.24   The new DSN file appears for this Text File as a valid selection in this dialog box each time an Excel report is created from an external data source.

> **MODIFYING THE SCHEMA.INI FILE**
>
> Changing the Schema.ini file has an immediate effect on the next refresh of an Excel report. For example, if you change the data type of AuthCode to Integer, save the updated Schema.ini, and then refresh the PivotTable report, AuthCode is treated as numeric and you see only integer values in that column.

Understanding the Schema.ini File

Each time Excel connects to the external text file data source, it reads the Schema.ini file that is saved in that same directory to determine the data type and name of each field. You can add or edit the values in this file using Notepad. Here is the Schema.ini file for the Expense Data.csv example used earlier in this section:

```
1.  [expense data.csv]
2.  ColNameHeader=True
3.  Format=CSVDelimited
4.  MaxScanRows=25
5.  CharacterSet=OEM
6.  Col1=MONTH LongChar
7.  Col2=TYPE LongChar
8.  Col3=CATEGORY LongChar
9.  Col4=AMOUNT Integer
10. Col5=AUTHCODE LongChar
```

As you can see, many of the lines are similar to the information you entered in Excel. Line 1 is the text file data source you selected in Figure 3.21. Line 2 identifies that the first row of the data contains column headings. The next line defines the file format, comma-delimited. Line 4 defines the number of preview rows, and Line 5 defines the character set as OEM. Lines 6–10 define the various columns, names and data types. (For more information about file format settings, read "Defining the Field Format" earlier in this chapter.)

Any file in the selected directory with a valid extension type can appear in the Define Text Format dialog box. If you define file formats for multiple files, all of these settings are stored in a single Schema.ini file of that directory. A new line is created for the filename with the corresponding formatting and field options listed below it.

Viewing the DSN File for a Text File

The DSN file stores the connection information used to access the external data source. It is used only for creating new reports and appears in the Choose Data

Source dialog box each time you create an Excel report from an external data source. Deleting the DSN file has no effect on existing reports that initially used this DSN to connect to the external data source. Remember, connection information is saved in the Excel report; the DSN is only used to keep you from having to re-enter the connection information each time you create a new report with the same data source.

Text File DSN's are stored in this directory:

```
C:\Program Files\Common Files\ODBC\Data Sources
```

Many of the lines in the DSN file correspond to options that were selected when the data source was defined. Here is the Weekly Expense Extract.dsn file for the Expense Data.csv example:

```
1.  [ODBC]
2.  DBQ=C:\EXPENSES
3.  DefaultDir=C:\EXPENSES
4.  Driver={Microsoft Text Driver (*.txt; *.csv)}
5.  DriverId=27
6.  Extensions=txt,csv,tab,asc
7.  FIL=text
8.  MaxBufferSize=2048
9.  MaxScanRows=25
10. PageTimeout=5
11. SafeTransactions=0
12. Threads=3
13. UserCommitSync=Yes
14. [Microsoft Office]
15. DefaultTable=Expense Data.csv
```

Just like the Schema.ini file, many of the lines in this file correspond to options and fields selected when you initially set up the data source. There are a few lines that are worth highlighting. First, line 3 controls the default directory that is searched when this DSN is selected. Line 6 shows the valid file extensions for text files that can be used for this data source. Line 15 stores the default file used for this data source. Leaving The Default Table set to blank, or removing the line altogether, directs you to select from a list of multiple text files in that directory. (Note that only the files that have an extension shown in Line 6 will appear.)

NOTE Remember that you are not able to change any lines in this DSN file from Excel. However, you can edit the file using a program such as Notepad.

Creating a Data Source for an SQL Database

Many enterprise software programs use Access, SQL, and Oracle databases to store critical business information. These programs sometimes have reporting and query tools for extracting data. However, as the database and reporting technology advance, many of these enterprise software publishers are unable to stay competitive with the cutting-edge report-development software applications in the marketplace. As a result of this and several other reasons identified in the Introduction, many organizations access the database directly, using more innovative and powerful reporting tools such as Excel Reports.

Figure 3.25 illustrates how Excel can access information from an enterprise system's OLTP database to instantaneously update reports. In this situation, the data can be pulled directly from the database and instantly imported into the report.

This section tells you how you can create a DSN in Excel for an SQL database. In order to maintain consistency, it references the NorthwindCS SQL database that is created from Microsoft Access. If you have not yet created this database, you should install it now so that you can follow along with the examples in this section.

CROSS-REFERENCE See Appendix A if you need help with creating the NorthwindCS database on an SQL Server.

When you create a DSN for an SQL database, you must specify the server and default database. After that, you can also assign a default database table or view to the data source. This option is useful if you are not familiar with SQL programming, because you can use the Query Wizard to generate basic SQL statements.

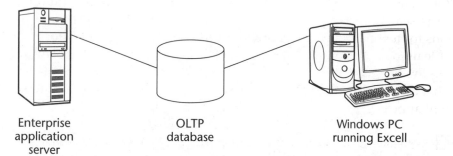

Enterprise   OLTP   Windows PC
application   database   running Excell
server

Figure 3.25   Excel can extract information from an OLTP database in near real-time.

CROSS-REFERENCE See Appendix A if you need help with creating the NorthwindCS database on an SQL Server.

When you create a DSN for an SQL database, you must specify the server and default database. After that, you can also assign a default database table or view to the data source. This option is useful if you are not familiar with SQL programming, because you can use the Query Wizard to generate basic SQL statements.

To create a DSN file for the NorthwindCS database, follow these steps:

1. From Excel, choose Data ⇨ PivotTable And PivotChart.

2. Select External Data Source and click Next.

3. Click the Get Data button when the Wizard's Step 2 dialog box appears.

WARNING The Typical installation of Excel does not include this feature for accessing external data. If it is not already installed, you need access to the original CD to complete the installation.

4. When the Choose Data Source dialog box appears, as shown in Figure 3.26, select <New Data Source> and click OK.

NOTE You might see about six to eight additional data sources below <New Data Source> in your view of the Choose Data Source dialog box. These data sources are created when this feature is installed. You can just ignore them for this exercise.

5. Type **NorthwindCS Sales Report** into the data source name field, select SQL Server as the data type, and then click the Connect button (see Figure 3.27).

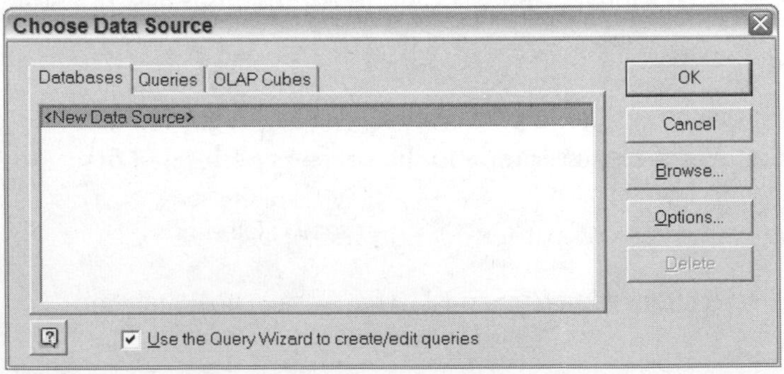

Figure 3.26 Selecting <New Data Source> creates a new DSN file.

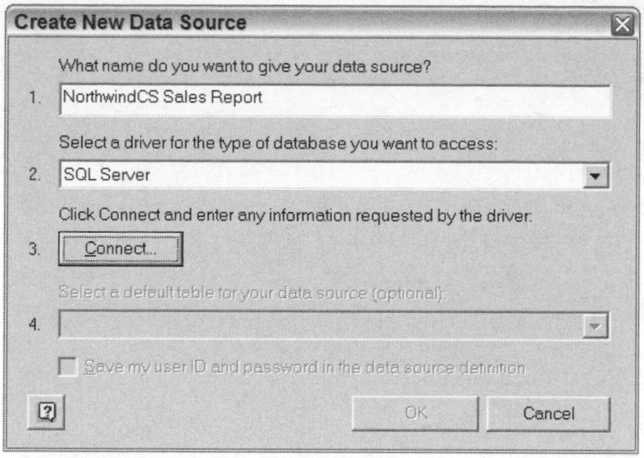

Figure 3.27 Type a meaningful name for the data source and choose SQL Server for the type of driver.

WATCH THE VIDEO Watch the video on how you can create a DSN file for a SQL database by downloading the ch0303_video.avi file from www.wiley.com/go/excelreporting.

Be sure to provide a meaningful name, because it will appear in the Choose Data Source dialog box each time a new Excel report is created from an external data source. Here are some of the data elements you might want to include in the name:

- SQL Server
- Default database
- Default database table or view

Authenticating to the Database

After selecting an SQL Server driver and clicking the Connect button, the SQL Server Login dialog box appears. Here, you enter in the name of the SQL server and the authentication credentials.

NOTE In order to determine whether a particular user or SQL login can access a database or database object, authentication to the server is performed first.

You can choose from two types of authentication methods:

- **Trusted Security:** The Windows domain user account or group and password of the user is used to authenticate to the SQL server.
- **SQL Login Account and Password:** A specific user account and password is specified to authenticate to the SQL server.

Table 3.2 Trusted Security and SQL Authentication Differences

DESIRED CAPABILITY	TRUSTED SECURITY	SQL AUTHENTICATION
To require users to enter a password each time the report is refreshed	No	Yes
To provide access based on the Windows NT domain account or group	Yes	No
To provide access based on the SQL login account	No	Yes

WARNING The SQL Server must be configured to Mixed Mode in order for an SQL login to be accepted. You can enable this mode in the Security tab of the SQL Server Properties dialog box.

In a general sense, one authentication method isn't better than another. Determining what method is best for your organization requires an evaluation of security policies and the existing network, operating system, and database security already in force. Depending on the results of this analysis and future goals, one of these authentication methods might be preferable over the other. An in-depth review of database security is outside the scope of this book, but Table 3.2 includes a brief summary of the differences to help you understand each option a little better.

WARNING If you opt to use a SQL login authentication method, I recommend that you do not use the sa account unless security isn't a concern.

When the SQL Server Login dialog box appears, as shown in Figure 3.28, follow these steps to connect to the SQL server and set the default database for this DSN to the NorthwindCS database:

1. In the Server field, type the SQL Server name or click the drop-down arrow to select a SQL Server from the list.

2. Select an authentication method by either clicking the Use Trusted Connection check box or providing a SQL Server Login ID and Password.

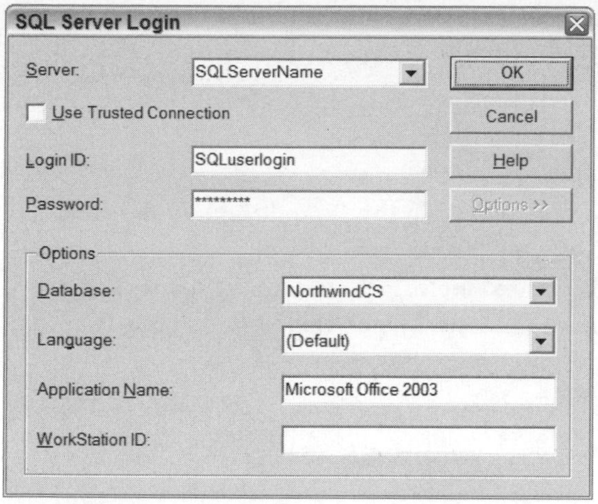

Figure 3.28 In this dialog box, you specify the SQL server, security credentials, and default database for the DSN file.

3. Select the NorthwindCS database from the Database drop-down box.

4. Verify that your dialog box looks similar to the one shown in Figure 3.28 and click OK.

   You should now be returned to the Create New Data Source dialog box shown in Figure 3.29. Notice that the default database now appears next to the Connect button. You can select a default table or view from the Select a Default Table for your Data Source drop-down box.

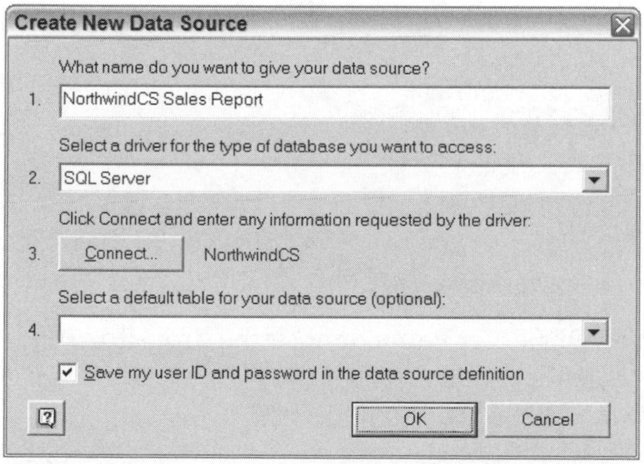

Figure 3.29 The default database selected earlier now appears next to Connect.

If you plan to extract data from the database using an SQL query, leave the Select a Default Table for Your Data Source drop-down box blank. Otherwise, select the default database table or view that should be used for this data source.

WARNING Object owners are not displayed in the Default Table drop-down box. Thus, the object owner (usually "dbo") is not explicitly defined. Rather, it is implicitly set by selecting an object. For example, if there are two database tables that have the same name but a different owner, the names simply appear twice in the drop-down box.

5. For this example, leave the Select A Default Table For Your Data Source box blank.

6. If you are using a SQL Server login account, check Save My User ID And Password in the Data Source Definition check box and then click OK.

You have now created a DSN for the NorthwindCS database. The DSN will appear in the Choose Data Source dialog box shown in Figure 3.30 whenever you create an Excel report that has an external data source. When you no longer plan to use this data source, you can click the Delete button to remove it from the list of valid data sources.

CROSS-REFERENCE Read Chapter 6 to learn how Excel reports can extract data from multiple SQL databases located on multiple SQL servers.

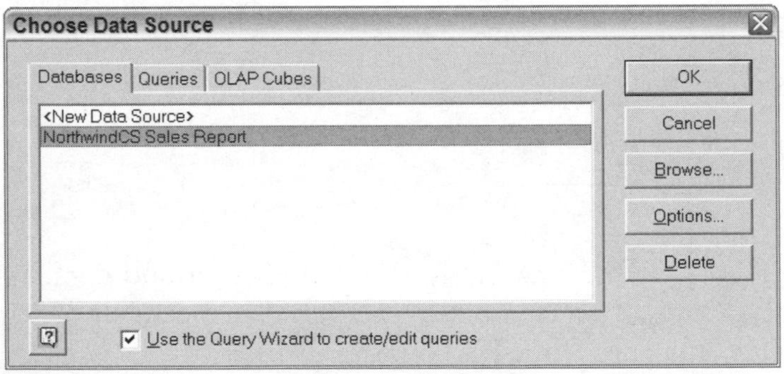

Figure 3.30   The new DSN file appears for this SQL database as a valid selection in this dialog box each time an Excel report is created from an external data source.

Supporting Files of Database DSNs

Unlike a text file, a Schema.ini file is not created for a database. Why? Because the database tables already store the field information such as the data type and the field width. The only file generated when a new database data source is created is the DSN file.

The DSN file stores the connection information for accessing a particular database on a particular database server. It is used only for creating new reports and appears in the Choose Data Source dialog box each time that you create a new Excel report from an external data source. Deleting the DSN file has no effect on existing reports that initially used this DSN to connect to the external data source. Remember, connection information is saved in the Excel report; the DSN is only used to keep you from having to re-enter the connection information each time you create a new report with the same data source.

Database file DSN's are stored in this directory:

C:\Program Files\Common Files\ODBC\Data Sources

This section provides examples of DSN files for both types of authentication methods for the NorthwindCS Sales Report example.

Viewing the DSN File for a Trusted Connection

Many of the lines correspond to options that were selected when the data source was defined. Here is the NorthwindCS Sales Report.dsn file that uses a Trusted Connection authentication method:

```
1. [ODBC]
2. DRIVER=SQL Server
3. SERVER=SQLSERVERNAME
4. APP=Microsoft Office 2003
5. WSID=DESKTOP
6. DATABASE=NorthwindCS
7. Network=DBMSSOCN
8. Trusted_Connection=Yes
```

Lines 1 and 2 define the ODBC data driver. The SQL Server and database name you specified in Figure 3.28 appear in Lines 3 and 6, respectively. If you opted to use a Trusted Connection, Line 8 is set to Yes.

Viewing the DSN File for an SQL Login

The DSN file for an SQL Server authentication method is similar to a Trusted Connection authentication method. The main difference is that the Trusted

Connection line is removed. Also, if the Save My User ID and Password in the Data Source Definition option is checked, the SQL login and password are also stored in this file.

```
1. [ODBC]
2. DRIVER=SQL Server
3. SERVER= SQLSERVERNAME
4. APP=Microsoft Office 2003
5. WSID=DESKTOP
6. DATABASE=NorthwindCS
7. Network=DBMSSOCN
8. [Microsoft Office]
9. UID=SQL LOGIN
10. PWD=PASSWORD
```

Lines 1 and 2 define the ODBC data driver. The SQL Server and database name you specified in the SQL Server Login dialog box appear in Lines 3 and 6, respectively. Lines 7–10 appear only when the Save My User ID and Password option is checked. Lines 9–10 store the SQL login and password.

WARNING If you are using a SQL Authentication method, you can see how easy it is to locate the User ID and password in the text file. If security is a concern, do not save these credentials to the DSN file.

Creating a Data Source for an OLAP Cube

Accessing data from an Online Transaction Processing (OLTP) database is useful when Excel report updates need to be rapidly processed without numerous procedures. However, when a data set becomes very large, you may encounter some problems, including the following:

- A lengthy period of time to import the data into Excel
- Processing delays when the report is modified
- Database locking that interferes with normal operations of the enterprise system
- Adverse performance impact on users accessing the OLTP database or enterprise system

When any of these problems arise, you can either reduce the size of the data set or build an Offline Analytical Processing (OLAP) cube of the data. An OLAP cube usually resolves all the performance, locking, and processing issues. However, it also comes at a cost. With an OLAP cube, you can no longer extract the data in near real-time because the OLAP cube must first be built from the applicable data in the OLTP database. (This can take awhile, depending on the storage design options you select.) Additionally, because the underlying data has been aggregated to increase performance, you cannot drill down on the data in Excel.

An in-depth analysis of OLAP cubes is outside the scope of this book. However, I have included a brief summary of the differences between an OLTP database and an OLAP cube in Table 3.3 to help you understand the differences in these technologies a little better.

When you create a DSN for an OLAP cube, you specify the Analysis Server, database, and OLAP cube. You can also connect to offline cube files that can be created from an Analysis Server or even from the Microsoft Query program.

CROSS-REFERENCE Read Chapter 10 for information on creating offline cube files.

The following is a detailed, step-by-step example on how to create a data source for an OLAP cube using the Foodmart 2000 database installed by default with Analysis Services.

To create a DSN file for the FoodMart 2000 database, follow these steps:

1. From Excel, choose Data ⇨ PivotTable And PivotChart.

2. Select External Data Source and click Next.

3. Click Get Data when the PivotTable and PivotChart Wizard - Step 2 of 3 dialog box appears.

4. When the Choose Data Source dialog box appears, click the OLAP Cubes tab at the top of the dialog box, select <New Data Source>, and click OK, as shown in Figure 3.31.

Table 3.3 OLTP Databases and OLAP Cubes Differences

CAPABILITY	OLTP DATABASE	OLAP CUBE
Extracts enterprise data in near real-time	Yes	No
Includes a drill-down capability	Yes	No
Imports each row of data into the report	Yes	No
Provides pre-aggregated totals for ultra-fast performance	No	Yes
Provides fast connection to the data source	No	Yes
Offers the capability to analyze extremely large data sets	No	Yes

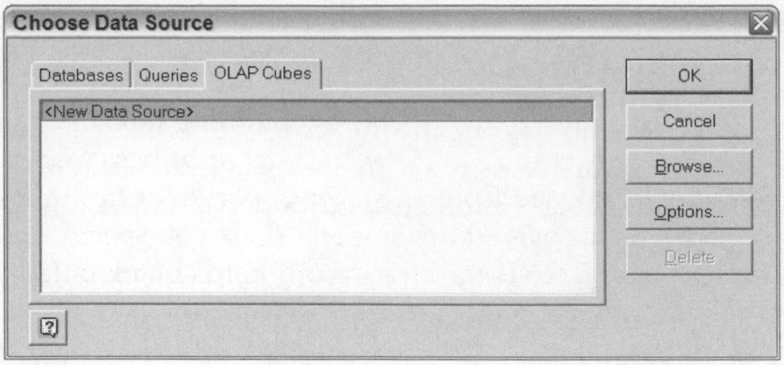

Figure 3.31 Click the OLAP Cubes tab in this dialog box to access or create an OLAP data cube.

5. Type **Foodmart Sales Report** into the data source description field, select Microsoft OLE DB Provider For OLAP Services 8.0 as the type of data, and then click Connect (see Figure 3.32).

You choose the type of data driver and provide a name for the DSN in the Create New Data Source dialog box. The name should be meaningful because it will appear in the dialog box each time a new Excel report is created from an OLAP cube or cube file. Here are some of the data elements you might want to include in the name:

- Analysis Server
- Database
- Cube

NOTE Select the OLAP 8.0 driver for a SQL Server 2000 data cube and the OLAP 9.0 driver for SQL Server 2005 data cube.

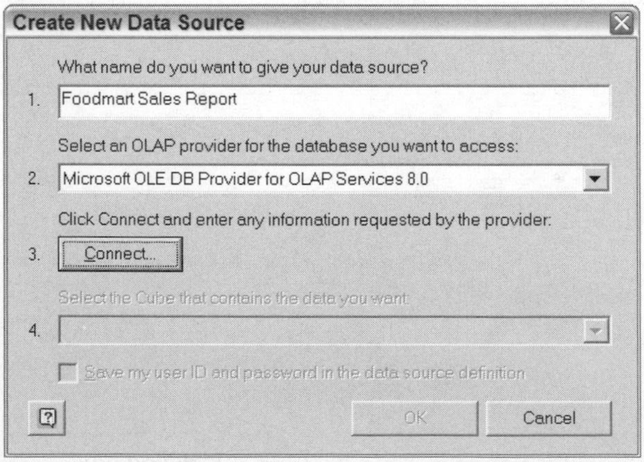

Figure 3.32 In box 1, type a name that provides a meaningful description of the data, and then select an OLAP Driver.

Accessing the OLAP Cube

After you click the Connect button in the Create New Data Source dialog box, you are presented with the Multidimensional Connection dialog box. In this dialog box, you can choose to connect to an Analysis Server or browse for an OLAP cube file. Cube files can be created from an Analysis Server or from the Microsoft Query program (which is covered in Chapter 10). If you specify an Analysis Server, you can leave the User ID and Password fields blank unless you are establishing an HTTP connection.

NOTE Accessing an OLAP cube requires that the Windows user login be added to the OLAP Administrators group.

Follow these steps to connect to an Analysis Server and select the Sales cube in the Foodmart 2000 database:

1. Type the name of the Analysis Server that you want to access in the Server field, and then click Next, as shown in Figure 3.33.

2. The next view of the dialog box appears, showing all the valid databases on the Analysis Server. Select FoodMart 2000 and click Finish, as shown in Figure 3.34.

   You should now be returned to the Create New Data Source dialog box, as shown in Figure 3.35. Notice that the database you selected appears next to the Connect button.

3. Select the Sales cube from the Select The Cube That Contains The Data You Want drop-down box and click OK.

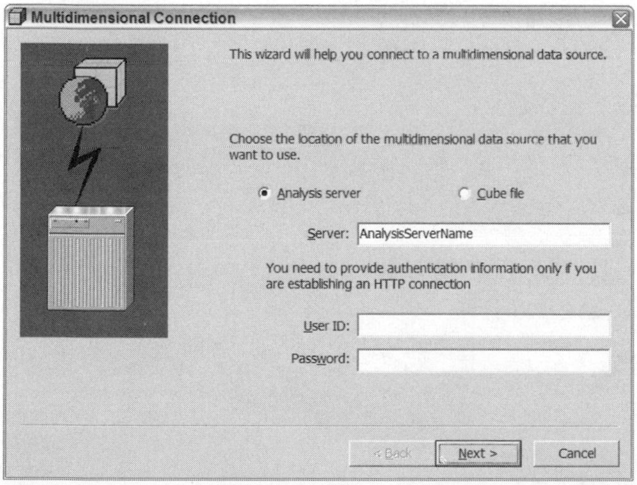

Figure 3.33   You can connect to an Analysis Server or cube file from this dialog box.

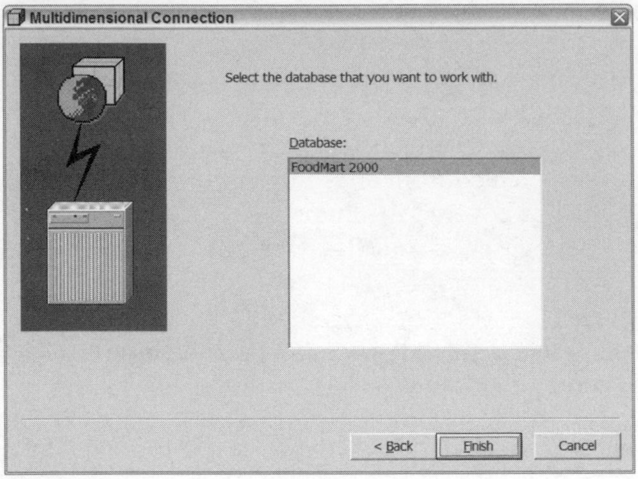

Figure 3.34   In this box, select a database on the Analysis Server.

WARNING   **You must select a cube from the drop-down box shown in Figure 3.35, otherwise the DSN will fail to work.**

You have now created a DSN for the Sales cube on the Foodmart 2000 database. The DSN will appear under the OLAP Cubes tab in the Choose Data Source dialog box, as shown in Figure 3.36, whenever you create an Excel report that uses an OLAP cube. If you no longer plan to reference this data source, you can click the Delete button to remove it from the list of valid data sources.

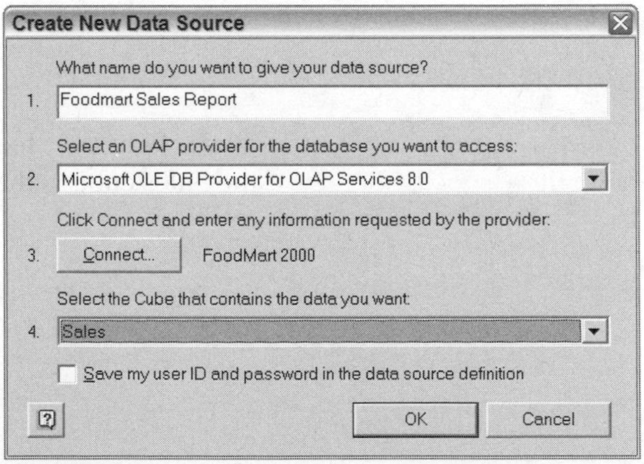

Figure 3.35   The FoodMart 2000 database that you selected in step 2 is now shown here.

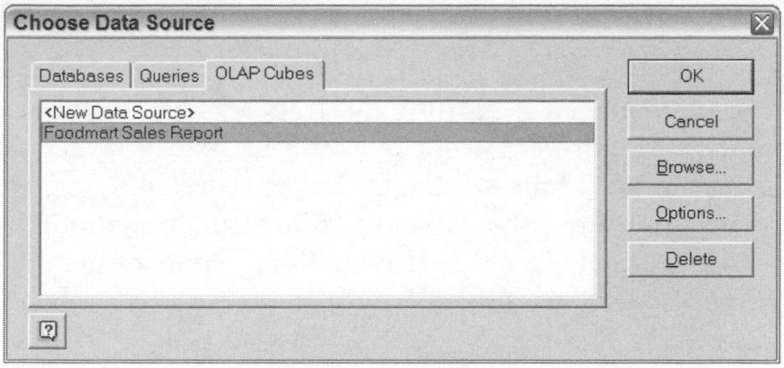

Figure 3.36 The new DSN file for this OLAP cube appears as a valid selection in this dialog box each time an Excel report is created from an external data source.

Supporting Files of OLAP Cube DSNs

The DSN file stores the connection information for accessing a particular OLAP cube in a specified OLAP database and Analysis Server. It is only used for creating new reports and appears in the Choose Data Source dialog box each time you create a new Excel report with an OLAP cube data source. Deleting the DSN file has no effect on existing reports that initially used this DSN to connect to the external data source. Remember, connection information is saved in the Excel report; the DSN is only used to keep you from having to re-enter the connection information each time you create a new report with the same data source.

OLAP cube DSN's are stored in this directory:

C:\Documents and Settings\{User}\Application Data\Microsoft\Queries

Viewing the DSN File for an OLAP Cube

Many of the lines in the DSN file correspond to options that were selected when the data source was defined. Here is the DSN file for the Sales cube in the Foodmart 2000 database:

```
1. QueryType=OLEDB
2. Version=1
3. CommandType=Cube
4. Connection=Provider=MSOLAP.2;Data Source=SERVERNAME;Initial
Catalog=FoodMart 2000;Client Cache Size=25;Auto Synch Period=10000
5. CommandText=Sales
```

Line 4 contains the connection information for the Analysis Server (Data Source) and database name (Initial Catalog). The OLAP cube name is referenced in Line 5 (Command Text).

Trying It Out in the Real World

Steven Buchanan, the sales manager at Northwind Traders, has negotiated with his suppliers to obtain a return credit for discontinued stock on hand. Steven has assigned the database administrator to develop an SQL query to extract the required information from the database and calculate the return-credit amount. They need your help to create a PivotTable report of the discontinued product by company that uses the following SQL query developed by the database administrator:

```
SELECT pro.ProductName
                                                AS [PRODUCT],
                                       pro.UnitsInStock

AS [QTY],
                                                pro.UnitPrice

AS [UNIT PRICE],
          ((pro.UnitsInStock * pro.UnitPrice) * 0.50) AS [RETURN CREDIT],
                                       sup.CompanyName

AS [COMPANY NAME]
FROM                                                Products pro
INNER JOIN Suppliers sup ON pro.SupplierID = sup.SupplierID
WHERE               (pro.Discontinued = 1 AND pro.UnitsInStock > 0)
```

ON THE WEB You can download the Northwind0301.sql file to your computer from the web site www.wiley.com/go/excelreporting.

Getting Down to Business

After you download the Northwind0301.sql file to your computer, follow these steps to complete the exercise:

1. From Excel, choose Data ⇨ PivotTable And PivotChart Report.

2. Select External Data source, and click Next when the PivotTable Wizard appears.

3. Click Get Data when the next view of the Wizard appears.

4. When the Choose Data Source dialog box appears, select <New Data Source> and click OK.

5. Type **NorthwindCS Database** into the data source name field, select SQL Server as the type of data, and click Connect.

6. In the Server field, type the name of the SQL Server that you will access; and then select an authentication type, set the default database to NorthwindCS, and click OK.

TIP The description for a database DSN should typically include the server, database, and object. If you have only one database server and you use a SQL query instead of an object, only the database should be entered in the name field.

7. When you are returned to the Create New Data Source dialog box, leave the default table field blank. Verify that your dialog box looks like Figure 3.37. Note that you can optionally choose to save the user id and password in the DSN file. Click OK.

8. When you are returned to the Choose Data Source dialog box, uncheck the Use the Query Wizard To Create/Edit Queries option.

9. Verify that your dialog box looks like Figure 3.38 and click OK to continue.

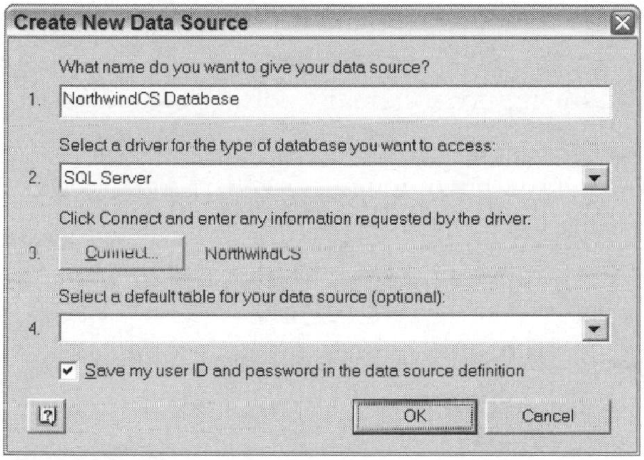

Figure 3.37 Leave the default table field blank when you are using SQL queries to create a PivotTable report.

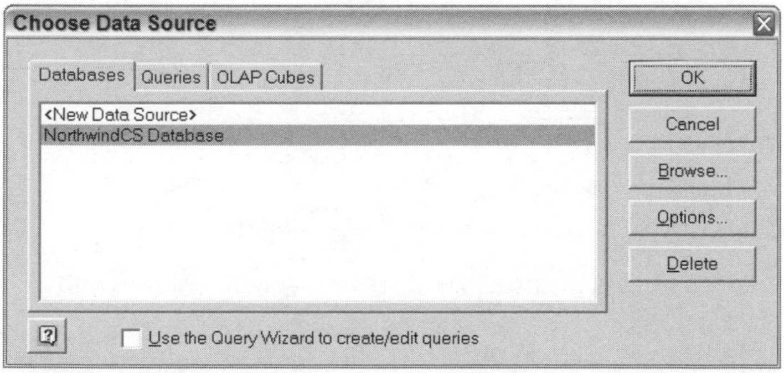

Figure 3.38 Select the NorthwindCS Database, and then uncheck the Use The Query Wizard To Create/Edit Queries option to bypass the Query Wizard.

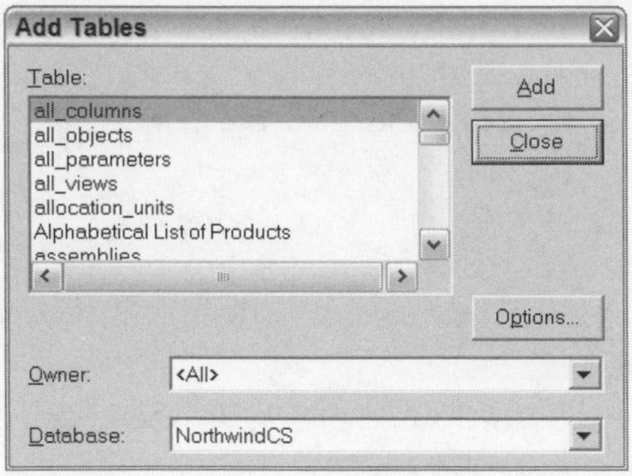

Figure 3.39 When a default table is not defined in the DSN file, the Add Tables dialog box appears. You simply close this box if you are pasting an SQL query into the PivotTable.

10. The Microsoft Query program is started, and the Add Tables dialog box shown in Figure 3.39 appears. Click Close in this box, because you will be pasting a SQL query into the report. (Manually adding the tables is not necessary.)

11. In the Microsoft Query dialog box shown in Figure 3.40, click the SQL button to open the SQL dialog box where you can paste a query.

12. Copy and then paste the SQL query into the SQL dialog box, as shown in Figure 3.41, and click OK.

13. Click OK when the Microsoft Query dialog box appears, warning you that the query cannot be displayed graphically.

SQL button

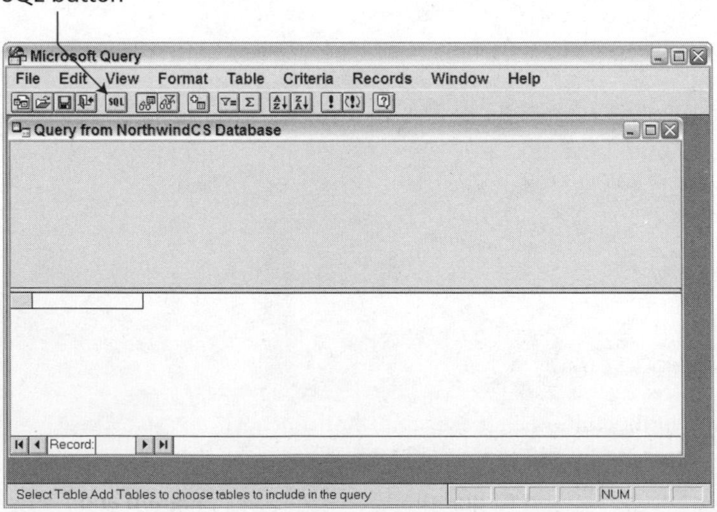

Figure 3.40 Click the SQL button to use a query instead of a table or view.

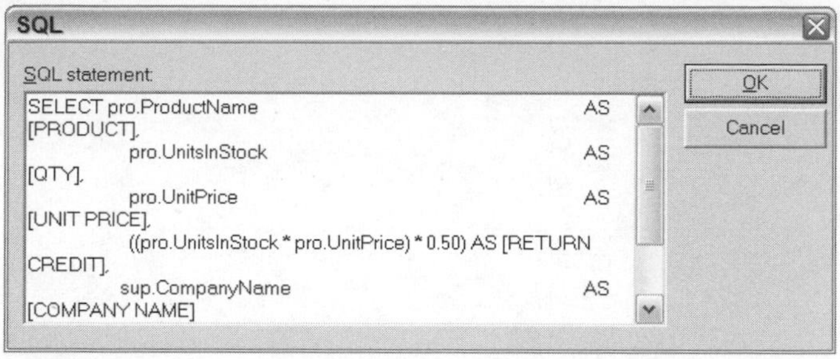

Figure 3.41   The SQL dialog box allows you to paste an SQL query that identifies the fields, field names, tables, and conditions of your report.

NOTE Microsoft Query attempts to display queries graphically, showing the table names, fields, and relationships. Complex SQL queries often cannot be displayed graphically — and that's ok. Just ignore this warning.

14. You are returned to the Microsoft Query window, except this time the dataset is returned from the executed SQL query. Click the Open Door button as shown in Figure 3.42.

15. When the PivotTable and PivotChart wizard appears, click Finish.

16. When you are returned to Excel, drag Company Name to the Page area, Product to the Row area, QTY to the Column area, and Return Credit to the Data area.

17. Verify that your PivotTable report looks like Figure 3.43.

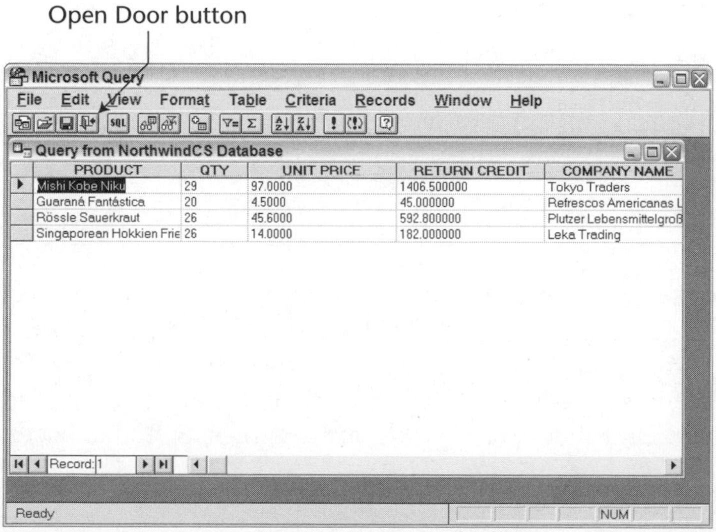

Open Door button

Figure 3.42   Click the Open Door button to quit the Microsoft Query program and return the SQL query's data set to Excel.

	A	B	C	D	E	F	G	H	I	J	
1	COMPANY NAME	(All) ▼									
2											
3	Sum of RETURN CREDIT	QTY ▼									
4	PRODUCT ▼	20	26	29	Grand Total						
5	Guaraná Fantástica	45			45						
6	Mishi Kobe Niku			1406.5	1406.5						
7	Rössle Sauerkraut		592.8		592.8						
8	Singaporean Hokkien Fried Mee		182		182						
9	Grand Total	45	774.8	1406.5	2226.3						
10											
11											
12											
13											
14											
15											
16											
17											
18											
19											

Sheet1 / Sheet2 / Sheet3 /

Figure 3.43   If you did everything right, the PivotTable report should look like this.

Reviewing What You Did

I used this exercise to demonstrate what follows after a data source is created. Some of the steps in this exercise were already covered in this and earlier chapters. However, some of the material is new (such as accessing the Microsoft Query program and using an SQL query for the PivotTable report) and some is covered in later chapters. Don't worry if you didn't get it all this time. I simply wanted to demonstrate the full development cycle in a real-world situation. After you read the later chapters, you can repeat this exercise again to ensure that you fully understand it. Also, don't forget to watch the video of how this is done if you get stuck in any of the steps.

WATCH THE VIDEO **Watch the ch0304_video.avi video on how the PivotTable report is created at** `www.wiley.com/go/excelreporting`**.**

Chapter Review

This chapter outlined the various methods for getting source data into an Excel report. It showed you how delimited and fixed-width files can be imported into Excel, while explaining how to define the data type of fields in a text file to ensure that the data is properly imported. Finally, this chapter described how to create, interpret, and modify DSN files for text files, SQL databases, and OLAP cubes.

CHAPTER 4

Using the
Query Wizard

This chapter focuses on the Query Wizard program that is integrated into Microsoft Excel. Using this Wizard, users can choose fields, apply filters, and add sort instructions using simple and easy graphical screens. This program can be especially valuable for organizations with only a limited supply of SQL knowledge, because the Query Wizard enables users to build basic SQL queries from existing database tables and views.

In this chapter, I cover all four dialog boxes of the Query Wizard. I use a single example for building the query from the Wizard, and I show you how that query is saved and accessed. This discussion includes a detailed explanation of the query itself, similar to Chapter 3, where I reviewed the DSN file. I finish this chapter with another real-world example that you can use for additional practice.

Overview of the Query Wizard

The Query Wizard guides you through four different dialog boxes where you define the key components for building an SQL query. In the first dialog box, you start by choosing the fields you want to include in your Excel report. Here, you can even arrange the order in which fields are displayed (left to right) in the query. In the second dialog box of the Wizard, you can apply filters to any of the fields you selected in the first dialog box. You define the filters by first selecting a string or mathematical operator from a drop-down list of available ones and then specifying a value. In the third dialog box, you can sort the result set by choosing an ascending or descending sort order for one or more columns. You finish in the fourth and last dialog box by choosing either to return the data to Excel or launch the Microsoft Query program (covered in Chapter 5) to further tweak the SQL query.

Table 4.1 lists each dialog box with a brief explanation of its purpose and an explanation of what part of the query is being generated. Notice that only the first three dialog boxes actually build the query; the fourth dialog box is used as a bridge to either return to Excel or launch the Microsoft Query program. Keep in mind that you only have to complete the information in the first dialog box shown in Figure 4.2; filtering (second dialog box) and sorting (third dialog box) are not mandatory steps.

Table 4.1   Explanation of the Query Wizard Dialog Boxes

DIALOG BOX	PART OF SQL QUERY	EXPLANATION
1 – Choose Columns	`Select <Columns>` `From <Objects>`	Here you choose the fields, the order of the fields in the query, and the objects from which these fields are selected.
2 – Filter Data	`Where <Conditions>`	Here you specify the conditions for data to be extracted from its data source. Note that you can specify conditions only on fields or columns selected in the first dialog box.
3 – Sort Order	`Order By`	Here you define how the resulting data set is sorted. An ascending or descending sort order can only be defined on fields that were selected in the first dialog box.
4 – Finish	This area is not applicable to the SQL query, as it only acts as a bridge to either return the query created in the first three steps to Excel or edit the query in the Microsoft Query program.	Here you can choose to a.) Return the Data to Excel, b.) View and/or edit the Data in the Microsoft Query program, or c.) Create an OLAP cube from the data. You can also save the Query that you built in the first three dialog boxes here.

The Wizard is capable of generating only basic SQL queries. Field concatenation, aggregate functions, conditional logic, and sub-queries are beyond the scope of what can be accomplished with the Query Wizard program.

TIP Some organizations have succeeded in creating SQL database views to solve multiple table joins, aggregate functions, and complex filter conditions. These views can also replace the database field names with more understandable names (CUSNUM could be CustomerNumber, for example) and eliminate fields that report users don't need. This enables novice report users to rely on the database views and easy-to-understand field headings to obtain their data.

The following sections describe how to start the Wizard and explain in more detail what features and functions are available in each of the four dialog boxes.

Starting the Wizard

The Wizard enables users who are unfamiliar with SQL programming to build basic SQL queries by specifying the query components in the first three graphical dialog boxes of the program. Using this Wizard, you can

- Select specific columns or fields that should be included in the report
- Filter data using several types of mathematical and string operators
- Sort on columns or fields in ascending or descending order

In order to invoke the Query Wizard, you must be accessing data from an external data source, and you must have the Wizard enabled by checking that option from the Choose Data Source dialog box shown in Figure 4.1. (Refer to Chapter 3 if you are not familiar with how to bring up this dialog box.) Clicking to select the Use The Query Wizard To Create/Edit Queries option in Figure 4.1 enables the Query Wizard to start when the data source is accessed by either double-clicking it or selecting it and then clicking OK. If this option is unchecked, the Wizard is bypassed and you are routed directly to the Microsoft Query program.

If you click the various tabs at the top of this dialog box, you'll notice that the Query Wizard is only enabled for the Databases and Queries tabs. It is not used for OLAP Cubes, because the data has already been aggregated and typically filtered to meet a specific business need or purpose.

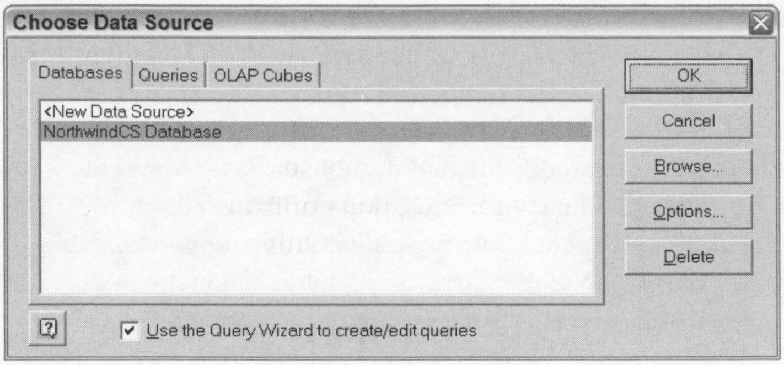

Figure 4.1   Check the Use The Query Wizard To Create/Edit Queries option to enable the Query Wizard for new Excel reports.

> **NOTE** If you choose to save a query, it can be accessed from the Queries tab in Figure 4.1. Read the section "Opening a Saved Query" later in this chapter for more information about how this works.

Selecting Objects

Chapter 3 showed you how to create a Data Source Name (DSN) file for connecting to external data sources. After you create a DSN, you can select data from it using the Query Wizard (explained in this chapter) or the Microsoft Query program (covered in Chapter 5). For this example, select the NorthwindCS database you created in the last chapter. Make sure that you check the Use The Query Wizard To Create/Edit Queries option at the bottom of the Choose Data Source dialog box before clicking OK. This should bring up the Query Wizard – Choose Columns dialog box, shown in Figure 4.2.

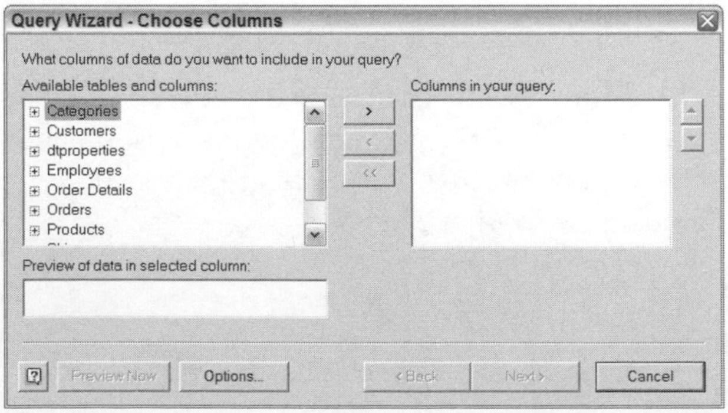

Figure 4.2   When the data source is a database, the first view of the Query Wizard shows the various tables, views, and synonyms in the database.

Figure 4.2 shows the first of the Query Wizard's four dialog boxes. Here, you choose the fields you want to include in your report. You select the fields from various types of objects in the external data source. Depending on how you have the Table Options set, you may see a list of different objects than the ones shown in Figure 4.2 for the NorthwindCS database. You can modify the view to match this dialog box by clicking the Options button. When the Table Options dialog box opens, you can click Show Tables Only.

Using Table Options for Object Selection

The Table Options dialog box (see Figure 4.3) lets you choose whether tables, views, system tables, and/or synonyms are shown in the Available Tables And Columns pane of the Choose Columns dialog box. This dialog box offers you a couple of other options. In the Owner field, you can opt to show only the objects for a particular database owner. And if you want your tables and columns displayed in alphabetical order, you can check the box near the bottom of the dialog box. I usually display objects in alphabetical order when I am not familiar with the database entities and need to locate specific columns and tables. If you are already familiar with the table layout, you may find that this option is more of a nuisance than a help.

TIP Synonyms act as aliases for your objects, enabling you to simplify the naming of objects (including remote objects in another database or another schema). They are available only in SQL 2005 and Oracle databases.

The meaning of Tables, Views, and System Tables in Figure 4.3 varies with the type of external data source you are accessing. Table 4.2 includes a list of several external data sources with a short explanation of what each corresponding Table Option value means.

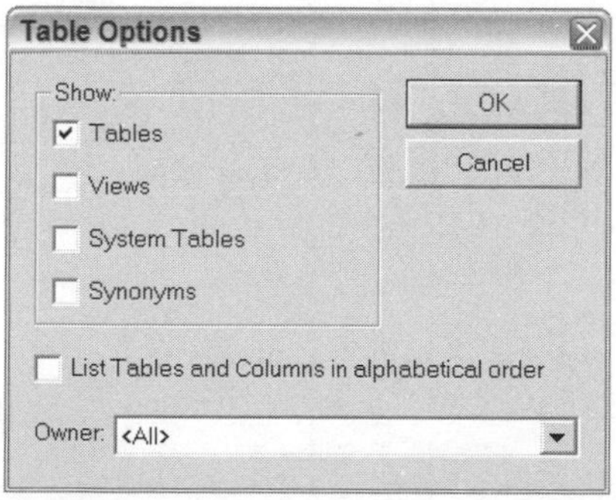

Figure 4.3   You can choose to show only specific database objects from this dialog box.

Table 4.2 Table Option Meanings Based on Data Source

TYPE	TABLES	VIEWS	SYSTEM TABLES	SYNONYMS	OWNER
Access database	Tables are shown as Tables	Queries are shown as Views	Hidden system tables are shown as System Tables		
Excel workbook	Used in conjunction with System Tables to show worksheet tabs and data	Used in conjunction with Tables to show worksheet tabs and data			
Oracle database	User tables are shown as Tables	Database views are shown as Views	Database system Tables are shown as System Tables	Public and private synonyms are shown as Synonyms	Database schemas are shown as Owners
SQL Server database	Database user tables are shown as Tables	Database views are shown as Views	Database system tables are shown as System Tables	This is a new SQL 2005 feature still in beta release at the time of this writing; information not yet available	Database owners are shown as Owners (usually dbo)
Text file or directory	Files are shown as Tables				

To set the Table Options to match the screen shown in Figure 4.2 and follow the example in this chapter, complete these steps:

1. Check Tables and uncheck System Tables, Views, and Synonyms.

2. Uncheck List Tables And Columns In Alphabetical Order.

3. Select <All> as the Owner.

4. Click OK to return to the first view of the Wizard.

5. Verify that your dialog box looks like Figure 4.2.

Choosing Fields

After you are returned to the first view of the Wizard, you can choose the specific fields you want to include in your Excel report. The pane on the left shows the available objects and the fields in each object. The pane on the right shows the fields you have selected for your report.

From the dialog box shown in Figure 4.4, you can expand the tree to select fields from individual tables. Clicking a table name in the left pane and then clicking the right-pointing single arrow button moves all the fields from that table to the Columns In Your Query pane. You can select a single field in the Columns In Your Query pane and click the left-pointing arrow button to move it back to the Available Tables And Columns pane. Or you can click the double left-arrow button to move all the fields back. The up and down arrows to the right of the Columns In Your Query pane control the order of the columns in the query (explained in the "Adjusting Field Order" section of this chapter).

To follow along with the example used in this chapter, select these fields for your report:

- Product ID, ProductName, and Discontinued from the Products table

- EmployeeID, ShipCountry, and ShipVia from the Orders table

- UnitPrice, Quantity, and Discount from the Order Details table

Figure 4.4 Choose the fields you want to include in your report from the available objects in this dialog box.

Previewing Object Data

Selecting a field name from either the Available Tables And Columns or the Columns In Your Query window and clicking the Preview Now button shows a list of the unique values in the selected field. Figure 4.5 shows how this works for the ProductName field.

CROSS-REFERENCE The default number of preview rows that you can see by scrolling with the up and down arrows is 100. Read Chapter 5 to learn how you can change this option setting in the Microsoft Query program.

Adjusting Field Order

As you select the various fields for your report, you may find it necessary to adjust the order in which they are displayed. Keep in mind that you can also arrange the order of fields from the Microsoft Query program or from Excel.

NOTE Adjusting field order primarily applies to Spreadsheet reports. In a PivotTable, the fields are meant to be dynamically dragged to different locations in the report, so the field order applies only to the PivotTable Field List.

Try moving the ProductName field ahead of the ProductID field by selecting ProductID and clicking the down arrow to move the field down. Alternatively, you can select ProductName and click the up arrow once to move it up. Verify that your dialog box looks like Figure 4.6.

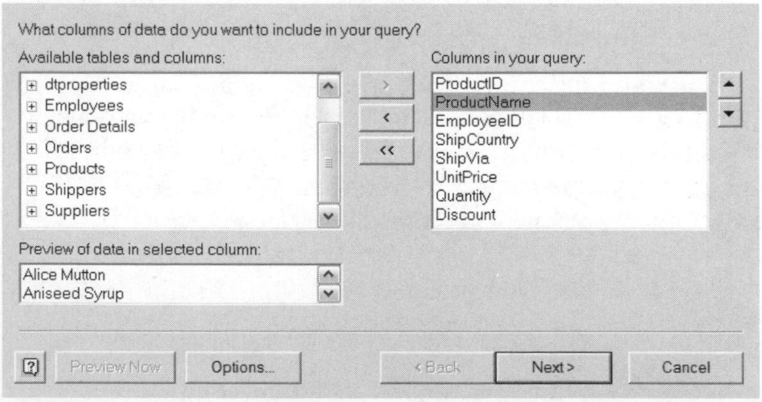

Figure 4.5 Selecting ProductName and clicking Preview Now causes a sample list of values for that field to be displayed in the Preview of Data In Selected Column window.

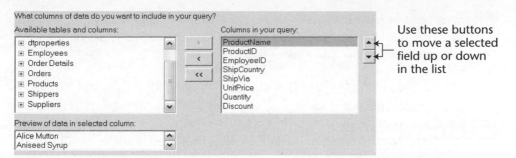

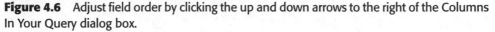

Figure 4.6 Adjust field order by clicking the up and down arrows to the right of the Columns In Your Query dialog box.

Filtering Data

Filters are used to limit the amount of data returned or displayed in a report. For example, a sales database might have 10 years of sales data, but only the last three years are applicable for revenue forecasting. So, if you are creating a sales forecast report from this data source, you might want to apply a filter against a field such as Order Date to extract only the transactions for the last three years. This filter can be applied in one of two ways:

- **Before the data is returned to Excel:** This method uses a condition specified in the Where clause of an SQL query. The Wizard creates the Where clause from the operators and values you input into the fields of the Query Wizard's Filter Data dialog box.

- **After the data is returned to Excel:** This method uses the drop-down arrows in the Excel report to limit the data displayed. This option was demonstrated in Chapter 2.

CROSS-REFERENCE The first option for filtering described in the preceding list can be further classified into two categories. A filter applied as part of the query (for example, quantity > 10) or a filter specified each time the report is updated. The latter is called a *parameter query* and is covered in Chapter 11.

The first option controls the amount of data that is returned and displayed, while the second option controls only the amount of data displayed. In the first option, only the last three years of sales data are imported into the Excel report. Contrast that with the second option, in which 10 years are loaded into the report. Depending on the number of rows being imported, this could result in a significant performance difference. This section focuses exclusively on the first option because this is what the Wizard accomplishes.

TIP Unless you need the additional data, use a filter to import only the necessary information you need. This results in faster report updates, improved performance, and reduced disk space requirements.

The Wizard builds the Where clause in an SQL query by using the operators and values that you select in this second view of the dialog box. There are numerous operators in the drop-down list; but keep in mind that this only a small subset of what is actually available to users who are knowledgeable about SQL programming. Nevertheless, the available options are a good start and usually sufficient for novice users who do not have complex requirements.

CROSS-REFERENCE See the SQL reference in Appendix B for a more complete list of operators and some examples of their use.

In order to simplify the organization of the available operators, I have classified them into a mathematical category for numeric data and into a string category for alphanumeric data. That is not to say that you cannot use a mathematical operator on a string field or vice-versa, but just be sure to think about the results. For example, using "Greater than or Equal To" a "W" results in the values W, X, Y, and Z being returned.

Using the Wizard to Filter Data

In the second view of the Query Wizard, the Filter Data box, you can select fields and then apply a filter condition or conditions. In the left-most pane, Columns To Filter, a list of all the fields you selected in the previous dialog box is presented. After you select a field, you can choose an operator and enter a numeric or string value in the Filter Value field. Note that you can only select from the list of available operators. (Refer to Tables 4.3 and 4.4 for a complete list of mathematical and string operators.) The Filter Value field, which is a drop-down box next to the Operator field, shows a preview of data in the selected field. This can be helpful if you are selecting a particular value or just want to validate that the field data is correct. Unlike the Operator drop-down box, you do not have to select a particular value; it is only meant to be used as a reference or as a shortcut.

NOTE By the way, you won't see the Filter Value and Operator fields labeled as such in the Filter Data dialog box. I have assigned these names to the fields to help you better understand the figures and text in this chapter.

In the example shown in Figure 4.7, I have selected the ProductName field and specified two conditions. The first is that the ProductName is not Aniseed Syrup. The second condition is that the ProductName begins with a C. In layman terms, this means that only the records that have a product name not beginning with a C or a product name of Aniseed Syrup will be selected from the data source when this query is run.

NOTE You can get a full list of the Product Names by analyzing the Products database table or by clicking the drop-down arrow in the Filter Value field when ProductName is selected.

NOTE Remember, you do not have to specify a filter. This is an optional step in the Query Wizard process.

When you specify multiple conditions for a particular field, as is the case in Figure 4.7, you must specify And or Or to evaluate them. If I had used Or instead of And, all the products would have been selected. Why? Because, although the first condition states that product names cannot be equal to Aniseed Syrup, that condition is negated by an Or that states product names can start with any letter except a C. So basically, the first condition allows all the products except Aniseed Syrup to be pulled (including products that start with the letter C), whereas the second condition allows all the products except those that start with the letter C to be pulled (including Aniseed Syrup). All this is just to say that using an And or an Or can make a big difference in how a filter is actually applied in an SQL query.

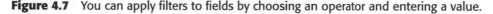

Figure 4.7 You can apply filters to fields by choosing an operator and entering a value.

Applying Multiple Filters

After you apply a filter to a field, the field name appears in bold in the Columns To Filter pane, on the left side of the dialog box. You can apply multiple filters by simply selecting another field and defining the operator type and value. In Figure 4.8, I selected UnitPrice and defined the filter criteria to be greater than $2.50 and less than $50.00.

Mathematical Operators

Table 4.3 lists all the mathematical operators available from the Query Wizard, along with their SQL programming equivalents and a short explanation of what the operator is intended to accomplish.

Table 4.3 Mathematical Operators and SQL Interpretations

OPERATOR	EXPLANATION	SQL EQUIVALENT
Equals	Equals the number or text specified in the Filter Value drop-down field	=
Does not equal	Does not equal the number or text specified in the Filter Value drop-down field	<>, !=
Is greater than	Is greater than the number specified in the Filter Value drop-down field	>
Is greater than or equal to	Is greater than or equal to the number in the Filter Value drop-down field	>=
Is less than	Is less than the number specified in the Filter Value drop-down field	<
Is less than or equal to	Is less than or equal to the number specified in the Filter Value drop-down field	<=

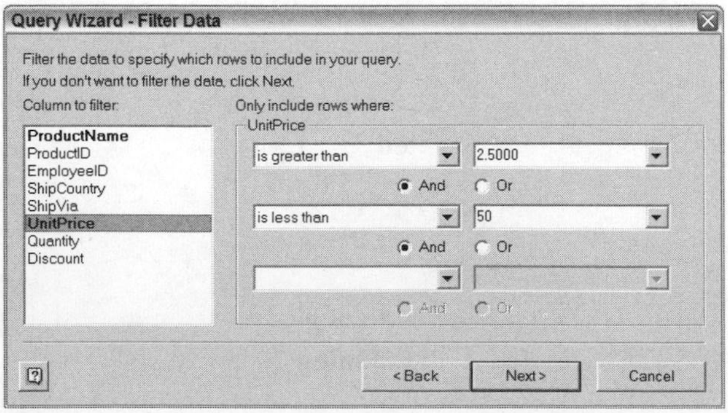

Figure 4.8 After you apply a filter, the field appears in bold, as is the case for ProductName.

CROSS-REFERENCE The SQL reference in Appendix B provides a more complete list of mathematical operators available with SQL programming.

String Operators

Table 4.4 lists all the string operators available from the Query Wizard, along with the SQL programming equivalent and a short explanation of what the operator is intended to accomplish. I use the letter A in the SQL Equivalent column to represent a string value. Replace A with the particular text you want to use with the string operator.

Table 4.4   String Operators and SQL Interpretations

OPERATOR	EXPLANATION	SQL EQUIVALENT
Begins with	Begins with the character or text specified in the Filter Value drop-down field	LIKE A%
Does not begin with	Does not begin with the character or text specified in the Filter Value drop-down field	NOT LIKE A%
Ends with	Ends with the character or text specified in the Filter Value drop-down field	LIKE %A
Does not end with	Does not end with the character or text specified in the Filter Value drop-down field	NOT LIKE %A
Contains	Contains the character or text specified in the Filter Value drop-down field	LIKE %A%
Does not contain	Does not contain the character or text specified in the Filter Value drop-down field	NOT LIKE %A%
Like	Contains the text specified in the Filter Value drop-down field	LIKE A%
Not Like	Does not contain the text specified in the Filter Value drop-down field	NOT LIKE A%
Is Null	Has a null value for the selected field	IS NULL
Is Not Null	Does not have a null value for the selected field	IS NOT NULL

CROSS-REFERENCE The SQL reference in Appendix B gives a more complete list of string filters available with SQL programming.

Viewing and Changing Filter Conditions

If you want to remove a filter or just a particular filter condition, simply select the bold field in the Column to Filter pane, and the filter conditions automatically appear on the right. You can then remove the filter conditions by deleting the data in the Filter Value field to the right of the Operator drop-down field.

NOTE You cannot remove the operator type in the Operator field because a blank operator value is not accepted until after the field has been reinitialized with a blank value.

Now that you've seen how this works, try it for yourself. Complete these steps to practice filtering data and follow along with my example in this chapter:

1. Select ProductName and apply the conditions Does Not Equal Aniseed Syrup and Does Not Begin With C.

2. Select UnitPrice and apply the conditions Is Greater Than 2.50 (in the first filter) and Is Less Than 50.00 (in the second filter). (Refer back to Figure 4.8 if you want to see how I entered these filter conditions.)

3. Click Next to continue to the Sort Order dialog box of the Wizard.

Sorting Data

After you click Next in the Filter Data dialog box, the Sort Order dialog box appears. Here, you define the sort order of the data set that is returned from the data source. The data set, as a whole, is sorted when you choose a field in the Sort By drop-down list and select an ascending or descending sort order. You should use this dialog box to sort records for Spreadsheet reports, not for PivotTable reports. Why? Because the unique field values are individually sorted as fields are dropped into a PivotTable report location. Thus, sorting the entire result set each time the report is updated makes no sense.

NOTE Remember, choosing a sort order is an optional step. You do not have to specify a sort.

In Figure 4.9, I first selected ProductName and specified a descending sort order. Next, I selected ShipCountry and specified an ascending sort order. If you want to remove a sort, simply select the field and choose the blank value in the drop-down list.

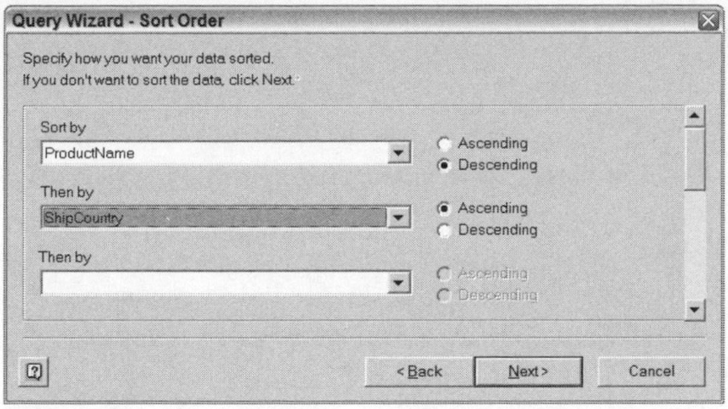

Figure 4.9 You sort the data set by selecting fields and specifying an ascending or descending sort order.

NOTE In Figure 4.9, I demonstrate how to apply a sort order for a PivotTable report. This doesn't provide any useful utility and only serves to increase the amount of time it takes to execute the query. You should use this dialog box only when you are creating a Spreadsheet report. I've done this here just so you can how this dialog box works and how the SQL statement is generated.

To practice choosing a sort order and continue with my example, follow these steps:

1. Select ProductName and specify a Descending sort order.

2. Select ShipCountry and specify an Ascending sort order.

3. Click Next to continue to the Finish dialog box of the Wizard.

Finishing Up

After you click Next in the Sort Order dialog box of the Query Wizard, the Finish dialog box appears, as shown in Figure 4.10. This is the fourth and last dialog box of the Wizard. Here, you can perform the following functions:

- Return Data to Microsoft Excel to finish creating the report
- View data or edit the query in the Microsoft Query program
- Create an OLAP cube from the query
- Save the query

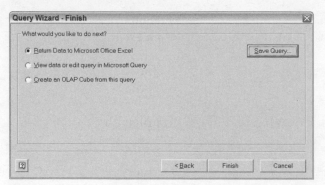

Figure 4.10   Use this last view of the Wizard to return data to Excel, tweak the query in the Microsoft Query program, or create an offline OLAP cube.

If you want to modify the SQL query or view the data returned from the data source, select the second option, View Data Or Edit Query in Microsoft Query to start the Microsoft Query program. If no changes are required, you can select the first option, Return Data To Microsoft Office Excel. This option takes you back to the Excel program so that you can finish creating your Excel report. The last option, Create An OLAP Cube From This Query, starts the OLAP Cube Wizard.

CROSS-REFERENCE   Read Chapter 10 to learn more about the OLAP Cube Wizard and how OLAP cubes are created.

Saving the Query

Queries created from the Query Wizard or from the Microsoft Query program can be saved and accessed whenever you create a new Spreadsheet or Pivot-Table report. Keep in mind that the query file stores both the connection information used to access the external data source and the SQL query used to extract the data. It is used only for creating new reports and appears in the Queries tab of the Choose Data Source dialog box each time you create an Excel report from an external data source. Deleting the query file has no effect on existing reports that initially used this query to connect to the external data source. Remember, connection information and query information are saved in the Excel report; the query is used only to keep you from having to re-enter the connection information and build the SQL query each time you create a new report.

By default, queries are saved to this location:

```
C:\Documents and Settings\{User}\Application Data\Microsoft\Queries
```

> **WARNING** Saving a query to another location may require you to manually browse for that location when the query is accessed from Excel.

When you click the Save Query button in the final Query Wizard box to save the SQL query you created in the Wizard, the Save As dialog box appears, as shown in Figure 4.11.

To continue following along with my example, complete these steps:

1. Click the Save Query button in the Finish dialog box.

2. When the Save As dialog box appears, save the query as the default name **Query from NorthwindCS Database.dqy**.

3. Open the file in Notepad.

Viewing a Saved Query

When you look at the query you saved earlier, notice that many of the lines correspond to query parameters entered in the various dialog boxes of the Query Wizard. Here is the query file for the NorthwindCS database example covered in this chapter. Some of the lines are very long, so I split them apart to make them easier for you to read here by using a letter after the number (3a, 3b, 3c, and so on). In order for the query to be read by Excel, however, the format cannot be changed:

```
1a. XLODBC
2a. 1
3a. DRIVER=SQL Server;
3b. SERVER=SQLSERVERNAME;
3c. UID=SQL LOGIN;
3d. APP=Microsoft Office 2003;
3e. WSID=DESKTOP;
3f. DATABASE=NorthwindCS;
3g. Trusted_Connection=Yes
4a. SELECT Products.ProductName,
4b. Products.ProductID,
4c. Products.Discontinued,
4d. Orders.EmployeeID,
4e. Orders.ShipCountry,
4f. Orders.ShipVia,
4g. "Order Details".UnitPrice,
4h. "Order Details".Quantity,
4i. "Order Details".Discount
4j. FROM NorthwindCS.dbo."Order Details" "Order Details",
4k. NorthwindCS.dbo.Orders Orders,
4l. NorthwindCS.dbo.Products Products
4m. WHERE "Order Details".OrderID = Orders.OrderID AND
```

```
4n. "Order Details".ProductID = Products.ProductID AND
4o. ((Products.ProductName<>'Aniseed Syrup' And
4p. Products.ProductName Not Like 'C%')
4q. ("Order Details".UnitPrice>$2.5000 And
4r. "Order Details".UnitPrice<$50))
4s. ORDER BY Products.ProductName DESC,
4t. Orders.ShipCountry
5a. ProductName<tab>
5b. ProductID<tab>
5c. Discontinued<tab>
5d. EmployeeID<tab>
5e. ShipCountry<tab>
5f. ShipVia<tab>
5g. UnitPrice<tab>
5h. Quantity<tab>
5i. Discount
```

Lines 1–3 contain the connection information. Line 4 contains the SQL query that was created in the various dialog boxes of this chapter. Lines 4a–4i contain the fields and field objects specified in the first dialog box of the Query Wizard. Note that the database, the database owner, and the object are all specified in lines 4j–4l. Lines 4m and 4n contain the instructions for joining the Products, Order, and Order Detail tables to one another. Lines 4o–4r contain the filter conditions that were entered in the second dialog box of the Query Wizard. Lines 4s and 4t contain the sort order specified in the third dialog box of the Query Wizard. Finally, lines 5a–5i contain the field names. Each field name is separated by a <tab>.

CROSS-REFERENCE Read Chapter 3 to learn more about the connection information shown in Lines 1 through 3 of the preceding query.

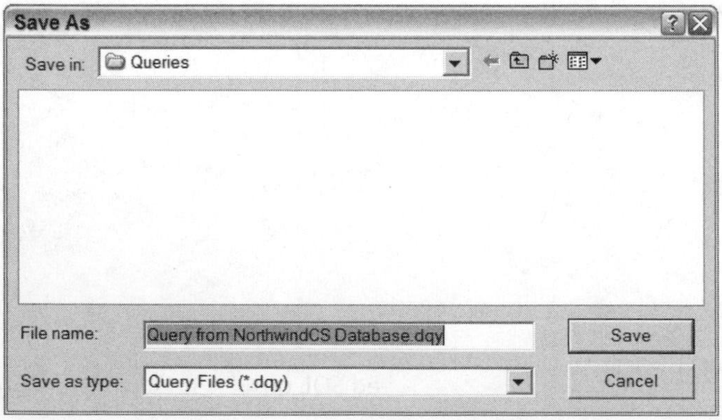

Figure 4.11 You can save the query that you created in the Wizard for later access or use.

Opening a Saved Query

Once a query is saved, you can access it when new Excel reports are created. To access the data source, follow these steps:

1. From Excel, choose Data ➪ PivotTable And PivotChart.

2. Select External Data Source and click Next.

3. Click Get Data when the PivotTable And PivotChart Wizard appears.

4. Click the Queries tab when the Choose Data Source dialog box appears, as shown in Figure 4.12.

NOTE Don't forget that the connection information is also saved along with the SQL query.

5. Uncheck the Use The Query Wizard To Create/Edit Queries option.

NOTE I unchecked this option because the query cannot be edited by the Query Wizard program. This isn't uncommon considering that the program performs only very basic functions. Don't forget to recheck that option should you want to use the Query Wizard in the future — it's an easy one to overlook.

6. Verify that Query from NorthwindCS Database is selected and click OK to continue.

The Microsoft Query program should now be started, and you should see a window that looks like Figure 4.13. This is the same window you would have seen if you had selected the second option, View Data Or Edit Query In Microsoft Query, in Figure 4.10.

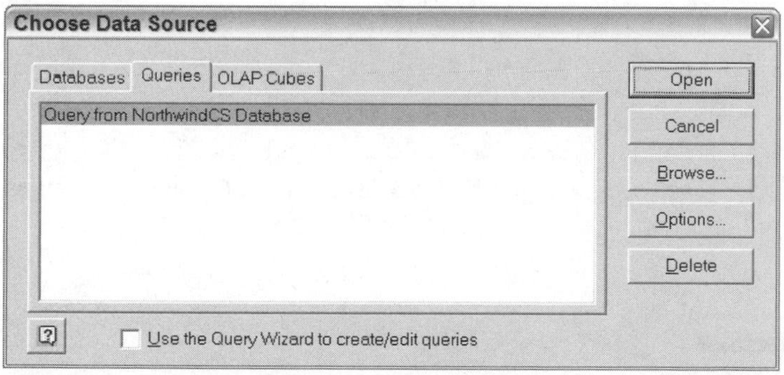

Figure 4.12 Click the Queries tab to access previously saved SQL queries for creating new Excel reports.

Editing with Microsoft Query

After you have created a basic SQL query from the Query Wizard, you can edit or tweak the query from the Microsoft Query program. Notice that the three tables — Products, Orders, and Order Details — selected in the first dialog box of the Wizard all appear in the upper part of the program window shown in Figure 4.13. The fields that were selected in this first dialog box of the Query Wizard also appear in the bottom portion of the window. Notice that the fields are also arranged (left to right) in the same order as Figure 4.6. The filters that were applied in the second dialog box of the Wizard appear in the Criteria Fields section displayed in the middle of the program window.

NOTE Chapters 5 and 6 cover the Microsoft Query program.

You can close the program from Microsoft Query by choosing File ⇨ Cancel And Return Data To Microsoft Office Excel.

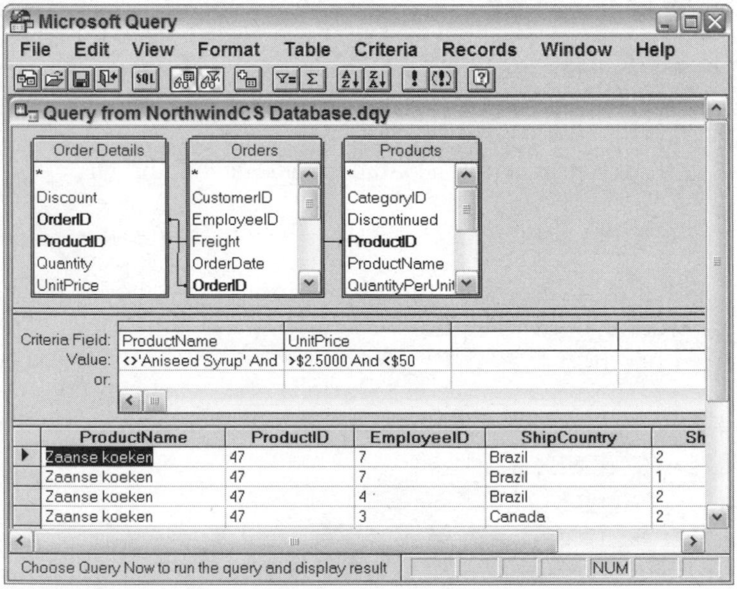

Figure 4.13 The Microsoft Query program graphically displays the SQL query that was created in the Query Wizard program.

Trying It Out in the Real World

Andrew Fuller, the Vice President of Sales at Northwind Traders, has just learned that the shipments of discontinued products in April of 1998 were a mistake. He has asked you to provide him with a report of the contact names, product IDs, and quantities of items sold so that he can personally contact the customer. Andrew has already asked the database administrator to research what database tables need to be accessed for creating the PivotTable report. The database administrator communicated that the following fields are required:

- ContactName from the Customers table
- ShippedDate from the Orders table
- Discontinued from the Products table
- ProductID and Quantity from the Order Details table

Getting Down to Business

Follow these steps to complete this exercise:

1. From Excel, choose Data ➪ PivotTable And PivotChart Report.

2. Select External Data Source and click Next when the PivotTable And PivotChart Wizard appears.

3. Click Get Data when the next view of the Wizard appears.

4. When the Choose Data Source dialog box appears, verify that Use The Query Wizard To Create/Edit Queries is checked; and then select the NorthwindCS database and click OK.

5. The Query Wizard - Choose Columns dialog box appears. Move the following fields from the Available Tables And Columns pane to the Columns In Your Query pane:

   - ContactName from the Customers table
   - ShippedDate from the Orders table
   - Discontinued from the Products table
   - ProductID and Quantity from the Order Details table

6. Verify that your dialog box looks like Figure 4.14, and then click Next to continue.

7. Click Discontinued in the Column To Filter pane; and then select Equals in the Operator drop-down list and type **1** in the Filter Value field, as shown in Figure 4.15.

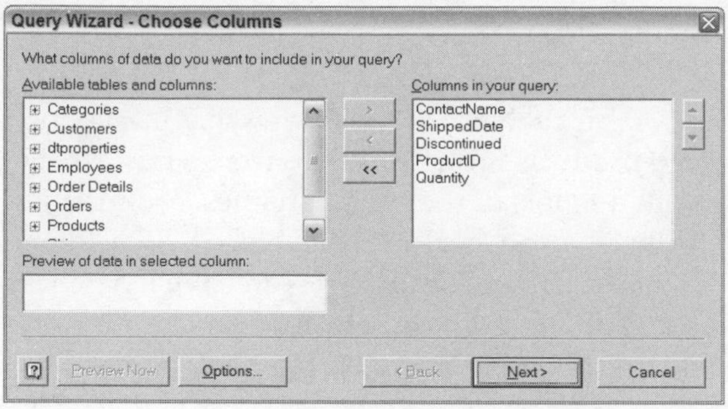

Figure 4.14 Select fields from the various tables in the NorthwindCS database.

8. Click ShippedDate and then select Is Greater Than Or Equal To in the Operator drop-down list and type **4/1/1998** in the Filter Value field.

9. Press the Tab key twice to add a second filter condition for the Shipped-Date field. This time, select Is Less Than Or Equal To in the Operator drop-down list and type **4/30/1998** in the Filter Value field.

10. Verify that your dialog box looks like Figure 4.16, and then click Next to continue.

11. Click Next to bypass the Sort Order dialog box.

12. When the fourth and last dialog box of the Wizard appears, verify that the Return Data To Microsoft Office Excel option is checked, and then click Finish.

13. Click Finish when the PivotTable And PivotChart Wizard dialog box appears.

14. When you are returned to Excel, drag ContactName to the Row area, ProductID to the Column area, and Quantity to the Data area.

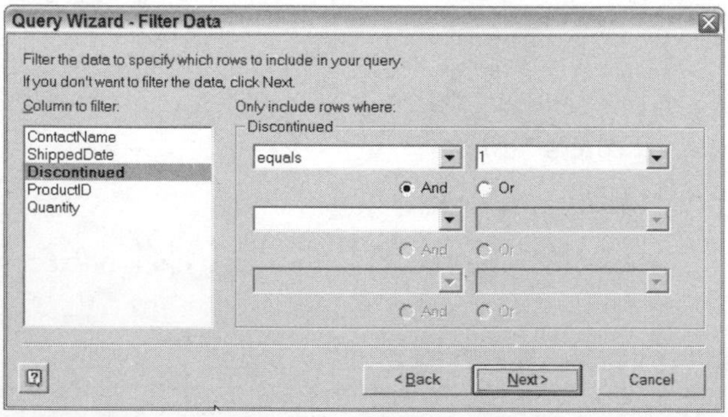

Figure 4.15 A value of 1 means True for the Discontinued field.

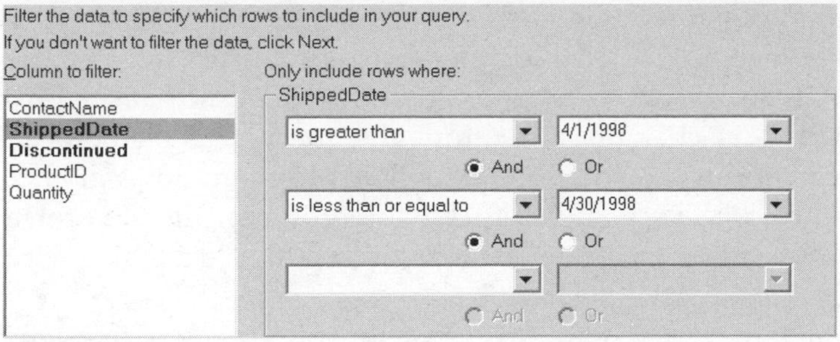

Figure 4.16 Two filter conditions are required in ShippedDate to extract only the shipments in April 1998.

NOTE The fields ShippedDate and Discontinued do not need to be displayed in the PivotTable. However, they must be selected in order for a filter to be applied when the Query Wizard is used.

15. Verify that your PivotTable report looks like Figure 4.17.

Reviewing What You Did

This exercise provided you with some more practice with using the Query Wizard program while demonstrating a real-world scenario. Notice that while the Wizard provides some useful functions, it is also very limiting and requires that you conform to a sometimes rigid template. For example, you didn't need to include the Discontinued or ShippedDate fields in the report, but you were forced to select them in order to apply the filter.

	A	B	C	D	E	F	G	H	I
1		Drop Page Fields Here							
2									
3	Sum of Quantity	Pro							
4	ContactName	5	24	28	29	42	53	Grand Total	
5	Alejandra Camino					4		4	
6	Carine Schmitt				14			14	
7	Carlos Hernández		10	20				30	
8	Christina Berglund			30				30	
9	Elizabeth Lincoln		30					30	
10	Horst Kloss					40		40	
11	Howard Snyder				2			2	
12	Isabel de Castro				10	14		24	
13	Jose Pavarotti	70	41		60	24		195	
14	José Pedro Freyre		12					12	
15	Maria Larsson				50			50	
16	Maurizio Moroni		10					10	
17	Michael Holz						70	70	
18	Pascale Cartrain					30		30	
19	Paula Wilson		30					30	
20	Zbyszek Piestrzeniewicz		12					12	
21	Grand Total	70	145	50	136	112	70	583	

Figure 4.17 If you did everything right, the PivotTable report should look like this.

Despite the limitations and the sometimes awkward interface, this Query Wizard can still be very helpful, especially for novice report users. You can use it to build a basic SQL query and then continue to the Microsoft Query program to make the necessary changes to fine-tune the query. This method can assist report users who are just beginning to learn SQL programming. Another option that I've found to be very successful in some organizations is for a savvy database administrator to create database views that several novice report users can access for creating their reports.

Don't forget to watch the video if you were not sure about any of the steps in this exercise or you just want to verify that you did everything right.

WATCH THE VIDEO Watch the ch0401_video.avi video on how to create this PivotTable report using the Query Wizard at www.wiley.com/go/ excelreporting.

Chapter Review

This chapter started by outlining the general purpose and use of each of the four dialog boxes of the Query Wizard program. It went on to describe how the Wizard is started when Excel reports are created. It then walked you through the details of the four dialog boxes and showed you how to select fields from various objects, arrange the order of fields in the query, select the type of filter to apply, and change and remove filter conditions. This chapter also discussed why you should use the sort order only for Spreadsheet reports and showed you how to save, access, and interpret a saved query.

For readers who are not familiar with SQL programming, this chapter can be used as a bridge to the next chapter, which describes the various functions and features of the Microsoft Query program.

CHAPTER 5

Getting Started with Microsoft Query

This chapter focuses on the Microsoft Query program that is integrated into Microsoft Excel. Microsoft Query acts as an intermediary between an Excel report and an external data source. Novice users can use this program to build a new SQL query using the program's graphical tools, or even fine-tune one that was started from the Query Wizard. Advanced users can use this program to simply paste in an SQL query that was created from an external SQL development program or just type in the SQL directly into an SQL window in the Microsoft Query program.

In a general sense, Microsoft Query is the next level up in complexity over the Query Wizard you learned about in Chapter 4. Although you are still constrained by some of the program's limitations, it offers many new, powerful tools that are easy to use for building SQL queries. Using Microsoft Query, you can perform several types of table joins, design complex filter conditions, create calculated fields, and insert parameters. There are also tools for managing database objects, editing table data, and creating offline OLAP cubes.

This chapter provides an overview of the Microsoft Query program and shows you how to start the program from new and existing Excel reports. It then takes you on a tour of the program environment, menu items, and toolbar. It organizes many of the program functions into the various parts of an SQL query and shows you how to handle them using the program's graphical tools. In the last section, the chapter provides another real-world example that you can use for additional practice.

Introducing the Microsoft Query Program

The Microsoft Query program acts as an intermediary between an Excel report and an external data source. You can use this program to tweak a query that was initially created from the Query Wizard (covered in Chapter 4), build a query from scratch using the program's graphical tools, or simply paste in an SQL query that was already created using SQL development programs such as:

- Query Analyzer (Microsoft SQL Server 7.0/2000 databases)
- SQL Server Management Studio (Microsoft SQL Sever 2005 databases)
- SQL*Plus (Oracle databases)
- Toad (Oracle databases)

The Microsoft Query program includes several graphical tools for building all the fundamental parts of an SQL query from the Select to the Order By parts, and it includes tools for creating aggregate functions, expressions, and even parameters. There is also an SQL window available for pasting or entering more complex SQL queries created from external SQL development programs.

If you choose to build a query using the program's graphical tools, an SQL query is generated in the background. Adding or removing a field, modifying a filter condition, or changing a sort order using the program's graphical tools produces a corresponding change to the background SQL query.

Although Microsoft Query has many more capabilities than the Query Wizard, it still has many limitations. For example, you can use Microsoft Query to perform single query operations only. Queries that produce more than one result set are problematic in the sense that Microsoft Query reads only the first result set. Some examples that involve multiple query operations include

- Multiple queries separated by a GO statement
- Stored procedures that produce more than one result set
- Compute By statements

Additionally, although you can paste queries into the SQL dialog box that utilizes Case logic, subqueries, correlated subqueries, and union operators, there are no graphical tools for building these query components. Of course, these are more advanced programming topics and are probably best handled through a more robust development tool, anyway.

CROSS-REFERENCE Read Chapter 6 to learn more about using SQL queries in the Microsoft Query program and Appendix B for more information about SQL programming, including Case logic.

Beyond the tools included for building SQL queries, the Microsoft Query program also includes several other tools for analyzing data, managing database objects, and creating offline OLAP cube files. Using this program, you can

- Create, edit, and drop database tables and views
- Create, edit, and drop stored procedures
- Index fields on a database table or view
- Edit table data
- Create offline OLAP cubes

With the exception of creating offline OLAP cubes, however, the functions just listed are best handled in a database management program. But they are briefly covered in the next chapter. That way, you know they exist in the event you need immediate access to them to support users who don't have a database management program installed on their computers.

Starting Microsoft Query

There isn't a hot-key or a menu item in Excel that launches the Microsoft Query program. The program can be started only when you create or modify an existing report that uses an external data source. Reports that can use Microsoft Query include the following:

- PivotTable reports
- PivotChart reports
- Spreadsheet reports

There are a few different methods for starting the Microsoft Query program that vary with the type of report you are using and whether it is a new report or an existing report. The various options are outlined here.

With New Reports

The Microsoft Query program is launched when you create a new PivotTable or Spreadsheet report that utilizes an external data source. You have the following options for starting the program when a new Excel report is created:

1. Choose Data ⇨ PivotTable And PivotChart Report.
2. Choose Data ⇨ Import External Data ⇨ New Database Query.
3. Choose Data ⇨ Import External Data ⇨ Import Data.

CROSS-REFERENCE Chapter 4 demonstrates how a PivotTable accesses the Microsoft Query program using the first option, PivotTable And PivotChart report. Chapter 11 shows how a Spreadsheet report accesses the Microsoft Query program, using the second option, New Database Query. The third option, using the Import Data command, is not covered in this book. It provides the same basic functionality as the second option, with some different screens and options.

When you create a new report by choosing either the first or second option (listed in the preceding bullet list) and specifying an external data source, the Choose Data Source dialog box shown in Figure 5.1 appears. As demonstrated in Chapter 4, you can either start building a basic query using the Query Wizard or route directly to the Microsoft Query program by unchecking the Use The Query Wizard To Create/Edit Queries option, selecting a data source, and then clicking OK.

When the Microsoft Query program is launched for a new report, you are presented with the Add Tables dialog box shown in Figure 5.2. You can either close the dialog box to paste in or open a saved SQL query, or you can select the various objects (tables, views, and synonyms) to start building a query using the program's graphical tools. The "Trying It Out in the Real World" section of this chapter provides a brief demonstration of how this is done.

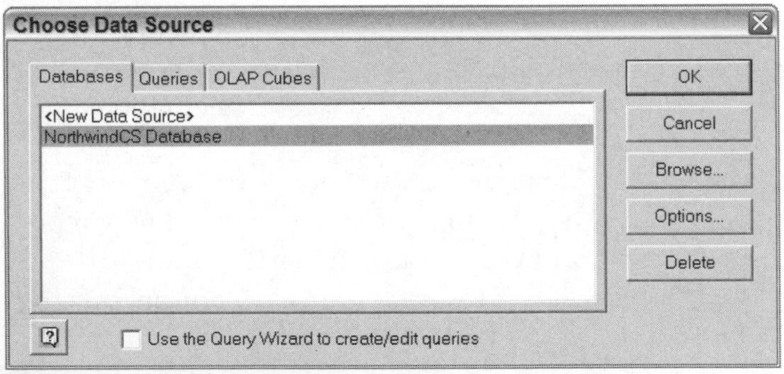

Figure 5.1   Make sure that Use The Query Wizard To Create/Edit Queries is unchecked to start Microsoft Query; otherwise, you have to first route through the four dialog boxes of the Query Wizard before getting to Microsoft Query.

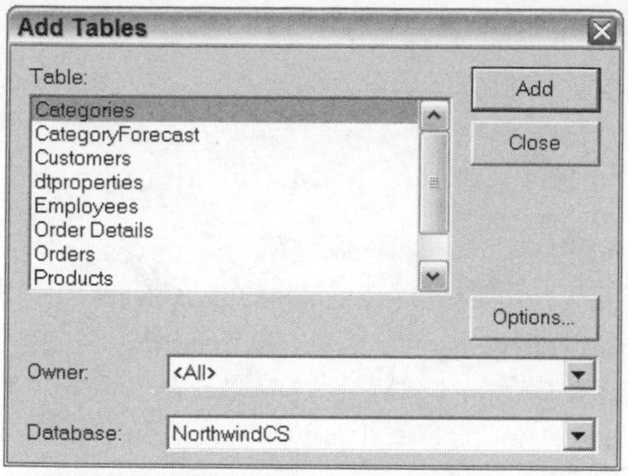

Figure 5.2 Select the various tables or views to build a query, or close the dialog box to either open or paste a saved query into the SQL dialog box.

With Existing Reports

Accessing the Microsoft Query program from an existing report is necessary when the underlying SQL query must be modified, as for the following tasks:

- Adding or removing report fields
- Changing the filter conditions to adjust the amount of data being imported into the report
- Fixing an error or modifying a calculated field formula in the query
- Adjusting, adding, or removing a table join in the query
- Inquiring on the query of an Excel report that uses an external data source for its report data

There are slightly different methods for starting the Microsoft Query program for the different types of Excel reports. PivotTable and PivotChart reports require that you first choose the PivotTable Wizard, whereas Spreadsheet reports provide a more immediate pathway.

PivotTable and PivotChart Reports

Follow these steps to start the Microsoft Query program from an existing PivotTable or PivotChart report:

1. Choose PivotTable Wizard from the PivotTable toolbar or right-click the report and select the PivotTable Wizard from the pop-up menu.
2. Click Back when the PivotTable And PivotChart Wizard — Step 3 of 3 appears.
3. Click Get Data to start the Microsoft Query program when the PivotTable And PivotChart Wizard — Step 2 of 3 appears.

TURNING OFF THE QUERY WIZARD

If the Query Wizard option is checked and the report can be edited by the Query Wizard, the Query Wizard appears before the Microsoft Query program can be launched. If you want to bypass the Query Wizard, just follow these steps to quickly turn off the Query Wizard program:

1. Click off the Excel report and then choose Data ⇨ Import External Data ⇨ New Database Query.

2. Uncheck the Use The Query Wizard To Create/Edit Queries box.

3. Click Cancel to return to Excel.

NOTE If the Query Wizard option is checked and the report can be edited by the Query Wizard, the Query Wizard appears before the Microsoft Query program can be launched. Just click Next to get to the Finish dialog box of the Wizard. In that last dialog box, you can select View Data Or Edit Query in Microsoft Query and then click Finish to start the program.

Spreadsheet Reports

Launching the Microsoft Query program from an existing Spreadsheet report is much easier. Simply right-click on the report and choose Edit Query from the pop-up menu. Keep in mind that the Query Wizard appears first if the Use The Query Wizard To Create/Edit Queries option is checked in the Choose Data Source dialog box.

Understanding the Basics

The Microsoft Query program is a basic visual development program that you can use to build SQL queries. It's similar to the Visual Basic Editor available in most Office applications. Microsoft Query, however, is used only for queries, and it is a much less robust development program than Visual Basic Editor. Nevertheless, there's still a lot to take in the first time you see it, especially for those without a programming background. This section covers the basics of the program and familiarizes you with its various windows, toolbar buttons, and objects. It starts by reviewing the environment, briefly describing the purpose of each section, menu item, and toolbar button. Following this introduction, the section describes how you can customize the environment and configure query options to your own particular preference.

Getting to Know the Environment

When the Microsoft Query program starts, you see a few different sections. The menu and toolbar buttons are displayed at the top of the window, followed by the Table and Criteria sections. You can toggle the display of these last two sections, and they are suppressed when a query cannot be displayed graphically (explained later). The Results section is next. Here is where the selected fields in the query are displayed. If a query has been executed, the results are also displayed. The Status Bar section is the fifth and last section. Here, toolbar tips, keyboard settings, and the Record Box are displayed.

Let's take a closer look at the Microsoft Query program by opening the NorthwindCS Database.dqy query file you created in Chapter 4 (using the Query Wizard program). If you have already read over Chapter 4 and completed the examples, the basic framework of this query should be familiar to you. If you are a more advanced user, you can simply download the query file from the companion website.

ON THE WEB You can download the NorthwindCS Database.dqy file to your computer from this book's companion website at `www.wiley.com/go/ excelreporting`.

You can open this file from the Microsoft Query program by following these steps:

1. Download the Query From NorthwindCS Database.dqy file from the website or create it by completing the instructions in Chapter 4. If you download the file, save it to this location (be sure to replace `{User}` with your Windows login):

   `C:\Documents and Settings\{User}\Application Data\Microsoft\Queries`

2. From Excel, choose Data ➪ PivotTable And PivotChart Report.

3. Select External Data Source and click Next.

4. When the PivotTable And PivotChart Wizard — Step 2 of 3 appears, click Get Data.

5. When the Choose Data Source dialog box appears, verify that the Use The Query Wizard To Create/Edit Queries box is unchecked and then click the Queries tab at the top of the dialog box.

6. Select Query From NorthwindCS Database, as shown in Figure 5.3, and click Open.

7. Verify that your Microsoft Query window looks similar to the one shown in Figure 5.4.

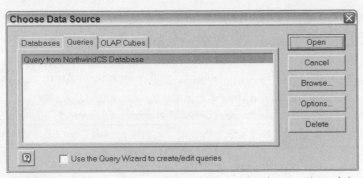

Figure 5.3   The saved query file appears under the Queries tab in the Choose Data Source dialog box.

As you can see in Figure 5.4, each section of the Microsoft Query program is labeled with a letter. Table 5.1 identifies the section name and provides a brief description of its purpose.

You can toggle the display of the Tables and Criteria sections by using the relevant toolbar buttons (these buttons are described a little later in Table 5.2). If the query results do not appear in the Results section, you can press the F9 key to execute the SQL query.

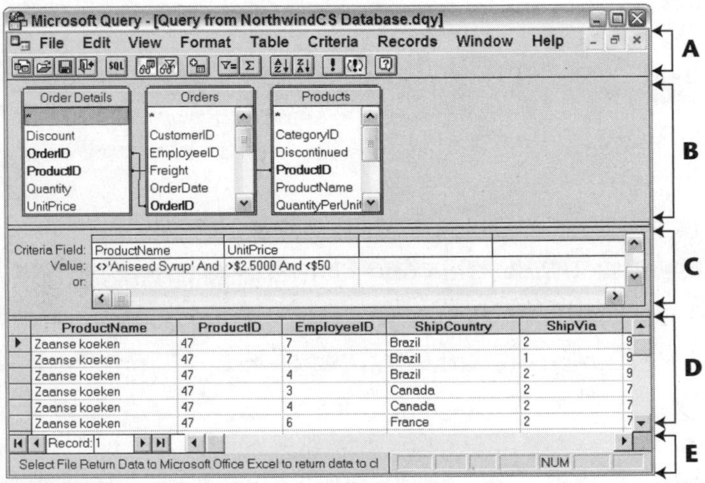

Figure 5.4   The Microsoft Query environment includes several areas for developing an SQL query using the program's graphical tools.

Table 5.1   Explanation of the Microsoft Query Sections

ID	SECTION	PURPOSE
A	Menu and toolbar	Enables you to perform program functions; access utilities; configure options; and open, save, and run queries
B	Tables	Enables you to view tables and manage joins
C	Criteria	Enables you to view and manage filters
D	Results	Enables you to view, modify, delete, and add fields; view query results; sort columns; and arrange the order of fields in the query (left to right)
E	Status Bar and Record Box	Record Box enables you to go to a particular record number and the Status Bar enables you to view toolbar button explanations and keyboard settings such as Num or Caps lock

Menu and Toolbar Section

You can use the menu and toolbar to perform all the functions for managing a query. Table 5.2 provides a brief description of all menu items and buttons. Many of these items are also covered in more detail throughout this chapter, under their relevant sections. I include them here, as I think it provides a handy reference. Keep in mind that there are a few toolbar buttons that do not have an associated menu item. I have included a button name next to each toolbar button that I reference in various examples throughout this chapter.

Table 5.2   Microsoft Query Toolbar Menus and Associated Buttons

MENU	MENU ITEM OR BUTTON NAME	BUTTON	DESCRIPTION
File	New Query		Creates a new query.
	Open Query		Opens a saved query.
	Save Query		Saves the current query. If the file already exists, it is just overwritten with the updated one.
	Save As		Saves the current query as a different filename.
	Table Definition		Opens a dialog box to view, create, delete or index a table.

(continued)

Table 5.2 *(continued)*

MENU	MENU ITEM OR BUTTON NAME	BUTTON	DESCRIPTION
	Execute SQL		Opens a dialog box to run an SQL query.
	Create OLAP Cube		Starts the OLAP cube wizard to create offline cube files using the current query.
	Return Data		Exits the Microsoft Query program and return the data to the Excel report.
	Cancel and Return to Microsoft Excel		Exits the Microsoft Query program without returning the data to the Excel report.
Edit	Redo		Redoes the last Undo operation.
	Cut		Cuts the selected data and copies it into memory.
	Copy		Copies selected data to the clipboard.
	Copy Special		Copies the selected data and optionally row numbers and column headings into the clipboard.
	Paste		Pastes the contents from the clipboard.
	Delete		Deletes selected data.
	Options		Opens a dialog box to set Microsoft Query program options.
	Show/Hide Tables		Toggles the display of the Tables section.
	Show/Hide Criteria		Toggles the display of the Criteria section.
	Zoom Field		Opens the Zoom dialog box to view data in the selected cell.
	Query Properties		Opens the Query Properties dialog box to extract only unique records or to group records.
	Parameters		Opens the Parameter dialog box to edit Parameter prompts.
	View SQL		Opens the SQL dialog box to view or edit the SQL query.

Table 5.2 *(continued)*

MENU	MENU ITEM OR BUTTON NAME	BUTTON	DESCRIPTION
Format	Font		Opens the Font dialog box to set font type, font style, and font size for records in the Results section.
	Row Height		Opens the Row Height dialog box to configure the row height of cells in the Results section.
	Column Width		Opens the Column Width dialog box to configure the column width of cells in the Results section.
	Hide Columns		Hides the selected column or columns.
	Show Columns		Opens the Show Columns dialog box to hide or show columns.
	Add Tables		Opens the Add Table dialog box to add tables, views, and synonyms to the query.
	Remove Table		Removes the selected table from the Query.
	Joins		Opens the Joins dialog box to manage table joins.
Criteria	Add Criteria		Opens the Add Criteria dialog box to create an aggregate function and/or add a filter condition.
	Remove All Criteria		Removes all defined criteria.
Records	Insert Column		Opens the Add Column dialog box to add an additional field to the query.
	Remove Column		Deletes the selected column or columns from the query.
	Edit Column		Opens the Edit Column dialog box to modify the field, field name, and/or aggregate function.
	Sort		Opens the Sort dialog box to add, view, modify, and remove existing sorts.
	Go To		Opens the Go To dialog box to route to a specific record number in the query result set.

(continued)

Table 5.2 *(continued)*

MENU	MENU ITEM OR BUTTON NAME	BUTTON	DESCRIPTION
	Allow Editing		Allows data to be edited in the result set of a single table.
	Query Now	!	Executes the current SQL query.
	Auto Query	(!)	Toggles whether the SQL query is automatically executed.
Window	Tile		Tiles the display of multiple query windows.
	Cascade		Cascades the display of multiple query windows.
Help	Help	[?]	Opens the Help dialog box to review online help.
	About Microsoft Query		Opens the About Query dialog box to review license and release information.
Not listed on any menu*	Cycle Through Totals	Σ	Applies an aggregate function to the selected field. Continued mouse clicks cycle through the aggregation functions Sum, Avg, Count, Min, Max, and <none>. There is no associated menu item for this toolbar button.
	Sort Ascending	A Z↓	Removes all existing sorts and then applies an ascending sort on the selected column or columns. There is no associated menu item for this toolbar button.
	Sort Descending	Z A↓	Removes all existing sorts and then applies a descending sort on the selected column or columns. There is no associated menu item for this toolbar button.

*The last three buttons shown in this table are not associated with any menu in the Microsoft Query program.

Tables Section

You can toggle on the display of the Tables section by choosing View ➪ Tables from the menu or by clicking the toolbar button. Queries not created in the Microsoft Query program often cannot be displayed graphically in the Tables or Criteria sections. When this happens, several toolbar and menu functions are also disabled. A warning message is displayed that reads SQL Query can't be represented graphically. Continue Anyway? and requires you to acknowledge it by clicking OK. (Read the "Displaying Queries Graphically" section of this chapter for more information about the implications of not being able to graphically display an SQL query.)

> **NOTE** The tables and the table joins of an SQL query are displayed in the Tables section of the Microsoft Query program. The fields in each table are listed in alphanumeric order. The primary key fields are shown in bold; table joins are represented by connection lines. An Inner Join is represented by a line with a ball on either side, whereas a Left or Right Join is represented by a ball on one side and an arrow on the other side.

The NorthwindCS Database Query example from Chapter 4 is shown in Figure 5.5. Double.clicking a connection line launches the Table Joins dialog box, where you can view all the table joins. Double.clicking a field in a table adds that field to the SQL query. Double.clicking the asterisk at the top of the table adds all the fields in that table to the SQL query.

Criteria Section

You can toggle on the display of the Criteria section by choosing View ⇨ Criteria or by clicking the toolbar button. The filter criteria are used to limit the number of rows returned from the external data source (which is akin to the Filter Data dialog box of the Query Wizard). The criteria can be entered by simply clicking a blank cell in the Criteria section, selecting a field from the drop.down list, and specifying the filter information in the Value cell. Less.experienced users can choose Criteria ⇨ Add Criteria to launch a dialog box where the fields, field operators, and values can be selected using graphical tools. The criteria specified in the Query Wizard's Filter Data dialog box from Chapter 4 (refer back to Figures 4.7 and 4.8) are displayed in the Criteria section shown in Figure 5.6.

> **CROSS-REFERENCE** Chapter 6 provides more information on using criteria fields.

Figure 5.5   Table joins are represented by connection lines; primary key fields are displayed in bold.

Criteria Field:	ProductName	UnitPrice	
Value:	<>'Aniseed Syrup' And	>$2.5000 And <$50	
or:			

Figure 5.6 The filters in the Where or Having part of an SQL query are displayed in the Criteria section.

Results Section

The field headings and results are displayed in the Results section of the Microsoft Query program. Unlike the Tables and Criteria sections, the results can always be displayed in this section, regardless of whether the query can be graphically displayed.

Fields can be added to the query by simply clicking a blank cell and then selecting a field from the drop-down list. You can also create a calculated field by selecting a blank cell in the Results section and typing a formula.

The NorthwindCS Database Query example from Chapter 4 is shown in Figure 5.7. Notice that ProductName is sorted in reverse alphanumeric order. This aligns with the instructions specified in the Query Wizard's Sort Order dialog box from Chapter 4.

Record Box and Status Bar

The Record Box and Status Bar include the three components shown in Figure 5.8. The Record Box shows the record number currently selected. Pressing the F5 key routes your cursor to this area, where you can type the number of the record you want to have displayed in the Result section. You can use the arrows on either side of the Record Box to move to the previous or next record or the first or last record of the result set. The Status Bar displays tooltips in the bottom-left of the status bar when you glide your mouse over a toolbar button. Keyboard settings such as Caps Lock, Num Lock, and Scroll Lock appear in the bottom-right of the Status Bar. The Scroll Bar is simply used for scrolling left or right through the fields in the Result section when there are more fields in the result set than can be displayed in the Results section at one time.

ProductName	ProductID	EmployeeID	ShipCountry	ShipVia
Zaanse koeken	47	7	Brazil	2
Zaanse koeken	47	7	Brazil	1
Zaanse koeken	47	4	Brazil	2
Zaanse koeken	47	3	Canada	2
Zaanse koeken	47	4	Canada	2
Zaanse koeken	47	6	France	2
Zaanse koeken	47	4	France	2
Zaanse koeken	47	6	Germany	2

Figure 5.7 The Results section shows a preview of the data generated by the SQL query.

Figure 5.8 Tooltips, record selection, and keyboard settings are all displayed in the Record Box and Status Bar sections of the Microsoft Query program.

Customizing the Environment

Now that you have a better grasp on the various sections of the Microsoft Query program, you're ready to start customizing the program to your own preference. This section describes how you can

- Manage the display of columns
- Change row and column sizes in the Results section
- Modify the font style used in the Results section
- Work with multiple Microsoft Query windows

Before I delve into these topics, the next section provides a brief overview of how SQL queries are graphically displayed.

Displaying Queries Graphically

Queries generated by Microsoft Query can usually be graphically displayed, meaning that the tables and table joins, and the filter fields and filter criteria, are displayed in the Table and the Filter sections, respectively. However, queries pasted or typed into the SQL dialog box cannot always be graphically displayed. When this happens, Microsoft Query prompts you with the warning message SQL Query can't be displayed graphically. Continue Anyway? You must acknowledge this message by clicking OK. This message isn't a problem, but it does have some effect on what functions are enabled and what sections are displayed in the Microsoft Query environment. For example, the Tables and Criteria sections are not displayed because the program is unable to graphically represent the query. Several functions for adjusting the SQL query are also disabled in the program's menu, requiring you to perform them by editing the SQL query. Table 5.3 identifies many of these disabled functions and describes how to perform them under both circumstances.

TIP If the SQL query cannot be graphically displayed, you're most likely using advanced SQL. If that's the case, you're probably savvy enough to adjust the query to perform many of the functions that are disabled in the Microsoft Query program.

Table 5.3   Performing Functions Based on Whether the Query Can Be Graphically Displayed

FUNCTION	GRAPHICALLY DISPLAYED	NOT GRAPHICALLY DISPLAYED
Hide Fields	Fields can be hidden or deleted using the program's graphical tools.	Fields can be hidden using the program's graphical tools, but only deleted by removing the fields in the Select part the SQL query.
Adding a Table	Add Tables feature enabled.	Tables can only be added by adding them to the Join part of the SQL Query.
Modify Sort Order	Columns can be sorted using the toolbar icons and menu items.	Columns can only be sorted by editing the Order By part of the SQL query.
Modify Field Order	Fields can be rearranged using drag-and-drop features.	Field order can only be adjusted by rearranging the order of the fields (left to right) in the Select part of the SQL query.
Modify Criteria	Criteria can be modified using the graphical tools.	Criteria can only be modified by editing the Where or Having part of the SQL query.
Modify Fields in Query	Fields can be added, removed, and renamed using graphical tools.	Fields can only be modified by editing the fields and formulas in the Select part of the SQL query.

Managing the Display of Columns

When using the Microsoft Query program, you may want to suppress the display of particular columns or fields to troubleshoot a query or to focus on some particular column. This can be accomplished by moving a field to a different position in the query, by temporarily hiding it, or even by permanently deleting it.

You can move a column in the query by simply selecting it in the Results section, dragging it left or right, and then dropping it in the desired location. You can also permanently delete a column by selecting it and choosing Records ➪ Remove Column or by pressing the Delete key.

WARNING If an SQL query cannot be displayed graphically, you will not be able to drag fields to a different position in the Results section. See Table 5.3 for a more complete list of functions that are disabled for queries that cannot be graphically displayed.

If you only want to temporarily hide a column, you can select the column or columns and then choose Format ➪ Hide Columns. If you want to hide or show multiple columns, choose Format ➪ Show Columns to launch the Show Columns dialog box shown in Figure 5.9. Here, you can select which columns to display or hide by selecting a field and clicking Hide or Show.

NOTE Showing or hiding a column has no effect on the Excel report. If you want to permanently remove the column from the report, you have to delete it.

Changing Row and Column Sizes

By default, Microsoft Query displays the result set in a standard row height and column width. Depending on the type of data being extracted, you may want to adjust these settings. For example, if you include a field with a Text data type, such as the Notes field in the Employees table of the NorthwindCS database, the information in that field is not fully displayed. You can increase the row height and adjust the column width in order to see most of the information in that field. Of course, you could also use the Zoom feature (explained later in this chapter) to display all the data of a particular cell in a single dialog box.

WARNING Row and Column size settings are discarded when the Microsoft Query program is closed.

Row and Column sizes are adjusted in a manner similar to how the cells of an Excel spreadsheet are adjusted. In order to increase the row height, simply move the mouse pointer to the left of the cells, until it changes to a bar with arrows that point both up and down, as shown in Figure 5.10, and then click the mouse and move it up or down to adjust the row height.

Alternatively, you can adjust the row height by choosing Format ➪ Row Height. This brings up the dialog box shown in Figure 5.11, where you can specify a particular row height or reset it to a Standard Height.

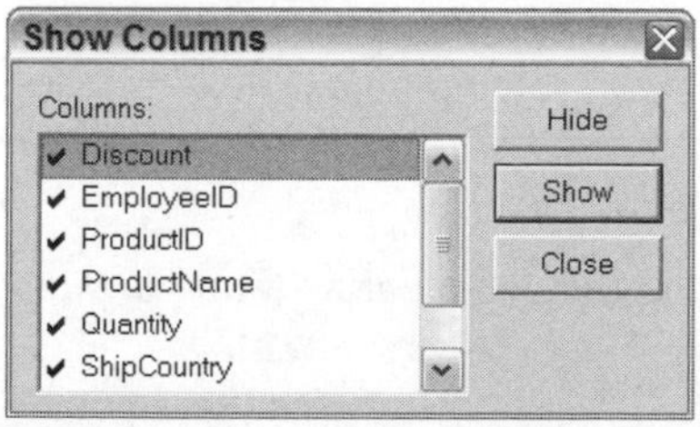

Figure 5.9   Temporarily show or hide columns in this dialog box.

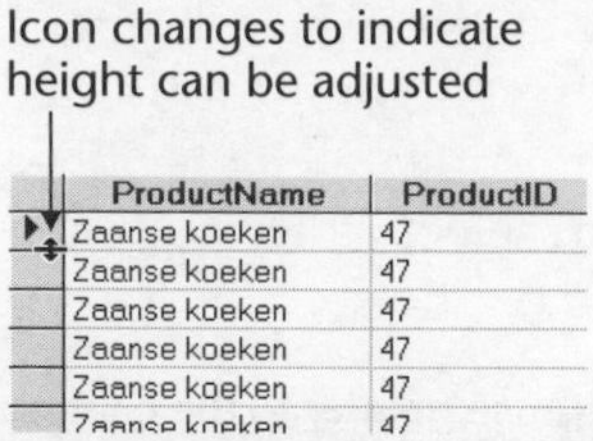

Icon changes to indicate
height can be adjusted

ProductName	ProductID
Zaanse koeken	47
Zaanse koeken	47
Zaanse koeken	47
Zaanse koeken	47
Zaanse koeken	47
Zaanse koeken	47

Figure 5.10   You can adjust row height by moving the mouse pointer to the row area and dragging the cell border down or up.

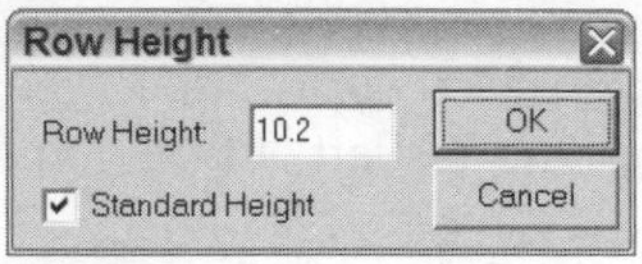

Figure 5.11   To reset the default height, check the Standard Height check box.

> **NOTE** Unlike with a column cell, you cannot double-click a row cell to set the row height to a Best Fit in the Microsoft Query program.

You can adjust the width of a column by choosing Format ⇨ Column Width. When the dialog box shown in Figure 5.12 appears, you can reset the column width to the standard width or to a specific size by typing a number.

The Standard Width includes some additional space over the Best Fit. The default setting is to use the Standard Width. Notice that you can also apply the Best Fit option by double-clicking the right side of the cell border after the button changes, as shown in Figure 5.13.

> **NOTE** The standard height and width vary with the type of font, the font style, and the font size being used.

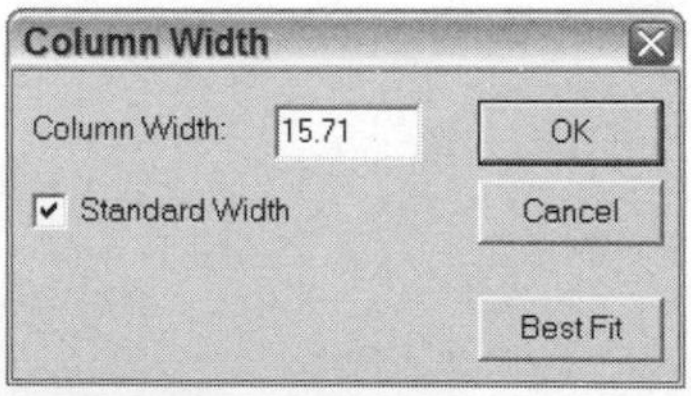

Figure 5.12   Unlike with the Row Height dialog box, you can set either a Standard Width or a Best Fit size for column cells.

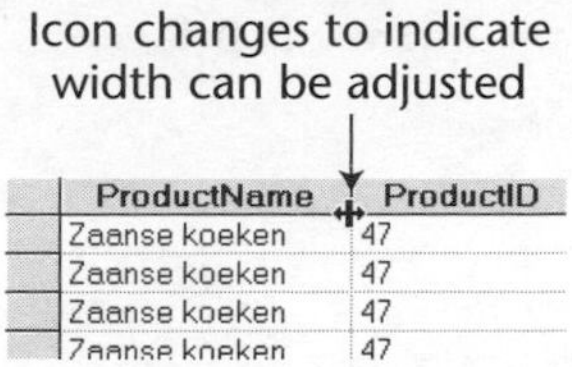

Icon changes to indicate
width can be adjusted

ProductName	ProductID
Zaanse koeken	47
Zaanse koeken	47
Zaanse koeken	47
Zaanse koeken	47

Figure 5.13 You can adjust the column width by moving the mouse pointer to the column cell area and dragging the cell border right or left.

Row height settings apply to all rows, while column width settings can be individually applied. If you want to apply the same column width to multiple cells, click each column and then choose Format ⇨ Columns to apply a specified width, Standard Width, or a Best Fit. Click the cell in the upper-left of the Result section to select all columns.

NOTE Multiple columns can be selected only when they are next to one another.

Modifying the Font Style

You can modify the font and font style by choosing Format ⇨ Font. Selecting this option brings up the Font dialog box shown in Figure 5.14. Here, you can choose to display the Results section in various types of available fonts, font styles, and font sizes. Unlike column settings, you cannot apply font styles to individual cells. Keep in mind that the font style applied here does not impact the Excel report; it applies only to the data displayed in the Results section.

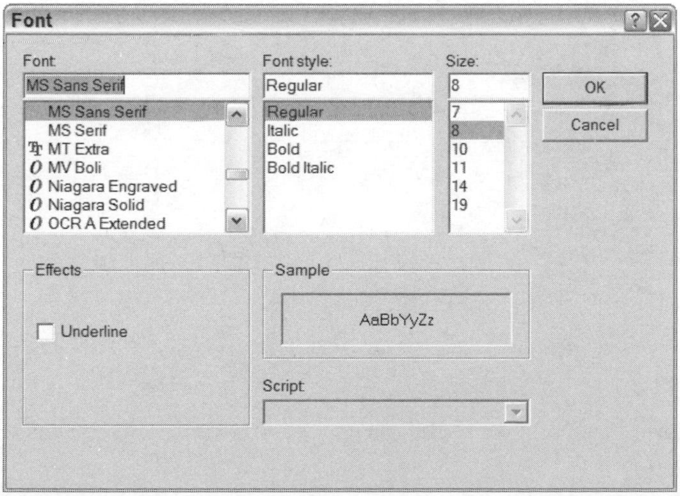

Figure 5.14 You can change the Fonts in the Results section from the Font dialog box.

WARNING Font settings are discarded when you close the Microsoft Query program.

Working with Multiple Query Windows

Multiple query windows can be helpful for querying on data in another table or comparing the result sets between a test and a production database server. The various query windows can be vertically tiled (side by side) or cascaded (accessed in a full window view by choosing Window ⇨ *Query Name*).

Choose Window ⇨ Tile or Window ⇨ Cascade to toggle how multiple query windows are displayed. Figure 5.15 shows how two query windows can be tiled to compare the results between two database servers.

Setting Program Options

Program options are maintained in the Options dialog box shown in Figure 5.16. These options, a potpourri of connection and query property settings, affect how Microsoft Query connects and interacts with external data sources. Connection properties, preview rows, and query edit features are all configured here. You can open this dialog box by choosing Edit ⇨ Options.

WARNING Unlike font and column settings, options modified here are saved and affect future Query Wizard and Microsoft Query sessions.

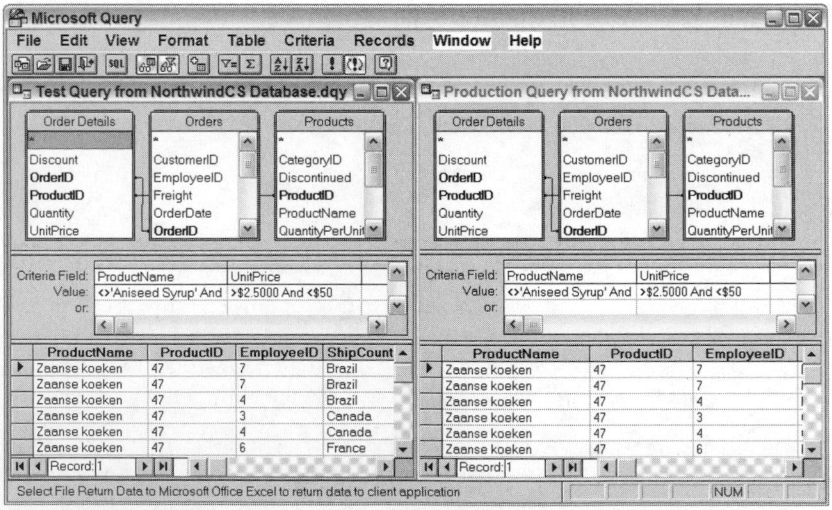

Figure 5.15 Tiling query windows can be useful for comparing the results between production and test databases.

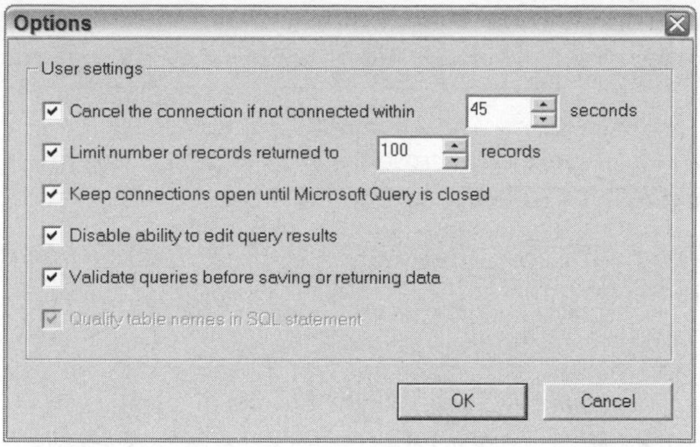

Figure 5.16 You can control query and connection properties from this dialog box.

The first option for connection time should need adjustment only when the initial connection to the database server or servers is taking longer than the time specified in that field. The next option for limiting rows applies only to the number of records read by the Microsoft Query program for previewing the result set. It does not control the number of records actually imported into the Excel report.

TIP **If you want to control the number of records imported into the Excel report, use the** SET ROWCOUNT n **function before the query (SQL Server) or use** Rownum = n **in the Where part of the query (Oracle).**

The third option, for keeping the connection open, can be useful if it takes a long time to connect to the data source (use this option in conjunction with the first option). The fourth option enables the data from a single table query to be edited. It is used in conjunction with the Allow Editing item in the Records menu. Queries can optionally be validated before saving or returning data. Table 5.4 provides a more detailed explanation of each option.

Table 5.4 Explanation of Query Options

USER SETTING	EXPLANATION
Cancel the connection if not connected with *n* seconds	Use this option to control the query timeout period. If you have a slow network and you are accessing a couple of database servers in a single query, you might have to adjust this value upward.
Limit number of records returned to *n* records	Use this option to control the number of records returned and displayed in the Results section and in some preview functions. Note that this setting does not affect the number of records actually returned to the Excel report.

(continued)

Table 5.4   *(continued)*

USER SETTING	EXPLANATION
Keep Connections Open Until Microsoft Query is Closed	When checked, this option keeps the connection open until the Microsoft Query program is closed. Use this option when making a connection to the external data source takes a long time.
Disable Ability to Edit Query Results	By default, this option is checked in order to prevent an accidental table update through the Microsoft Query program.
Validate Queries before Saving or Returning Data	Use this option to have the Microsoft Query program validate that the query works before returning data to Excel.

Working in the Environment

This section covers how you can use some of the basic navigation and operations functions of the Microsoft Query program environment. It shows you the primary features you're likely to use on a regular basis as you develop, manage, and save queries for Excel reports, including the following topics:

- Running a query
- Retrieving and saving queries
- Accessing the generated SQL
- Go to and zooming
- Editing data
- Creating an OLAP cube from a saved query

Running a Query

A query can automatically be executed whenever it is opened or modified using the Automatic Query option. This option is toggled by clicking the Auto Query toolbar button or by choosing Records ➪ Automatic Query.

TIP Enabling the Automatic Query option can be a nuisance when multiple changes to the SQL query are required because each change triggers a refresh.

If the automatic query option is disabled, the SQL query can be run using the following methods:

- Clicking the Query Now toolbar button
- Choosing Records ⇨ Query Now
- Pressing the F9 key

Retrieving and Saving Queries

Queries developed with the Query Wizard or with the Microsoft Query programs can be saved for use in future Excel reports. Keep in mind that the SQL query is automatically embedded in the Excel report, so saving the query is only helpful if you plan to use it for creating *new* reports. The default location for retrieving or saving a query is (replace *User* with your Windows login):

```
C:\Documents and Settings\User\Application Data\Microsoft\Queries
```

You can retrieve queries from the Microsoft Query program by choosing File ⇨ Open to open a dialog box or by clicking the Open toolbar button.

WARNING Microsoft Query can only retrieve query files that have a file extension of .dqy (database query), .qry (query), or .oqy (OLAP cubes).

Queries created in SQL development programs such as Query Analyzer (SQL Server 7.0/2000), Microsoft SQL Server Studio (SQL Server 2005), or Toad (Oracle) are best loaded into the Microsoft Query program using a cut-and-paste operation. Simply copy the query to your clipboard from the development program, press Alt+Tab to move to an open Microsoft Query session, click the View SQL button, and then paste the query into the SQL dialog box.

Accessing the Generated SQL

If you choose to build an SQL query using the program's graphical tools, an SQL query is still generated in the background. Adding or removing fields, modifying a filter condition, or changing a sort order using the program's graphical tools produces a corresponding change to the background SQL query. You can access this query at any time by clicking the View SQL button. Advanced users typically ignore the program's graphical tools and click the View SQL button to paste in queries developed from external SQL development programs.

Go To and Zooming

Although there is not a Find Text function, you can route to a specific record by choosing Records ⇨ Go To or by pressing the F5 key. The F5 key brings the cursor to the Record Box where you can type a record number to go to, use the buttons to move back or forward one record, or scroll to the first or last record in the Results section.

TIP There is no Find function for locating specific text in the Results section. I recommend that you perform this type of operation in a real SQL development program.

The Zoom function is useful for inquiring on data in fields where there is a lot of information and it cannot be fully displayed in the Results section. For example, clicking the Notes field in the Employees table of the NorthwindCS database provides a dedicated dialog box for examining the full contents of that particular cell, as shown in Figure 5.17.

You can zoom on a field by either right-clicking it twice or by choosing View ⇨ Zoom.

Editing Data

You can use Microsoft Query to add or modify the data in a database table. This feature can be useful when you are running a test or just need to modify or insert a few records into a table. In order for this function to work, the following conditions must be met:

- The Disabled Editing option must be unchecked.
- The query must utilize only a single table.
- The query must include all the required fields.
- The query cannot contain any Identity columns.
- The Allow Editing option must be enabled. (Choose Records ⇨ Allow Editing to toggle the setting of this option.)

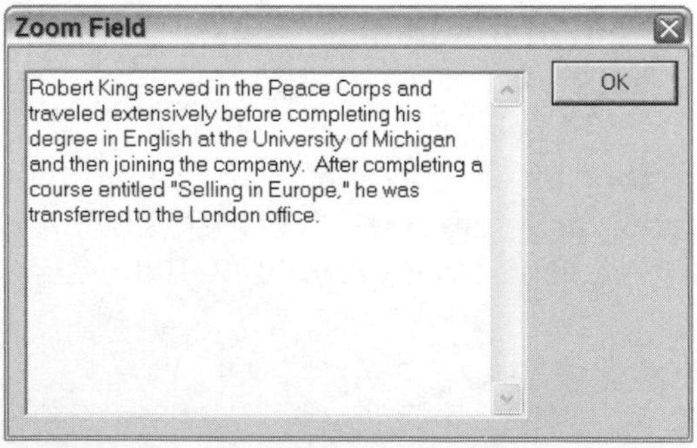

Figure 5.17   The Zoom feature is ideal for adding, editing, or viewing long strings of data in a single dialog box.

Creating an OLAP Cube from a Saved Query

From the Microsoft Query program, you can start the OLAP Cube Wizard to build an offline OLAP cube using the current query. This is a useful tool when the result set becomes too large (usually indicated by noticeably slowed performance).

CROSS-REFERENCE Read Chapter 3 for an overview of OLAP cubes and Chapter 10 for creating offline cube files.

Trying It Out in the Real World

Laura Callahan, an inside Sales Coordinator in the Northwind Trader's Seattle office, is responsible for ensuring that product stock levels are appropriately managed. Laura is concerned that there might be too much inventory on hand for some products. She has requested that you provide her with a PivotTable report that summarizes the units of stock for available products where there are over 100 units in stock. Laura is not familiar with ID numbers and has communicated that the full names should be used for products, categories, and suppliers.

Getting Down to Business

Follow these steps to complete this exercise:

1. From Excel, choose Data ⇨ PivotTable And PivotChart Report.
2. Select External Data Source, and then click Next.
3. When PivotTable And PivotChart Wizard — Step 2 of 3 appears, click Get Data.
4. When the Choose Data Source dialog box appears, verify that the Use The Query Wizard To Create/Edit Queries is unchecked, select the NorthwindCS Database data source, and then click OK.
5. When the Microsoft Query program is launched, you are presented with the Add Tables dialog box. Add the following Tables to the Tables section:
    - Categories
    - Suppliers
    - Products
6. Click Close to close the Add Tables dialog box.

7. Double-click the CategoryName field in the Categories table to add this field to the Results section.

8. Double-click the CompanyName field in the Suppliers table to add this field to the Results section.

9. Double-click the ProductName and UnitsInStock fields in the Products table to add these fields to the Results section.

10. Choose View ➪ Criteria if the Criteria section is not displayed.

11. Select Products.Discontinued or just type **Discontinued** in the Criteria Field of the Criteria section, and then type **0** in Value, under Discontinued.

12. Select Products.UnitsInStock or type **UnitsInStock** in the Criteria field (directly to the right of Discontinued); then type **> 100** in Value, under `UnitsInStock`.

13. Choose Records ➪ Query Now if Automatic Query is not enabled.

14. Verify that your Microsoft Query window looks like Figure 5.18.

15. Click the Return Data button to exit the Microsoft Query program and bring up the PivotTable And PivotChart Wizard - Step 2 Of 3 dialog box.

16. Click Finish in the Wizard dialog box to return the data to Excel and create the PivotTable report.

17. Drag CategoryName and CompanyName to the Page area, ProductName to the Row area, and UnitsInStock to the Data area of the PivotTable report.

18. Verify that your PivotTable report looks like Figure 5.19.

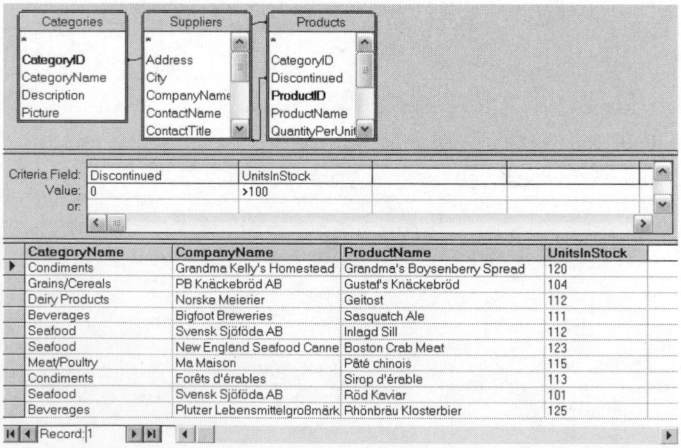

Figure 5.18 If you did everything right, the Microsoft Query window should look like this.

	A	B	
1	CompanyName	(All)	▼
2	CategoryName	(All)	▼
3			
4	Sum of UnitsInStock		
5	ProductName ▼	Total	
6	Boston Crab Meat	123	
7	Geitost	112	
8	Grandma's Boysenberry Spread	120	
9	Gustaf's Knäckebröd	104	
10	Inlagd Sill	112	
11	Pâté chinois	115	
12	Rhönbräu Klosterbier	125	
13	Röd Kaviar	101	
14	Sasquatch Ale	111	
15	Sirop d'érable	113	
16	Grand Total	1136	

ᴵ◀ ◀ ▶ ▶ᴵ \ **Sheet1** / Sheet2 / Sheet3 /

Figure 5.19   The PivotTable report for Laura appears as shown here.

WATCH THE VIDEO To see how this PivotTable report is created using the Microsoft Query program, click the file ch0501_video.avi at www.wiley.com/ go/excelreporting to watch the video.

Reviewing What You Did

This example gave you some practice building a basic SQL query using the graphical tools of the Microsoft Query program. I recommend that you review the functions and tools covered in this chapter to get more familiar with the environment and how queries are executed. Chapter 6 continues the discussion of the Microsoft Query program but picks up with more advanced SQL topics.

Chapter Review

This chapter reviewed the graphical tools of the Microsoft Query program and described how you can use them to customize and work in the environment. You learned how to access the Microsoft Query program for different types of Excel reports. In addition, the chapter discussed the purpose of each section of the Microsoft Query environment, how to toggle the display of different sections, how to configure program options, customize the environment, and perform basic functions.

CHAPTER 6

Working with SQL in Microsoft Query

As you continue the examination of Microsoft Query started in Chapter 5, this chapter shows you how to build and use SQL queries in the Microsoft Query program.

The chapter starts with a review of the graphical tools and how they are mapped to the various parts of an SQL query. The various types of table joins are covered, along with an explanation of the returned dataset. The chapter covers advanced SQL topics, such as how to extract data from multiple database servers in a single session. Finally, this chapter provides another real-world example at the end so you can practice what you learned.

Managing the SQL Query

This section shows you how to use Microsoft Query's graphical tools to build and adjust an SQL query. In Table 6.1, these tools are organized into the various parts of an SQL query to which they apply.

I intentionally left out the join part of the SQL query and moved it to the next section of this chapter. I did this because I've included a lot of information on table joins, and I thought it deserved its own section. There is also a lot of helpful information in the "Managing Table Joins" section for users who need a primer on the material, or for users who are unfamiliar with how the Microsoft Query program handles the various table joins and want to learn more.

Table 6.1 Graphical Tools to SQL Statement

SQL PART	GRAPHICALLY SUPPORTED FUNCTIONS
Select	Adding and removing fields Creating calculated fields Renaming fields Arranging the order of fields (left to right) in a query Aggregating fields Using Distinct
From	Adding tables
Where	Using criteria
Group By	Grouping records
Having	Using criteria with aggregated data

Before You Begin

To set things up so you can follow along with the examples in this section, complete these steps:

1. From Excel, choose Data ⇨ PivotTable And PivotChart Report.

2. Select External Data source and then click Next.

3. When the PivotTable And PivotChart Wizard - Step 2 of 3 appears, click Get Data.

4. When the Choose Data Source dialog box appears, verify that Use The Query Wizard To Create/Edit Queries is unchecked, select the NorthwindCS Database data source, and click OK.

CROSS-REFERENCE If you need help with creating the Northwind CS database on an SQL Server, read the section "Creating the NorthwindCS SQL Database" in Appendix A.

5. When the Microsoft Query program is launched, you are presented with the Add Tables dialog box. Select the Products table, click Add to add the table to the query, and then click Close to close the Add Tables dialog box.

6. Verify that your Microsoft Query window looks like Figure 6.1.

After you have completed these steps, you're set up to follow along with the examples in the rest of this section.

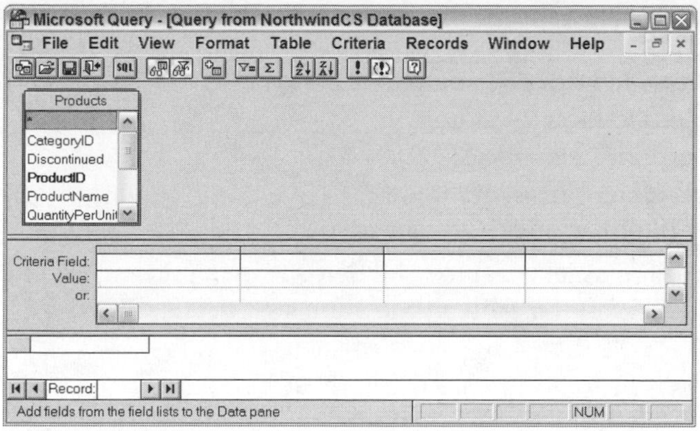

Figure 6.1 Add the Products table to follow along with the examples in this section.

Working in the Select Part of an SQL Query

The Select part of an SQL query includes the fields, field names, and the order of the fields (left to right) in the query. Calculated fields, aggregate functions, and keywords, such as Distinct, are also included here. This section reviews how you can use the Microsoft Query program to include these components in the Select part of your SQL query.

NOTE All the functions in this section assume that the query can be displayed graphically. If the query cannot be displayed graphically, you need to perform these functions by editing the SQL query.

Adding and Removing Fields

In the Tables section, the fields in each table are listed in alphanumeric order. Looking at the Products table in Figure 6.1, notice that an asterisk is displayed at the top of the table, followed by all the table's field names (in alphanumeric order). You can either choose to add individual fields to the query or add all the fields. The easiest way to add a single field to the query is usually to just double-click it. If you want to add all the fields to the query, just double-click the asterisk.

TIP Double-clicking the asterisk performs a SELECT * from {*Table Name*}. Thus, the fields in the query appear in the order in which they are defined in the database table, not in alphanumeric order as they are in the Tables section.

Like most things in Excel, you can choose from several methods to accomplish common tasks. Adding a field to a query is no exception; there are several ways to complete this task, and each method does something slightly different. Table 6.2 provides a list of these various methods with a short description about when to use each one.

It's just as easy to delete fields from the query. Just select the column (or columns) in the Result section and press the Delete key or choose Records ⇨ Remove Column. If you want to quickly remove all fields from a particular table in the Results section, just click on the table in the Tables section and press the Delete key.

Complete the following steps to add fields using these different methods:

1. Double-click the SupplierID field in the Products table to add the field to the query.

2. Double-click the UnitsinStock field in the Products table to add the field to the end of the query.

3. Select UnitsInStock in the Results section (the column is highlighted), and then Choose Records ⇨ Insert Column.

4. When the Add Column dialog box appears, select ProductName from the Field drop-down list, click Insert to add this field to the query, and then click Close to close the Add Column dialog box.

5. Verify that ProductName is inserted before UnitsInStock, and then drag UnitsOnOrder from the Products table and drop it on top of UnitsIn-Stock in the Results section to add it between ProductName and UnitsInStock.

TIP If you make a mistake, just select Edit ⇨ Undo to start over.

Table 6.2   Methods for Adding a Field to the Query

METHOD	USE WHEN
Double-click a field in a table	Quickly adding a field to the end of the query.
Drag-and-drop	Adding a field to a specific place in the query.
Results	Adding expressions or calculated fields at the end of the query.
Records ⇨ Add Column*	Adding a field to a particular location, specifying a name and/or applying an aggregate function.

*If a cell is selected in the Results section, Records ⇨ Add Column is replaced with Records ⇨ Insert Column.

6. Select Discontinued from a blank cell in the Results section.

7. Now, try removing that column from the query by selecting the Discontinued column and pressing the Delete key.

8. Select Records ➪ Query Now if Automatic Query is not enabled.

9. Verify that your Results section looks like Figure 6.2.

Creating Calculated Fields

Calculated fields are useful when you need to add a field to the query that doesn't currently exist in the database. This might include concatenating two or more fields into a single field or performing some type of mathematical or string operation on a field. For example, you could add the quantity in UnitsOnOrder to the quantity in UnitsInStock to create a new calculated field called TotalExpectedUnits.

Follow these steps to create a calculated field:

1. Verify that no records are selected in the Results section, and then choose Records ➪ Add Column.

2. When the Add Column dialog box appears, type **UnitsOnOrder+ UnitsInStock** in the Field field and press the Tab key to move to Column Heading.

3. Type **TotalExpectedUnits** in the Column Heading field and verify that your dialog box looks like Figure 6.3.

4. Click the Add button to the insert the new calculated field into the query, and then click Close to close the Add Column dialog box.

5. Select Records ➪ Query Now if Automatic Query is not enabled.

6. Verify that the Results section looks like what is shown in Figure 6.4.

You can also create a calculated field by selecting a blank cell in the Results section and then simply typing a formula into the column heading cell. Table 6.3 lists a few calculated field formulas that you can use in a query.

You can also combine several operations into a single one. For example, instead of just using LEFT(ProductName,10) to obtain the first 10 positions of the product name, you could use UPPER(LEFT(ProductName,10)) to also obtain the results in uppercase, as shown in Figure 6.5.

SupplierID	ProductName	UnitsOnOrder	UnitsInStock
1	Chai	0	39
1	Chang	40	17
1	Aniseed Syrup	70	13
2	Chef Anton's Cajun Seasoning	0	53
2	Chef Anton's Gumbo Mix	0	0
3	Grandma's Boysenberry Spread	0	120

Figure 6.2 If you did everything right, your Results section should look like this.

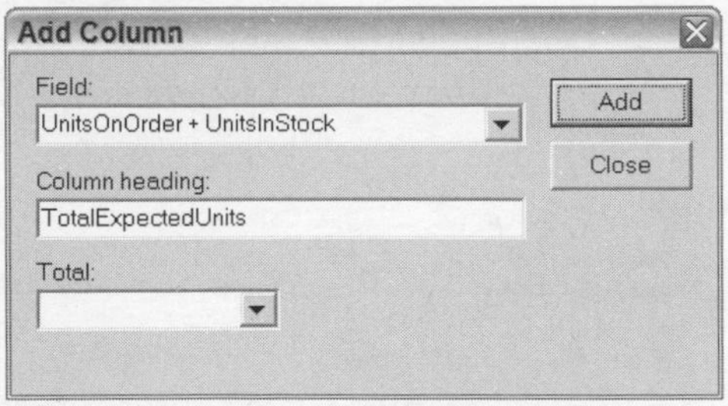

Figure 6.3 You can enter formulas, expressions, and operators into the Field box to create calculated fields in the query.

SupplierID	ProductName	UnitsOnOrder	UnitsInStock	TotalExpectedUnits
1	Chai	0	39	39
1	Chang	40	17	57
1	Aniseed Syrup	70	13	83
2	Chef Anton's Cajun Seaso	0	53	53
2	Chef Anton's Gumbo Mix	0	0	0
3	Grandma's Boysenberry S	0	120	120

Figure 6.4 You can easily add calculated fields to the query; they are useful when that particular field doesn't already exist in a database table.

Table 6.3 Some Examples of Calculated Fields

CALCULATION	EXPLANATION
GETDATE()	Produces the current date.
UPPER(ProductName)	Uppercases ProductName.
UnitPrice*1.10	Adds 10 percent to the value of UnitPrice.
1	Shows a 1 in the column.
'XYZ'	Shows XYZ in the column.
CategoryID + 'XYZ' + ProductId	Concatenates Category ID, XYZ, and ProductID to make a new field (e.g., ProductCode).
LEFT(ProductName,10)	Shows the first 10 positions of ProductName.

UnitsInStock	TotalExpectedUnits	UPPER(LEFT(ProductName,10))
39	39	CHAI
17	57	CHANG
13	83	ANISEED SY
53	53	CHEF ANTON
0	0	CHEF ANTON
120	120	GRANDMA'S

Figure 6.5 You can combine multiple operations to create a calculated field.

CROSS-REFERENCE Read the SQL reference in Appendix B for a more complete list of available string functions and some examples of how you can use them to modify column text.

Changing a Column Name

The field names used in the NorthwindCS database tables are easy to understand. That's rarely the case, however, when you're working with enterprise databases. There's usually some type of sensible technical naming convention in place, but rarely is the name entirely spelled out. There are also several other reasons why you might want to change a column name. Perhaps the name isn't descriptive or suitable enough for the report. Renaming fields, such as Discount to Sales Discount, or Amount to Amount Paid, may lead to a more understandable Excel report. If calculated fields are being added to the report, an appropriate name should also be assigned to it. In Figure 6.3, this was accomplished in a single step. In Figure 6.5, however, the name of the field is the same as the formula.

In order to modify a column name, simply double-click the field or select the field and choose Records ➪ Edit Column. Either method brings up the Edit Column dialog box.

Follow these steps to practice changing the names of columns in the Results section:

1. Add the calculated field shown in Figure 6.5 by selecting a blank cell in the Results section and typing the formula.

2. Select the calculated field column and choose Records ➪ Edit Column to launch the Edit Column dialog box.

3. Type **ShortName** in the Column Heading field, verify that your dialog box looks like Figure 6.6, and then click OK to close the Edit Column dialog box.

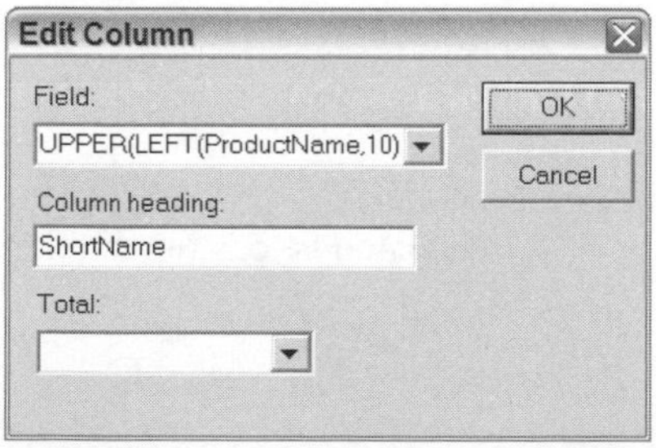

Figure 6.6 The Edit Column dialog box allows you to change the field name.

4. Double-click the ProductName column (second field from the left) to open the Edit Column dialog box.

5. Type **LongName** in the Column Heading field, and then click OK to close the Edit Column dialog box.

6. Select Records ➪ Query Now if Automatic Query is not enabled.

7. Verify that the Results section looks like Figure 6.7.

When the field heading is renamed, the background SQL statement is also modified by including an AS 'Field Heading' after the column name. You can click the View SQL button to review the SQL query shown here:

```
SELECT  Products.SupplierID,
        Products.ProductName        AS 'LongName',
        Products.UnitsOnOrder,
        Products.UnitsInStock,
        UnitsOnOrder+UnitsInStock   AS 'Total Expected Units',
        Upper(Left(ProductName,10)) AS 'ShortName'
FROM    NorthwindCS.dbo.Products Products
```

WARNING Although Microsoft Query puts the field heading in a single quote, this can be problematic when SQL queries are pasted into the SQL window. Try to use brackets ([ ]) instead of single quotes (' ') to ensure that Microsoft Query can properly read the field headings (explained later in the "Using SQL Functions" section).

Keep in mind that the Edit Column dialog box is only enabled when the query can be graphically displayed. If it cannot be graphically displayed, you need to specify the field names by modifying the underlying SQL query. In the PivotTable and Spreadsheet Report chapters (see Chapters 2 and 11), I also show you how to rename fields from the Excel report, regardless of whether the query can be graphically displayed in the Microsoft Query program.

SupplierID	LongName	UnitsOnOrder	UnitsInStock	TotalExpectedUnits	ShortName
1	Chai	0	39	39	CHAI
1	Chang	40	17	57	CHANG
1	Aniseed Syrup	70	13	83	ANISEED SY
2	Chef Anton's Cajun Seaso	0	53	53	CHEF ANTON
2	Chef Anton's Gumbo Mix	0	0	0	CHEF ANTON
3	Grandma's Boysenberry S	0	120	120	GRANDMA'S
3	Uncle Bob's Organic Dried	0	15	15	UNCLE BOB'

Figure 6.7 ProductName is renamed to LongName and the calculated field is renamed to ShortName.

CROSS-REFERENCE In Chapters 7 and 11, you learn how to change field names from the Excel report.

Arranging the Order of Fields in a Query

Arranging the order of the fields in a query (left to right) is just as easy as adding or removing a field. Just select the column, and then drag it to a new position in the query.

Complete these steps to follow my example in this chapter:

1. Click ShortName and verify that the column heading and its cell below are highlighted.

2. Drag ShortName between LongName and UnitsOnOrder.

3. Verify that the Results section looks like Figure 6.8.

As soon as you perform this step, the underlying SQL query is immediately modified. You can click the View SQL button to verify that the following query appears:

```
SELECT  Products.SupplierID,
        Products.ProductName        AS 'LongName',
        UPPER(LEFT(ProductName,10)) AS 'ShortName',
        Products.UnitsOnOrder,
        Products.UnitsInStock,
        UnitsOnOrder+UnitsInStock   AS 'TotalExpectedUnits'
FROM    NorthwindCS.dbo.Products Products
```

NOTE Adjusting the order of the fields in a query primarily applies to Spreadsheet reports. In a PivotTable, the fields are meant to be dynamically dragged to different locations in the report; so the order of fields in a query applies only to the PivotTable Field List.

SupplierID	LongName	ShortName	UnitsOnOrder	UnitsInStock	TotalExpectedUnits
1	Chai	CHAI	0	39	39
1	Chang	CHANG	40	17	57
1	Aniseed Syrup	ANISEED SY	70	13	83
2	Chef Anton's Cajun Seaso	CHEF ANTON	0	53	53
2	Chef Anton's Gumbo Mix	CHEF ANTON	0	0	0
3	Grandma's Boysenberry S	GRANDMA'S	0	120	120
3	Uncle Bob's Organic Dried	UNCLE BOB'	0	15	15

Figure 6.8 You can change field order by using the drag-and-drop features of Microsoft Query.

Using Aggregate Functions

Aggregate functions compute a single value result for a particular column (or columns). For example, calculating the total of UnitsOnOrder by SupplierID requires that you perform the aggregate SUM function on UnitsOnOrder. The aggregate functions include the following:

- **AVG:** Computes an average
- **COUNT:** Counts the number of records
- **MAX:** Finds the maximum value
- **MIN:** Finds the minimum value
- **SUM:** Computes a sum

NOTE Review the online help included in your database software for a complete list of aggregate functions.

All of these aggregate functions are supported through the graphical tools of the Microsoft Query program. You can create an aggregate function by double-clicking a column name or by choosing Records ⇨ Edit Column.

To see how this works, try this example:

1. Delete all columns in the query, except SupplierID and UnitsOnOrder.
2. Select UnitsOnOrder (the field heading and the cells below are highlighted), and then click the Cycle Totals toolbar button once to cycle the aggregation type to SUM.
3. Select Records ⇨ Query Now if Automatic Query is not enabled.
4. Verify that the Results section looks like Figure 6.9.

In the example shown in Figure 6.9, you might want to rename the field to something like TotalUnitsOnOrder. In practice, you may find it preferable to add an aggregated column through the Add Column dialog box by choosing Records ⇨ Add Column because you can define the field, the field heading, and the aggregation method all at the same time.

SupplierID	Sum of UnitsOnOrder
1	110
2	100
3	0
4	20
5	30
6	0
7	10

Figure 6.9 The Cycle Totals toolbar button cycles through each aggregate function for a selected column, each time it is clicked.

Here's the SQL generated by the Microsoft Query program. Notice that the Group By statement is automatically added:

```
SELECT    Products.SupplierID,
          Sum(Products.UnitsOnOrder) AS 'Sum of UnitsOnOrder'
FROM      NorthwindCS.dbo.Products Products
GROUP BY Products.SupplierID
```

NOTE A Group By **statement is required for all the non-aggregated fields in an SQL query when an aggregate function is used.**

Using Distinct

You can use the Distinct function when you want to obtain only the unique rows of a result set. For example, you can use Distinct to create a unique list of category ID's in the Product Table. Simply add CategoryID to the query results in repeating values of CategoryID, as shown in Figure 6.10. This happens because CategoryID is pulled once for each product record in the Products table.

The SQL query produced for this query is as follows:

```
SELECT Products.CategoryID
FROM   NorthwindCS.dbo.Products Products
```

In order to obtain only the unique values by adding the Distinct keyword to the SQL query, follow these steps:

1. Choose View ➪ Query Properties.

2. When the Query Properties dialog box shown in Figure 6.11 appears, check Unique Values Only, and then click OK.

3. Select Records ➪ Query Now if Automatic Query is not enabled.

4. Verify that the Results section looks like Figure 6.12.

CategoryID
1
1
1
1
1
1
1
1

Figure 6.10 A CategoryID is shown for each record in the Products table.

Figure 6.11 Check Unique Values Only to add the Distinct keyword to the fields in the Select part of an SQL Query.

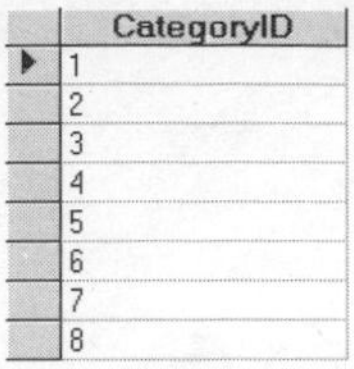

Figure 6.12 Only the unique values of CategoryID are returned when the Unique Values Only option is checked.

As soon as you perform this step, the underlying SQL query is modified. You can click the View SQL button to verify that the query looks like this:

```
SELECT DISTINCT Products.CategoryID
FROM NorthwindCS.dbo.Products Products
```

Working in the Where and Having Parts

You can add filter conditions to either the `Where` or the `Having` clause of an SQL query to restrict the type of data returned. The principal difference between these two clauses is that the `Where` clause is used for filtering non-aggregated data, whereas the `Having` clause is used for filtering aggregated data. So if you want to select only the product categories having a certain average price, you put the filter criteria in the `Having` clause because `AVG` is an aggregate function. If you are not familiar with SQL programming, this might sound a little confusing. Don't worry, a couple of examples are included in this section to help contextualize how this works.

WARNING The Microsoft Query program usually builds either a `Having` clause or a `Where` clause, not both. If not properly corrected, this can lead to substantially reduced performance. See the "Distinguishing between Where and Having" section of this chapter for more information about this topic.

Introducing Some New Operators

Chapter 4 provided a list of the valid mathematical operators (Table 4.3) and string operators (Table 4.4) that could be used in a filter. All of these operators are available in the Microsoft Query program, along with four new ones listed in Table 6.4.

CROSS-REFERENCE Read the SQL reference in Appendix B for a more complete list of the operators available with SQL programming.

Adding Criteria to a Query

Microsoft Query includes a few different graphical tools for creating filter conditions. You can choose to create them using the following methods:

- Choose Criteria ➪ Add Criteria to open the Add Criteria dialog box where you can pick from a list of valid operators.
- Select a field from a blank Criteria Field cell in the Criteria section, and then specify an operator and value in the Value field.
- Select a value in the Results section, and then click the Criteria Equals toolbar button to apply a filter that pulls only those records with the selected value in that column.

Using the Add Criteria Dialog Box

Using the Add Criteria dialog box, you can choose from a list of predefined mathematical and string operators. This is similar to the Filter Data dialog box of the Query Wizard that you saw in Chapter 4, except that you have a few new operators and some additional features and functions.

Table 6.4 Additional Operators in Microsoft Query

OPERATOR	EXPLANATION	SQL EQUIVALENT
Is Between	Between x and y	BETWEEN x AND y
Is Not Between	Not between x and y	NOT BETWEEN x AND y
Is One Of	Contains the specified values A, B, C, n... (Use when selecting multiple values.)	IN ('A','B','C')
Is Not One Of	Does not contain the specified values A, B, C, n... (Use when excluding multiple values.)	NOT IN ('A','B','C')

Follow these steps to see how this method works:

1. Start with a new query that uses only the Products table in the North-windCS database.

TIP You can either remove all columns in the Products table (if you are following along from the previous section) or repeat the steps in the "Before You Begin" section to just select the Product table.

2. Verify that your Microsoft Query window looks like the Microsoft Query shown in Figure 6.2.

3. Double-click the fields CategoryID, ProductName, Discontinued, and UnitsInStock (in this order) to add these fields to the Query.

4. Choose Criteria ⇨ Add Criteria to launch the Add Criteria dialog box.

5. Select CategoryID in the Field drop-down box, and then select Is One Of in the Operator drop-down box, as shown in Figure 6.13.

6. Click the Values button to open the Select Value(s) dialog box where you can specify the values to include in the query.

7. Notice that the unique values in CategoryID appear in the Values dialog box. Select the values 2, 4, and 5.

8. Verify that the Select Value(s) dialog box looks like Figure 6.14; and then click OK to close this dialog box and return to the Add Criteria dialog box.

9. Notice that 2,4,5 is added to the Value field of the Add Criteria dialog box. Click the Add button to apply the filter, and then click Close to close the dialog box.

10. Select Records ⇨ Query Now if Automatic Query is not enabled.

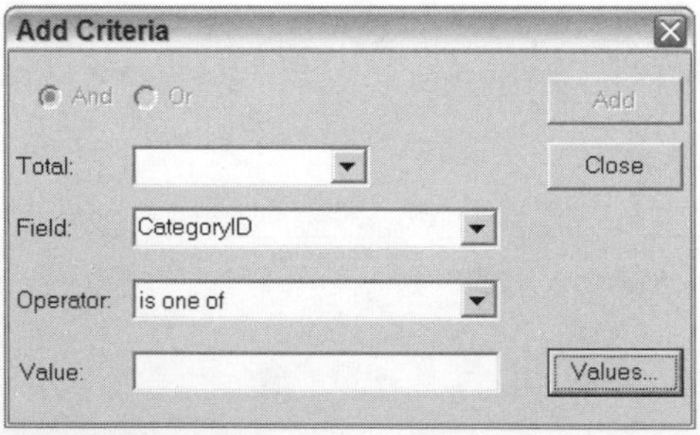

Figure 6.13 You select fields and operators from a drop-down list in the Add Criteria dialog box.

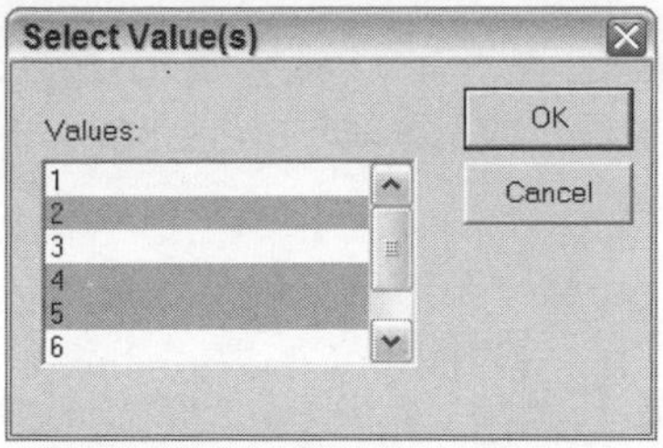

Figure 6.14   Select the unique values to include in the filter condition from the Select Value(s) dialog box.

11.   Verify that your Microsoft Query window looks like Figure 6.15.

As soon as you perform this step, the underlying SQL query is modified. You can click the View SQL button to verify that the query looks like this:

```
SELECT Products.CategoryID,
       Products.ProductName,
       Products.Discontinued,
       Products.UnitsInStock
FROM   NorthwindCS.dbo.Products Products
WHERE  (Products.CategoryID In (2,4,5))
```

Using the Criteria Section

You can also specify filter conditions in the Criteria section of the Microsoft Query program. This method provides some additional flexibility because you are not constrained to the list of valid operators in the Operator drop-down box. For example, the SQL function Soundex is not listed as a valid operator, but it is a supported SQL function that enables you to search for strings that "sound like" specified text: Soundex(Smith), for example, returns Smith, Smyth, and Smithe.

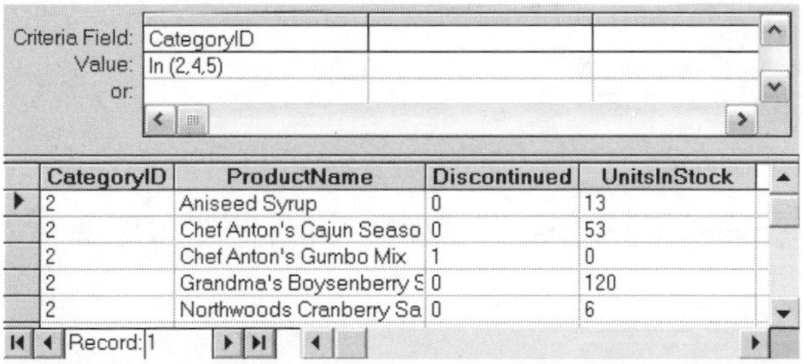

Figure 6.15   The filter criteria are automatically added in the Criteria section of the Microsoft Query program.

Looking at Figure 6.15, you can see that the Microsoft Query program simply added the filter criteria into the Criteria section from the Add Criteria dialog box. This time, bypass the Add Criteria dialog box and enter the filter conditions directly into the Criteria section.

To see how this works, follow these steps:

1. Click the Criteria Field cell to the right of CategoryID in the Criteria section, type **Soundex(ProductName)**, and press the down arrow to move to the Value field.

2. Type **Soundex('Seerup')** in the Value field.

3. Choose Records ➪ Query Now if Automatic Query is not enabled.

4. Verify that your Microsoft Query window looks like Figure 6.16.

You have now selected only the records that have a CategoryID of 2, 4, or 5 and a ProductName that sounds like the word *Syrup*. The SQL query has automatically been adjusted to include the new criteria shown here:

```
SELECT  Products.CategoryID,
        Products.ProductName,
        Products.Discontinued,
        Products.UnitsInStock
FROM    NorthwindCS.dbo.Products Products
WHERE   (Products.CategoryID In (2,4,5)) AND
        (Soundex(ProductName)=Soundex('Seerup'))
```

TIP You can use other functions such as LEFT, SUBSTRING, and UPPER by simply including the criteria field inside that function, just like I did in the Criteria section of Figure 6.16.

Criteria Field:	CategoryID	Soundex(ProductNa		^
Value:	In (2,4,5)	Soundex('Seerup')		
or:				v

	CategoryID	ProductName	Discontinued	UnitsInStock	
▶	2	Sirop d'érable	0	113	

|◀◀ Record: 1   ▶|▶| ◀| | ▶|

Figure 6.16   You can save time by entering Filter conditions directly into the Criteria section of Microsoft Query.

Using the Criteria Equals Button

The Criteria Equals button provides a quick and easy method for applying a column filter based on a particular cell value that is selected in the Results section. In order to use this feature, simply select a cell in the Results section and click the Criteria Equals button. Keep in mind that this method permits only one value to be selected at a time, and the only operator that is used for the filter is Equals. If you are doing some preliminary analysis or troubleshooting, this toolbar button can be helpful for quickly honing in on particular records that have the specified value in the selected column.

Adding and Removing Criteria

Remove criteria displayed in the Criteria section by first selecting the column (or columns) in the Criteria section and then pressing the Delete key. Choose Criteria ⇨ Remove All Criteria to remove all the criteria shown in the Criteria section.

Distinguishing between Where and Having

The Where clause of an SQL query is used for filtering non-aggregated data, while the Having clause of an SQL query is used for filtering aggregated data. A Group By statement is also required for all the non-aggregated fields in an SQL query whenever the Having clause is used. Keep in mind that although all of the filter conditions can be specified in the Having part of the SQL query, this can result in substantially reduced performance.

In order to illustrate the differences between the Where and Having clauses of an SQL query — and how the Microsoft Query program builds these parts of the query from its graphical tools — I've included an example.

Complete these steps to follow along with my example:

1. Start with a new query that uses only the Products table in the North-windCS database.

NOTE You can either remove all the columns in the Products table (if you are following along from the previous section) or repeat the steps in the "Before You Begin" section at the start of the chapter to select only the Product table.

2. Verify that your Microsoft Query window looks like Figure 6.1.
3. Double-click the fields SupplierID and UnitsOnOrder (in this order) to add these fields to the Query.

4. Choose Criteria ⇨ Add Criteria to launch the Add Criteria dialog box.

5. Select Discontinued in the Field drop-down box and Equals in the Operator drop-down box. Type **0** in the Value field and click the Add button to add the criteria to the Criteria section.

6. Keeping the Add Criteria dialog box open, select UnitsOnOrder in the Field drop-down box and Is Greater Than in the Operator drop-down box. Type **0** in the Value field; and then click the Add button to add the criteria to the Criteria section.

7. Click Close to close the Add Criteria dialog box.

8. Verify that your Criteria section looks like Figure 6.17.

9. Select SupplierID in the Results section and click the Sort Ascending button to sort the data in the result set in ascending order.

10. Select Records ⇨ Query Now if Automatic Query is not enabled.

You have now created an SQL query that extracts all the records in the Products table that are not discontinued and for which there are units on order. The query shows the SupplierID followed by the Units On Order. Clicking the View SQL button displays the query shown here:

```
SELECT    Products.SupplierID,
          Products.UnitsOnOrder
FROM      NorthwindCS.dbo.Products Products
WHERE     (Products.Discontinued=0) AND
          (Products.UnitsOnOrder>0)
ORDER BY Products.SupplierID
```

Now, how can you pull only the records for suppliers that have 100 or more units on order? Looking at Table 6.5, you can see that only a few suppliers have over 100 units. Supplier 1 has 110 total units (40 units and 70 units), Supplier 2 has 100 units, and Supplier 14 has 110 units (70 units and 40 units).

Now, let's aggregate UnitsOnOrder by SupplierID and apply a filter to select only the records that have more than 30 units on order.

NOTE If you want to compare the Results section and this table, sort the result set in the Results section by SupplierID.

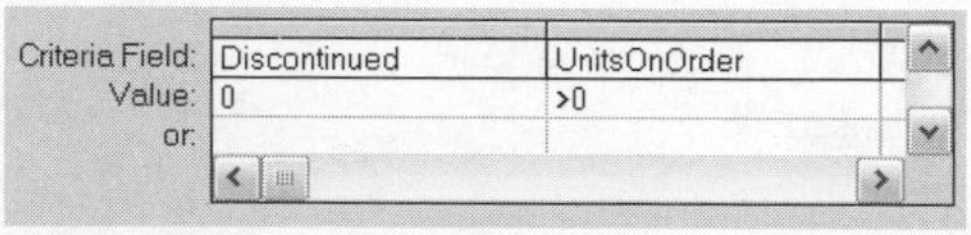

Figure 6.17   These filter criteria are added to the `Where` clause of the SQL query.

Table 6.5 Individual and Total Units on Order by SupplierID

SUPPLIERID	UNITS ON ORDER	TOTAL UNITS
1	40, 70	110
2	100	100
4	20	20
5	30	30
7	10	10
8	10, 40	50
12	80	80
14	70, 40	110
17	50	50
20	10	10
21	70	70
22	70	70
23	60	60
26	10	10

Follow these steps to aggregate Units On Order and apply the filter:

1. Double-click UnitsOnOrder in the Results section to bring up the Edit Column dialog box.

2. Type **Total Units** in the Column Heading, and then select Sum from the Total drop-down box to aggregate UnitsOnOrder by SupplierID.

3. Double-click the Value cell for UnitsOnOrder (the cell with >0 in it) in the Criteria section to bring up the Edit Criteria dialog box.

4. Delete the 0 and type **30** in Value; click OK to modify the filter; verify that the Edit Criteria dialog box looks like Figure 6.18; and close the Edit Query dialog box.

5. Choose Records ⇨ Query Now if Automatic Query is not enabled.

Clicking the View SQL button displays the following query:

```
SELECT    Products.SupplierID,
          Sum(Products.UnitsOnOrder) AS 'Total Units'
FROM      NorthwindCS.dbo.Products Products
WHERE     (Products.Discontinued=0) AND
          (Products.UnitsOnOrder>30)
GROUP BY Products.SupplierID
ORDER BY Products.SupplierID
```

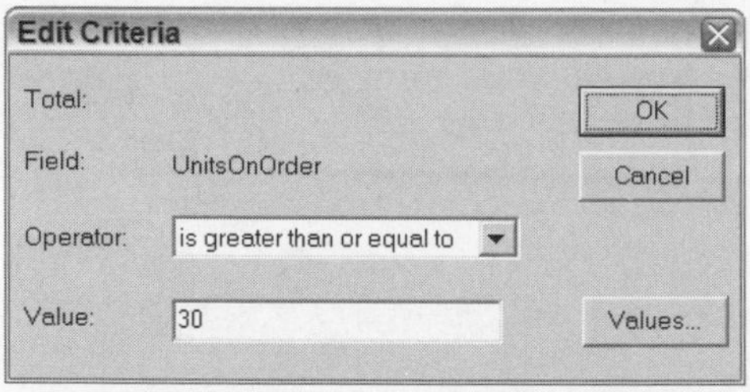

Figure 6.18 Filter criteria you define in the Criteria section can be modified from the Edit Criteria dialog box.

Notice that UnitsOnOrder was used instead of SUM(UnitsOnOrder) in the Criteria section. As a result, the criteria is place in the Where clause of the query instead of in the Having clause. This results in the query returning a Total Units of 40 for Supplier 8 instead of 50 units. Why? The query eliminated the row with 10 units before the data was even aggregated.

Now, try modifying the criteria to filter on total units on order rather than individual units on order:

1. Double-click the Criteria Field cell for UnitsOnOrder (the cell with UnitsOnOrder in it) in the Criteria section to bring up the Edit Criteria dialog box.

2. Select Sum from the Total drop-down field. Verify that the Edit Criteria dialog box looks like Figure 6.19; and then click OK to modify the criteria field and close the dialog box.

NOTE Two types of Edit Criteria dialog boxes are available. The first Edit Criteria dialog box is shown in Figure 6.18 and is launched when you double-click the Value cell in the Criteria section. In this box, you specify criteria in the Where clause of the SQL query. The second Edit criteria dialog box is shown in Figure 6.19 and is launched when you double-click the Criteria Field cell in the Criteria section. In this box, you can apply an aggregate function to the field, resulting in the criteria being evaluated in the Having clause of the SQL query.

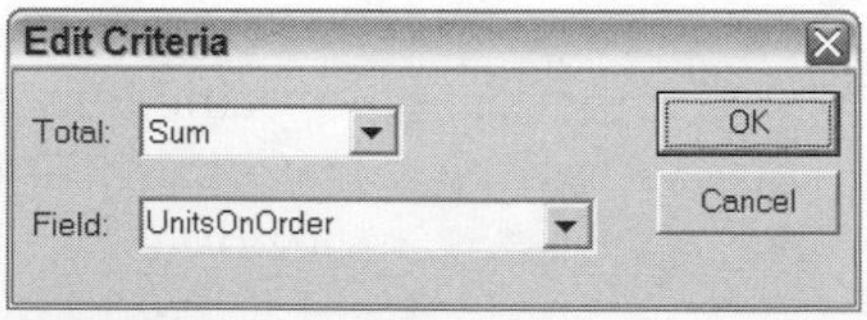

Figure 6.19 You can apply an aggregate function to the criteria field in this dialog box.

3. Double-click the Value cell for UnitsOnOrder (the cell with >30 in it) in the Criteria section to bring up the Edit Criteria dialog box.

4. Change the value in Operator to Is Greater Than Or Equal To. In the Value cell, delete the 30 and type **50.** Click OK to modify the filter and close the Edit Query dialog box.

5. Choose Records ⇨ Query Now if Automatic Query is not enabled.

Notice that Supplier 8 has total units of 50 displayed, instead of the 40 units in the previous example. This is because the filter criteria is included in the Having clause of the SQL query and is therefore not applied after the rows are aggregated. If you click the View SQL button, the query is displayed as follows:

```
SELECT     Products.SupplierID,
           Sum(Products.UnitsOnOrder) AS 'Total Units'
FROM       NorthwindCS.dbo.Products Products
GROUP BY   Products.SupplierID, Products.Discontinued
HAVING     (Products.Discontinued=0) AND
           (Sum(Products.UnitsOnOrder)>=50)
```

WARNING The Microsoft Query program often combines all the filter criteria into the Having part of an SQL query when a criteria field is aggregated. This can lead to performance problems because the Having statement is not optimized for performance.

Working in the Order By Part

The Order By part of an SQL query is used to sort the result set of an SQL query. Keep in mind that a sort order should only be specified for a Spreadsheet report and not on a PivotTable report (explained in Chapter 7). There are two methods for applying a sort order:

- Choose Records ⇨ Sort to view and modify the sort order information.
- Select a column (or columns), click the Ascending or Descending button to first remove all the existing sort order information; and then add a sort for the selected column (or columns).

In the Northwind Database Query example, the sort order was specified first on ProductName in descending order and then second on ShipCountry in ascending order. Choosing Records ⇨ Sort brings up the Sort dialog box shown in Figure 6.20.

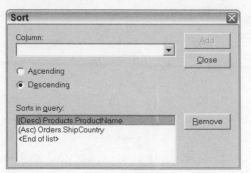

Figure 6.20   You manage the sort order information for a query by using the Sort dialog box.

You can add or remove column sorts in this dialog box. Unfortunately, there are no up or down arrows for changing the sort order priority. If you want to change the sort order priority, follow these steps:

1. In the Sorts In Query pane, select the field you want to delete from the sort order and click Remove.

2. In the Sorts In Query pane, select the field that you want to insert the new field in front of.

3. From the Column drop-down box, select the field you want to insert and click the Ascending or Descending button; and then click the Add button to insert this new field above the field you selected in step 2.

You can also apply a single sort order by selecting a column (or columns) and clicking the ascending or descending sort buttons. If you use this shortcut, keep in mind that it removes any existing sort order instructions defined in the query.

> **NOTE**   You should use a sort order only for Spreadsheet reports. A sort order doesn't provide any useful utility in PivotTable reports; it serves only to increase the amount of time it takes to execute the query.

Managing Table Joins

Table joins can be a confusing topic, especially for users who are not familiar with SQL programming. This section shows you how to use the graphical tools in Microsoft Query to create several types of table joins. It also describes each type of table join, demonstrates how different join types affect the result set produced from the query, and reviews the underlying SQL query that is produced. The joins described in this section include the following:

- Inner join
- Left joins
- Right join
- Cross join
- Self join
- Full join

All of the joins, except the Full join, are supported by the graphical tools in the Microsoft Query program. The Right join is supported insofar as the tables are reversed in the SQL query to create a Left join. The Cross join is created by removing any link between the two tables, whereas the Self join is created by adding the table to the Tables section twice.

If you are using the Microsoft Query program to create table joins, keep in mind that some restrictions are imposed that wouldn't normally apply if you were using an SQL development program to create the query. However, since the Microsoft Query program can handle only so much complexity through its graphical tools, you are limited in what you can do. These limitations are explained in the appropriate sections.

Before You Begin

In order to follow along with this section, you need to create the Categories-Forecast table in the NorthwindCS database, along with inserting some records into the new table.

To create the CategoriesForecast table in the NorthwindCS database, follow these steps:

1. Open a Microsoft Query dialog box using the NorthwindCS Database data source.

2. Choose File ⇨ Execute SQL to bring up an Execute SQL dialog box. Verify that the NorthwindCS database is selected in the bottom part of the dialog box.

3. Paste the following SQL query into the Execute SQL dialog box to create the CategoryForecast table and click Execute:

```
CREATE TABLE [dbo].[CategoryForecast]
          ([CategoryID] [int] NOT NULL,
          [ForecastAmount] [int] NOT NULL,
          [Active] [char](1) NOT NULL,
CONSTRAINT  [PK_CategoryForecast]
PRIMARY KEY CLUSTERED ([CategoryID] ASC) ON [PRIMARY])ON [PRIMARY]
```

ON THE WEB You can download the CategoryForecastTbl.txt file to your computer from this book's companion website at www.wiley.com/go/ excelreporting. **Look in the Chap06.zip file or the Chap06 directory, depending on which file you download.**

4. Click OK to acknowledge that the SQL command ran successfully, and then clear the contents of the Execute SQL dialog box.

TIP The Execute button becomes disabled when the Execute SQL window is completely cleared.

5. Paste the following SQL query into the Execute SQL dialog box to insert records into the CategoryForecast table, and then click Execute:

```
INSERT INTO CategoryForecast
SELECT '0', 4000,'N'
UNION ALL
SELECT '1',16500,'Y'
UNION ALL
SELECT '2', 9000,'Y'
UNION ALL
SELECT '3',12000,'Y'
UNION ALL
SELECT '4',10000,'Y'
UNION ALL
SELECT '5', 5000,'Y'
UNION ALL
SELECT '6',14000,'Y'
UNION ALL
SELECT '9', 3000,'Y'
```

ON THE WEB You can download the CategoryForecastVal.txt file to your computer from this book's companion website at www.wiley.com/go/ excelreporting. **Look in the Chap06.zip file or the Chap06 directory.**

6. Click OK to acknowledge that the SQL command ran successfully; then click Cancel to close the Execute SQL dialog box.

After you have created the CategoryForecast table, complete these steps to follow along with the examples in this section:

1. From Excel, choose Data ➪ PivotTable And PivotChart Report.
2. Select External Data source, and then click Next.

3. When the PivotTable And PivotChart Wizard appears, click Get Data.

4. When the Choose Data Source dialog box appears, verify that Use The Query Wizard To Create/Edit Queries is unchecked, select the NorthwindCS Database data source, and click OK.

5. When the Microsoft Query program is launched, you are presented with the Add Tables dialog box. First, add the CategoryForecast table; and then add the Categories table to the Tables section. Once the tables have been added, you'll notice that the tables are joined on CategoryID (the field name that is common to both tables). Click Close to close the Add Tables dialog box.

6. Add CategoryID from the CategoryForecast table to the query and rename it to **Forecast-CategoryID**.

7. Add CategoryID from the Categories table to the query and rename it to **Categories-CategoryID**.

8. Choose Records ⇨ Query Now if Automatic Query is not enabled.

9. Verify that your Microsoft Query window looks like Figure 6.21.

Before you start this section, carefully review the values in the CategoryForecast table (Table 6.6) and the Categories table (Table 6.7) to be sure that you understand the contents of each table and the differences.

NOTE The CategoryID's 0 and 9 are not in the Categories table.

The records for the Categories table are shown in Table 6.7. For simplicity, I've included only the first two columns of the table (there is no need to include Description and Picture since they aren't referenced in this section's examples).

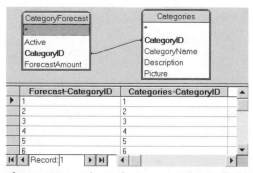

Figure 6.21   Microsoft Query automatically joins the tables on field names that are common to each table.

Table 6.6   Records in the CategoryForecast Table

CATEGORYID	FORECASTAMOUNT	ACTIVE
0	4000	N
1	16500	Y
2	9000	Y
3	12000	Y
4	10000	Y
5	5000	Y
6	14000	Y
9	3000	Y

Table 6.7   Records in the Categories Table

CATEGORYID	DESCRIPTION
1	Beverages
2	Condiments
3	Confections
4	Dairy Products
5	Grains/Cereals
6	Meat/Poultry
7	Produce
8	Seafood

NOTE The CategoryID's 7 and 8 are not in the CategoryForecast table.

After you have created the new CategoryForecast table in the NorthwindCS database and reviewed the contents of the Categories and CategoryForecast table, you're ready to begin learning about each table join.

Understanding Joins and Join Types

The tables and the table joins of an SQL query are displayed in the Tables section of the Microsoft Query program. The primary key fields are shown in bold, and table joins are represented by connection lines. An Inner join is represented by a line with a ball on either side, whereas a Left or Right join is represented by a ball on one side and an arrow on the other side. Cross joins are marked by the lack of any connection line in the Tables section.

NOTE Keep in mind that a table can be joined by more than one condition, and a join can be performed on fields with different names.

You can create table joins by choosing Table ⇨ Joins or by selecting a field from one table and dragging it on top of a field in another table. Figure 6.22 demonstrates how the ReportsTo field can be joined to EmployeeID.

After you create a join, you can remove it by clicking the line and pressing the Delete key. Alternatively, you can choose Tables ⇨ Joins and delete the join in the dialog box by selecting it and clicking Remove.

Inner Joins

An Inner join links the table together using a value (or values) in one or more fields that is common to both tables. This type of join selects only the rows where the joined fields have matching values. An Inner join on CategoryID between the CategoryForecast and Categories forecast table is graphically represented in the Tables section in Figure 6.23. Notice that the connection line has a ball on each end. Looking back at Tables 6.6 and 6.7, you can derive that only values 1–6 are selected because they are the only ones common to both tables. Although the Categories table has values 7 and 8 and CategoryForecast has values 0 and 9, they are not common to both tables; therefore, they are not returned when an Inner join is used.

Keep in mind that Microsoft Query creates Inner joins only when tables are added to the Tables section. These default joins are created on fields that have the same name with one or both of them being defined as a primary key field. If both of these conditions cannot be satisfied, Microsoft Query settles for just the field name being the same. If at least this second condition cannot be satisfied, a join is not created.

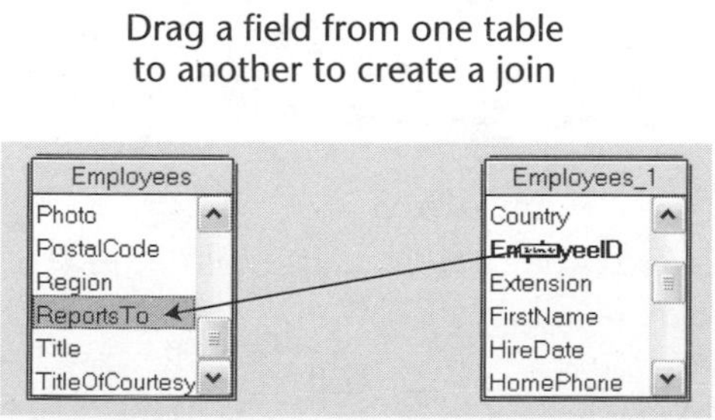

Drag a field from one table
to another to create a join

Figure 6.22 You can create a join by selecting a field and dragging it to another table.

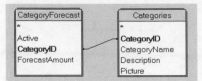

Figure 6.23   An Inner join is represented by a line with a ball on either side.

WARNING If a Join line is not shown in the Tables section, a Cross join is created. This type of join is rarely needed and produces a Cartesian product. Read the "Cross Joins" section a little later in this chapter for more information about this type of join.

Here is the SQL query generated for the Categories and CategoryForecast tables that were linked using an Inner join:

```
SELECT CategoryForecast.CategoryID AS 'Forecast-CategoryID',
       Categories.CategoryID       AS 'Categories-CategoryID'
FROM   NorthwindCS.dbo.Categories Categories,
       NorthwindCS.dbo.CategoryForecast CategoryForecast
WHERE  Categories.CategoryID = CategoryForecast.CategoryID
```

Left and Right Joins

Left and Right joins pull all the data in one table and only the data in the other table with a matching record on the joined field. Assuming that Category-Forecast is on the left and Categories is on the right, a Left join on CategoryID yields the values 0, 1, 2, 3, 4, 5, 6, and 9. A Right join yields 1, 2, 3, 4, 5, 6, and Null for values 7 and 8. The Null is used because there isn't a 7 or 8 to pull in the CategoryForecast table. Because something must be pulled, a Null value is used.

NOTE A Null means that the field value is missing or unknown. It is not the same as a <blank> value and must be treated differently.

In order to change the Inner join to a Left join, follow these steps:

1. Verify that your Microsoft Query Window looks like Figure 6.21.

2. Select Tables ➪ Joins or double-click the line that links the two database tables to bring up the Joins dialog box (see Figure 6.24).

3. Click the second button in the Join Includes section of the dialog box, and then click the Add button to modify the Inner join to a Left join. Click Close to close the dialog box.

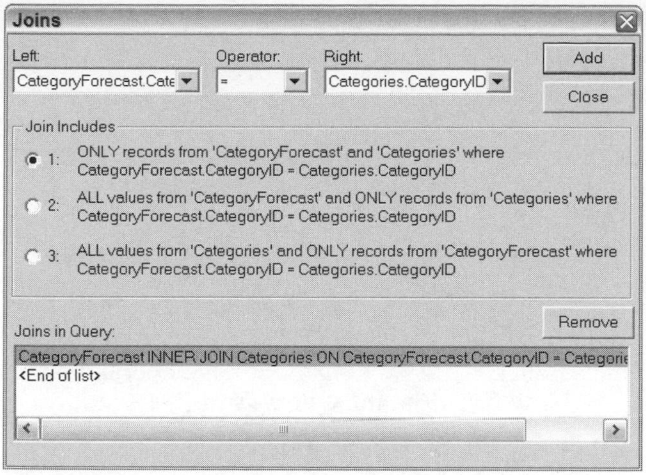

Figure 6.24 The first Inner join option is the default. You can change it to a Left join (Option 2) or a Right join (Option 3) in this dialog box.

4. Choose Records ⇨ Query Now if Automatic Query is not enabled.

5. Verify that the Microsoft Query window looks like Figure 6.25.

Here is the query generated by Microsoft Query:

```
SELECT CategoryForecast.CategoryID AS 'Forecast-CategoryID',
       Categories.CategoryID    AS 'Categories-CategoryID'
FROM  {oj NorthwindCS.dbo.CategoryForecast CategoryForecast
LEFT OUTER JOIN NorthwindCS.dbo.Categories Categories
            ON CategoryForecast.CategoryID = Categories.CategoryID}
```

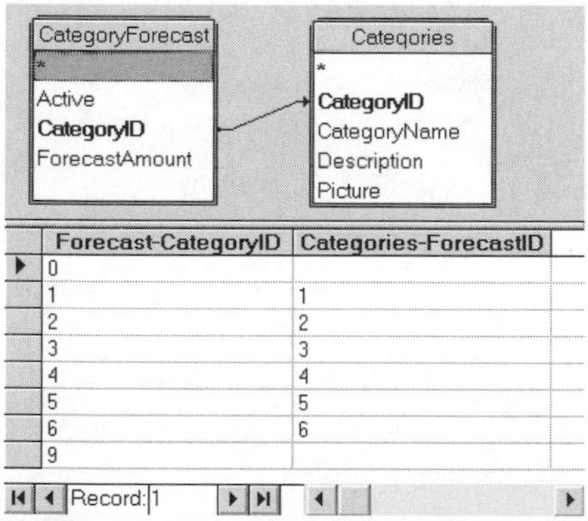

Figure 6.25 A right arrow indicates that the Categories table is left-joined to the Category-Forecast table, meaning that all of the CategoryForecast rows are returned and only the rows with a matching CategoryID in Categories.

Changing the join type to a Right join just switches the table in the SQL query to maintain a Left join. Essentially, the Categories table is moved to the FROM clause and the CategoryForecast table is moved to the JOIN clause to reflect how they appear in the query.

To modify the Left join to a Right join, follow these steps:

1. Choose Tables ⇨ Joins or double-click the line that links the two database tables together to bring up the Joins dialog box.

2. Click the third button in the Join Includes section of the dialog box; and then click the Add button to modify the Left join to a Right join. Click Close to close the dialog box.

3. Choose Records ⇨ Query Now if Automatic Query is not enabled.

4. Verify that the Microsoft Query window looks like Figure 6.26.

NOTE Microsoft Query will not generate a Right join. Regardless of the arrow direction, a Left join is always maintained.

Although you may be expecting the join to be a Right join, the Microsoft Query program simply switched the tables in the query to maintain a Left join. You can verify this in the SQL query by clicking the View SQL button to see the following query displayed:

```
SELECT CategoryForecast.CategoryID AS 'Forecast-CategoryID',
       Categories.CategoryID       AS 'Categories-CategoryID'
FROM   {oj NorthwindCS.dbo.Categories Categories
LEFT OUTER JOIN NorthwindCS.dbo.CategoryForecast CategoryForecast
          ON Categories.CategoryID = CategoryForecast.CategoryID}
```

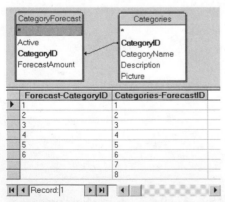

Figure 6.26 A left arrow shows that the CategoryForecast table is left-joined to Categories, meaning that all of the Categories rows are returned and only the rows with a matching CategoryID in CategoryForecast.

> **NOTE** A query created using the graphical tools of the Microsoft Query program allows only one Outer join to be created. You can circumvent this limitation only by editing the SQL statement, which also results in the Microsoft Query program being unable to display the query graphically.

Cross Joins

Cross joins produce a Cartesian product of the two tables, meaning that for each of the records in the first table, all the records in the second table are joined. This type of join is created by simply deleting the graphical join (selecting it and clicking Delete). Alternatively, the Cross join can be included in the SQL statement. Figure 6.27 shows how a Cross join is performed.

All the possible combinations of CategoryID in CategoryForecast and Categories are produced when tables are Cross joined. So, you have the pairs 0-1, 0-2, 0-3, 0-4, 0-5, 0-6, 0-7, 0-8, and then 1-1, 1-2, and so forth until all 64 unique combinations are exhausted (there are eight rows in each table, so 8 * 8 = 64). Notice that the Cross join clause is not inserted into the SQL query, as it isn't required:

```
SELECT CategoryForecast.CategoryID AS 'Forecast-CategoryID',
       Categories.CategoryID       AS 'Categories CategoryID'
FROM   NorthwindCS.dbo.Categories Categories,
       NorthwindCS.dbo.CategoryForecast CategoryForecast
```

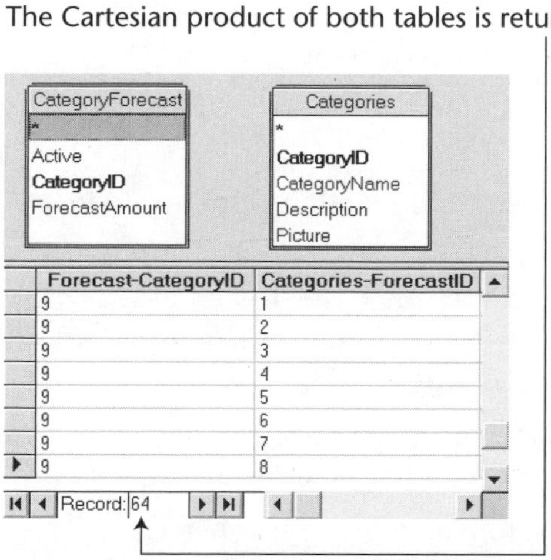

The Cartesian product of both tables is returned

Figure 6.27   When there are no lines or arrows that join the tables, a Cross join is produced.

Self Joins

Self joins are required when you need to access information that is included in the same table. For example, in the Employees table of the NorthwindCS database, there is a field for determining the employee manager. All the employees are included in the table; but if you want to provide a list of the employees with the employee manager name next to it, you need to create a Self join.

To create a Self join on the Employees table, follow these steps:

1. Start a new query or remove all current tables in the Tables section.

2. Click the Add Tables button to bring up the Add Tables dialog box.

3. Add the Employees table to the Tables section by selecting the table and clicking Add.

4. Add the Employees table to the Tables section again by selecting the table and clicking Add.

5. When you are prompted with the warning message that the table already exists, just click OK to acknowledge the warning and add the table.

6. Click Close to close the Add Tables dialog box.

7. Add the following fields to the query (in this order):

   a. EmployeeId from the Employees table

   b. LastName from the Employees table

   c. ReportsTo from the Employees table

   d. LastName from the Employees_1 table

8. Choose Tables ⇨ Joins to bring up the Joins dialog box.

9. Delete the current join by selecting it in the bottom pane of the Joins dialog box and clicking Remove.

10. Select Employees.ReportsTo in the Left field, = in the Operator field, and Employees_1.EmployeeId in the Right field.

11. Click the second button in the Join Includes pane to select all the records from Employees and only the records from Employees_1 where Employees.ReportsTo = Employees_1.EmployeeID.

12. Verify that the Joins dialog box looks like Figure 6.28, and then click Add to create the Self join. Click Close to close the Joins dialog box.

13. Choose Records ⇨ Query Now if Automatic Query is not enabled.

14. Verify that your Microsoft Query window looks like Figure 6.29.

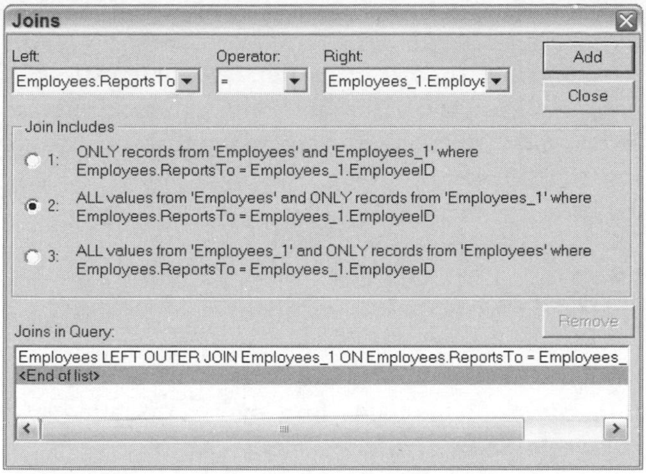

Figure 6.28 A Self join is created by joining the Employees table joining to itself using ReportsTo = EmployeesID.

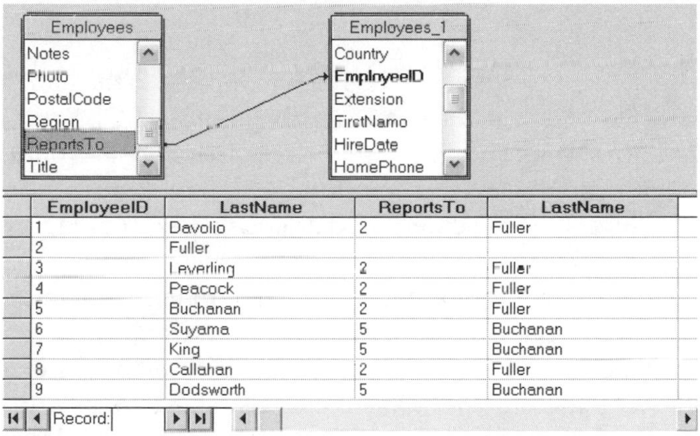

EmployeeID	LastName	ReportsTo	LastName
1	Davolio	2	Fuller
2	Fuller		
3	Leverling	2	Fuller
4	Peacock	2	Fuller
5	Buchanan	2	Fuller
6	Suyama	5	Buchanan
7	King	5	Buchanan
8	Callahan	2	Fuller
9	Dodsworth	5	Buchanan

Figure 6.29 This Self join on ReportsTo on EmployeeID shows employee names and their manager's last name.

The following SQL query is generated by the Microsoft Query program:

```
SELECT          Employees.EmployeeID,
                Employees.LastName,
                Employees.ReportsTo,
                Employees_1.LastName
FROM           {oj NorthwindCS.dbo.Employees Employees
LEFT OUTER JOIN NorthwindCS.dbo.Employees Employees_1
             ON Employees.ReportsTo = Employees_1.EmployeeID}
```

Full Joins

Full joins result in all rows being returned from either table, regardless of whether there is a record that matches in the other table. This can result in null values being produced. This join is not available through the graphical tools of the Microsoft Query program, but you can insert it by simply typing or pasting the query into the SQL dialog box.

Executing SQL Commands

Microsoft Query includes the Execute SQL dialog box for executing SQL commands and queries. This tool includes functionality for viewing, updating, and removing data and database objects. You can use this dialog box to

- Create database tables and views
- Delete, update, or select data in a table
- Insert records into a table
- Execute or view a stored procedure

I recommend you use this tool only when you do not have access to the native database development programs such as the Query Analyzer or the SQL Server Management Studio. These programs are much better suited for SQL programming and program development. However, if you find yourself without access to these programs, you can access the Execute SQL dialog box shown in Figure 6.30 by choosing File ➪ Execute SQL.

The permissions to the data source for executing SQL commands are determined by the SQL login account that is used to access the data source. If you need to log in using another account, click the Data Sources button to create or access another data source with the proper login credentials. The database currently selected to run the SQL commands is shown in the Database drop-down box at the bottom part of the Execute SQL dialog box. In Figure 6.30, the NorthwindCS database is selected in this box.

You can open and save queries in this dialog box by clicking the Open and Save buttons, respectively. Files can be saved and opened using a file extension type of .QRT (Query Template) only.

Clicking the Procedures button brings up the Select Procedure dialog box, shown in Figure 6.31, which lets you automatically paste a stored procedure into the Execute SQL dialog box.

Executing an SQL query that results in data being returned automatically creates a new query window and displays the data in the Results pane. Other SQL statements for creating or deleting database objects or modifying or inserting data just brings up a confirmation statement that prompts you with the message Executed SQL Statement Successfully, requiring you to acknowledge it by clicking OK.

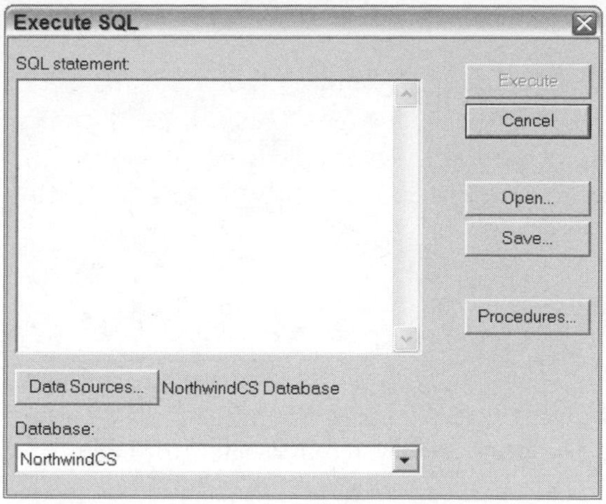

Figure 6.30   You can use the Execute SQL dialog box to run SQL commands from Microsoft Query.

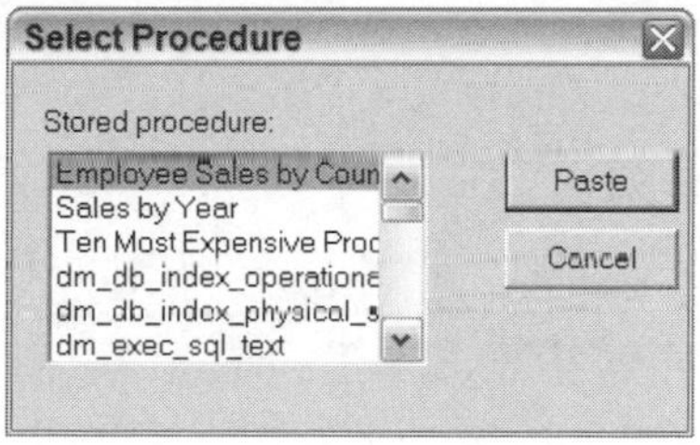

Figure 6.31   You can automatically paste a procedure into the Execute SQL dialog box from here.

Managing Tables

Microsoft Query includes the Select Tables dialog box for creating, viewing, updating, removing, and indexing database tables. You can also use it to view other types of files such as Excel workbooks and comma-delimited and fixed-width files. As with the Execute SQL dialog box, I recommend that you use the Select Tables dialog box tool only when you do not have access to the native database development programs. You can access this dialog box by following these steps:

1. Open a Microsoft Query dialog box and then choose File ➪ Table Definition to bring up the Choose Data Source dialog box.

2. Select the NorthwindCS Database data source, and then click OK to bring up the Select Table dialog box shown in Figure 6.32.

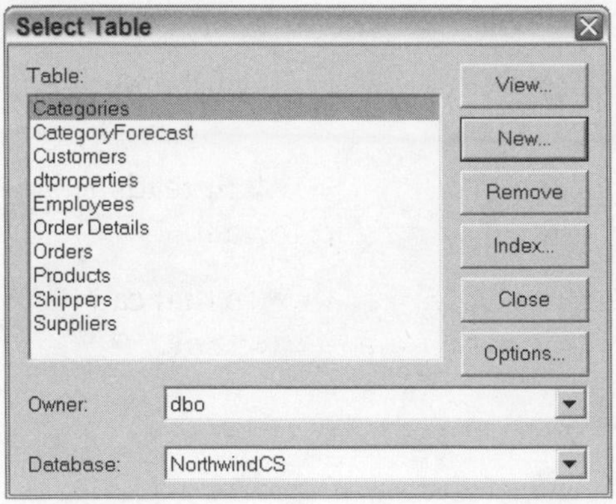

Figure 6.32   From this dialog box, you can create, modify, remove, and index tables.

Clicking the View button in the Select Table dialog box brings up the View Definition Table dialog box. Here, you can view all the fields and field data types. Even though this dialog box is intended for viewing the table design, you can also add or remove fields.

Clicking the New button brings up a dialog box that is just like the View Definition Table dialog box except that all the fields are empty.

NOTE You can copy an existing table by first selecting it in the View Definition Table dialog box, changing its name in the Table Name field, and then clicking Create.

Clicking the Remove button deletes the selected table. Clicking the Index button brings up the Create Index dialog box, where you can select a field to create a unique or non-unique index. Clicking the Close button closes the Select Table dialog box. Clicking the Options button brings up the Table Options dialog box, where you can determine which objects are displayed in the Table pane (see Figure 6.32).

Understanding How Microsoft Query Uses SQL

The Microsoft Query program has some interesting quirks that I've noticed over the years. I include a few of them here as I've found them to sometimes be problematic in report development. Once you understand them, however, you can easily circumvent them. Here's a list of the quirks I review in this section:

- A pasted query is automatically modified to conform to Microsoft Query's standard of SQL when the query can be displayed graphically.
- An SQL query is hidden when comments lines are added to the first line of the query statement.

- Field names should be put in brackets instead of single quotes.
- Criteria is incorrectly put into the `Having` clause instead of the `Where` clause.
- Stored procedures with input parameters work only with Spreadsheet reports and PivotTable lists and must use a particular format.

I review these quirks here and show you a couple of examples that can help you better understand the nuances of the Microsoft Query program.

Automatic Query Modification

When you paste a query into the SQL dialog box (accessed by clicking the View SQL button on the program's toolbar), Microsoft Query first parses the query to ensure that there are no syntax errors. After this step is completed, the program attempts to produce a graphical representation of the query by reading and trying to figure out the query instructions. If the program is successful, the query is modified to Microsoft Query's style and a graphical representation of the query is produced. By that, I mean the tables and the table joins are shown in the Table section, and the filter field and filter criteria are shown in the Criteria section. The sort instructions are also available in the Sort dialog box (accessed by choosing Records ⇨ Sort).

Try this example to see for yourself how this works:

1. Paste the following query into the SQL dialog box by clicking the View SQL button:

```
SELECT * FROM Categories
```

2. Click OK to close the SQL dialog box and execute the query.

3. Click the View SQL button to confirm that the query has been modified as shown in the following:

```
SELECT  Categories.CategoryID,
        Categories.CategoryName,
        Categories.Description,
        Categories.Picture
FROM    NorthwindCS.dbo.Categories Categories
```

There are numerous features available when the query can be graphically displayed. However, for SQL experts, this might be an annoying feature because editing the modified queries can take a little longer than you might prefer. You can work around this feature by *hiding* the SQL query (adding the /* */ comment in the first line of the query). The next section explains how you can hide the SQL query.

Hiding an SQL Query

You can hide the query for an Excel report by adding a single line comment (--) or a block comment (/* */) in the first line of the SQL query. This feature is also useful when you want to prevent a query from being graphically displayed (explained in the preceding section). After you add this comment line and leave the Microsoft Query program, the query will no longer appear in the SQL dialog box when a user attempts to access it. Instead, an empty dialog box is displayed and no rows are returned in the Results section.

> **WARNING** Adding the comment in the first line of the query disables users from looking at the underlying SQL query, but it does not prevent users from pasting another query into the SQL dialog box (this is controlled through the database security settings).

Although the query is hidden, it can be retrieved by temporarily disabling access to the external data source (in this case, the database) and switching the database in the Choose Data source dialog box to another database that doesn't include all the referenced tables in the SQL query. These are, of course, advanced options, so most users don't know how they work. (Welcome to the elite club of advanced Excel report developers; now, aren't you glad you purchased this book?)

> **CROSS-REFERENCE** Read Chapter 3 to learn how to temporarily disable access to an external data source and change the report's data source.

Use Brackets instead of Single Quotes

If you are pasting an SQL query into the SQL dialog box, always put field headings in brackets ([ ]) instead of single quotes (' '). Microsoft Query can get confused when trying to decipher date, string, and mathematical operators.

Follow these steps see how the Microsoft Query becomes confused when single quotes are used with a string operator:

1. Paste the following query into the SQL dialog box by clicking the View SQL button:

```
SELECT fcst.CategoryID                       AS 'ID',
       UPPER(LEFT(ctgy.CategoryName,10))     AS 'Short Name',
       fcst.ForecastAmount                   AS 'Amount'
FROM   CategoryForecast fcst
```

```
INNER JOIN Categories ctgy
        ON fcst.CategoryID = ctgy.CategoryID
```

2. Click OK to close the SQL dialog box and execute the query.

3. Click OK when you are prompted with a message stating that the query cannot be graphically displayed.

4. Verify that the Results pane looks like Figure 6.33.

All the fields that follow an unreadable field become corrupt. Although you can modify the field names from Excel, they are permanently lost once the query is edited in the Microsoft Query program. You can avoid this problem by using brackets for field headings instead of apostrophes.

Try the following simple queries, and you'll see the difference:

1. Clear out the existing query, and then paste the updated query with brackets instead of apostrophes into the SQL dialog box:

```
SELECT fcst.CategoryID                      AS [ID],
       UPPER(LEFT(ctgy.CategoryName,10))    AS [Short Name],
       fcst.ForecastAmount                  AS [Amount]
FROM   CategoryForecast fcst
INNER JOIN Categories ctgy
        ON fcst.CategoryID - ctgy.CategoryID
```

2. Click OK to close the dialog box and execute the query.

3. Click OK when you are prompted with a message stating that the query cannot be graphically displayed.

4. Verify that the Results pane looks like Figure 6.34.

CategoryID		ForecastAmount
1	BEVERAGES	16500
2	CONDIMENTS	9000
3	CONFECTION	12000
4	DAIRY PROD	10000
5	GRAINS/CER	5000
6	MEAT/POULT	14000

Figure 6.33 The field heading is missing for ShortName, and ForecastAmount is used instead of Amount.

ID	Short Name	Amount
1	BEVERAGES	16500
2	CONDIMENTS	9000
3	CONFECTION	12000
4	DAIRY PROD	10000
5	GRAINS/CER	5000
6	MEAT/POULT	14000

Figure 6.34 The field headings work properly when included in brackets instead of single quotes.

Criteria Incorrectly Put into the Having Clause

The problem of Microsoft Query putting criteria into the Having clause instead of the Where clause was observed in the "Distinguishing between Where and Having" section of this chapter. Recall that the Having clause is used when an aggregate function is used in the Criteria pane. There is no magical workaround for this situation except to manually edit the SQL query. If report developers are relying on the Microsoft Query program to develop their queries, SQL experts should watch out for this problem within their organizations.

Stored Procedures with Input Parameters

Stored procedures can accept input parameters that can be used to pull a range of data. For example, the Employee Sales By Country stored procedure included as part of the NorthwindCS database requires that a beginning and ending date be specified when the stored procedure is executed. If you do not want to prompt the user to input the parameters into the report, the stored procedure can work in both PivotTable and Spreadsheet reports. However, if you want to prompt the user to enter the value (or values) for the stored procedure, you can use only a Spreadsheet report or a PivotTable list with the stored procedure. You also have to input the stored procedure in exactly this format:

```
{Call "Stored Procedure Name" (?,?)}
```

This format assumes that the stored procedure has two parameter variables, which is why there are two question marks in the parenthesis. If you want to execute the Employee Sales By Country stored procedure with parameters, you should paste the query as follows:

```
{Call "Employee Sales by Country" (?,?)}
```

CROSS-REFERENCE The following sections, "Inserting a Stored Procedure" and "Using Parameters," along with Chapter 11, provide more information about this topic.

Inserting a Stored Procedure

Instead of pasting a query into the SQL dialog box, you can simply enter a stored procedure. Stored procedures typically run much faster than regular SQL queries because the *query plan* (that is, the instructions for how the database server calculates the most efficient path for obtaining the data) has already been created by the SQL query optimizer. Additionally, the stored procedure can simply be modified if fields are added or removed or the query logic is changed. A simple refresh of the report with the stored procedure automatically makes the corresponding changes to the Excel report.

WARNING **Stored procedures are stored with the database on the database server. If you plan to use stored procedures in your reports, ensure that you properly evaluate the organizational implications. This may include developing a sensible naming convention, implementing sound change control procedures, and creating a stored procedure library in the event that the database becomes corrupted.**

In order to use an SQL query with the report, just select the data source and enter the stored procedure name. If there are spaces in the stored procedure name, put the stored procedure in double quotes. For example, if you want to execute the Ten Most Expensive Products stored procedure that returns the 10 most expensive products in the ProductTable, simply enter the following text into the SQL dialog box:

```
"Ten Most Expensive Products"
```

If the stored procedure has input variables, specify them after the stored procedure name. To execute the Employee Sales By Country stored procedure, for example, a beginning and ending date are required. So you would enter the following text into the SQL dialog box to pull all sales transactions for 1997:

```
"Employee Sales by Country" '01-01-1997','12-31-1997'
```

If you want to prompt the user to specify the beginning and ending date each time the report is requested, you must use the following format:

```
{Call "Employee Sales by Country" (?,?)}
```

This prompts for a beginning and ending date referred to as a *parameter value*, and there are some restrictions and program options tied to it. The next section covers these options.

Using Parameters

A parameter allows the user to specify a value each time the report is refreshed. You can use parameters only with Spreadsheet reports and Pivot-Table lists, not with PivotTable reports. You can use parameters in queries that access tables and views, and in stored procedures. Chapter 11 provides some detailed examples of how to use parameter queries. This section includes a brief example of how they are used only in the context of the Microsoft Query program with the Employee Sales By Country stored procedure. There are numerous related topics included as part of parameter queries, so be sure to read Chapter 11 if you plan to implement this technology with your Excel reports.

In order to created parameters for the Employee Sales By Country, follow these steps:

1. Choose Data ➪ Import External Data ➪ New Database Query.

2. When the Choose Data Source dialog box appears, select the NorthwindCS Database data source, and then click OK to open the Microsoft Query program.

3. Close the Add Tables dialog box, and then click the View SQL button to open the SQL dialog box.

4. Type the following text into the SQL dialog box and click OK:

   ```
   {Call "Employee Sales by Country" (?,?)}
   ```

5. Click OK to acknowledge that the query cannot be displayed graphically.

6. When the Enter Parameter Value dialog box appears (see Figure 6.35), type **01-01-1997** and click OK.

7. When the second Enter Parameter Value dialog box appears, type **12-31-1997** and click OK.

8. Verify that your Microsoft Query window looks like Figure 6.36.

You can change the parameter names by choosing View ➪ Parameters to bring up the Parameters dialog box. Just select a parameter and click the Edit button. In Figure 6.37, I changed the name for Parameter 1 to BeginningDate and Parameter 2 to EndingDate.

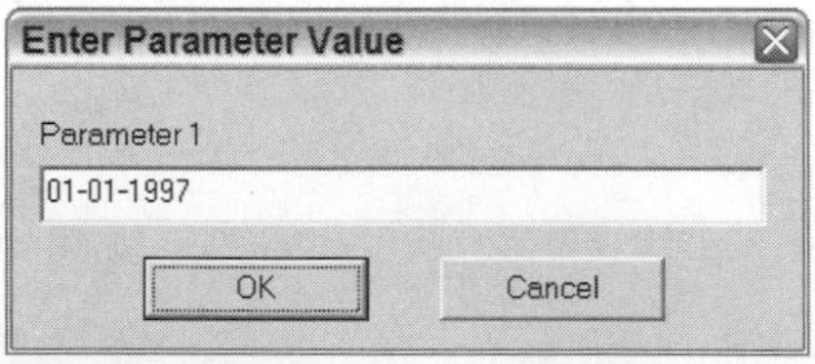

Figure 6.35 Enter a parameter value in this dialog box to limit the number of rows returned from a stored procedure or SQL query.

Country	LastName	FirstName	ShippedDate	OrderID	SaleAmount
USA	Callahan	Laura	1997-01-16 00:00:00.000	10380	1313.8200
USA	Fuller	Andrew	1997-01-01 00:00:00.000	10392	1440.0000
USA	Davolio	Nancy	1997-01-03 00:00:00.000	10393	2556.9500
USA	Davolio	Nancy	1997-01-03 00:00:00.000	10394	442.0000
UK	Suyama	Michael	1997-01-03 00:00:00.000	10395	2122.9200
USA	Davolio	Nancy	1997-01-06 00:00:00.000	10396	1903.8000
UK	Buchanan	Steven	1997-01-02 00:00:00.000	10397	716.7200
USA	Fuller	Andrew	1997-01-09 00:00:00.000	10398	2505.6000
USA	Callahan	Laura	1997-01-08 00:00:00.000	10399	1765.6000
USA	Davolio	Nancy	1997-01-16 00:00:00.000	10400	3063.0000

Figure 6.36   All sales transactions are returned for the beginning and ending dates specified in the parameter dialog boxes.

TIP   Try to use a consistent naming structure with parameters. For example, if you use Begin Date, don't switch some reports to Start Date, Beginning Date, From, and so forth. Implementing a uniform naming structure is easier for you and for the report user to understand and maintain.

With the parameter names changed, the dialog box prompts you for Beginning-Date (see Figure 6.38) instead of just Parameter 1.

WARNING   Don't use spaces in the parameter name. It often confuses the program, resulting in the parameter name being lost.

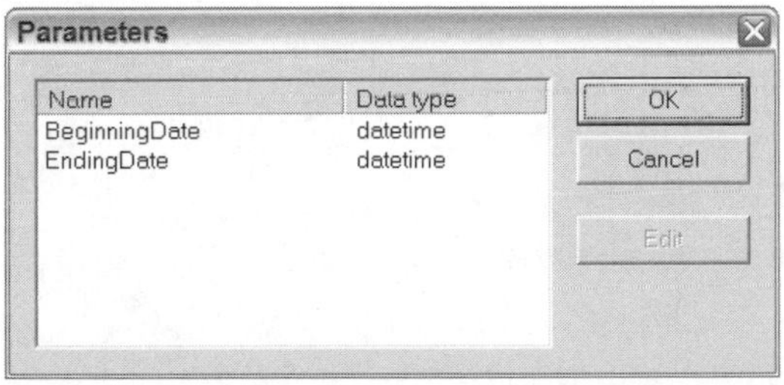

Figure 6.37   You can change the parameter name in the Parameters dialog box.

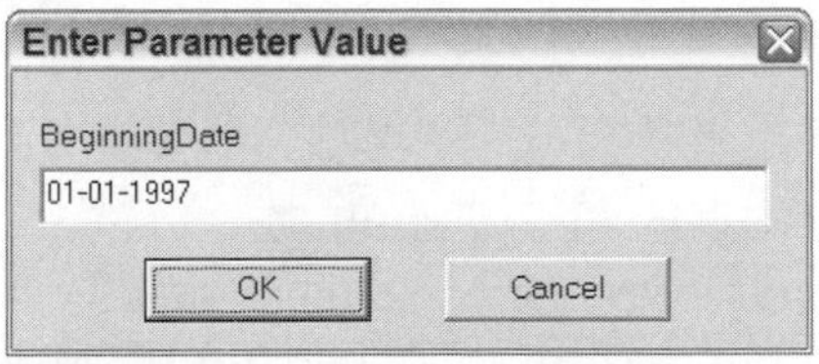

Figure 6.38   The parameter name has been renamed from Parameter 1 to BeginningDate.

Accessing Multiple Databases in a Single Session

The Microsoft Query program includes graphical tools that enable you to create a query that accesses multiple databases on a single server. However, it does not include graphical tools for accessing multiple databases on different servers. If you want to do that, you have to make adjustments in the SQL query. This section demonstrates how you can create a query for both circumstances.

Multiple Databases on a Single Server

In order to follow along with this example, you must have created the CategoryForecast table in the "Executing SQL Commands" section of this chapter. In addition, you must also have access to the original Northwind database that is included as part of a default installation of Microsoft SQL Server 2000. This database is different from the NorthwindCS database referenced throughout most of this chapter. You must have both databases installed because the SQL query in this exercise references both of them.

To create a query that accesses multiple databases on a single server, follow these steps:

1. Start a new query session in Microsoft Query that uses the NorthwindCS data source.

2. Click the Add Tables button and add the CategoryForecast table to the Tables Pane.

3. Change the database from NorthwindCS to Northwind in the Database drop-down list of the Add Tables dialog box. This action refreshes the tables shown in the Tables pane of the dialog box.

4. Add the Categories table to the query as shown in Figure 6.39, and then click Close to close the Add Tables dialog box.

5. Add the CategoryID field from the CategoryForecast table, the CategoryName from the Categories table, and the ForecastAmount from the CategoryForecast table (in this order) to the query.

6. Choose Records ⇨ Query Now if Automatic Query is not enabled.

7. Verify that your Microsoft Query window looks like Figure 6.40.

Congratulations! You have now successfully created a multiple database query that accesses tables in the Northwind and NorthwindCS databases. Clicking the SQL button shows the SQL query generated by the Microsoft Query program:

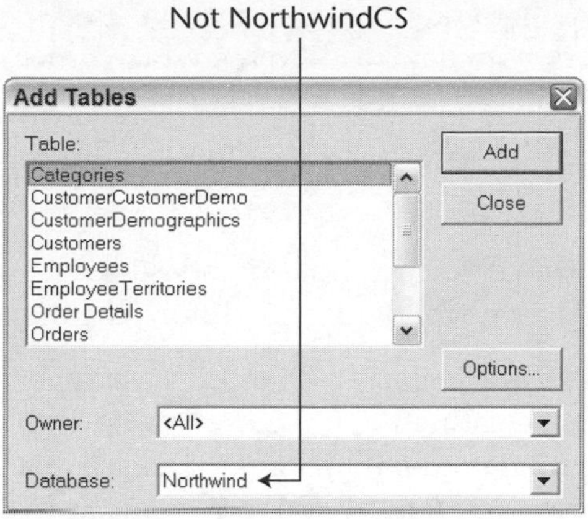

Not NorthwindCS

Figure 6.39   Change the database from NorthwindCS to Northwind in the Database drop-down list.

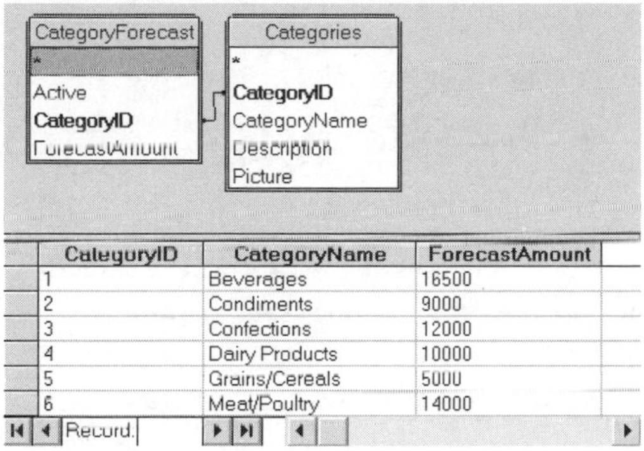

Figure 6.40   A query that accesses fields from two different databases in a single Microsoft Query session.

```
SELECT CategoryForecast.CategoryID,
       Categories.CategoryName,
       CategoryForecast.ForecastAmount
FROM   Northwind.dbo.Categories Categories,
       NorthwindCS.dbo.CategoryForecast CategoryForecast
WHERE Categories.CategoryID = CategoryForecast.CategoryID
```

Multiple Databases on Different Servers

Microsoft Query does not include graphical tools for accessing databases on different servers, but it's easy to do if you are familiar with SQL query programming. This is a useful function if you are trying to compare the differences between two database servers. For example, if you have one enterprise application used for order entry and another enterprise application used for warehouse management, you could query both databases to see which orders have been sent, but not shipped. You could even do this when one of the database servers is connected over a Virtual Private Network (VPN). I use a much simpler example in this section because the topic is already complex enough on its own.

Before you try to create a query that accesses multiple database servers, keep in mind that you'll need to ensure that the following conditions are met:

- You have already created a linked server using an SQL user login type (not a Windows login). I recommend creating the linked server on both servers and using the same SQL login name so that access can easily be performed both ways (assuming that this method does not create any security problems).

- The database servers are installed with the same collation type. If this isn't the case and can't be done, you may run into problems when trying to execute the multiple server queries.

- You have tested that the multiple server query works in the Query Analyzer or Microsoft Server Management Studio. If you can't get it to work there, it's probably not going to work in the Microsoft Query program.

- You understand which server is the source server and which server is the destination server in the context of your selected data source, because the linked server acts in only one direction.

Here's an example of a query that pulls all the category IDs in the Categories table of the Northwind database on one database server that are not in the CategoryForecast table of the second database server:

```
SELECT  CategoryID,
        CategoryName
FROM    {DatabaseServer1}.Northwind.dbo.Categories
WHERE   CategoryID NOT IN
        (SELECT CategoryID
         FROM  {DatabaseServer2}.NorthwindCS.dbo.CategoryForecast
         )
```

NOTE Notice that the objects are fully qualified in the `From` part of the SQL query: `ServerName.DatabaseName.ObjectOwner.TableName`. If the database server name was Jupiter, the fully qualified name in the subquery would be `Jupiter.NorthwindCS.dbo.CategoryForecast`.

If you did everything right, the Microsoft Query window should look like Figure 6.41.

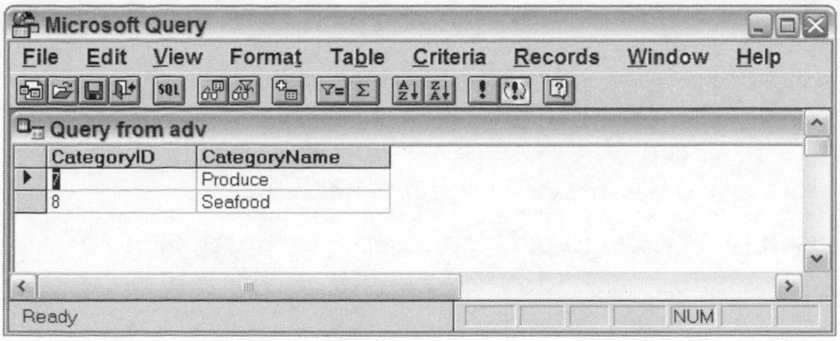

Figure 6.41   Result set returned from a multiple database server query.

This is a very advanced topic and requires you to be knowledgeable about SQL administration and SQL programming. To learn more about these topics, I suggest that you read the SQL books online or these Wiley Books: *Professional SQL Server 2000 Programming* by Robert Vieira, *SQL Server Developer's Guide* by Joseph J. Bambara and Paul R. Allen, and *MCSE SQL Server 2000 Administration For Dummies* by Rozanne Whalen and Dan Whalen.

Trying It Out in the Real World

Michael Suyama, a Sales Representative in the Northwind Trader's London office, has requested that you provide him with a report that compares the total value on hand against the forecasted value on hand for each product category that has not been discontinued. The report should sort the results from the largest negative variance to the highest positive variance. Michael has already discussed this requirement with the database administrator who has informed you that the following fields are required:

- CategoryName from the Categories table.
- ForecastAmount from the CategoryForecast table.
- The Sum of UnitsInStock multiplied by UnitsPrice from the Products table. The field heading should be titled as TotalValueOnHand.
- The Difference between ForecastAmount and TotalValueOnHand. The field heading should be titled as Variance.

Getting Down to Business

Follow these steps to complete this exercise:

1. From Excel, choose Data ➪ PivotTable And PivotChart Report.
2. Select External Data Source, and then click Next.

3. When the PivotTable And PivotChart Wizard - Step 2 of 3 appears, click Get Data.

4. When the Choose Data Source dialog box appears, verify that Use The Query Wizard To Create/Edit Queries is unchecked, select the NorthwindCS Database data source, and then click OK.

5. When the Microsoft Query program is launched, you are presented with the Add Tables dialog box. Add the following tables to the Tables section:

   - Categories
   - CategoryForecast
   - Products

NOTE To create the CategoryForecast database table, refer to the "Executing SQL Commands" section earlier in this chapter.

6. Double-click the CategoryName field in the Categories table to add this field to the Results section.

7. Double-click the ForecastAmount field in the CategoryForecast table to add this field to the Results section.

8. Choose Records ⇨ Add Column to bring up the Add Column dialog box.

9. Type **(Products.UnitsInStock * Products.UnitPrice)** in Field, tab to the Column Heading, type **TotalValueOnHand**, and then select Sum from the Total field.

10. Verify that the Add Column dialog box looks like Figure 6.42, and then click the Add button to add this field to the Results section. Click Close to close the Add Column dialog box.

11. Select a blank cell in the Results section and type (ForecastAmount - (SUM(Products.UnitsInStock * Products.UnitPrice))).

12. Double-click the new field to bring up the Edit Column dialog box. Type **Variance** in the Column Heading field and click OK.

13. Choose Criteria ⇨ Add Criteria to bring up the Add Criteria dialog box.

14. Select Products.Discontinued in Field, Equals in Operator, and 0 in Value. Click the Add button to add the criteria to the query, and then click Close to close the Add Criteria dialog box.

15. Select the Variance column in the Results section (the column is highlighted); and then click on the Sort Ascending button to sort the results from the largest negative variance to the largest positive variance.

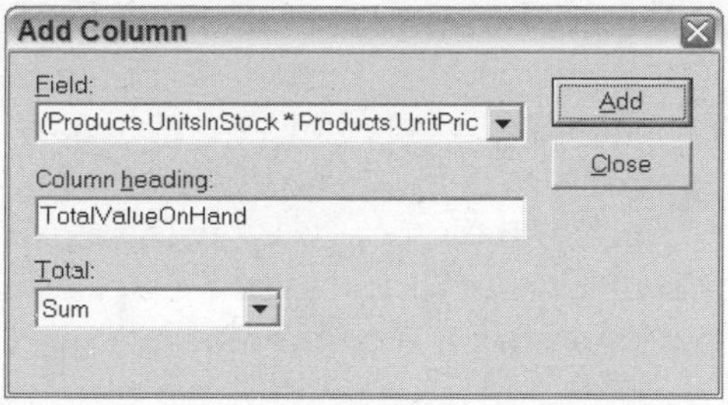

Add Column

Field:
(Products.UnitsInStock * Products.UnitPric ▼)   [Add]

Column heading:
TotalValueOnHand   [Close]

Total:
Sum ▼

Figure 6.42   Verify that your Add Column dialog box looks like this before adding it to the Results section.

16. Choose Records ⇨ Query Now if Automatic Query is not enabled.

17. Verify that your Microsoft Query window looks like Figure 6.43.

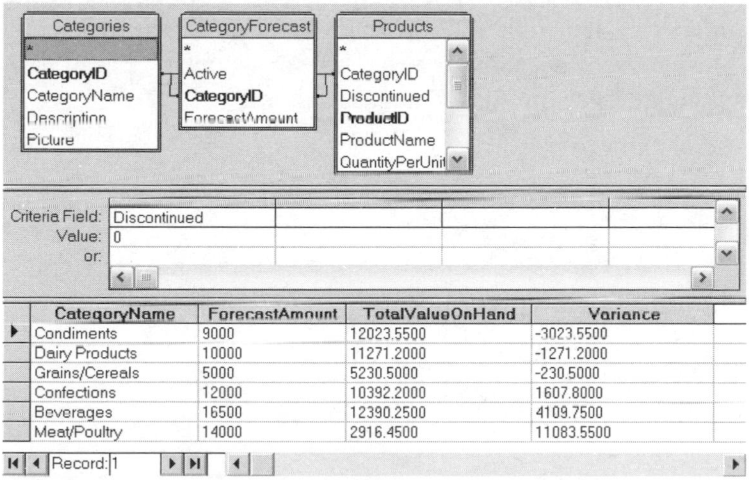

Categories	CategoryForecast	Products
CategoryID	Active	CategoryID
CategoryName	**CategoryID**	Discontinued
Description	ForecastAmount	**ProductID**
Picture		ProductName
		QuantityPerUnit

Criteria Field: Discontinued
Value: 0
or:

CategoryName	ForecastAmount	TotalValueOnHand	Variance
Condiments	9000	12023.5500	-3023.5500
Dairy Products	10000	11271.2000	-1271.2000
Grains/Cereals	5000	5230.5000	-230.5000
Confections	12000	10392.2000	1607.8000
Beverages	16500	12390.2500	4109.7500
Meat/Poultry	14000	2916.4500	11083.5500

◄◄ ◄ Record: 1 ► ►◄ ◄

Figure 6.43   If you did everything right, the Microsoft Query window should look like this.

WATCH THE VIDEO **To see how to build this SQL query in the Microsoft Query program, click the ch0601_video.avi file at** www.wiley.com/go/ excelreporting **and watch the video.**

Reviewing What You Did

This example provided you with a way to practice much of what you learned in this chapter. Although the Microsoft Query program includes many useful and powerful tools for building SQL queries that can be integrated into your reports, there are also several limitations. For example, using the graphical tools, I'm unable to create a calculated field that tests the variance for a positive or negative amount. As a report user with high expectations, I'd probably want a Variance Type field with the values Positive, Zero, and Negative in my report. However, the only way to add this field to the report is by using Case logic in the SQL query because that functionality is not included as a graphical tool in the Microsoft Query program. (See Appendix B for more information about Case logic and how it is used.)

Chapter Review

This chapter organized the various query tools into each part of an SQL query and identified which functions were disabled when a query could not be graphically displayed. It also described the various types of table joins and provided examples of how each one works using a new database table that was created in the NorthwindCS database. After reviewing the basics, the chapter provided a quick introduction to some of the more advanced features, such as parameter queries and queries that reference multiple database servers.

Advanced
Reporting Features

CHAPTER 7

Designing
PivotTable Reports

With the professional tools and functions included in Excel 2003, you can create professional-looking PivotTable reports; this chapter shows you how. This chapter assumes you are familiar with the basic features and functions of PivotTables covered in Chapter 2 and picks up with the more advanced design functions available in PivotTable reports. After working through this chapter, you can move on to Chapter 8, which focuses on the data management options available in PivotTable reports.

To start off, this chapter introduces you to the Layout Manager and the Pivot-Table toolbar. The Layout Manager lets you to design a PivotTable by moving fields on or off an unchanging diagram, an ideal alternative for report developers who prefer to see the changes applied all at once, rather than interactively. The PivotTable toolbar contains numerous functions and button shortcuts for managing the PivotTable report. You can add or remove buttons in this toolbar to customize it in a way that works best for your reporting needs.

Following the review of the PivotTable components, this chapter is divided into three sections. The first section focuses on formatting and includes information on field arrangement, report design features, and report options. The second section focuses on PivotTable design and covers aggregate functions, calculated fields, and formulas. The final section provides another real-world example that you can use as additional practice.

A Review of the PivotTable Components

Chapter 2 introduced the basic features of PivotTable reports. This included an explanation of the various areas of a PivotTable, an introduction to drag-and-drop technology, and some examples on drill-down functionality. This section covers the Layout Manager and the PivotTable toolbar. It starts by providing a more complex SQL query for this PivotTable toolbar that you can download from the Wiley website. This query will help you get a better grasp on some of the rich features and powerful capabilities of Excel PivotTable reports.

ON THE WEB You can download the ch07_example.txt query file to your computer from this book's companion website at www.wiley.com/go/ excelreporting. Look for this document in either the Chap07.zip file or Chap07 directory, depending on which .zip file you download.

Before You Begin

Start this chapter by creating a new PivotTable report from an external data source that accesses the NorthwindCS database.

Complete these steps to start this chapter and follow along with my examples:

1. From Excel, choose Data ➪ PivotTable And PivotChart Report.

2. Select External Data Source and click Next.

3. When the PivotTable And PivotChart Wizard - Step 2 of 3 appears, click Get Data.

4. When the Choose Data Source dialog box appears, verify that Use The Query Wizard To Create/Edit Queries is unchecked, select the NorthwindCS Database data source, and then click OK.

5. When the Microsoft Query program is launched, you are presented with the Add Tables dialog box. Close this dialog box and click the SQL button.

6. Paste or type the following query into the SQL dialog box and click OK:

```
SELECT CAST (cat.CategoryID AS CHAR(2))
        + ' - '
        + UPPER(cat.CategoryName)           AS 'CATEGORY DESC',
    Cat.CategoryName                         AS 'CATEGORY NAME',
    CAST (pro.ProductID AS CHAR(2))
        + ' - '
        + UPPER(pro.ProductName)             AS 'PRODUCT DESC',
    pro.ProductName                          AS 'PRODUCT NAME',
```

```
          pro.UnitPrice                            AS 'PRICE',
          (pro.UnitPrice * pro.UnitsInStock)       AS 'VALUE',
          pro.UnitsInStock                         AS 'QTY STOCK',
          pro.UnitsOnOrder                         AS 'QTY ORDER',
          UPPER(sup.CompanyName)                   AS 'SUPPLIER',
          CASE
               WHEN (pro.UnitPrice * pro.UnitsInStock) > 3000
                    THEN 'REQUIRED'
               WHEN (pro.UnitPrice * pro.UnitsInStock) > 2000
                    THEN 'RECOMMENDED'
                    ELSE 'NOT REQUIRED'
                    END                            AS 'INSURANCE'
FROM     Products pro
INNER JOIN Categories cat ON pro.CategoryID = cat.CategoryID
INNER JOIN Suppliers  sup ON sup.SupplierID = pro.SupplierID
```

NOTE A nice benefit of combining an SQL query with an Excel report is the capability to create fields that don't exist in the database. In this query, for example, I created the Insurance field to determine whether the product should be insured based on Its Total Value (Quantity in Stock * Price).

7. Click the Return Data to Microsoft Excel toolbar button to return the data to continue.

8. Click Next when PivotTable And PivotChart Wizard — Step 2 of 3 reappears.

9. Click Layout to bring up the Layout Manager dialog box.

WATCH THE VIDEO To see how this PivotTable report is created, click the ch0701_video.avi file at www.wiley.com/go/excelreporting to watch the video.

Layout Manager

Using the Layout Manager, you can design a PivotTable report without having to put up with a constantly changing report shape as fields are moved on or off the report. It takes a little longer to shape and customize the report using the Layout Manager, but it does provide a more fixed environment. I've found that users who are new to PivotTable report development and users who are not technology-savvy generally prefer using the Layout Manager to using the interactive drag-and-drop technology of the Excel worksheet.

This section covers only the basic features of the Layout Manager. There are numerous other functions available for setting field headings, changing aggregation types, hiding field values, and so forth. However, these functions are also available in the Excel worksheet, so I cover them in that section. The dialog boxes are still the same and accessed using the same methods, so it's only a matter of where you access the tools. I'm confident with some limited experimentation, you'll quickly get the hang of how this works from either the Layout Manager or the Excel Worksheet.

> **TIP** Don't forget to watch the videos posted on the www.wiley.com/go/excelreporting **web site. This will help reinforce the material covered in this chapter.**

Accessing the Layout Manager

You can access the Layout Manager when you create a new report or work with an existing report. If you are creating a new PivotTable report, click Next (instead of Finish) in Step 2 of 3, and then click the Layout button in Step 3 of 3 (as shown in Figure 7.1) to bring up the Layout Manager.

With an existing report, right-click the report, select PivotTable Wizard from the pop-up menu to bring up the Step 3 of 3 dialog box, and then click Layout to access the Layout Manager.

Using the Layout Manager

When the Layout Manager is displayed, as shown in Figure 7.2, you can move fields to various locations on the diagram. The areas are marked and outlined just as they are in the Excel worksheet. And just like with the worksheet, you can drop fields to any area on the diagram in the Layout Manager. Unlike working with the PivotTable from the Excel worksheet, however, you must have at least one field in the Data area in order for the Layout Manager to generate a PivotTable.

Figure 7.1 Click Layout to access the Layout Manager.

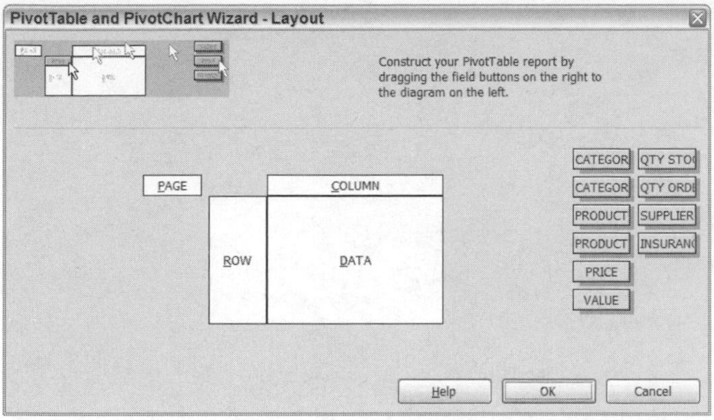

Figure 7.2   The Layout Manager maintains an unchanging canvas for building a PivotTable.

CROSS-REFERENCE   Review Chapter 2 if you need a refresher on the purpose and use of the various PivotTable areas.

When the Layout Manager appears, the fields in the query appear on the right side of the dialog box, and the PivotTable diagram appears in the middle. You can drag fields to any location on the diagram. The diagram does not change shape as fields are dragged on or off. Dropping fields in the Data section performs a Sum or Count, depending on whether the field is numeric (the default is Sum) or alphanumeric (the default is Count). You can modify the aggregation type by double-clicking the field and changing the summary function in the PivotTable field dialog box. (See the "Managing Data Area Fields" section later in this chapter to learn more about the functions available in the PivotTable Field dialog box for Data area items.)

The field names appear in the same order as they are listed in the query. The fields in the query appear from left to right and are shown down and then over in the Layout Manager. There is limited space for displaying field headings, so long field names can be displayed only if you double-click the field to bring up the PivotTable Field dialog box or move the mouse pointer over the field to reveal the full name in a toolbar tip, as shown in Figure 7.3.

In order to demonstrate some of the functionality in this dialog box, follow these steps:

1. Drag Category Desc and Product Desc to the Page area.

2. Drag Category Name to the Row area.

3. Drag Insurance to the Column area.

4. Drag Value to the Data area.

5. Verify that the Layout Manager looks like Figure 7.4.

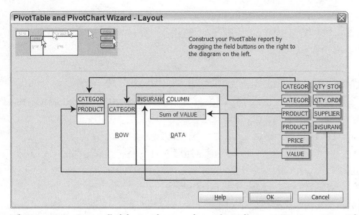

Figure 7.3 Move the mouse pointer over the field to reveal the full field name.

Figure 7.4 Drag fields to the unchanging diagram to create a PivotTable report.

With the exception of the Data area, a field can be added to only one area of the PivotTable report. The only reason the Data area can take a field multiple times is because this area performs some type of aggregate function on the field, thereby changing the meaning and use of the field to something else. For example, Value becomes Sum Of Value or Product Name becomes Count Of Product Name.

Try moving the Insurance column to the Row area (either from the Column section or from the list of fields on the right of the dialog box). Next, try moving fields to the Data area and to another area. Notice that the same field can be dragged to the Data area multiple times, but only to a Page, Row, or Column area once. When you're done, put everything back as shown in Figure 7.4.

TIP If you want the same field in more than one area of the report (for example, as a Page field and as a Row field), simply add it to the query another time. Keep in mind, however, that if you use the same field name for both fields, Microsoft Excel appends a 2 after the second field name to make it unique. Then, adding the field name to the Data area causes it to increment again from 2 to 3, and so on.

Next, double-click the Category Name in the Row area to bring up the PivotTable Field dialog box shown in Figure 7.5.

In this dialog box, you can perform several functions, including

- Changing the field name displayed in the report
- Setting a subtotal method
- Showing items in the report with no data
- Accessing the PivotTable Field Advanced Options dialog box to configure advanced display and sorting features (explained later)
- Accessing the PivotTable Field Layout dialog box to configure report-formatting options (explained later)

Clicking a Page or Data area field brings up a slightly different dialog box where you can choose to display or hide particular values (Page area field) or change the type of aggregate function performed on the field (Data area field).

To continue with this example, follow these steps:

1. Double-click Sum Of Value in the Data area to bring up the PivotTable field dialog box.
2. Type **TOTAL VALUE** in the Name field and click OK.
3. Click OK in the PivotTable Layout Manager.
4. Click Finish in the PivotTable And PivotChart Wizard – Step 3 of 3 dialog box to create the PivotTable report.
5. Verify that your PivotTable report looks like Figure 7.6.

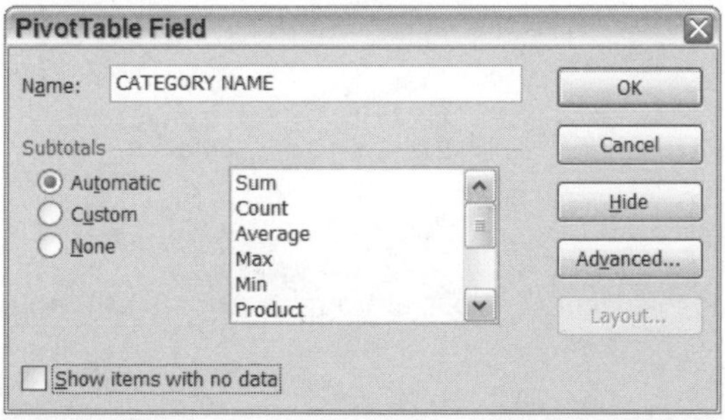

Figure 7.5 You can change the field heading, subtotal settings, sort options, field formatting, and filter conditions in this dialog box.

	A	B	C	D	E
1	CATEGORY DESC	(All)			
2	PRODUCT DESC	(All)			
3					
4	TOTAL VALUE	INSURANCE			
5	CATEGORY NAME	NOT REQUIRED	RECOMMENDED	REQUIRED	Grand Total
6	Beverages	8000.75		4479.5	12480.25
7	Condiments	5803.05	3000	3220.5	12023.55
8	Confections	5001.1	2151.1	3240	10392.2
9	Dairy Products	3658.2		7613	11271.2
10	Grains/Cereals	3410.5	2184		5594.5
11	Meat/Poultry	156.45	5573		5729.45
12	Produce	3549.35			3549.35
13	Seafood	5994.15	7016.2		13010.35
14	Grand Total	35573.55	19924.3	18553	74050.85

Sheet1 / Sheet2 / Sheet3 /

Figure 7.6 If you did everything right, the PivotTable report should look like this.

TIP When you drop fields into the Data area, Microsoft Excel adds a Count Of or Sum Of before the field heading. I usually modify the heading to achieve a better report meaning and presentation. In Figure 7.6, I changed Sum Of Value to Total Value.

Now, you're ready to start working with the PivotTable report. Let's start with a quick overview of the PivotTable Toolbar.

PivotTable Toolbar

You can access all the functions and features of a PivotTable from the PivotTable toolbar shown in Figure 7.7. You can toggle the display on or off by choosing View ➪ Toolbars ➪ PivotTable or by right-clicking the PivotTable and selecting Show PivotTable Toolbar from the pop-up menu. Some functions, such as creating calculated fields, can only be performed from this toolbar.

Clicking the down-arrow next to the Close box (X) in the top-right corner brings up the Add or Remove menu. This menu is where you can customize what buttons are displayed on the PivotTable toolbar; use this feature to make the toolbar suit your particular report development or report analysis needs.

Table 7.1 provides an explanation of the various graphical buttons shown by default in the PivotTable toolbar.

Figure 7.7 This is the default display of the PivotTable toolbar, although you can easily add or remove buttons.

Table 7-1 PivotTable Toolbar Button Descriptions

BUTTON	BUTTON NAME	DESCRIPTION
	Format Wizard	Launches the Format Wizard dialog box to apply predefined table and format styles.
	PivotChat Wizard	Creates a PivotChart from the selected PivotTable report.
	Hide Detail	Hides an Inner Row or Inner Column field.
	Show Detail	Shows an Inner Row or Inner Column field.
	Refresh Data	Refreshes the PivotTable report data.
	Display Hidden Totals	Displays totals for hidden items (note that this only works for OLAP data sources).
	Display Items	Always displays items.
	Field Settings	Brings up the Field Settings dialog box.
	Field List	Toggles the display of the field list.

These buttons and functions are explained in greater detail in the appropriate sections throughout this chapter.

Formatting the PivotTable Report

Microsoft Excel offers several tools and functions that help you present your report in the best possible light — on-screen or on paper. In this section, I cover various formatting topics to customize the look and function of your Pivot-Table reports, including

- Automatic and manual formatting features
- Formatting options
- Formatting for printing
- Designing and working with Page fields
- Sorting
- Conditional formatting
- Displaying data as columns

- Managing inner and outer fields
- Grouping items
- Renaming fields
- Formatting Data area fields

Auto and Manual Formatting Features

You can apply predefined formats to the PivotTable report by choosing Format Report from the PivotTable toolbar menu. This is a nice feature for quickly and easily adding some color and formatting to a PivotTable report. Personally, I prefer to apply my own style, format, and design using the functions included in Excel. I recommend that you check out a few of the available templates and decide for yourself.

To see how this works, follow these steps:

1. Choose Format Report from the PivotTable toolbar to bring up the AutoFormat dialog box shown in Figure 7.8.

2. Select Table 9 in the AutoFormat dialog box, and then click OK to apply the template style to the PivotTable report and close the dialog box.

3. Verify that your PivotTable report looks like Figure 7.9.

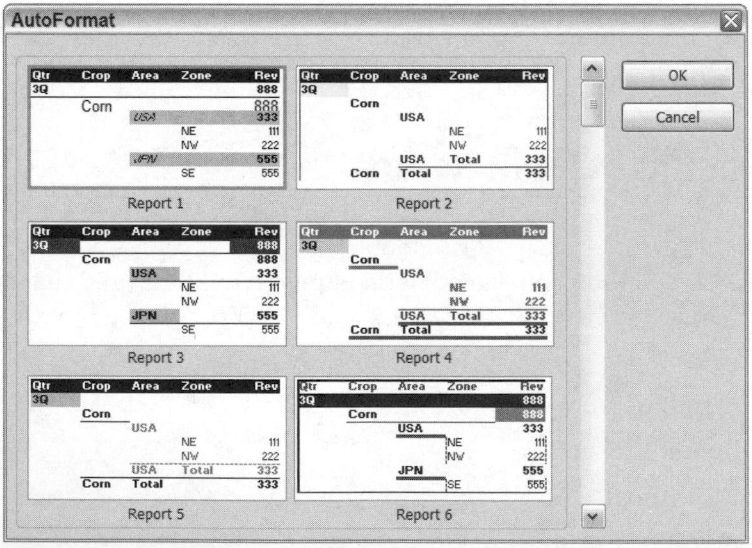

Figure 7.8 You can use the AutoFormat dialog box to apply various predefined table and report styles and formats.

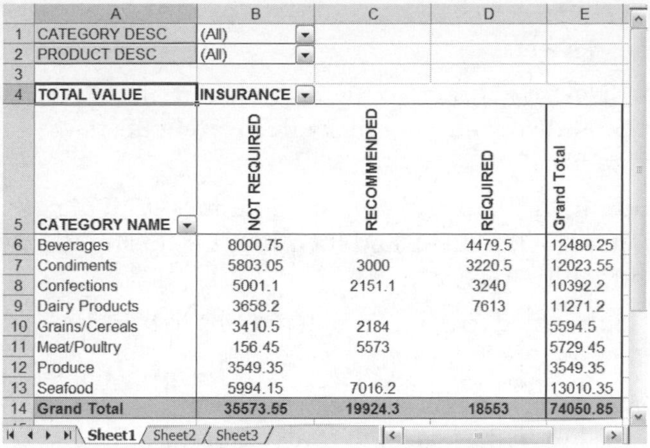

Figure 7.9   You can apply template formats to a PivotTable by selecting Format Report from the PivotTable toolbar.

Notice that the PivotTable report shown in Figure 7.9 has been modified to include shaded grand totals, bold field headings, and rotated column heading text — an ideal format when column heading values are lengthy. The columns are not stretched across the paper; instead they are rotated to fit in a smaller column width. Try a few different settings, and then reset the format back to PivotTable Classic.

It's also possible to apply manual formatting options by selecting column or row cells and then applying a particular font style or cell format. I prefer having this flexibility to selecting a style from an existing template. I've included an example here to give you an idea about how you can add some pizzazz and style to your own reports by using the readily available formatting features and functions included with Excel.

To apply the manual format changes and continue with the example, follow these steps:

1. Double-click Total Value in cell A4 to bring up the PivotTable Field dialog box.

2. Click Number in the PivotTable Field dialog box to bring up the Format Cells dialog box, and then select Accounting in the Category pane. Click the Symbol drop-down field, select None, and then click OK to return to the PivotTable Field dialog box.

TIP   Always format Data area fields in the Field Settings dialog box instead of from the Excel Formatting toolbar. Otherwise, the formats may be lost when the PivotTable shape changes, as fields are moved to different columns or rows where formats have not been defined.

3. Click OK to close the PivotTable Field dialog box.

4. Click the top-left cell where the rows and columns meet to highlight all the cells in the Excel worksheet.

5. Choose Format ⇨ Row Height to bring up the Row Height dialog box. Type **20** in the Row Height field, and then click OK to apply the new row height and return to Excel.

6. Choose Format ⇨ Column Width to bring up the Column Width dialog box. Type **16** in the Column Width field, and then click OK to apply the new column width and return to Excel.

7. With all the cells still highlighted, choose Format ⇨ Cells to bring up the Format Cells dialog box.

8. Click the Alignment tab, and then select Center in the Vertical drop-down box to vertically align the text in the increased row size of the cell.

9. Click the Fonts tab in the Format Cells dialog box, select Arial Narrow in the Font pane, and then click OK to apply the alignment and font changes to the Excel worksheet.

10. Right-align and bold the column field heading values by selecting cells B5 through E5 and clicking the align-right toolbar button and the Bold font button.

11. Verify that your PivotTable report looks like Figure 7.10.

I also suggest inserting a few rows at the top of the report so you have room to add a title, set the print date, and identify the database (for example, Production or Test). If you have a corporate logo, you can also insert it by choosing Insert ⇨ Picture ⇨ Clip Art. With some additional tweaks, I show how the report might look for Northwind Traders in Figure 7.11.

	A	B	C	D	E
1	CATEGORY DESC	(All)			
2	PRODUCT DESC	(All)			
3					
4	TOTAL VALUE	INSURANCE			
5	CATEGORY NAME	NOT REQUIRED	RECOMMENDED	REQUIRED	Grand Total
6	Beverages	8000.75		4479.5	12480.25
7	Condiments	5803.05	3000	3220.5	12023.55
8	Confections	5001.1	2151.1	3240	10392.2
9	Dairy Products	3658.2		7613	11271.2
10	Grains/Cereals	3410.5	2184		5594.5
11	Meat/Poultry	156.45	5573		5729.45
12	Produce	3549.35			3549.35
13	Seafood	5994.15	7016.2		13010.35
14	Grand Total	35573.55	19924.3	18553	74050.85

Figure 7.10 PivotTable report with manual formatting changes applied.

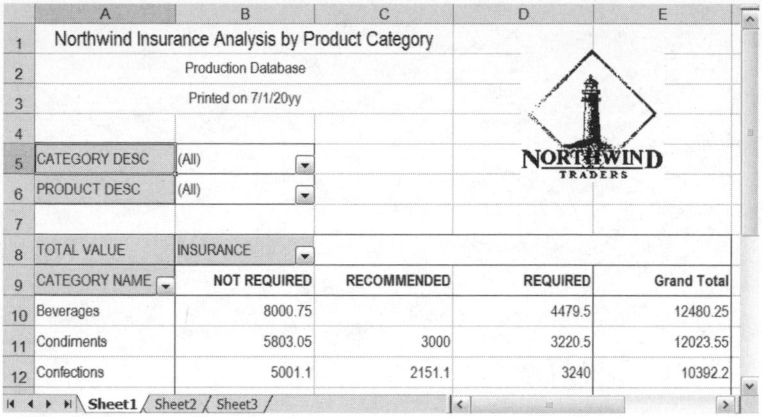

Figure 7.11 Add the report information and a corporate logo to produce a professional-looking report.

WARNING In practice, always leave blank rows between the Report Title and the Page Area of a PivotTable report. The PivotTable does not automatically shift down when additional fields are dropped into the Page area and there are rows above the Page area. Although this is easily resolved from the Excel worksheet by using the Insert Rows function, it can be problematic when you're working in the Layout Manager. Imagine making several changes in the Layout Manager, only to have them all be discarded because one or more new Page fields could not fit in the Page area.

Don't worry about trying to adjust the report to look like Figure 7.11. I provide it here only as an example to demonstrate how you might customize your Excel reports in the enterprise. Notice that Row 1 is just the report title, followed by the database that the report is accessing (in this case, the Production database), and lastly, the current date (which is just a formula field). I just pasted the corporate logo on the right from the Access database.

Formatting Options

Formatting options are accessed in the PivotTable Options dialog box. Here, you can configure the display of grand total fields, set display options for blank values and error values, set print titles, and control how Page fields are presented.

You can access the format options in the PivotTable Options dialog box by right-clicking the PivotTable and selecting Table Options from the pop-up menu. Alternatively, you can choose Table Options from the PivotTable toolbar. Either method brings up the dialog box shown in Figure 7.12.

Figure 7.12 The top-half of the PivotTable Options dialog box looks like what is shown here. This section controls PivotTable formatting options.

This section describes only the top portion of this dialog box, as the bottom portion is focused on data options, a topic covered in Chapter 9. There are several options in this dialog box for controlling the display and formatting of PivotTable reports, both on-screen and in print.

The AutoFormat and Preserve Formatting options are closely related. If you are making custom formatting changes to the PivotTable, be sure to uncheck AutoFormat and check Preserve Formatting.

WARNING Always uncheck the AutoFormat option and check the Preserve Formatting option before you start making formatting changes to the PivotTable report. If you forget to do so before refreshing the report, the formatting changes are discarded, often requiring you to reapply the formatting.

The Merge Labels option is useful for centering outer row fields in cells, rather than putting them at the top of the cell, as demonstrated in Figure 7.13.

The Page Layout option is used in conjunction with the option below it: Fields Per Column or Fields Per Row. These options control how Page area fields are displayed. You can choose to first display them horizontally across the report and then vertically down, or vertically down and then horizontally across. In Figure 7.14, I changed the option to display the second Page field, Product Desc, across and to the right of Category Desc rather than under Category Desc, as shown earlier in Figure 7.11.

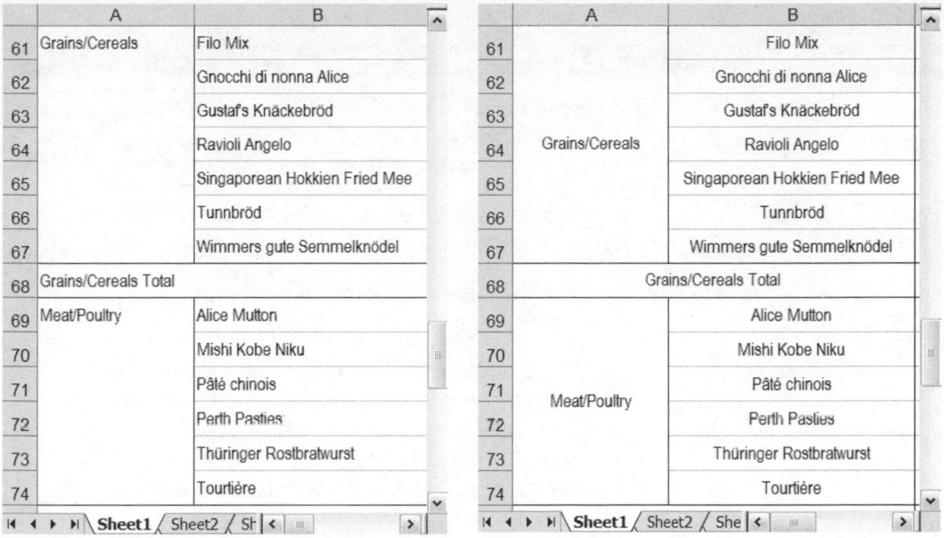

Figure 7.13 Labels not merged (left) and labels merged (right).

Table 7.2 provides a brief explanation of each formatting option available in the PivotTable Options dialog box.

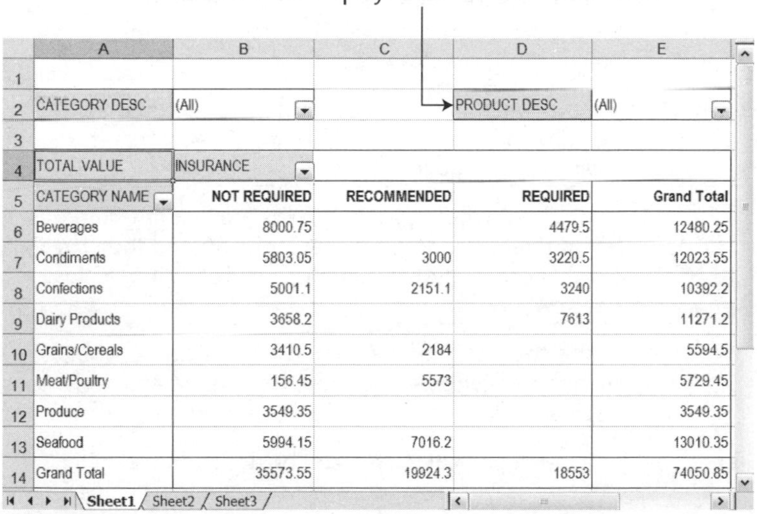

Product Desc displayed across rather than down

	A	B	C	D	E
1					
2	CATEGORY DESC	(All)		PRODUCT DESC	(All)
3					
4	TOTAL VALUE	INSURANCE			
5	CATEGORY NAME	NOT REQUIRED	RECOMMENDED	REQUIRED	Grand Total
6	Beverages	8000.75		4479.5	12480.25
7	Condiments	5803.05	3000	3220.5	12023.55
8	Confections	5001.1	2151.1	3240	10392.2
9	Dairy Products	3658.2		7613	11271.2
10	Grains/Cereals	3410.5	2184		5594.5
11	Meat/Poultry	156.45	5573		5729.45
12	Produce	3549.35			3549.35
13	Seafood	5994.15	7016.2		13010.35
14	Grand Total	35573.55	19924.3	18553	74050.85

Figure 7.14 Page fields can be placed over and then down (shown here) or down and then over. Use this option in conjunction with Fields Per Row (or Column).

Table 7.2 Available Options in the PivotTable Options Dialog Box

OPTION NAME	DESCRIPTION
Name	Sets the name of the PivotTable report (optional). You can ignore this field unless you plan to incorporate Visual Basic for Applications (VBA) code.
Grand Totals For Columns	Toggles the Grand Totals display for report columns (row 14 of Figure 7.10).
Grand Totals For Rows	Toggles the Grand Totals display for report rows (column E in Figure 7.10).
AutoFormat Table	Toggles whether the PivotTable is automatically formatted. This option is useful if you want Excel to automatically format the PivotTable report whenever the report is refreshed or field arrangement is modified. If you apply your own format, be sure to uncheck this option or you risk losing all your manually applied formatting. Use this option in conjunction with Preserve Formatting.
Subtotal Hidden Page Items	Toggles whether hidden page items are included in subtotals.
Merge Labels	Toggles whether Outer Row and Outer Column field headings are merged into the middle of the cell.
Preserve Formatting	Toggles whether formatting changes made to the PivotTable report are saved. Use this option in conjunction with AutoFormat Table.
Repeat Item Labels On Each Printed Page	Toggles whether Outer Row and Outer Column field headings are printed on the second page when they break across a page.
Page Layout	Controls whether Page area fields are laid out from left to right first and then over, or down and then over. Used in conjunction with Fields per Column or Fields per Row.
Field Per Column (or Fields per Row)	Name changes with the Page Layout. It controls how many page items can be dropped into the area before Page fields start a new column or a new row.
For Error Values, Show	Displays a particular character or string in place of an error message when box is checked and text string is entered in the box to the right.
For Blank Values, Show	Displays a particular character or string in place of blank values when box is checked and text string is entered in the box to the right.
Set Print Titles	Controls whether column and row headings are automatically printed on additional pages.

Preparing the Report for Printing

If you plan to print the PivotTable report for offline analysis, you may want to configure the PivotTable format options and Excel's print options for the report to look best on paper. The items in your checklist should include the following:

- Printer orientation
- Field labels
- Headings and footers
- Layout options with Outer Row and Column fields

TIP If you have several worksheets that have the same PivotTable, set all the print features in the first PivotTable worksheet before copying the worksheet.

Setting and Adjusting the Printer Orientation

The printer orientation can be set either to Portrait or Landscape in the Page Setup dialog box accessed by choosing File ➪ Page Setup. If the report is wider than it is long, set the orientation to Landscape. If the report is longer than it is wide, set the orientation to Portrait.

Choose View ➪ Page Break Preview to ensure that the report is properly displayed on the page. Then choose View ➪ Normal to return to the normal worksheet view.

WARNING Customizing the Page Break Preview automatically adjusts the scaling in the Page Setup dialog box. If you change the printer orientation of a report that already has customized Page Break settings, reset the scaling to 100 percent Of Normal Size in the Page Setup dialog box and reapply the Page Break Preview settings. If you don't follow this procedure, the report size may not be optimized in the new page orientation, making it smaller than it might otherwise appear.

Working with Field Labels

You can configure Field Labels to be repeated on each printed page from both the Sheet tab of the Page Setup dialog box and from the PivotTable Options dialog box. If you are using a report title and logo, you should probably use the Page Setup dialog box to repeat column headings because the Rows To Repeat At Top option allows you to also print the report title and related information on each page. If you aren't using a report title or logo, just check the option Set Print Titles in the PivotTable Options dialog box.

If the report has Outer Row or Outer Column fields and does not fit on one page, check the Repeat Item Labels On Each Printed Page option to automatically print the field label on the second page when it splits across a single page.

Using Headers and Footers

Many organizations already have guidelines in place for what information should be included in Header and Footers. This might include some confidentiality warning, a corporate name or logo, or some particular font style. I generally try to include the following information in a report header or footer:

- **Report title:** The name of the report
- **Database area:** Production, Test, Staging, and so on
- **Print date:** The date that the report is printed
- **Report revision number:** Important in early parts of the development cycle
- **Page number:** Usually in the form of Page *n/n* (for example, Page 1/3)

I've found that questions or reported problems related to a report are often more easily diagnosed when you have a report name, print date, report revision, and Database area included with the report.

Setting Print Options for Outer Row and Outer Column Fields

If the PivotTable report has multiple Row area fields or multiple Column area fields, you can configure the report to automatically insert a page break before each new Outer Row or Outer Column field. You set this option in the Pivot-Table Layout dialog box that you can access by clicking the Layout button in the PivotTable Field dialog box of an Outer Row or Outer Column field. (To learn more about inserting page breaks for each new group, read the "Managing Inner and Outer Fields" section later in this chapter.)

Designing and Working with Page Area Fields

Page area fields act much differently than Column and Row fields in a Pivot-Table report. Selecting a value in the Page area filters what is displayed in the Column, Row, and Data areas. And unless you are working with an OLAP data source, you can select only one value or all values from the drop-down list; you can't pick and choose multiple values. Because these fields are so unique, I generally try to identify what fields are going to be in the Page area when initially developing an SQL query so that I can customize how the values are displayed in the drop-down list.

This section covers some topics on Page area fields that I think you will find useful.

Selecting Multiple Items from a Page Area Field

I'm not sure why Microsoft designed it this way, but you can select only a single value or all values from the drop-down field list of a Page area field unless the data source is an OLAP cube. However, despite this feature, it's easy to work around. One method is to drag the Page area field to a Row or Column area, select the values you want to display, and then drag it back to the Page area where it will then show "(Multiple Items)." Another, easier method is to just double-click the field to bring up the PivotTable Field dialog box shown in Figure 7.15. In this dialog box, you can choose to display or hide items in the Hide Items pane.

If items are hidden in a Page area field, and the field is dragged off the report, the filter is immediately removed. However, Excel remembers the filter settings once the item is dragged back to the report.

WARNING It's easy for report users to forget or not notice that filter settings have been applied to the PivotTable report, especially when a Page area field with filter settings was once removed and then dragged back to the report a few weeks or a few months later. Because the filter settings are saved with the field, the user doesn't expect or notice that the filter settings have been reapplied. To avoid this problem, train report users to remove filter settings on Page area fields before the settings are dragged off the report.

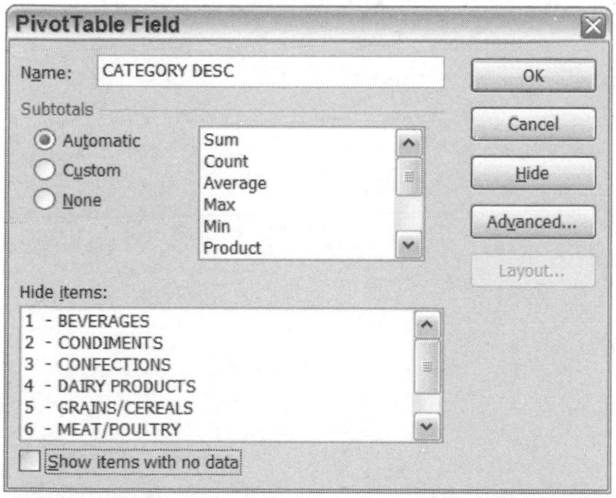

Figure 7.15 Double-click a Page area field to select multiple fields to be displayed or hidden.

Designing a Page Area Field

In the example used in this chapter, the Page area fields Product Desc and Category Desc are created by concatenating the field code with its description. For Category Desc, I've changed the datatype from Identity to Character and concatenated a dash and then the category description to make this new field:

```
CAST (cat.CategoryID AS CHAR(2))
        + ' - '
        + UPPER(cat.CategoryName)              AS 'CATEGORY DESC',
```

Although the Category code for Northwind Traders might be more database-oriented, this is not always the case for many organizations that use codes to track important business data. Common ones include promotion codes, sales analysis codes, and customer contact codes. Several pieces of logic might also be embedded into a particular code (for example, date information, market segment, market channel, and product information). Although this kind of complexity is not built into the NorthwindCS database, I include this reference because it can be useful for your PivotTable report development. Basically, you can break apart the different positions of a single field code and display each component as if it were a real field. In my experience, I've found that this method of separating the various positions of a field code into multiple fields is often seen as innovative and valuable to key decision-makers in an organization.

Following the simpler example used in the SQL query, Product and Category codes are assigned to each category and product in the database. For example, the category Beverages has a category ID of 1, Condiments a category ID of 2, Confections a category ID of 3, and so on. I concatenated Product and Category codes with their descriptions in the SQL query, so report users could see the code and the description as a single field in the report. Figure 7.16 shows the drop-down list for the Category Desc.

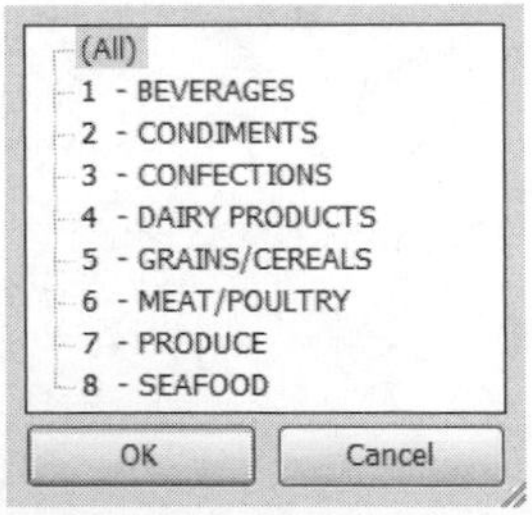

Figure 7.16 Concatenating codes with a dash and its description provides an innovative method for Page area fields.

Sorting

Field items are sorted when a field is dropped into the PivotTable report. You can sort in a few different ways with a PivotTable. The following options are available:

- Ascending alphanumeric sort
- Descending alphanumeric sort
- Sort based on a value in the Data area
- Custom sort

TIP In a PivotTable, the unique items of a Column or Row field are sorted alphanumerically when the field is dropped into the report. As a result, you should never use an Order By statement in the SQL query for a PivotTable. This statement works on the entire dataset and only serves to increase the amount of time it takes to execute the query and refresh the report.

Sorting in Ascending or Descending Order

You can apply ascending or descending sort order to fields in the Row or Column area by first clicking the field, and then clicking the A ⇨ Z button or the Z ⇨ A button in the Standard toolbar. You can also sort the data based on the values in the Data area, the Grand Total Row area, or the Grand Total Column area. Just highlight the desired area and click the applicable sort button to sort the data.

TIP Page area fields are often not sorted in alphanumeric order, and you cannot sort a field that is in dropped in this location. However, you can drag it to a Row or Column area, sort it there, and then drag it back to the Page area where the sort will be maintained. You can even apply a custom sort before moving it back to the Page area.

It's also possible to sort data by choosing Data ⇨ Sort to bring up the Sort dialog box. In this dialog box, you can also automate the sort order by days of the week or months of the year by clicking Options.

NOTE "Trying It Out in the Real World," at the end of this chapter, demonstrates how to sort the data by months of the year.

Sorting on a Data Area Field

You can also set the sort order based on the values in the Data area. Double-click a Row or a Column field to bring up the PivotTable Field dialog box; and then click the Advanced button to bring up the PivotTable Field Advanced Options dialog box, as shown in Figure 7.17.

In the AutoSort Options section of this dialog box, you can choose to sort the field values in an Ascending, Descending, or Manual (custom) order. The Using Field at the bottom shows the field currently selected and all the fields in the Data area. In this example, I've chosen to sort the product categories by Total Value (the Data area value) in ascending order. Using this feature, you can sort or rank report data. Imagine automatically sorting the profit, sales, cost, productivity, incidents counts, or shipments against items in the Row or Column area.

Top n and Bottom n Display

The display of the top *n* or bottom *n* values is controlled in the Top 10 AutoShow section of the PivotTable Field Advanced Options dialog box. Just click the On button, select Top or Bottom from the Show drop-down list, and enter the number of items that should be displayed. Once a Top *n* or Bottom *n* is applied, the field's drop-down arrow turns blue to indicate that not all the items are being displayed.

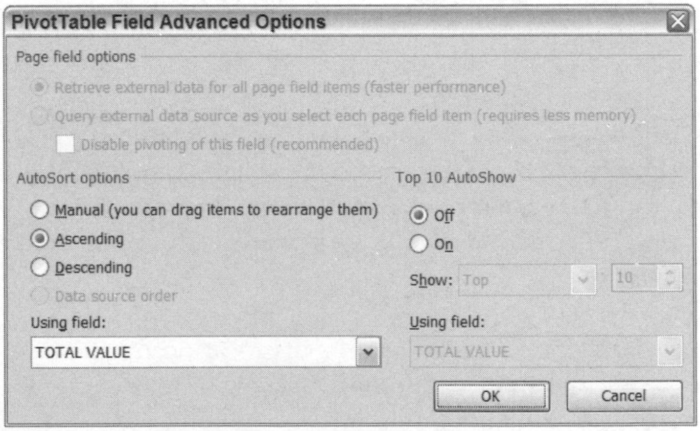

Figure 7.17 In this dialog box, you can sort PivotTable fields in the Row or Column area based on a value in the Data area.

Custom Sort Order

You can also perform a custom sort can by simply selecting a field and dragging it to the preferred location in the Column or Row area. The field is ready to be moved when the button changes from a plus sign to the mouse pointer combined with an arrow that points in four directions. Try organizing the fields as shown in Figure 7.18.

WARNING If the button does not change shape, the sort order is not set to manual. Double-click the field to bring up the PivotTable Field dialog box, click the Advanced button and click Manual in the Sort Order section of the dialog box.

Conditional Formatting

Conditional formatting has only limited application in PivotTable reports because it is not automatically applied like it is with Spreadsheet Reports. If you find that this feature is valuable in your PivotTable report, I suggest incorporating the conditional formatting into some VBA program that can be accessed from a toolbar button or embedded into an operation, such as Refresh Data.

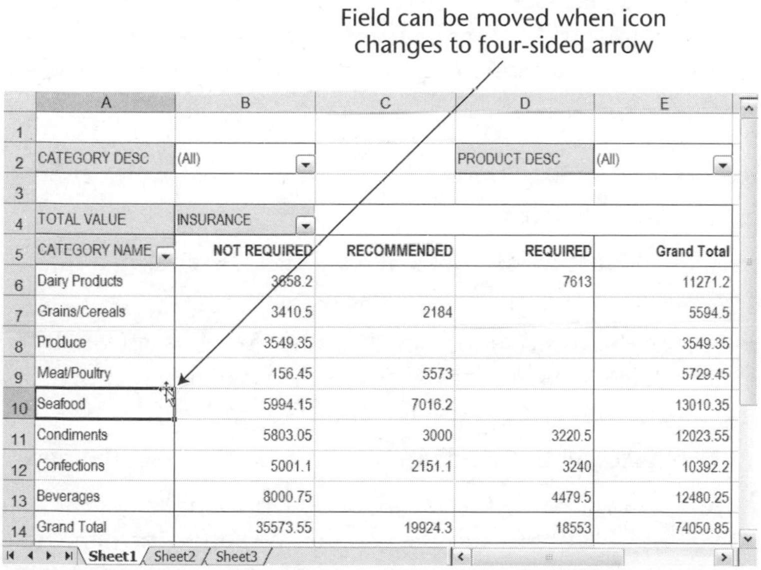

Field can be moved when icon
changes to four-sided arrow

	A	B	C	D	E
1					
2	CATEGORY DESC	(All)		PRODUCT DESC	(All)
3					
4	TOTAL VALUE	INSURANCE			
5	CATEGORY NAME	NOT REQUIRED	RECOMMENDED	REQUIRED	Grand Total
6	Dairy Products	3658.2		7613	11271.2
7	Grains/Cereals	3410.5	2184		5594.5
8	Produce	3549.35			3549.35
9	Meat/Poultry	156.45	5573		5729.45
10	Seafood	5994.15	7016.2		13010.35
11	Condiments	5803.05	3000	3220.5	12023.55
12	Confections	5001.1	2151.1	3240	10392.2
13	Beverages	8000.75		4479.5	12480.25
14	Grand Total	35573.55	19924.3	18553	74050.85

◄ ◄ ► ►◄ \ **Sheet1** / Sheet2 / Sheet3 /

Figure 7.18   You can sort fields in a custom way by dragging them to the preferred location in the Column or Row area.

Having dispensed with the customary warnings that this feature is not particularly useful for PivotTable reports, you can still manually apply the format by choosing Format ⇨ Conditional Formatting. This brings up the Conditional Formatting dialog box in which you can set a font style, a font color, and border and shading effects.

CROSS-REFERENCE Read Chapter 11 to learn more about conditional formatting as it applies to Spreadsheet reports.

Grouping Items

You can group items in the Row or Column area into a new field. This function can be useful for grouping particular months into a specific fiscal quarter, sales representatives into a designated territory, or geographic locations into a region.

In order to create a group for the items, highlight the items you want to group, right-click the report, and then choose Group and Show Detail ⇨ Group from the pop-up menu.

TIP The Group function performs the same type of function that the SQL query (earlier in this chapter) does for the Insurance field. I generally try to keep all the report logic in a single location (the SQL query) when it's possible. However, if you are not familiar with SQL programming, you are not able to access the data source, or the data source is an OLAP cube, the Group function is an ideal alternative.

To group the categories in the Excel report into different Meal Types, follow these steps:

1. Verify that your PivotTable report looks like Figure 7.18, and then highlight cells A6–A7.

2. Right-click the highlighted cells and choose Group And Show Detail ⇨ Group. Notice that Excel creates a new field in the PivotTable report called Category Name2 and a new group called Group 1.

3. Click Group 1 in cell A6, type **Breakfast**, and press Enter to set the new group name.

4. Click cell A5, type **MEAL TYPE**, and press Enter to change the name of the field to Meal Type. Notice that the field name is also changed in the Field List dialog box.

5. Select cell A8, type **Lunch**, and press Enter to set the new group name.

6. Highlight cells B9–B10, right-click the highlighted cells, and choose Group and Show Detail ⇨ Group to create a new group under Meal Type called Group2 for Meat/Poultry and Seafood.

7. Select cell A9, type **Dinner**, and press Enter to set the new group name.

8. Highlight cells B11–B13, right-click on the highlighted cells, and choose Group and Show Detail ⇨ Group. This creates a new group under Meal Type called Group 3 for the remaining items in Category Name.

9. Select cell A11, type **All**, and press Enter to set the new group name.

10. Right-click the report and select Table Options from the pop-up menu to bring up the PivotTable Options dialog box. Check the Merge Labels option, and then click OK to merge the labels on Meal Type and close the dialog box.

11. Verify that your PivotTable report looks like Figure 7.19.

WATCH THE VIDEO To see how the categories are grouped into Meal Type, click the ch0702_video.avi file at www.wiley.com/go/excelreporting to watch the video.

	A	B	C	
1				
2	CATEGORY DESC	(All)		PROD
3				
4	TOTAL VALUE		INSURANCE	
5	CATEGORY NAME	CATEGORY NAME	NOT REQUIRED	RECO
6	Breakfast	Dairy Products	3658.2	
7		Grains/Cereals	3410.5	
8	Lunch	Produce	3549.35	
9	Dinner	Meat/Poultry	156.45	
10		Seafood	5994.15	
11	All	Condiments	5803.05	
12		Confections	5001.1	
13		Beverages	8000.75	

Sheet1 / Sheet2 / Sheet3 /

Figure 7.19 You can group fields in the Row or Column area into new fields by using the Group function in the PivotTable toolbar or pop-up menu.

If you accidentally grouped an item in the wrong category, you must ungroup the category the item is currently in and the category that the item should be in. After that, you can rearrange the items to the correct location and re-create the group.

After the group field is created, it exists as its own field name in the PivotTable report. Dragging the Category Name field off the PivotTable report doesn't remove the field from the PivotTable Field List. The only way to remove the new item is to ungroup all the items in the group.

Managing Inner and Outer Fields

When more than one field is dragged to a Column or Row field, the field on the right side is referred to as an Inner Row or Inner Column field, while the field on the left side is referred to as an Outer Row or Outer Column field. There are a few things to keep in mind when working with Inner and Outer fields:

- Inner fields can be displayed multiple times for each unique value of the Outer field.
- Inner fields are subtotaled for each unique Outer field.
- Only Inner Fields that have a value for an Outer field are displayed.
- The Layout button in the PivotTable Field dialog box is enabled for Outer fields.

Displaying Inner and Outer Row or Column Fields

Inner Row fields can be displayed multiple times for each valid combination of an Outer Row field, as shown in Figure 7.20. Notice that the left-most Outer Row fields are only displayed once. By default, an Inner Row field is not displayed if it does not have a valid combination with an Outer Row field.

The Layout button in the PivotTable Field dialog box is enabled for Outer Row and Outer Column fields. You can access this dialog box by double-clicking the field heading or right-clicking the field and then selecting Field Settings from the pop-up menu. Figure 7.21 shows the PivotTable Field dialog box for Category Name.

Clicking the Layout Button brings up the PivotTable Field Layout dialog box shown in Figure 7.22.

In this dialog box, you can choose to display the PivotTable in tabular or outline form. The default display is tabular; changing it to outline inserts a blank Inner Row at the top of each new group. The option below it, Display Subtotals At Top Of Group, is also enabled when an Outline form is selected.

Requested multiple times for each Outer Row item

	A	B	C	D
1	CATEGORY DESC	(All)		
2	PRODUCT DESC	(All)		
3				
4	TOTAL VALUE		INSURANCE	
5	CATEGORY NAME	SUPPLIER	NOT REQUIRED	RECOMMI
6	Grains/Cereals	G'DAY, MATE ◄	266	
7		LEKA TRADING	364	
8		PASTA BUTTINI S.R.L.	1500	
9		PB KNÄCKEBRÖD AB	549	
10		PLUTZER LEBENSMITTELGROßMÄRKTE AG	731.5	
11	Grains/Cereals Total		3410.5	
12	Produce	G'DAY, MATE ◄	1000	
13		GRANDMA KELLY'S HOMESTEAD	450	
14		MAYUMI'S	813.75	
15		PLUTZER LEBENSMITTELGROßMÄRKTE AG	1185.6	
16		TOKYO TRADERS	40	
17	Produce Total		3549.35	
18	Meat/Poultry	G'DAY, MATE ◄	0	
19		MA MAISON	156.45	

Sheet1 / Sheet2 / Sheet3 /

Figure 7.20   Inner Row fields are repeated and subtotaled for each Outer Row field.

PivotTable Field

Name: CATEGORY NAME

Subtotals
○ Automatic   Sum
○ Custom   Count
○ None   Average
               Max
               Min
               Product

☐ Show items with no data

[OK] [Cancel] [Hide] [Advanced...] [Layout...]

Figure 7.21   The Layout button is enabled for Outer Row and Outer Column fields.

PivotTable Field Layout

Display Options
◉ Show items in tabular form
○ Show items in outline form
   ☐ Display subtotals at top of group
☐ Insert blank line after each item

Print Option
☐ Insert page break after each item

[OK] [Cancel]

Figure 7.22   You can configure Display Options and a Print Option for Outer Row and Outer Column fields in the PivotTable Field Layout dialog box.

NOTE Subtotals can be displayed at the top of the group only when the Display Subtotals At Top Of Group is checked and there is only one subtotal calculation.

The Insert Blank Line After Each Item option adds a blank line before each new group. This additional line provides some more separation between each new group.

The Insert Page Break After Each Item option inserts a page break for each new group. This option is useful for inserting automatic page breaks for each new group. Trying to do that manually can be very difficult, especially if the report consumes numerous pages.

Managing Grand Totals and Subtotals

The default handling for PivotTable reports is to display Grand Totals for columns and rows, and to subtotal Inner Row and Inner Column fields for each Outer Row or Outer Column field. The Grand Total options are controlled in the PivotTable Options dialog box, in the top-left corner (refer to Figure 7.12), while subtotals are controlled from the Outer Row field.

Double-clicking an Outer Row field brings up the PivotTable Field dialog box, where you can set subtotals in one of three ways:

- **Automatic:** Default subtotal (Count or Sum)
- **Custom:** More than one subtotal or a different subtotal than the default
- **None:** No subtotals displayed

In Figure 7.23, I have selected Sum, Count, and Average in the PivotTable Field dialog box for Category Name.

Setting the subtotals as shown in Figure 7.23 configures the PivotTable report to look like Figure 7.24.

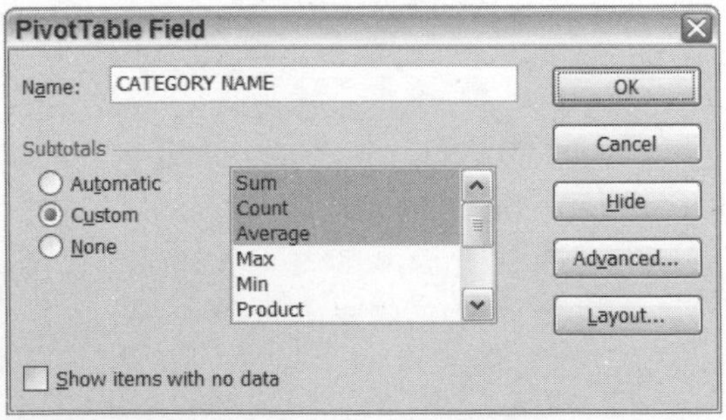

Figure 7.23   Subtotals are always set in the Outer Row field.

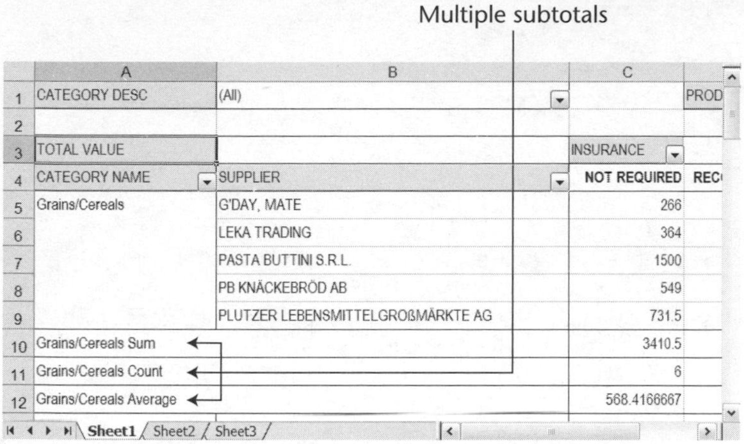

Multiple subtotals

Figure 7.24 Multiple subtotals calculated for an Inner Row field.

Managing Blank Values

You can opt to show all Inner Row fields, even if there is not a valid combination with an Outer Row field, by double-clicking the Inner Row field to bring up the PivotTable Field dialog box. Then check the Show Items With No Data option, as shown in Figure 7.25.

After this option is checked, all the valid suppliers for the item appear, even if there is not a valid combination of the Inner and Outer fields. This can be useful when the combination is expected to take place but hasn't happened yet because of latency issues (for example, a direct mail promotion where the second group of offers was sent out a few weeks after the first group). You can also use the For Empty Cells Show option in the PivotTable Options dialog box in conjunction with the Show Items with No Data option in the PivotTable Field dialog box to format the report. I checked the option Show Items with No Data for the Supplier field (refer to Figure 7.25) and also set For Empty Cells Show to "*" in the PivotTable Options dialog box. (You can bring up this dialog box by right-clicking the PivotTable and choosing Table Options from the pop-up menu.) The result is shown in Figure 7.26.

> **TIP** I've often found that report users are confused when they see a 0 in the Data area for a Column or Row field. Typically, they don't understand why a 0 appears if blank values are not normally displayed. Until they drill down on the data, they don't realize that there are one or more records behind that 0. If you decide to display some text for blank values, I don't recommend using a 0 because you lose the capability to readily distinguish a blank value from a 0.

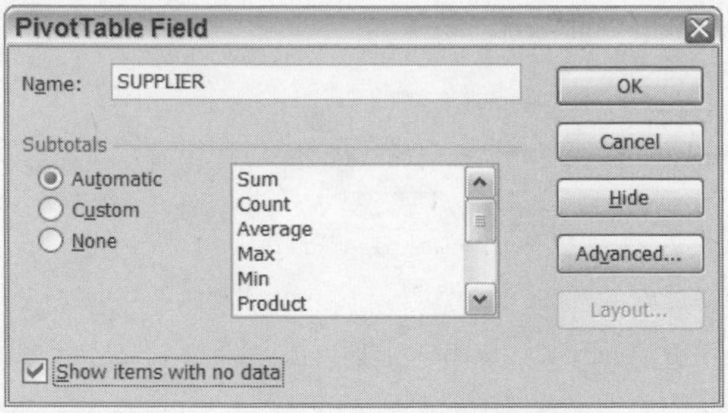

Figure 7.25   Check Show Items With No Data to display all Suppliers, regardless of whether a valid combination exists.

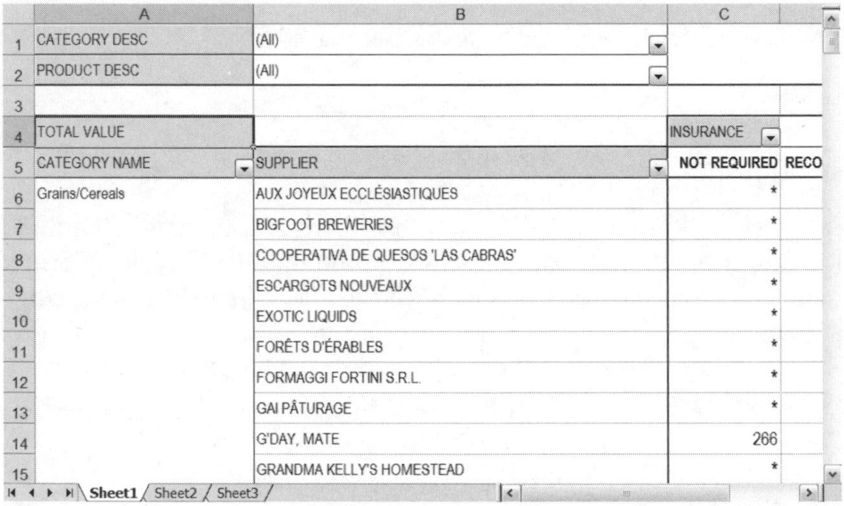

Figure 7.26   All values are shown for Supplier, and the * is used for blank items.

Renaming Fields

You can rename fields by double-clicking the field to bring up the PivotTable Field dialog box. After the dialog box opens, you can enter the new name into the Name field.

If the item is a data item, just type the name directly into Excel. There's no need to even bring up the PivotTable Field dialog box. When there are multiple data items, the Field Heading is changed to Data. However, you can still enter the new name wherever a current one is displayed.

If you are changing the name from the Layout Manager, just double-click the field on the right or in the diagram to bring up the PivotTable Field dialog box, and then enter the new name into the Name field.

Managing How Data Items Are Displayed

The default display for showing multiple Data area fields is to display them in rows rather than in columns, as shown in Figure 7.27. This display can be changed to show the data as an outer row (see Figure 7.28) or as columns (see Figure 7.29).

To move the Data items before Category Name, follow these steps:

1. Right-click Data in Cell B4 of Figure 7.27, and then choose Order ⇨ Move Left from the pop-up menu.

2. Verify that your PivotTable report now looks like Figure 7.28.

To move the Data items to columns, follow these steps:

1. Right-click Data in A4 of Figure 7.28 and choose Order ⇨ Move To Column from the pop-up menu.

2. Verify that your PivotTable report now looks like Figure 7.29.

Formatting Data Area Fields

You should format fields in the Data area from the PivotTable Field dialog box because formats applied from the worksheet columns or rows can be lost when the shape of the PivotTable is changed (by modifying a filter, dragging in a new field, or refreshing the report).

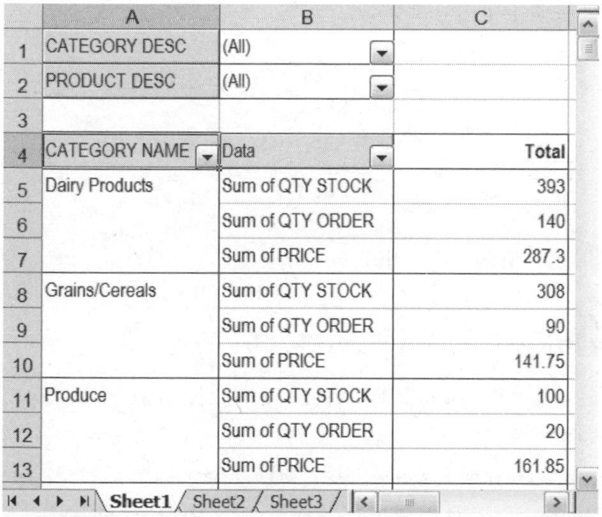

	A	B	C
1	CATEGORY DESC	(All)	
2	PRODUCT DESC	(All)	
3			
4	CATEGORY NAME	Data	Total
5	Dairy Products	Sum of QTY STOCK	393
6		Sum of QTY ORDER	140
7		Sum of PRICE	287.3
8	Grains/Cereals	Sum of QTY STOCK	308
9		Sum of QTY ORDER	90
10		Sum of PRICE	141.75
11	Produce	Sum of QTY STOCK	100
12		Sum of QTY ORDER	20
13		Sum of PRICE	161.85

H ◀ ▶ H \ **Sheet1** / Sheet2 / Sheet3 / |<   >|

Figure 7.27   By default, multiple Data items are displayed as rows.

	A	B	C
1	CATEGORY DESC	(All)	
2	PRODUCT DESC	(All)	
3			
4	Data	CATEGORY NAME	Total
5	Sum of QTY STOCK	Dairy Products	393
6		Grains/Cereals	308
7		Produce	100
8		Meat/Poultry	165
9		Seafood	701
10		Condiments	507
11		Confections	386
12		Beverages	559
13	Sum of QTY ORDER	Dairy Products	140
14		Grains/Cereals	90
15		Produce	20

Sheet1 / Sheet2 / Sheet3 /

Figure 7.28 Data items shown as an Outer Row field.

	A	B	C	D
1	CATEGORY DESC	(All)		
2	PRODUCT DESC	(All)		
3				
4		Data		
5	CATEGORY NAME	Sum of QTY STOCK	Sum of QTY ORDER	Sum of PRICE
6	Dairy Products	393	140	287.3
7	Grains/Cereals	308	90	141.75
8	Produce	100	20	161.85
9	Meat/Poultry	165	0	324.04
10	Seafood	701	120	248.19
11	Condiments	507	170	276.75
12	Confections	386	180	327.08
13	Beverages	559	60	455.75
14	Grand Total	3119	780	2222.71

Sheet1 / Sheet2 / Sheet3 /

Figure 7.29 Data items displayed in columns rather than in rows.

To set the format for Sum Of Price shown in Figure 7.29, follow these steps:

1. Select Sum Of Price in cell D5, right-click the field, and choose Field Settings from the pop-up menu.

2. Click Number to bring up the Format Cells dialog box, and then choose Accounting in the Number pane and None in the Symbol drop-down field.

3. Verify that your dialog box looks like Figure 7.30; and then click OK to close the Format Cells dialog box.

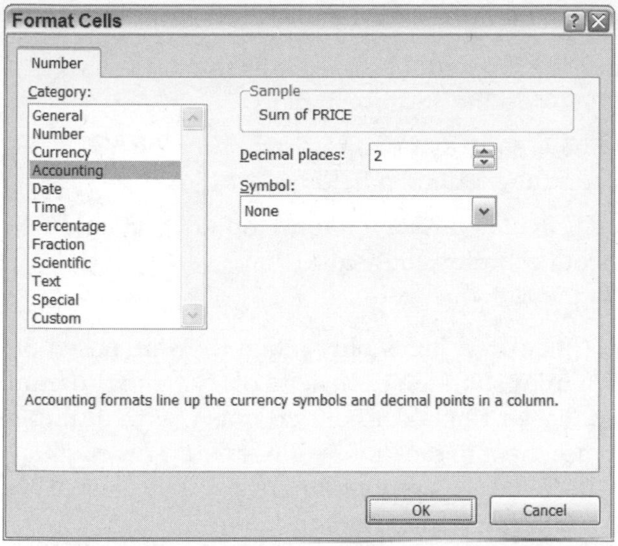

Figure 7.30   Set the format of Data fields in the Format Cells dialog box.

4. Click OK to close the PivotTable field dialog box and apply the Accounting format to all the values in Sum Of Price.

After you have applied a format to a Data area field, it is maintained for all the items, regardless of what shape the PivotTable takes. You can remove the format only by applying a new format or dragging it out of the PivotTable report.

Managing PivotTable Functions

Now that you know about the formatting features available in Excel PivotTable reports, you're ready to learn more about how to create and manage PivotTable fields. This includes a review of Calculated Fields, Calculated Expressions, and Data Field Options.

Creating Calculated Items and Calculated Fields

The PivotTable toolbar includes functions for creating Calculated Items and Calculated Fields. A Calculated Item is essentially a new item that appears in the drop-down list of a Row or Column area field. When it is created, the formula is based on some existing item in the field list. A Calculated Field is a little different from a Calculated Item. A Calculated Field actually appears as a new Data area field, rather than just an item in an existing field.

Calculated Field and Calculated Item are useful in the following situations:

- The report user does not have the technological skills to modify the SQL query or OLAP cube to add the additional field.

- The report user does not have security or access to modify the SQL query or OLAP cube to add the additional field.

- The Calculated Field and Calculated Item reference other Total fields that have been derived from complex, high-cost (that is, extensive CPU processing time) fields in the SQL query.

I use Calculated Fields and Calculated Items only when they are based on multiple fields derived from complex subqueries. Instead of trying to program these fields into the SQL query by writing a convoluted query with multiple subqueries, I can simply reference them in the PivotTable report. This can save a lot of processing time, since the fields are simply numerical values in the PivotTable report, and I do not have to run numerous subqueries to calculate the value or item.

WARNING Using Calculated Fields and Calculated Items spreads the report logic into more locations than just the SQL query, stored procedure, or OLAP cube. This adds an additional burden for managing change and configuration.

In this section, I provide more information about these special fields and demonstrate how you can use them in a PivotTable report.

Before You Begin

In order to follow along with the examples in this section, you must customize the PivotTable report. Before you begin, complete these steps:

1. Using the PivotTable in this chapter, drag Category Name to the Row area, and Value to the Data area.

2. Right-click the PivotTable and choose Table Options from the pop-up menu. Uncheck the option Grand Totals For Rows, and then click OK to close the PivotTable Options dialog box and suppress the grand total calculation for rows in the PivotTable reports.

3. Verify that your PivotTable report looks like Figure 7.31.

Creating a Calculated Item

A Calculated Item appears as a value in a Row or Column area field that is selected. Use this feature to create new values by referencing ones that already exist as values in that field. With Category Name in this example, you could create a new field that shows the estimated spoilage of the perishable product categories, such as Dairy Products and Produce. In the real world, this might be used for assessing the total value of stock at the end of the year and would include specific spoilage rates for each product category. However, to keep things simple, I'm going to forego complex formulas and just demonstrate how you can use this feature.

To create a Calculated Item field for Estimated Spoilage that estimates the cost of spoilage for Dairy Products and Produce at 15 percent, follow these steps:

1. Click the Category Name in cell A5 and choose Formulas ➪ Calculated Item from the PivotTable toolbar to bring up the Calculated Item dialog box.

2. Type **Estimated Spoilage** in the Name field and press Tab to move to the Formula field.

3. Type = (**'Dairy Products' + Produce)*-0.15** in the Formula field.

4. Verify that the Calculated Item dialog box looks like Figure 7.32, and then click the Add button to add Estimated Spoilage as a new value in Category.

5. Click OK to close the dialog box and add the Calculated Item to the PivotTable report.

6. Verify that your PivotTable report looks like Figure 7.33.

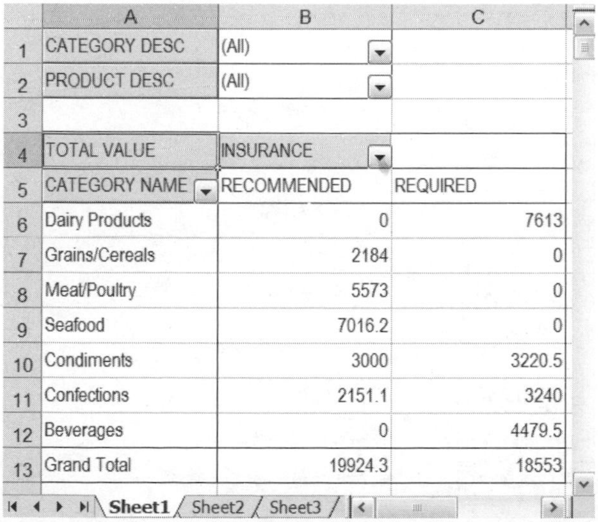

	A	B	C
1	CATEGORY DESC	(All)	
2	PRODUCT DESC	(All)	
3			
4	TOTAL VALUE	INSURANCE	
5	CATEGORY NAME	RECOMMENDED	REQUIRED
6	Dairy Products	0	7613
7	Grains/Cereals	2184	0
8	Meat/Poultry	5573	0
9	Seafood	7016.2	0
10	Condiments	3000	3220.5
11	Confections	2151.1	3240
12	Beverages	0	4479.5
13	Grand Total	19924.3	18553

◄ ◄ ► ►► \ **Sheet1** / Sheet2 / Sheet3 / ◄

Figure 7.31   Start with this PivotTable to follow the examples in this section.

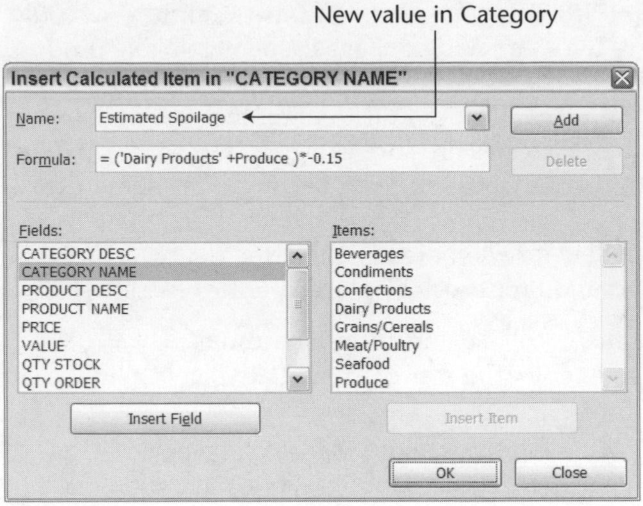

New value in Category

Figure 7.32 You can add Calculated Items as new values to a Row or Column area field.

You have now created a new Calculated Item field that estimates the cost of spoilage at 15 percent of the total inventory value of Dairy Products and Produce.

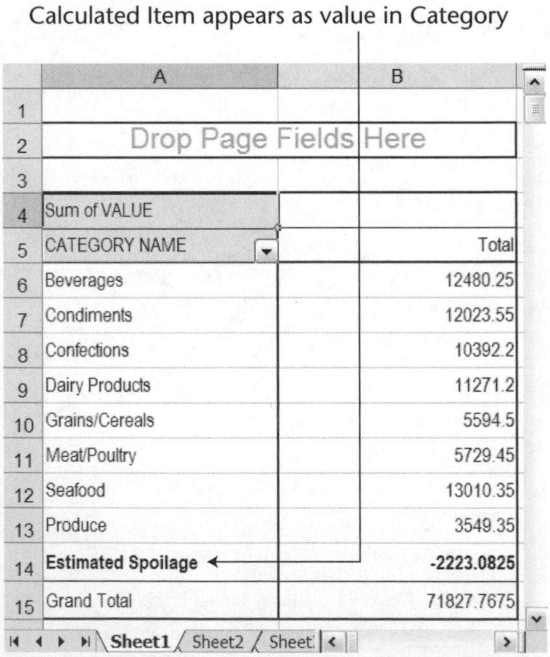

Calculated Item appears as value in Category

Figure 7.33 The Calculated Item, Estimated Spoilage, is added as a new value in the Category Name field, reducing the overall stock value by 15 percent for Dairy Products and Seafood.

After the Calculated Item is created, you can delete it by opening the Calculated Items dialog box, selecting the Calculated Item field, and clicking Delete.

Creating a Calculated Field

Calculated Fields appear only in the Data area of a PivotTable report. Unlike a Calculated Item that appears as an item in a Column or Row area field, a Calculated Field is a new field that is added to the Data area of the PivotTable report. The following example demonstrates how the inventory value can be increased by 10 percent for all product categories.

To create a new Calculated Field value that increases the total inventory value by 10 percent, follow these steps:

1. Starting with the PivotTable report in Figure 7.31, click any cell in the PivotTable and choose Formulas ⇨ Calculated Field from the PivotTable toolbar to bring up the Calculated Field dialog box.

2. Type **Value Next Year** in the Name field and press Tab to move to the Formula field.

3. Type **=VALUE * 1.10** in the Formula field.

4. Verify that the Insert Calculated Field dialog box looks like Figure 7.34, and then click the Add button to add COST as a new Calculated Field.

5. Click OK to close the dialog box and add the Calculated Field to the PivotTable report.

6. Type **Current Year Value** over Sum Of Value and **Next Year Value** over Sum Of Value Next Year in the Data area field headings to change the name of the Data fields. (Note that these fields are also changed in the PivotTable Field List Window.)

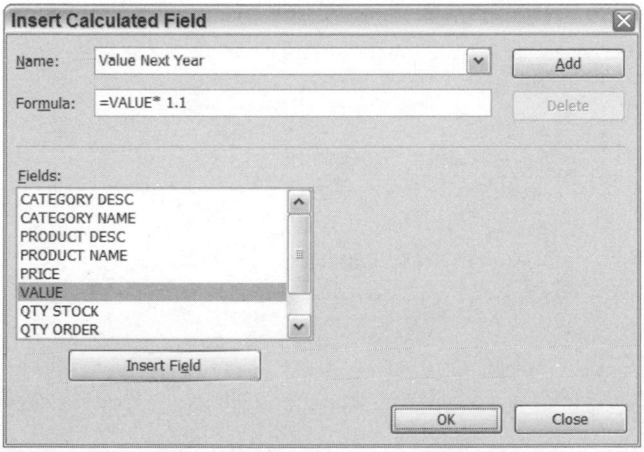

Figure 7.34   Calculated Fields can be displayed only in the Data area of a PivotTable report.

7. Right-click the Data area field heading and choose Order ⇨ Move to Column to display Current Year Value and Next Year Value as columns, rather than as rows.

8. Verify that the PivotTable report looks like Figure 7.35.

NOTE The only aggregate function that can be performed on a Calculated Field is Sum.

After the Calculated Item is created, you can delete it by opening the Calculated Fields dialog box, selecting the Calculated Item field from the drop-down box, and clicking Delete. You can also change the formula of these fields by selecting the field from the drop-down list, entering the new formula, and clicking Modify.

Displaying Formulas

You can display all the formulas for Calculated Items and Calculated Fields by choosing Formulas ⇨ List Formulas from the PivotTable toolbar menu. Selecting this function creates a new worksheet that lists all the formulas, as shown in Figure 7.36.

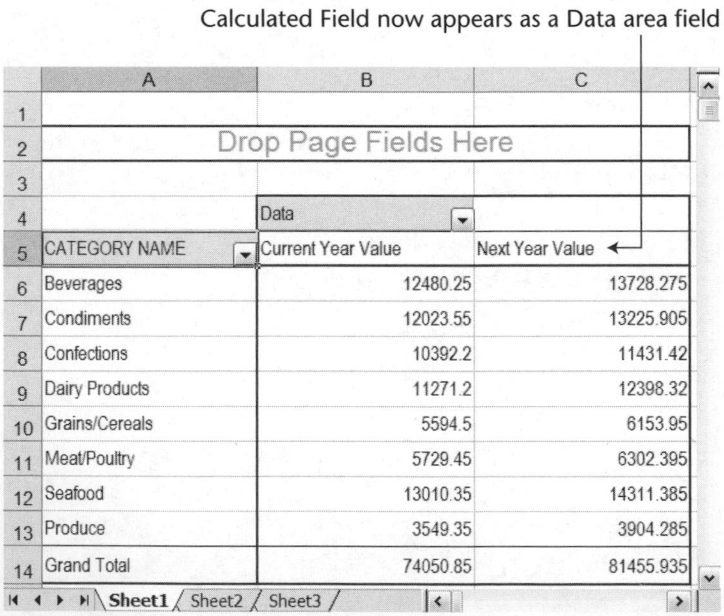

Calculated Field now appears as a Data area field

	A	B	C
1			
2		Drop Page Fields Here	
3			
4		Data	
5	CATEGORY NAME	Current Year Value	Next Year Value
6	Beverages	12480.25	13728.275
7	Condiments	12023.55	13225.905
8	Confections	10392.2	11431.42
9	Dairy Products	11271.2	12398.32
10	Grains/Cereals	5594.5	6153.95
11	Meat/Poultry	5729.45	6302.395
12	Seafood	13010.35	14311.385
13	Produce	3549.35	3904.285
14	Grand Total	74050.85	81455.935

◄ ◄ ► ►◄ \ **Sheet1** / Sheet2 / Sheet3 /

Figure 7.35 The Calculated Field, Next Year Value, has been added to the PivotTable Report as a new Data area item, calculating the inventory value at 110 percent of the Current Year Value.

	A	B	C	D
1	*Calculated Field*			
2	Solve Order	Field	Formula	
3		1	Value Next Year	=VALUE* 1.1
4				
5	*Calculated Item*			
6	Solve Order	Item	Formula	
7		1	'Estimated Spoilage'	= ('Dairy Products' +Produce)*-0.15
8				
9				
10	Note:		When a cell is updated by more than one formula,	
11			the value is set by the formula with the last solve order.	
12				
13			To change formula solve orders,	
14			use the Solve Order command on the PivotTable command bar.	

Figure 7.36 You can display the formulas for Calculated Fields and Calculated Items by choosing the List Formulas function from the PivotTable toolbar menu.

Handling Error Conditions

Error conditions in a PivotTable report usually result from division-by-zero errors. Although the message doesn't cause any problems with the PivotTable, it can certainly ruin the presentation effect, as demonstrated in Figure 7.37.

You can fix division-by-zero problems from the PivotTable Options dialog box. (You can open this dialog box by right-clicking on the PivotTable and choosing Table Options from the pop-up menu.) Just check the option For Error Values, Show, and then enter the text string you want to display in place of the error message. The text string can be up to 255 characters, although I recommend leaving the box blank (to display empty cells) or using a 0 or an asterisk, as shown in Figure 7.38.

	A	B	C
1	CATEGORY DESC	(All)	
2	PRODUCT DESC	(All)	
3			
4	STD DEV VALUE	INSURANCE	
5	CATEGORY NAME	RECOMMENDED	REQUIRED
6	Dairy Products	#DIV/0!	761.5540033
7	Grains/Cereals	#DIV/0!	#DIV/0!
8	Meat/Poultry	37.4766594	#DIV/0!
9	Seafood	256.9653933	#DIV/0!
10	Condiments	#DIV/0!	#DIV/0!
11	Confections	#DIV/0!	#DIV/0!

Figure 7.37 Unless fixed, division by zero errors can ruin your presentation.

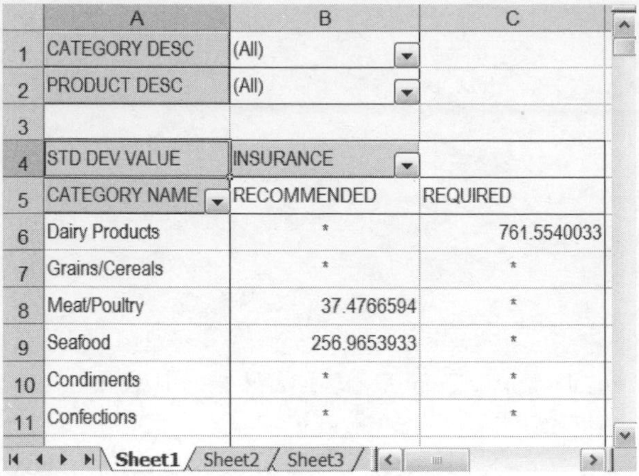

	A	B	C
1	CATEGORY DESC	(All)	
2	PRODUCT DESC	(All)	
3			
4	STD DEV VALUE	INSURANCE	
5	CATEGORY NAME	RECOMMENDED	REQUIRED
6	Dairy Products	*	761.5540033
7	Grains/Cereals	*	*
8	Meat/Poultry	37.4766594	*
9	Seafood	256.9653933	*
10	Condiments	*	*
11	Confections	*	*

Sheet1 / Sheet2 / Sheet3 /

Figure 7.38　An asterisk is now displayed instead of the division-by-zero error message.

Managing Data Area Fields

As you probably already know from practicing with the PivotTable reports and reading earlier sections of this book, PivotTables essentially perform some type of aggregate function on the field in the Data area. This might be a Count, a Sum, an Average, or a Min or Max. In addition to these well-known functions, you can also configure fields in the Data area to perform several other types of custom calculations, including

- Running totals
- Percentage of a specified cell, row, column, or grand total value
- Difference or percentage-difference from a base item, row, or column value

This section covers the basics of managing Data area fields and shows you how to change the type of aggregate function, calculate running totals, and display data as a percentage of a particular base item (that is a row total, column total, or grand total).

Changing the Aggregate Function and Using Custom Calculations

Fields dropped into the Data area of a PivotTable are automatically aggregated. If the field is an alphanumeric field, it is counted. If the field is a numeric field, it is summed. You can change this aggregate function — or summary type — by double-clicking the field in the Layout Manager or the Excel worksheet to bring up the PivotTable Field dialog box (see Figure 7.39).

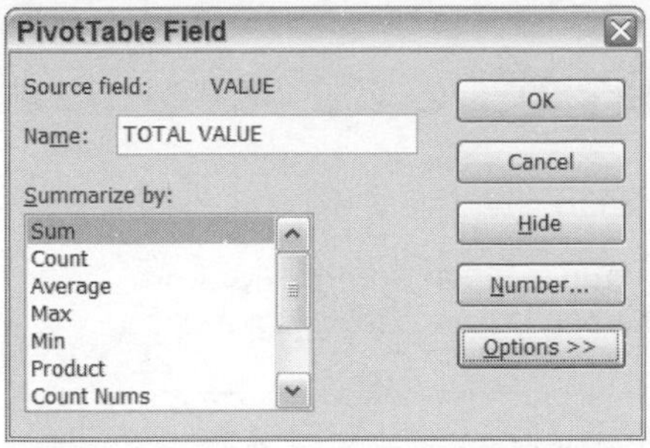

Figure 7.39   The aggregate function of a Data field is modified in the PivotTable Field dialog box.

The various types of aggregate functions are displayed in the Summarize By pane of the dialog box. Clicking the Hide button removes the field from the PivotTable report. Clicking the Number button brings up the Format Cells dialog box, where you can format the display of this Data area field. Clicking the Options button reveals the bottom part of this dialog box, as shown in Figure 7.40.

In the Show Data As drop-down box, you can select from the options listed in Table 7-3. Keep in mind that the aggregate function you select in the Summarize By pane in the top part of the PivotTable Field dialog box is closely related to the option you select in this Show Data As drop-down box. For example, a Count function used with a Running Total produces much different results than a Sum function used with a Running Total.

These options add a new dimension to how the data can be displayed in the PivotTable. Rather than just looking at numerical values, you can also examine how they are allocated as a percentage of some base field item, column, row, or report total. Using this feature, you can examine product revenue or cost as a percentage of a particular product category or compared to another product category. There are almost endless possibilities for how you can choose to display the data.

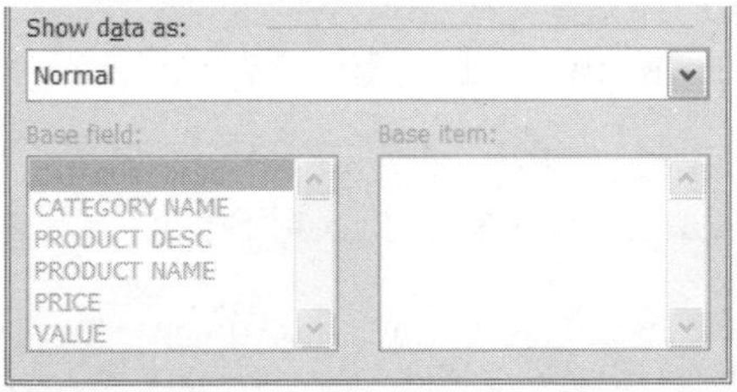

Figure 7.40   The bottom part of the PivotTable Field dialog box is displayed when you click Options.

Table 7.3 Custom Calculations

OPTION	DESCRIPTION
Normal	The Data area field is summarized in its normal way without any special function.
Difference From	The Data area field is summarized as a difference from a base field item. The next or previous item can also be selected.
% Of	The Data area field is shown as a percentage of a base field item.
% Difference From	The Data area field is shown as a percentage-difference from a base field item.
Running Total In	The Data area field is shown as a running total in a base field.
% Of Row	The Data area field is shown as a percentage of the total row value.
% Of Column	The Data area field is shown as a percentage of the total column value.
% Of Total	The Data area field is shown as a percentage of the total value displayed in the report.

Calculating Running Totals

Starting with a fresh view of the PivotTable report, complete these steps to configure a running total of Total Value by Category Name:

1. Drag Category Name to the Row area, Insurance to the Column area, and Value to the Data area of the PivotTable report.

2. Drag Value again (a second time) to the Data area of the PivotTable report.

3. Right-click the Data label in cell C4 and choose Order ⇨ Move To Column to display the Data area items in columns rather than in rows.

4. Verify that your PivotTable report looks like Figure 7.41.

5. Right-click Sum Of VALUE2 in cell C6, and then select Field Settings from the pop-up menu.

6. Type **RUNNING TOTAL** in the Name field, and then click the Options button to reveal the bottom part of the PivotTable Field dialog box.

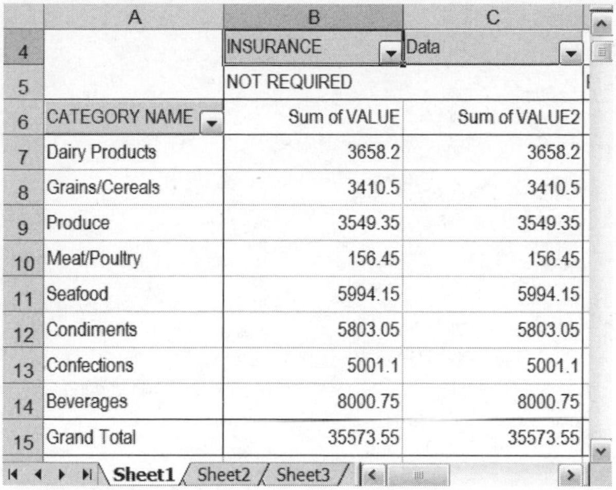

Figure 7.41   Start with this view of the PivotTable report that includes Value twice to see how a Running Total works.

7. Select Running Total In from the Show Data As drop-down box, and then select Category Name in the Base Field pane.

8. Verify that your PivotTable Field dialog box looks like Figure 7.42, and then click OK to change the field name, apply the running total calculation, and close the dialog box.

9. Verify that your PivotTable report now looks like Figure 7.43.

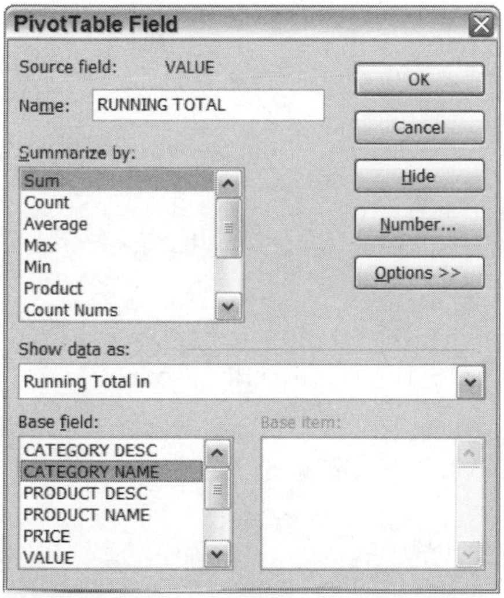

Figure 7.42   A running total of the Sum Of Total Value is calculated by Category Name.

	A	B	C
4		INSURANCE ▾	Data ▾
5		NOT REQUIRED	
6	CATEGORY NAME ▾	Sum of VALUE	RUNNING TOTAL
7	Dairy Products	3658.2	3658.2
8	Grains/Cereals	3410.5	7068.7
9	Produce	3549.35	10618.05
10	Meat/Poultry	156.45	10774.5
11	Seafood	5994.15	16768.65
12	Condiments	5803.05	22571.7
13	Confections	5001.1	27572.8
14	Beverages	8000.75	35573.55
15	Grand Total	35573.55	

Sheet1 / Sheet2 / Sheet3 /

Figure 7.43　A Running Total Of Value By Category Name is now displayed.

Showing Data as a Percentage of a Base Value

You can show Data area values as a percentage or percentage-difference of

- A row
- A column
- An item in a field (specific item, next item, or previous item)
- The total value displayed in the report

Complete these steps to use a custom calculation that shows the total value of Category Name as a percentage of the report total:

1. Using the PivotTable in this chapter, drag Category Name to the Row area, Insurance to the Column area, and Value to the Data area.

2. Right-click Sum Of VALUE in cell A4, and choose Field Settings from the pop-up menu to bring up the PivotTable Field dialog box.

3. Type **% OF INSUR CATG** in the Name field and click the Options button to reveal the bottom part of the PivotTable field dialog box.

4. Select % Of Total from the Show Data As drop-down box, and then click OK to change the field name, apply the calculation, and close the dialog box.

5. Verify that your PivotTable report now looks like Figure 7.44.

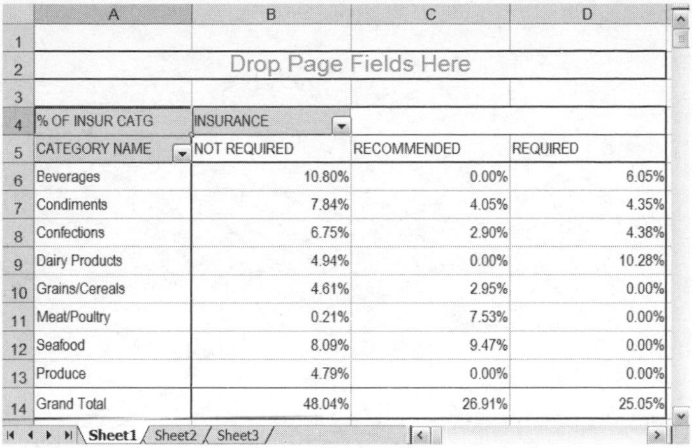

	A	B	C	D
1				
2		Drop Page Fields Here		
3				
4	% OF INSUR CATG	INSURANCE		
5	CATEGORY NAME	NOT REQUIRED	RECOMMENDED	REQUIRED
6	Beverages	10.80%	0.00%	6.05%
7	Condiments	7.84%	4.05%	4.35%
8	Confections	6.75%	2.90%	4.38%
9	Dairy Products	4.94%	0.00%	10.28%
10	Grains/Cereals	4.61%	2.95%	0.00%
11	Meat/Poultry	0.21%	7.53%	0.00%
12	Seafood	8.09%	9.47%	0.00%
13	Produce	4.79%	0.00%	0.00%
14	Grand Total	48.04%	26.91%	25.05%

H ◀ ▶ H \ **Sheet1** / Sheet2 / Sheet3 /

Figure 7.44 Total Value By Category Name shown as a percentage of the insurance category.

Trying It Out in the Real World

Robert King, a Sales Representative in the Northwind Trader's London office, is preparing an historical sales report for his supervisor, Steven Buchanan. Robert has heard that you are a magician with PivotTable reports and has enlisted your support to help him develop a report that shows the total net sales by country, month, and year. Robert knows that his supervisor will want to see the results ranked, and he also wants to display all countries, regardless of whether any sales were made that month. Robert has already obtained a database query that extracts the results from the NorthwindCS database. However, there was a small problem in the query that caused sales not to be included; only the component fields NetUnitPrice and Quantity were in the query results.

You are asked to help Robert complete the following objectives:

1. Create a PivotTable report from the SQL query created by the database administrator.

2. Create a calculated field called Sales that computes the product of NetUnitPrice and Qty.

3. Sort or rank the Total Sales by Country Within Year.

4. Display month in calendar order in the Column area of the PivotTable.

5. Display Total Sales in Accounting format with no decimal points.

Robert has provided you with the query shown here.

```
SELECT   Orders.ShipCountry                        AS [Country],
         Details.ProductID                         AS [Product],
         (Details.UnitPrice * (1-Discount))        AS [NetUnitPrice],
         Details.Quantity                          AS [Qty],
         LEFT(CONVERT(Char(10),OrderDate, 109),3)  AS [Month],
         DATEPART(Year,OrderDate)                  AS [Year]
FROM Orders Orders
INNER JOIN "Order Details" Details
ON Orders.OrderID = Details.OrderID
```

ON THE WEB You can download the ch07_realworld.txt query file to your computer from the website www.wiley.com/go/excelreporting.

When you're finished, the PivotTable report should look like Figure 7.45.

Getting Down to Business

Follow these steps to complete this exercise:

1. From Excel, choose Data ⇨ PivotTable And PivotChart Report.

2. Select External Data Source, and then click Next.

3. When the PivotTable And PivotChart Wizard – Step 2 Of 3 appears, click Get Data.

	A	B	J	K	L	M	N	O
1								
2								
3	Total Sales							
4	Year ▾	Country ▾	Aug	Sep	Oct	Nov	Dec	Grand Total
5	1996	Germany	172,227	16,590	140,976	81,136	7,923	2,383,670
6		USA	37,248	114,928	133,181	19,606	149,104	2,376,347
7		Austria	-	-	-	130,058	100,370	800,382
8		Brazil	59,256	676		3,039	73,719	638,458
9		France	1,215	10,922	11,684	150,585	73	608,081
10		Venezuela	5,677	3,391	3,360	3,591	8,282	221,537
11		UK	1,349	1,021	1,314	33,100	21,784	194,987
12		Ireland	-	40,360	6,412	-	20,590	184,872
13		Sweden	17,086	-	7,090		5,351	118,944
14		Mexico	7,221	5,664	6,307	5,208	-	112,004
15		Canada	-	-	24,652	-	12,903	73,234
16		Spain	1,170	9,917	3,546	272	-	50,002
17		Switzerland	-	-	-	-	2,967	37,426
18		Belgium	-	8,352	-	-	-	36,086
19		Denmark	-	-	670	3,367	7,228	31,482
20		Finland	2,860	-	5,263	-		21,880
21		Portugal	-	-	6,671	258	1,200	18,643

H ◀ ▶ H \Sheet1 / Sheet2 / Sheet3 /

Figure 7.45 Format the PivotTable to look as shown here.

4. When the Choose Data Source dialog box appears, verify that Use The Query Wizard To Create/Edit Queries is unchecked, and then select the NorthwindCS Database data source and click OK.

5. When the Microsoft Query program is launched, you are presented with the Add Tables dialog box. Close this dialog box, and then click the SQL button to paste in the SQL query.

6. Click OK to close the SQL dialog box, and then click OK again to acknowledge that the query cannot be displayed graphically.

7. Click the Return Data To Excel button to return the data to Microsoft Excel.

8. Click Finish when the PivotTable And PivotChart Wizard – Step 2 of 3 appears.

9. Drag Year and then Country to the Row area. Keep in mind that Country should be in the Inner Row field.

10. Double-click Country to bring up the PivotTable Field dialog box, click Show Items With No Data, and then click OK.

11. Drag Month to the Column area.

NOTE If Month does not automatically sort, select the Column Heading in cell C3 and choose Data ➪ Sort to bring up the Sort dialog box. Click the Options button to bring up the Sort Options dialog box where you can sort by month.

12. Click anywhere in the Data area; and then choose Formulas ➪ Calculated Field from the PivotTable toolbar to bring up the Calculated Field dialog box.

13. Type **Sales** in the Name field and **= NetUnitPrice * Qty** in the Formula field. Click OK to create the calculated field, add it to the PivotTable report, and close the Calculated Field dialog box.

14. Double-click Sum Of Sales in cell A3 to bring up the PivotTable Field dialog box. Type **Total Sales** in the Name field, and then click the Number button to bring up the Format Cells dialog box.

15. Select Accounting in the Category pane, 0 in the Decimal Places field, and None in Symbol drop-down box. Click OK to close this dialog box, and then click OK again to close the PivotTable Field dialog box.

16. Double-click Country to bring up the PivotTable Field dialog box. Click the Advanced button to bring up the PivotTable Field Advanced Options dialog box.

17. Click Descending in the AutoSort options, and then select Total Sales from the Using Field drop-down box.

18. Click OK to close this dialog box, and then click OK again to close the PivotTable Field dialog box.

WATCH THE VIDEO **To see how this example is completed, click the** **ch0703_video.avi file at** www.wiley.com/go/excelreporting **and watch the video.**

Reviewing What You Did

This example provides you with some more practice with some of the material covered in this chapter, including how to create a calculated field, apply an advanced sort based on the data in the Data area, and format fields in the Data area. There's a tremendous amount of material in this section, and I recommend that you experiment with numerous options, functions, and tools to get a better handle on how they affect the report.

Chapter Review

This chapter showed you how to design and format PivotTable reports using the powerful tools and functions available in Excel. It assumed that you had already read Chapter 2 or were at least familiar with the basic features and functions of PivotTable reports. The chapter started with an introduction to the Layout Manager and the PivotTable toolbar, which demonstrated how reports could be shaped and formatted from a static, unchanging diagram. After that, the chapter focused on the numerous formatting tools available and provided several examples of how they affect the PivotTable report. Next, you learned about the various functions included with PivotTable reports for creating calculated fields and modifying the aggregate function type of Data area fields.

CHAPTER 8

Managing PivotTable Data

You can manage the data in PivotTable reports in a number of ways. You can trigger automatic data refreshes, toggle whether the underlying dataset is saved with the PivotTable, and configure multiple PivotTables to share the same source data. This chapter covers the data management features available with PivotTable reports and provides a perspective on how you can use these various features to simplify the management and operation of your reports.

This chapter starts by describing the various data options available in the PivotTable Options dialog box. It then shows you how to change the PivotTable to use a different database or OLAP data source. Following that, it walks you through copying PivotTable reports and configuring them to either share the same dataset or use a separate dataset. It also discusses how ghost values can appear when an underlying SQL query is modified. The chapter concludes with a real-world exercise that helps bring together some of the topics covered into a realistic scenario that you might actually encounter in your organization.

Before You Begin

Start this chapter by creating a new PivotTable report from an external data source that accesses the NorthwindCS database.

To create the PivotTable report and follow along with the example used here, complete these steps:

1. From Excel, choose Data ➪ PivotTable And PivotChart Report.

2. Select External Data Source and click Next.

3. When the PivotTable And PivotChart Wizard Step 2 of 3 appears, click Get Data.

4. When the Choose Data Source dialog box appears, verify that Use The Query Wizard To Create/Edit Queries is unchecked, select the NorthwindCS Database data source, and then click OK.

5. When the Microsoft Query program is launched, you are presented with the Add Tables dialog box. Close this dialog box and click the SQL button in the toolbar.

6. Paste or type the following query into the SQL dialog box and click OK:

```
SELECT ord.ShipCountry                    AS [SHIP COUNTRY],
       shp.CompanyName                    AS [SHIPPER],
       CASE
         WHEN ord.ShippedDate IS NULL
               THEN 'NOT SHIPPED'
               ELSE 'SHIPPED'
               END                        AS [SHIP STATUS],
       CASE
         WHEN ord.ShippedDate IS NULL
               THEN 'LATE'
         WHEN ord.ShippedDate > ord.RequiredDate
               THEN 'LATE'
               ELSE 'ON TIME'
               END                        AS [SCHEDULE],
       1                                  AS [# SHIPMENTS]
FROM Orders ord
INNER JOIN Shippers shp ON ord.ShipVia = shp.ShipperID
```

ON THE WEB You can download the ch08_example.txt query file to your computer from the companion website at `www.wiley.com/go/ excelreporting`. Look for this document in either the Chap08.zip file or Chap08 directory, depending on which .zip file you download.

7. Click the Return Data To Microsoft Excel button to return the data and continue.

8. Click Finish to create the PivotTable report outline.

9. Drag Shipper to the Row area, Schedule to the Column area, and # Shipments to the Data area.

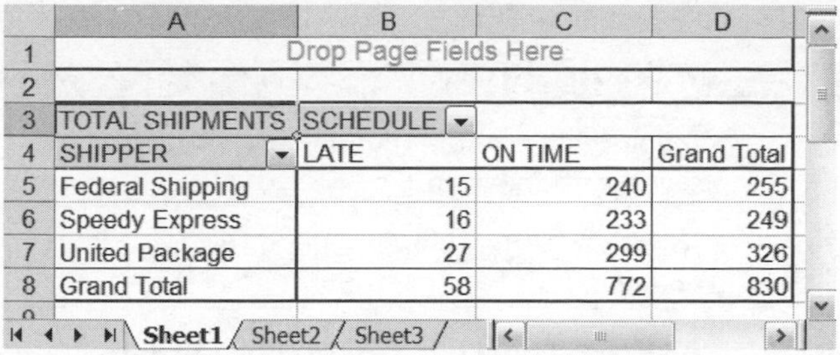

	A	B	C	D
1	Drop Page Fields Here			
2				
3	TOTAL SHIPMENTS	SCHEDULE		
4	SHIPPER	LATE	ON TIME	Grand Total
5	Federal Shipping	15	240	255
6	Speedy Express	16	233	249
7	United Package	27	299	326
8	Grand Total	58	772	830

Figure 8.1 You use this PivotTable report for the examples in later sections of this chapter.

10. Rename the Data area field Sum Of # Shipments to **Total Shipments**.
11. Verify that your PivotTable report looks like Figure 8.1.

WATCH THE VIDEO **To see how the PivotTable report shown in Figure 8.1 is created, watch the video ch0801_video.avi at** `www.wiley.com/go/excelreporting`.

Configuring PivotTable Data Options

You configure PivotTable data options from the PivotTable options dialog box. Right-click the report and choose PivotTable Options from the pop-up menu. Alternatively, you can choose Table Options from the PivotTable toolbar to bring up the PivotTable Options dialog box shown in Figure 8.2.

The options in the bottom half of the dialog box are separated into Data Source Options and External Data Options. The Data Source Options control refresh frequency, drill-down functionality, and whether data is saved with the report. The External Data Options control password, query, and memory functions. Table 8.1 provides a description of each option in this dialog box.

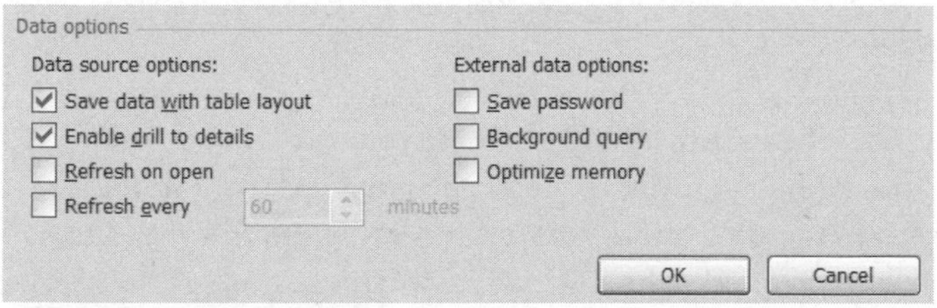

Figure 8.2 Data options are controlled in the bottom half of the PivotTable Options dialog box shown here.

Table 8.1 Explanation of PivotTable Data Options

OPTION NAME	DESCRIPTION
Save Data With Table Layout	Toggles whether the underlying dataset is saved with the report.
Enable Drill To Details	Toggles whether drill-down features are enabled.
Refresh On Open	Toggles whether the report is immediately refreshed when it is first opened.
Refresh Every	Refreshes the report every *n* minutes.
Save Password	Toggles whether the password is saved with the report.
Background Query	Toggles whether the report refresh halts all operations in the Excel worksheet until the refresh is completed or whether the user can continue working while the refresh query runs in the background.
Optimize Memory	Toggles whether Excel should optimize available memory during a refresh. Check this option if you encounter an insufficient memory error message.

Saving Data with the Table Layout

Unchecking the Save Data With Table Layout option removes the underlying dataset from the worksheet when the report is saved and closed. This can be useful if you need to email the report to a programmer for troubleshooting or to another user who can refresh it. Rather than trying to send a huge file, you can just send the PivotTable report shape with the SQL query and DSN connection information. The report looks exactly the same with this option checked; it's just that the underlying data is not available, so changes to the report cannot be made until the report is refreshed.

TIP I uncheck this option when I provide a PivotTable report to a user who does not want the underlying dataset. This option is also a good workaround when the user has access to the data source but can't receive the file with the dataset included because of email attachment size restrictions.

Enable Drill To Details

The Enable Drill To Details option toggles whether users are allowed to drill down on the details. When this option is checked, users are not able to drill down on report data. This can be useful when you want to prevent users from creating new worksheets that result from drilling down on report data.

> **NOTE** This option does not pertain to data sources such as OLAP where drill-down functionality is not available.

Refresh On Open

Check the Refresh On Open option to automatically refresh the PivotTable report when the Excel document is first opened. This feature can be useful when the report user has no experience with PivotTable reports. Simply check this option, and the report automatically refreshes whenever it is first opened. (Note that the user must click on Enable Automatic Refresh when the Query Refresh dialog box comes up, as explained in the next paragraph.)

As an added security measure, Excel prompts the user with the Query Refresh dialog box shown in Figure 8.3 if the Refresh On Open or the Refresh Every options is checked. Users must click on Enable Automatic Refresh to enable automatic refreshes to work.

> **WARNING** Keep in mind that it is possible that a malicious query could update or delete rows from the database tables. So be sure the query is verified to be safe and that you trust the source of this report before enabling the automatic refresh feature.

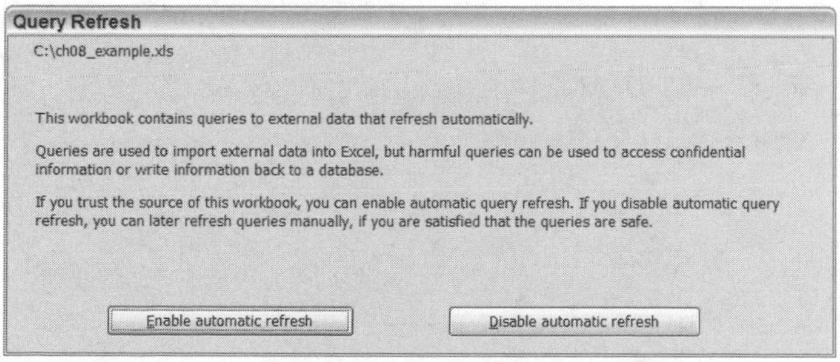

Figure 8.3 The Query Refresh message appears when PivotTable reports are set to automatically refresh or refresh at specific intervals.

Refresh Every

The Refresh Every option schedules the report to be refreshed every *n* minutes. The value for minutes must be an integer between 1 and 9999. This option is useful for reports designed to regularly monitor transactions or statistics. For example, a data entry processing manager might want to monitor the total number of transactions processed throughout the day and the average transaction processed each hour. Using this option, the report can automatically be updated every 15 minutes to show the updated transactions processed by the data entry staff.

Complete these steps to see how the Refresh Every option works using the NorthwindCS database:

1. Verify that your Excel report looks like Figure 8.1.

2. Right-click the PivotTable, and then select Table Options from the pop-up menu to bring up the PivotTable Options dialog box.

3. Check the option Refresh Every, set the minutes to 1, and click OK to set the refresh frequency to every minute and to close the PivotTable Options dialog box (Figure 8.4).

4. Open the NorthwindCS.adp database from Microsoft Access.

5. Click OK to close the Northwind start-up screen.

6. Click on Orders in the Main Switchboard dialog box to bring up the Orders dialog box.

7. Change the Ship Via on the first order (order 10248) from Federal to Speedy and close the Orders dialog box.

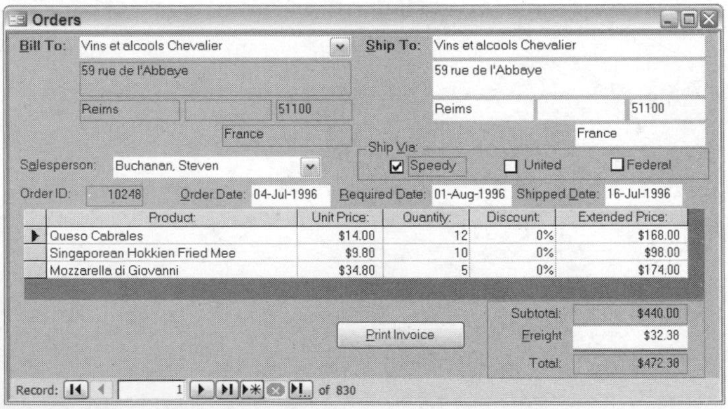

Figure 8.4 The PivotTable report picks up the Ship Via change during its next automatic refresh that is scheduled to run in one-minute intervals.

8. Switch back to the Excel report. If you compare what's shown in Figure 8.5 with what was shown in Figure 8.1, you can see that the count of On Time shipments has increased by 1 for Speedy and decreased by 1 for Federal.

NOTE It may take up to one minute for the refresh operation to run.

Keep in mind that as with the Refresh On Open option, when you use the Refresh Every option, the Query Refresh dialog box still appears when the report is initially opened. The report user must click the Enable Automatic Refresh button in this dialog box to enable the Refresh Every feature to work.

Save Password

The Save Password option toggles whether the password to the external data source is saved with the report. Although this option may be accessible, it is only relevant when the PivotTable accesses an external data source where a password is actually required. For example, if the PivotTable report uses an SQL database as its data source, and the database is authenticated to using SQL Server security, this option toggles whether the password is saved along with the user login or not. However, if Windows NT authentication is used instead, this option has no effect on the PivotTable, even though it is still accessible.

Uncheck this option if you want the user to specify a password in order to refresh the report or to edit the SQL query. You can also uncheck this option when you want to change the data source. (Read the section "Uncheck Save Password" a little later in this chapter to find out more about changing the data source of a PivotTable report when SQL authentication is used to access the database.)

Updated numbers from refresh

	A	B	C	D
1	Drop Page Fields Here			
2				
3	TOTAL SHIPMENTS	SCHEDULE ▾		
4	SHIPPER ▾	LATE	ON TIME	Grand Total
5	Federal Shipping	15	239	254
6	Speedy Express	16	234	250
7	United Package	27	299	326
8	Grand Total	58	772	830

Sheet1 / Sheet2 / Sheet3 /

Figure 8.5 The Refresh Every option automatically updates the report with the new shipping information.

Managing Data Sources

Sometimes it's necessary to change the PivotTable report to use another database or database server. This section outlines the various methods available for changing the report to use another data source. It also covers how to configure reports to share the same dataset, thereby reducing the size of the Excel workbook and the amount of memory required to open the reports in the workbook.

Identifying and Changing Valid Data Sources

If you have several database servers and/or databases that you use for testing, production, and development, you might find it necessary to change the PivotTable report's data source. There are three methods for changing a valid data source outlined in this section:

- Edit the SQL query
- Uncheck Save Password
- Temporarily disable access

Editing the SQL Statement

In the example shown in the "Before You Begin" section earlier in this chapter, the table names are not fully qualified in the SQL query:

```
FROM Orders ord
INNER JOIN Shippers shp ON ord.ShipVia = shp.ShipperID
```

The data source can be changed by either fully qualifying the table names with the new data source information or by modifying the existing qualification (if the objects are already fully qualified). For example, to modify the query to use the Northwind database on the Wiley server, all the tables in the query should be fully-qualified in the format: Server.Database.Owner.Object. Thus, the updated query with fully qualified table names looks like this:

```
FROM Wiley.Northwind.dbo.Orders ord

INNER JOIN Wiley.Northwind.dbo.Shippers shp

      ON ord.ShipVia = shp.ShipperID
```

If the database server has not changed, only the Database, Owner, and Object must be included in the qualification. Unless otherwise specified, dbo is the default owner for most objects created in an SQL database.

I generally avoid using this method to change the data source because it's a lot of work, especially when there are numerous tables used throughout the query. This method also does not work for OLAP data sources because queries are not used to access the cube's data.

Uncheck Save Password

If you are using an SQL login account and password to access an SQL database, just follow these steps to change the data source:

1. Uncheck Save Password in the PivotTable Options dialog box.
2. Save and then close the PivotTable report.
3. Reopen the report, right-click the report, and select Refresh Data from the pop-up menu.
4. When the SQL Server Login dialog box appears, enter the new database server, user login account, and password.
5. Click the Options button (notice that the bottom portion of this dialog box appears and the Options button becomes disabled). Select the new database, as shown in Figure 8.6.
6. Recheck Save Password in the PivotTable Options dialog box (assuming that this is the desired setting).

I think that this is the most efficient and simplest way to change the data source of a PivotTable report. However, it only works when a user login and password are specified with a database data source.

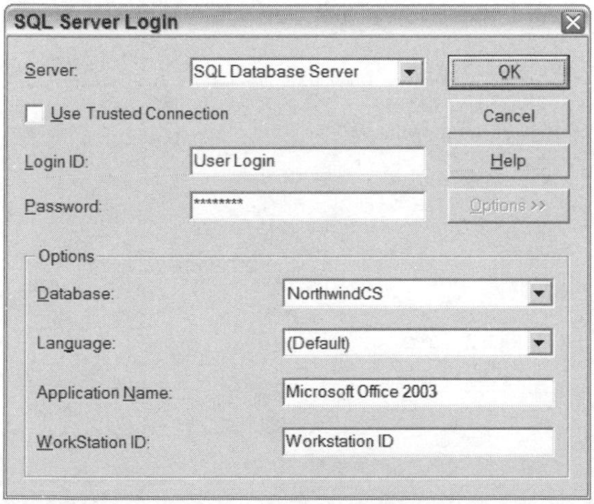

Figure 8.6   You can select a new SQL server and database from this dialog box.

Temporarily Disable Access

If the report uses an OLAP data source or an SQL database with Windows NT authentication, you can change the data source by temporarily disabling access to it. How can you disable access, you ask? You can either unplug the network cable from your computer or disable the local area network connection from the Windows operating system. Considering that the network cable might be buried under your desk, I generally recommend disabling the network connection. You'll probably get fewer strange looks from your colleagues by using this latter method.

You can disable the local area connection from the Windows operating system by following these steps:

1. From the Windows operating system, choose Start ⇨ Programs ⇨ Accessories ⇨ Communication ⇨ Network Connections to bring up the Network Connections dialog box.

NOTE If you are not using the Classic Start Menu with Windows XP, choose All Programs instead of Programs from the Windows XP Start button.

2. Under LAN or High-Speed Internet, right-click Local Area Connection, and choose Disable from the pop-up menu.

3. Open the PivotTable report, right-click it, and select Refresh Data.

4. Wait about one minute for the Refresh Data operation to time out. If the data source is an SQL database, the Microsoft SQL Server Login message appears, as shown in Figure 8.7.

If the data source is an OLAP cube, a failed initialization message appears, as shown in Figure 8.8.

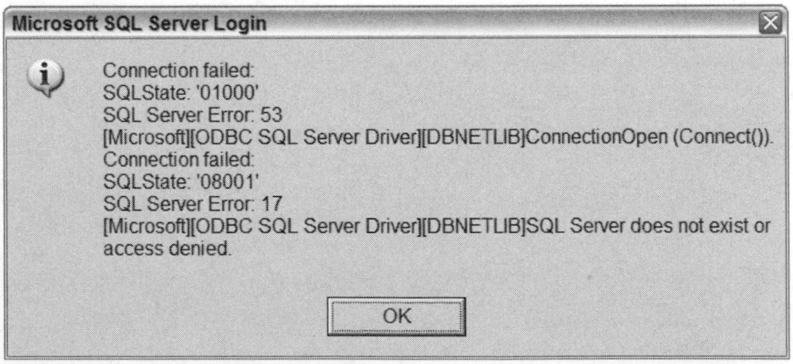

Figure 8.7 This message box appears when the PivotTable is unable to connect to an SQL database data source.

Figure 8.8 This message box appears when the PivotTable is unable to connect to an OLAP data source.

5. Click OK to acknowledge the message shown in Figure 8.7 or in Figure 8.8.

6. Under LAN Or High-Speed Internet, right-click Local Area Connection, and choose Enable from the pop-up menu.

7. Enter the new data source information and click OK to refresh the report with the updated data source.

As soon as the Local Area Network connection is re-enabled, you can access the database or OLAP cube from Excel. If you've spent a lot of time creating and formatting the PivotTable report, this can be a nifty alternative to re-creating the report from scratch.

Configuring a PivotTable to Share Source Data

Multiple PivotTable reports that exist in the same Excel workbook can share the same source data. I've found this to be particularly useful when there are several PivotTables reports that all use the same query but have a different layout or view. This configuration provides the following benefits:

- Reduced file size and memory requirements because only one copy of the source data has to be stored

- Refreshing one PivotTable report refreshes the data for all the reports that share the same source data

- Changes made to the SQL query in one PivotTable report are automatically applied to all reports that share the same source data

- Changes to Data Options in one PivotTable report are automatically applied to all reports that share the same source data

In order to configure another PivotTable report to share the same source data, just copy and paste the PivotTable report. You can also choose Edit ➪ Move Or Copy Sheet to copy the entire worksheet. This latter method works best when you want to copy everything in the worksheet, including the PivotTable, formats, titles, and printer settings.

Follow these steps to configure the PivotTable report to share the same source data:

1. Select all the cells in the PivotTable report and choose Edit ⇨ Copy to copy the PivotTable into memory.

2. Move to another worksheet in the workbook or to another location in the same worksheet and choose Edit ⇨ Paste to paste the PivotTable report.

WARNING Copying the cells or the worksheet to another workbook creates a separate memory space for the workbook, resulting in the PivotTable using its own copy of source data.

Configuring a PivotTable to Use Separate Source Data

There are two ways you can copy an existing PivotTable report while configuring it to use its own copy of source data. The first method is to copy the PivotTable into memory and paste it into a different workbook. (If required, it can then be moved or copied back to the original workbook.) The second method is to create a PivotTable report based on another PivotTable. The option to create Another PivotTable Report Or PivotChart Report (shown in Figure 8.9) appears only when a PivotTable already exists in the Excel workbook.

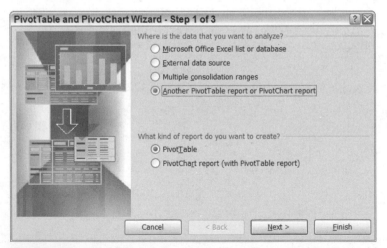

Figure 8.9   PivotTable reports can be based on another PivotTable report in the same workbook.

I prefer using the first option when the layout, formatting, and printer settings must be retained. Of course, the second method is more efficient when these elements are not required. I demonstrate how to use the second method here.

To copy a PivotTable report that uses its own copy of source data, follow these steps:

1. Click the worksheet and cell where the new PivotTable is to be copied (keep in mind that the existing PivotTable must be in the same workbook).

2. From Excel, choose Data ⇨ PivotTable And PivotChart Report.

3. Select Another PivotTable Report or PivotChart Report, and then click Next to bring up the PivotTable And PivotChart Wizard Step 2 of 3 dialog box shown in Figure 8.10.

4. Select the desired PivotTable report to copy, and then click Finish to copy the PivotTable report.

This method copies an existing PivotTable report and configures it to use its own copy of source data. Keep in mind that this method requires you to refresh each PivotTable report individually. Changes made to the Data Options or SQL query are not automatically replicated to the other copies of the PivotTable reports as they are when the reports are configured to use the same copy of source data.

TIP The PivotTable toolbar includes a button to refresh all PivotTable reports in the workbook. Just add the button by clicking the down arrow next to the X in the top-right of the toolbar.

Purging Ghost Values

Sometimes items that once appeared in the PivotTable drop-down list continue to appear in the drop-down list, even though the item no longer exists in the dataset. This can happen when the dataset becomes very large, the data source is a database, and the query or dataset is modified. The only way to clear these old items from the report is to recreate the PivotTable report from scratch.

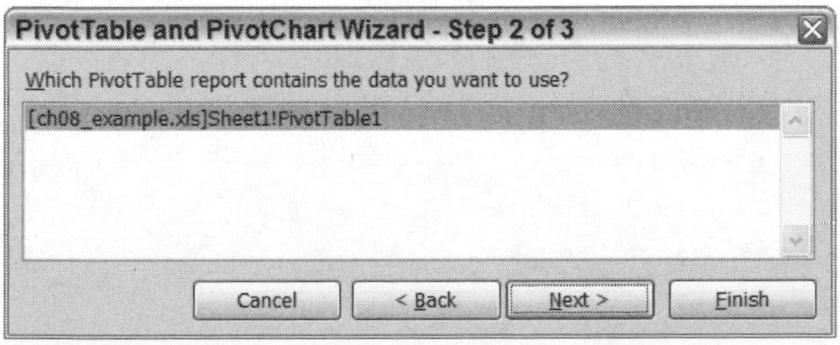

PivotTable and PivotChart Wizard - Step 2 of 3

Which PivotTable report contains the data you want to use?

[ch08_example.xls]Sheet1!PivotTable1

Cancel   < Back   Next >   Finish

Figure 8.10 Select the PivotTable Report that you want to copy in this dialog box.

TIP This software bug is particularly bothersome when you have put a lot of work into formatting the PivotTable report. Hold off on adding labels, page breaks, and formats until you are sure that the query and the dataset are correct, as the ghost values are often confusing and frustrating for report users.

Trying It Out in the Real World

Margaret Peacock, a Sales Representative in the Seattle, Washington, office of Northwind Traders has been asked by her manager, Andrew Fuller, to identify and delete all the orders in the NorthwindCS database that have not been shipped. Margaret has enlisted your help to develop a PivotTable report that displays the Order ID, Shipper, and Customer ID for all orders that have not yet shipped. She needs two copies of the report. The first report should contain the original data before any modifications were made. The second report should automatically query the database every minute and update the report with the new information. Margaret will delete one order at a time, so the first report should provide the Order ID, Shipper Name, and Customer ID, while the second report shows only a total count of remaining orders that need to be deleted from the database.

Getting Down to Business

Follow these steps to complete this exercise:

1. From Excel, choose Data ⇨ PivotTable And PivotChart Report.

2. Select External Data Source and click Next.

3. When the PivotTable And PivotChart Wizard Step 2 of 3 appears, click Get Data.

4. When the Choose Data Source dialog box appears, verify that Use The Query Wizard To Create/Edit Queries is unchecked, select the North-windCS Database data source, and then click OK.

5. When the Microsoft Query program is launched, you are presented with the Add Tables dialog box. Close this dialog box and click the SQL button.

6. Paste or type the following query into the SQL dialog box and click OK:

```
SELECT shp.CompanyName   AS [SHIPPER],
       ord.OrderID       AS [ORDER ID],
       ord.CustomerID    AS [CUSTOMER ID]
```

```
FROM    Orders ord
INNER JOIN Shippers shp ON ord.ShipVia = shp.ShipperID
WHERE ShippedDate is Null
```

ON THE WEB You can download the ch08_rwe.txt query file to your computer from the companion website at www.wiley.com/go/ excelreporting.

7. Click the Return Data To Microsoft Excel button to return the data and continue.

8. Click Finish when the PivotTable And PivotChart Wizard Step 2 of 3 dialog box appears to create the PivotTable report outline.

9. Drag Shipper, Customer ID, and Order ID to the Row area, ensuring that the Shipper is the outermost Row area field and Order ID is the innermost Row area field.

10. Double-click Customer ID to bring up the PivotTable Field dialog box. Click None for Subtotals, and then click OK to suppress subtotals by Customer ID and close the dialog box.

11. Drag Shipper from the PivotTable Field List to the Data area.

12. Rename the Data area field Count of Shipper to # **Orders**.

13. Verify that your PivotTable report looks like Figure 8.11.

14. Click on cell A1 in Sheet2 of the Excel workbook, and then choose Data ↪ PivotTable And PivotChart Report.

	A	B	C	D
1		Drop Page Fields Here		
2				
3	# ORDERS			
4	SHIPPER	CUSTOMER ID	ORDER ID	Total
5	Federal Shipping	BLAUS	11058	1
6		ERNSH	11008	1
7		GREAL	11040	1
8			11061	1
9		LAMAI	11051	1
10		RANCH	11019	1
11	Federal Shipping Total			6
12	Speedy Express	CACTU	11054	1
13		LEHMS	11070	1
14		LILAS	11065	1
15			11071	1
16	Speedy Express Total			4
17	United Package	BONAP	11076	1

Sheet1 / Sheet2 / Sheet3

Figure 8.11 Format the first PivotTable report to look like this.

15. Select Another PivotTable Report Or PivotChart Report, and then click Finish to copy the PivotTable report shown in Figure 8.11 to Sheet2 of the Excel workbook.

16. Drag Shipper to the Data area, and then rename the field from Count of Shipper to **# Orders**.

17. Right-click the PivotTable report and select Table Options from the pop-up menu to bring up the PivotTable Options dialog box.

18. Check the option Refresh Every, set the minutes to 1, and click OK to set the refresh frequency to one minute and to close the PivotTable Options dialog box.

WATCH THE VIDEO You can see how this PivotTable report is created and formatting by watching video ch0802_video.avi at www.wiley.com/go/ excelreporting.

Reviewing What You Did

This example provides you with some additional perspective on why you might copy an existing PivotTable report and configure it to uses its own copy of source data, rather than share the source data with another PivotTable report. In the real world, you're likely to encounter an array of situations where you must determine whether the source data should be shared among the various PivotTable reports in an Excel workbook or stored as separate copies. This is also true for the other data options covered in this chapter. I recommend that you experiment with the other Data options and with changing the data source of PivotTable reports that use Windows NT authentication and SQL Server authentication.

Chapter Review

This chapter focused on the data options available with PivotTable reports. It covered how to change the source data location for a PivotTable report using a variety of different methods. It also described how each method works and what method is most appropriate for a particular situation. Finally, this chapter showed you how to copy PivotTable reports and configure them to share or not share the same source data.

CHAPTER 9

Exploring PivotChart
Functionality

A PivotChart report is similar to a PivotTable report in many ways. Fields can be dragged on or off the report, the shape and data summarization methods are easily customized, and changes can be made interactively. The principal difference is that information is graphically displayed in a PivotChart as opposed to numerically displayed in a PivotTable.

Entire books have been dedicated to Excel charts because there is a substantial amount of material to cover. I don't try to include all that information in this chapter. Instead, this chapter covers only the core chart features with an emphasis on the narrower topic of a PivotChart, and how this technology can be used to complement or even supplement a PivotTable report.

This chapter starts by providing an example of how you can create a PivotChart from scratch using the NorthwindCS database. After you've created the PivotChart, the chapter identifies the major components and outlines the similarities and differences between a PivotChart and a PivotTable. It also covers the terminology and the various components of a PivotChart, including a brief explanation of the PivotChart layout. It outlines the basic formatting functions available, including how to customize the chart type, use 3-D charts, and configure display settings. Following that, it discusses PivotChart options for setting a chart title, displaying a chart legend, and adding a data table. The chapter concludes with a real-world exercise that ties together several of the topics covered into a realistic scenario that you might encounter in your own organization.

Before You Begin

Start this chapter by creating a new PivotTable and PivotChart report from an external data source that accesses the NorthwindCS database.

Complete these steps to create the PivotChart report and follow along with the example used here:

1. From Excel, choose Data ➪ PivotTable And PivotChart Report to bring up the PivotTable And PivotChart Wizard - Step 1 of 3 dialog box.

2. Select External Data Source from the top of the dialog box, PivotChart Report (With PivotTable Report) at the bottom of the dialog box, and click Next to continue to the next step (see Figure 9.1).

3. When the PivotTable And PivotChart Wizard - Step 2 of 3 dialog box appears, click Get Data to bring up the Choose Data Source dialog box.

4. When the Choose Data Source dialog box appears, verify that Use The Query Wizard To Create/Edit Queries is unchecked, select the NorthwindCS Database data source, and click OK.

5. When the Microsoft Query program is launched, you are presented with the Add Tables dialog box. Close this dialog box and click the SQL button.

6. Paste or type the following query into the SQL dialog box and click OK:

```
SELECT ProductName                        AS [Product Name],
       (dtl.UnitPrice * dtl.Quantity)     AS [Order Amount],
       ord.Freight                        AS [Freight],
       dtl.Quantity                       AS [Quantity],
       cat.CategoryName                   AS [Category Name],
       DATEPART(YEAR, ShippedDate)        AS [Year],
       DATEPART(MONTH, ShippedDate)       AS [Month],
        CASE
            WHEN pro.Discontinued = '0'
                THEN '0 - Available'
                ELSE '1 - Discontinued'
                END                       AS [Status]
FROM "Order Details" dtl
INNER JOIN Orders ord ON dtl.OrderID = ord.OrderID
INNER JOIN Products pro ON dtl.ProductID = pro.ProductID
INNER JOIN Categories cat ON pro.CategoryID = cat.CategoryID
WHERE ShippedDate is NOT NULL
```

ON THE WEB You can download the ch09_example.txt query file to your computer from the companion website at www.wiley.com/go/excelreporting. Look for this document in either the Chap09.zip file or Chap09 directory, depending on which .zip file you download.

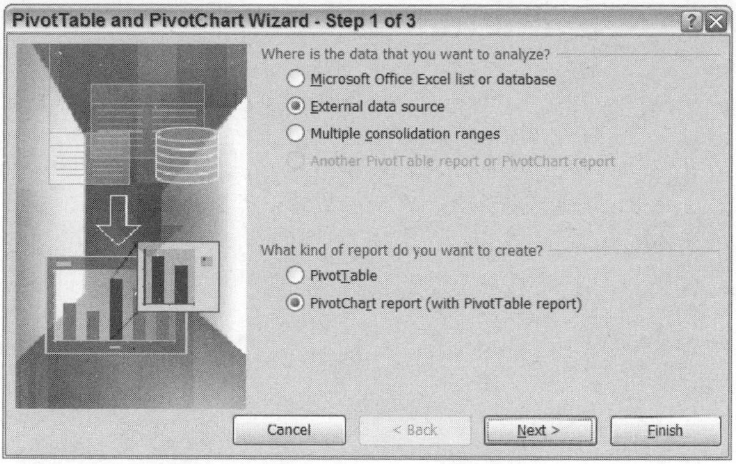

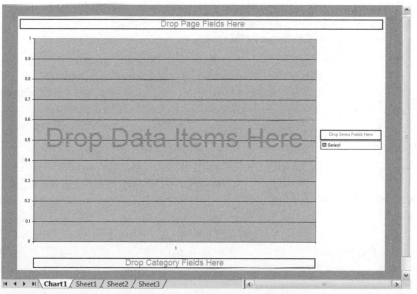

Figure 9.1 Click the PivotChart Report option near the bottom of this dialog box to create a PivotChart that is linked to a PivotTable.

7. Click the Return Data To Microsoft Excel button to return the data to Excel and continue.

8. When the PivotTable And PivotChart Wizard — Step 2 of 3 dialog box appears, click Finish to create the PivotTable and the PivotChart.

9. Verify that you see a blank PivotChart in the Chart1 worksheet tab as shown in Figure 9.2.

Figure 9.2 The PivotTable report appears in the Sheet1 workbook tab, and the PivotChart appears in the Chart1 workbook tab, as shown here.

Basic Components and Terminology

Many of the same concepts, terminology, and features of a PivotTable also apply to a PivotChart. This section highlights the similarities and explains the differences between these two types of reporting tools. It also identifies the major components and introduces some new terminology. This section covers these topics :

- Creating a PivotChart
- Terminology and display
- PivotChart toolbar
- PivotChart Field List
- PivotChart location

Creating a PivotChart

You can create a PivotChart by using either the PivotTable And PivotChart Wizard or by clicking the Chart Wizard button in the PivotTable toolbar. The preceding "Before You Begin" section provided an example of how the Wizard is used to create both a PivotTable and a PivotChart at the same time. Using the Chart Wizard button, the PivotChart is generated from an existing PivotTable report. Note that both methods require that a PivotTable be linked to the PivotChart.

> **NOTE** A PivotChart is always linked to a PivotTable; a PivotChart cannot exist on its own. Many of the advanced functions, such as modifying the underlying SQL query, must be initiated from the PivotTable as these functions are not accessible from the PivotChart.

The PivotChart can be displayed on its own worksheet tab or as an object in the same worksheet of the PivotTable. Regardless of the display, a change to the PivotTable results in a corresponding change to the PivotChart, and vice-versa.

Terminology and Display

A PivotChart uses much of the same terminology as a PivotTable. For example, in a PivotTable there is a Page area, a Row area, a Column area, and a Data area. In a PivotChart, the same areas are available except that the Row area fields of a PivotTable are called Category Axis fields in a PivotChart, and Column area fields are called Series Axis fields. The location is also different for these two types of fields. Series Axis fields are usually shown on the right, and Category Axis fields are usually shown at the bottom of a PivotChart.

To see how this works with the PivotChart you created in the "Before You Begin" section of this chapter, follow these steps:

1. Drag Category Name to the Category Axis, Status to the Series Axis, Year to the Page area, and Quantity to the Data area.

2. Verify that your PivotChart looks like Figure 9.3.

As you can see in Figure 9.3, there are many similarities between a PivotChart and a PivotTable. For example, clicking a field label, such as Year, shows a drop-down field list of the valid items in that field. Fields can also be interactively dragged on or off the PivotChart. And, as with a PivotTable report, double-clicking a Data area field brings up the PivotTable Field List window where you can change the summary type. Table 9.1 identifies and provides a brief explanation of the various components of the PivotChart shown in Figure 9.3.

NOTE Even though you are working with a PivotChart, the fields are stored in a PivotTable Field List window, not a PivotChart Field List window.

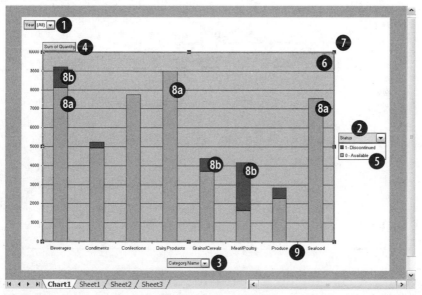

Figure 9.3 A sample PivotChart (the numbered primary components are described in Table 9-1).

Table 9.1 PivotChart Components (see corresponding numbers in Figure 9.3)

SECTION	ITEM	DESCRIPTION
1	Page Area Field	This is also the Page area in the linked PivotTable. Use this area to display data as if it were on separate pages.
2	Series Axis Area	This is the Column area in the linked PivotTable. Use this area to display fields that have only a few unique items. The items in this area are also shown in the Chart legend (see #5 in this table).
3	Category Axis Area	This is the Row area in the linked PivotTable. Use this area to display fields that have several items.
4	Data Area	This is also the Data area in the linked PivotTable. Use this area to graphically represent some type of aggregated data against Category Axis and Series Axis items.
5	Legend	Provides a color code explanation of the Series Axis fields that are represented as Data Items in the Chart (see #8a and #8b in this table).
6	Plot Area	The area where the Data Area items are graphically plotted. Right-clicking in this area brings up the Plot Area pop-up menu.
7	Chart Area	This includes all the components of the PivotChart, including the field buttons, the Plot area, and the Legend. Right-clicking in this area brings up the Chart Area pop-up menu.
8	Data Series	The Data Items represented graphically in the chart. 8a is the Sum of Quantity for Discontinued product categories, and 8b is the Sum of Quantity for Available product categories.
9	Items	The valid items in the Category Axis (Row area) fields.

Figure 9.4 shows how the PivotTable and PivotChart are related to one another. Carefully review this diagram if you are uncertain about the relationship between how these two reports display data.

	A	B	C	D
1	Year	(All)		
2				
3	Sum of Quantity	Status		
4	Category Name	0 - Available	1 - Discontinued	Grand Total
5	Beverages	8115	1095	9210
6	Condiments	4937	298	5235
7	Confections	7742		7742
8	Dairy Products	8997		8997
9	Grains/Cereals	3701	697	4398
10	Meat/Poultry	1636	2519	4155
11	Produce	2289	542	2831
12	Seafood	7551		7551
13	Grand Total	44968	5151	50119

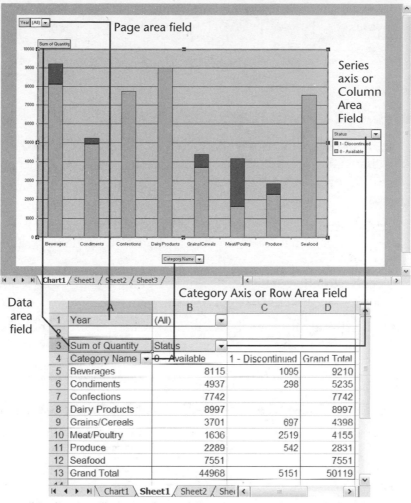

Figure 9.4 This diagram illustrates how objects in a PivotChart are linked to objects in a PivotTable.

PivotChart Toolbar

The PivotChart toolbar, shown in Figure 9.5, looks like the PivotTable toolbar except that the left-most button is labeled *PivotChart* instead of *PivotTable*.

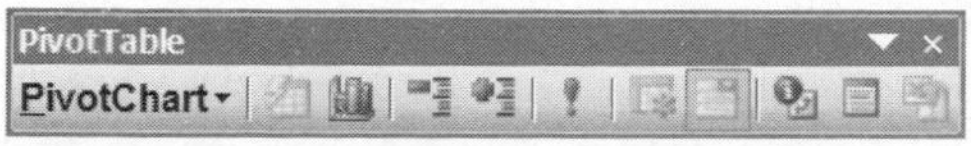

Figure 9.5 The PivotChart drop-down button (left-most button) replaces the PivotTable toolbar button.

Many of the menu items accessed under the PivotChart button are the same as the ones accessed under the PivotTable toolbar button. There are a couple of different ones, such as Hide PivotChart Field Buttons and Remove Field, but the others are just the same. Table 9.2 provides a brief explanation of these buttonfunctions.

Changing the PivotChart's Location

The default setting is to display the PivotChart in its own worksheet tab. In order to change the location of the PivotChart to another worksheet tab or to display the PivotChart in the same worksheet as the linked PivotTable, follow these steps:

1. Right-click in the Chart Area of the PivotChart and select Location from the pop-up menu to bring up the Chart Location dialog box shown in Figure 9.6.

2. Select the location to display the report, and then click OK to close the dialog box and set the new location.

In order to display the PivotTable and PivotChart report in the same worksheet, select that worksheet name from the As Object In drop-down field list.

Table 9.2 Summary of PivotChart Functions

FUNCTION	DESCRIPTION
Field Settings	After you click a field in the PivotChart, choosing this menu item brings up the PivotTable Field List window.
Options	Brings up the PivotTable Options dialog box.
Refresh Data	Refreshes the data in the PivotTable and PivotChart reports from the data source.
Hide PivotChart Field Buttons	Hides the field buttons displayed in the PivotChart.
Formulas	After you click a field in the PivotChart, choosing this menu item creates a Calculated Item or a Calculated Field.
Remove Field	After you click a field in the PivotChart, choosing this menu item removes a field from the PivotChart.

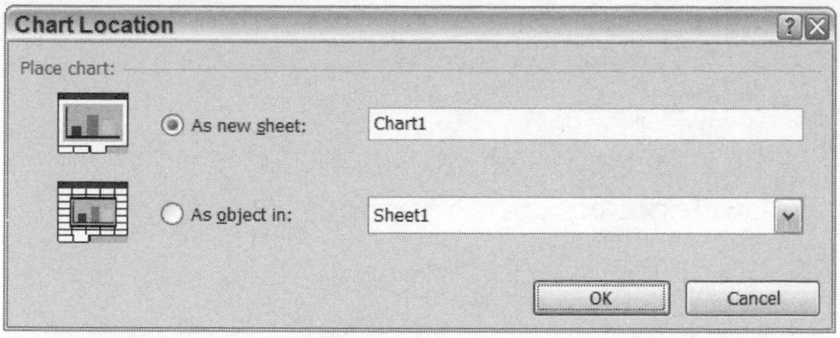

Figure 9.6   You can change the location of the PivotChart in this dialog box.

Field List Window

The PivotChart Field List window shown in Figure 9.7 looks like the Pivot-Table Field List window, except that it shows Category Axis instead of Row Area, and Series Axis instead of Column Area in the drop-down box next to the Add To button.

You can drag fields from the Field List to the selected entity only. For example, if the PivotChart is selected, fields from the PivotTable Field List can be dragged only to the PivotChart report and not to the PivotTable report.

> **TIP**   Displaying the PivotTable Field List can help show you which object is selected when the PivotChart and the PivotTable are both displayed in the same worksheet.

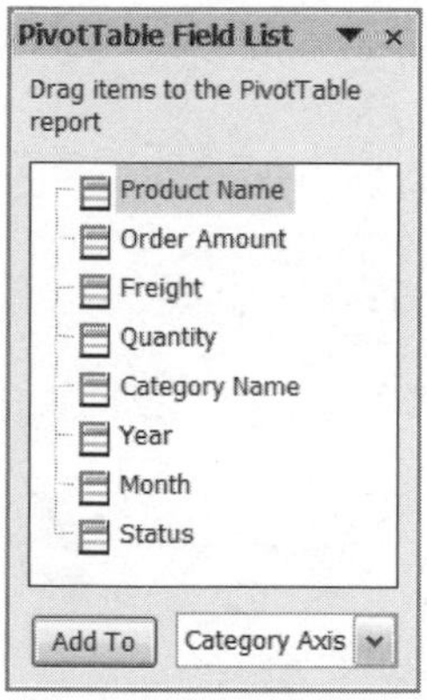

Figure 9.7   The PivotTable Field List window for a PivotChart should look familiar. It's very similar to the one used for a PivotTable.

Formatting the PivotChart

You can choose from several types of charts and formatting options in controlling how a PivotChart is displayed. This section outlines some of the core functions available and demonstrates how you can use them to customize your PivotChart report.

This section covers the following topics:

- Selecting a Chart Type
- Using 3-D Charts
- Formatting the Plot Area
- Formatting the Data Series

Selecting a Chart Type

You can choose from several types of charts in the Chart Type dialog box shown in Figure 9.8. You can select from Column, Bar, Area, Pie, and Radar charts to name just a few. And under each chart type, there are typically several sub-types. If those choices aren't enough, just click the Custom Types tab at the top of the dialog box to choose from numerous other types of charts.

To bring up the Chart Type dialog box, right-click in the Chart Area of the PivotChart and select Chart Type from the pop-up menu.

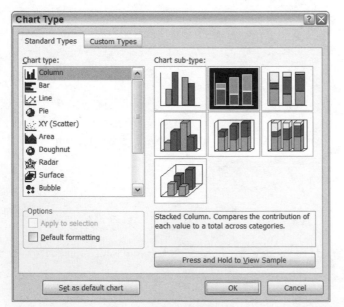

Figure 9.8   This dialog box offers two tabs for selecting chart types.

There are many types of charts available in this dialog box. They are the same ones that are used to create a standard Excel chart. I suggest using Excel's Online Help if you need more information on which type of chart is best suited for displaying a particular kind of report data. I also recommend the following books that are available from Wiley Publishing if you need additional information on chart types and chart functionality: *Excel Charts For Dummies* by John Nicholson (ISBN: 0-7645-8473-1), *Excel 2003 For Dummies* by Greg Harvey (ISBN: 0-7645-3756-3), and *Excel 2003 Bible* by John Walkenbach (ISBN: 0-7645-3967-1).

TIP Click the Press And Hold To View Sample button in the Chart Type dialog box to preview what a chart will look like before making the change.

Managing the View of 3-D Charts

If you decide to use a three-dimensional chart, you can choose from some additional functions to manage the display. This section briefly demonstrates how you can modify the 3-D display of the chart. You can opt to use the mouse to change the rotation and elevation of the chart or use the 3-D View dialog box to further customize more advanced chart settings, such as the perspective, height, and scale.

To set a 3-D display for the PivotChart that was shown earlier in Figure 9.3, follow these steps:

1. Verify that the PivotChart looks like Figure 9.3; and then right-click in the Chart Area and select Chart Type to bring up the Chart Type dialog box.

2. Verify that Column is selected in the Chart Type pane (left side), and then, in the Chart Sub-type pane, select the 3-D Column chart in the bottom-left corner.

3. Verify that the description shown in the box beneath the Chart Sub-Type pane displays the text 3-D Column. Compares values across categories and across series. Click OK to change the chart type to 3-D.

4. Verify that your PivotChart now looks like Figure 9.9.

Using the Mouse

You can use the mouse to modify the rotation and elevation of a chart. Follow these steps to see how this works:

1. Click the intersection of any two axes of the chart (the corners of the chart are highlighted with square black markers).

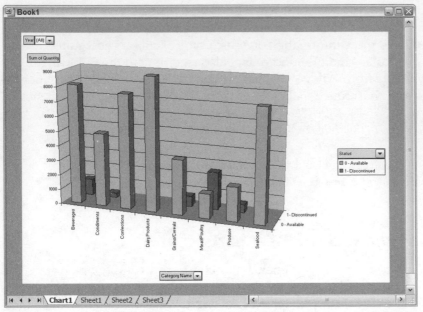

Figure 9.9: If you did everything right, your 3-D PivotChart should look like this.

2. Click one of the corner markers and move the chart in any direction to adjust the elevation or rotation of the chart. (The chart turns to an outline view as shown in Figure 9.10.)

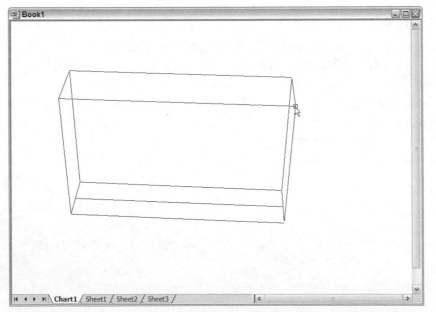

Figure 9.10 Click a corner marker to adjust the 3-D chart elevation and rotation.

It may be necessary to select different corners of the chart in order to obtain a specific rotation and elevation. Although this can be a useful feature for configuring a particular view, more advanced settings for the chart height and the chart perspective can be configured only from the 3-D View dialog box, which is discussed in the next section.

The floor is a useful feature for understanding the chart's orientation as you adjust the chart settings using the mouse. The number of lines shown in the floor of the chart is always one less than the number of items in the Series Axis area. In Figure 9.9, you can see that there are two items in the Series Axis area (Discontinued and Available), so there is only one line displayed in the chart floor in Figure 9.10.

Using the 3-D View Dialog Box

The 3-D View dialog box includes more robust functions for managing the display of a 3-D chart than what is available by simply using the mouse. You can only modify the chart's height and perspective, for example, from this dialog box.

To bring up the 3-D View dialog box shown in Figure 9.11, right click in the Chart Area and select 3-D View from the pop-up menu.

In the 3-D View dialog box, you can see an outline of the PivotChart in the center. You can either use the buttons to make discrete adjustments to the elevation, rotation, and perspective, or you can type in a specific value in the field. Any changes to the elevation, rotation or perspective are interactively depicted in the center diagram. Clicking the Right Angle Axes box shows the chart with right angles and disables any change to the chart's perspective. Clicking the Default button resets the display of the chart to its default setting.

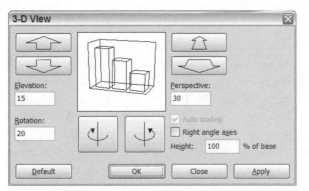

Figure 9.11 The elevation, rotation, perspective, and height of a 3-D chart can all be controlled from this dialog box.

TIP If you somehow manage to completely mess up the elevation and rotation of the chart, you can reset the 3-D chart back to the default display by clicking Default in the 3-D View dialog box.

Formatting the Plot Area

You use the Format Plot Area dialog box to modify the border and background color of the Plot Area of the chart. Right-click the Plot area and select Format Plot Area from the pop-up menu to bring up the dialog box shown in Figure 9.12.

You can customize the Plot Area border by choosing options in the Border section (left side) of this dialog box. You can set the type of border outline, the border color, and the border weight. The Plot Area background is controlled in the Area section (right side), where you can choose from various types of colors for the background setting. Clicking the Fill Effects button brings up the Fill Effects dialog box shown in Figure 9.13. In this box, you can configure more advanced background settings.

The Fill Effects dialog box offers four tabs for customizing the background of the PivotChart:

- **Gradient:** Enables you to set background colors, transparency, shading styles, and shading variants.

- **Texture:** Lets you choose from numerous types of background textures.

- **Pattern:** Enables you to apply patterns and select background and foreground colors.

- **Picture:** Lets you import and format a picture for the background.

Formatting the Data Series

Each Series Axis item is displayed as a Data Series item in the chart. If you look back at the PivotChart shown in Figure 9.3, you can see that two items, Discontinued and Available, are displayed for Status As Data Series items. You can configure the format of these items by double-clicking any of the Data Series items. In this example, that would be the blue or the red (appearing as gray or darker gray in this book) part of a particular Category Axis value (refer to the areas labeled as 8a or 8b in Figure 9.3).

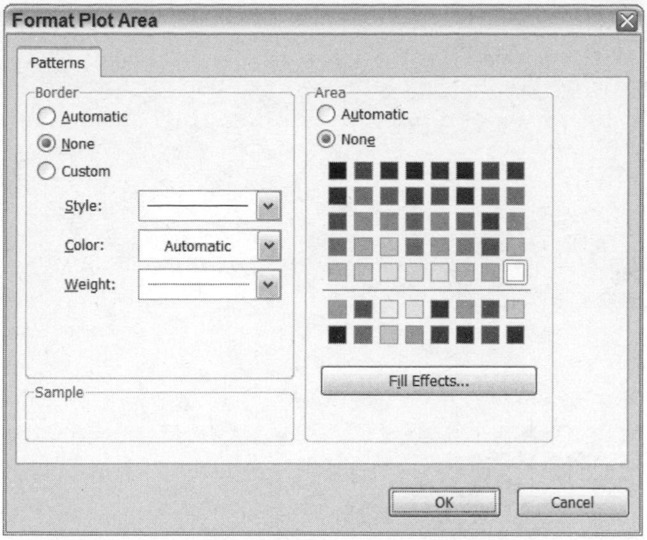

Figure 9.12   You can customize the background, patterns, and fill effects for the Plot Area of the PivotChart in the Format Plot Area dialog box.

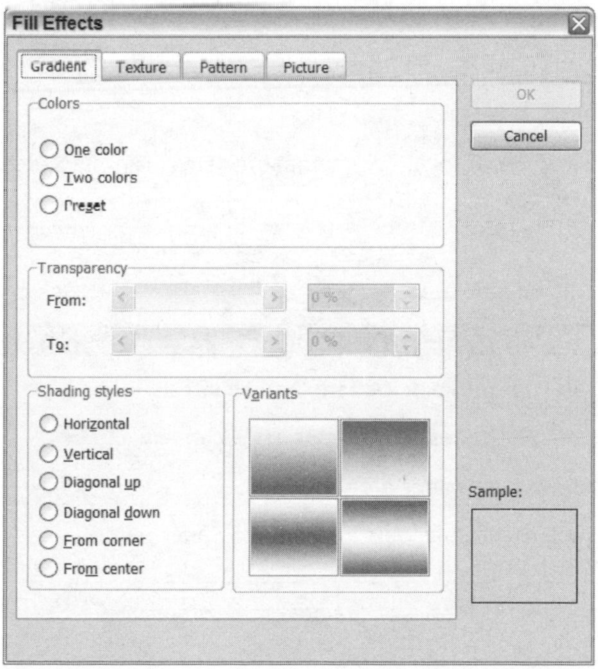

Figure 9.13   You control the more advanced Plot Area formatting from this dialog box.

Double-click the blue (or lighter gray) part of the Beverages category to bring up the Format Data Series dialog box (see Figure 9.14).

The Format Data Series dialog box has six tabs you can use for formatting the Data Series items. Table 9.3 provides a brief description of what functions are available on each tab.

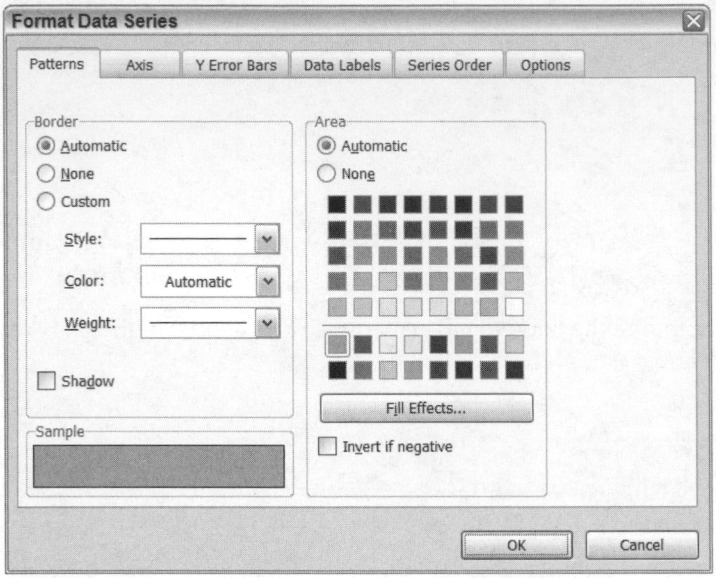

Figure 9.14 You can use the Format Series dialog box to format the items in a Data Series.

Table 9.3 Explanation of Format Data Series Tabs

TAB	DESCRIPTION
Patterns	Configures the border, color, pattern, and fill effects
Axis	Configures the plot series on a primary or secondary axis
Y Error Bars	Configures how error values are displayed
Data Labels	Configures the display of labels to show the Series name, Category name, or value
Series Order	Configures the order for how Data area series items are displayed
Options	Configures the gap between bars and whether series trend lines are displayed

Working with PivotChart Options

You can choose from several types of graphical display options to customize the display of a PivotChart report. By using the Chart Options dialog box, you can choose to display titles, configure axis and gridline settings, toggle and format the display of a chart legend, format data labels, and even add a data table. This section covers the options available in this dialog box with a specific emphasis on the following topics:

- Setting the chart title
- Configuring the chart legend
- Adding a data table

All of these options are controlled in the Chart Options dialog box. Right-click in the Chart Area and select Chart Options from the pop-up menu. The dialog box shown in Figure 9.15 appears.

You can use the six tabs in the Chart Options dialog box to control various display and formatting options of the chart. Table 9.4 provides a brief description of what functions are available on each tab.

NOTE The Data Labels tab in the Chart Options dialog box provides the same functionality as the Data Labels tab in the Format Plot Area dialog box.

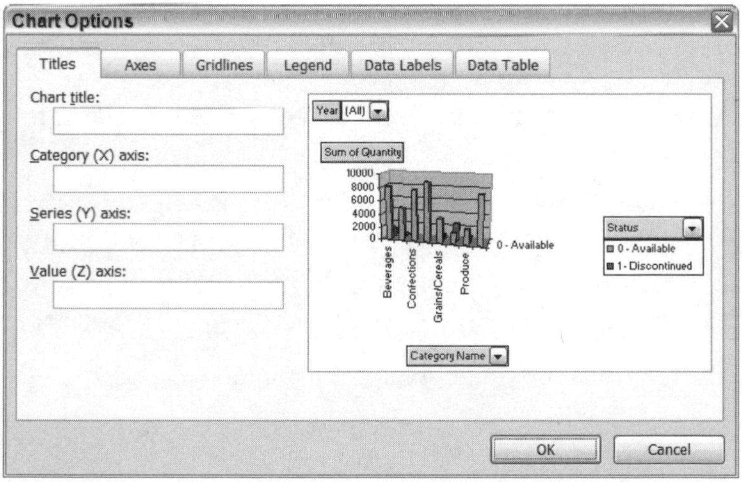

Figure 9.15   You can control how a number of items are displayed from the Chart Options dialog box.

Table 9.4 Explanation of Chart Options Tabs

TAB	DESCRIPTION
Titles	Adds or changes labels for the Chart title, Category (X) Axis area, Series Axis (Y) area, and Value (Z) Axis area
Axes	Toggles the display of Category Axis and Series Axis field labels on the chart
Gridlines	Toggles the display of minor and major gridlines for Category (X) Axis, Series Axis (Y) area, and Value (Z) Axis fields
Legend	Toggles the display of a legend for Category Axis fields and the location of the Chart Legend in the Chart Area
Data Labels	Configures the display of labels to show the Series name, Category name, or Value
Data Table	Toggles the display of a data table in the Chart Area

The following sections highlight some of the principal functions that are accessible in the Chart Options dialog box. I suggest that you experiment with some of the dialog box tabs not covered here to learn more about these features and formatting tools. Most of these options are straightforward and easy to learn, just a little outside the scope of this book.

Setting the Chart Title

The chart title and labels for the various chart axes are defined in the Titles tab of the Chart Options dialog box. You can also individually customize the font, font style, font size, and font color for each label.

Complete these steps to add labels to the chart and customize the label font settings using the 3-D PivotChart:

1. Verify that the PivotChart looks like Figure 9.9, and then right-click in the Chart Area and select Chart Options from the pop-up menu.

2. Click the Titles tab of the Chart Options dialog box.

3. Type **Product Category Sales Analysis** in the Chart Title field.

4. Type **Product Category** in the Category (X) Axis field.

5. Type **Product Status** in the Series (Y) Axis field.

6. Type **Quantity Sold** in the Value (Z) Axis field.

7. Click OK to add the labels to the chart and to close the Chart Options dialog box.

8. Click the text in the Chart Title box to select it, and then set the font to Arial Narrow bold with a font size of 18 and a font color of Red.

9. Set the remaining labels for each chart axis to Arial Narrow italic with a font size of 10 and a font color of Red.

10. Verify that your PivotChart now looks like Figure 9.16.

Configuring the Chart Legend

The Chart Legend provides a color code explanation of the Series Axis fields that are represented as Data Items in the Chart. You can toggle the Chart Legend display or move it to the top, bottom, left, or right in the Chart area. If more than one item is in the Series Axis area, all the permutations of the items are displayed.

To follow along with the example and configure the chart legend, complete these steps:

1. Verify that the PivotChart looks like Figure 9.16, and then right-click in the Chart Area and select Chart Options from the pop-up menu.

2. Click the Legend tab of the Chart Options dialog box. Notice that the legend can be displayed at the bottom, top, right, left, or corner of the Chart area.

3. After you review the legend placement options, uncheck Show Legend and click OK to suppress the display of the chart legend (in preparation for the next exercise) and close the Chart Options dialog box.

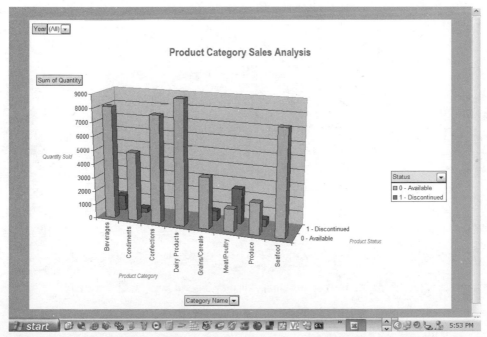

Figure 9.16 The PivotChart after a chart title and axes labels have been added.

Adding a Data Table

A data table usually appears at the bottom of the Chart area and looks something like a PivotTable, except that fields cannot be dragged on or off it. It is essentially a grid that shows the numerical data in a format similar to a PivotTable.

To add a data table to the PivotChart, follow these steps:

1. Verify that the PivotChart looks like Figure 9.16 (except that the chart legend is suppressed), and then right-click in the Chart Area and select Chart Options from the pop-up menu.

2. Click the Data Table tab of the Chart Options dialog box.

3. Check Show Data Table and Show Legend Keys, and then click OK to add the data table and to close the Chart Options dialog box.

4. Verify that your PivotChart now looks like Figure 9.17.

You can also customize the data table format in the Format Data Table dialog box. Right-click the data table and select Format Data Table from the pop-up menu to bring up the Format Data Table dialog box shown in Figure 9.18.

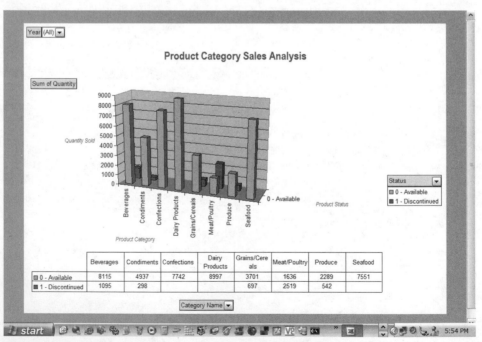

Figure 9.17: The data table can optionally display legend keys, as shown here.

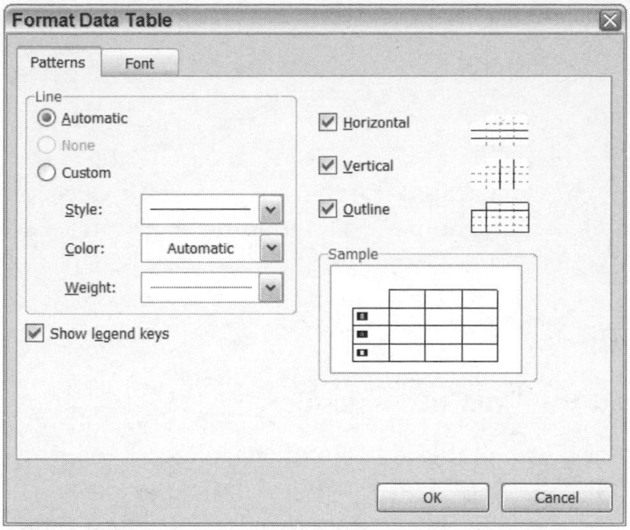

Figure 9.18 You can configure borders, border styles, and fonts for the Data Area table in this dialog box.

You can configure the border line style, border color, and border weight in the Patterns tab of the Format Data Table dialog box. In this box, you can also toggle the legend key display and the display of horizontal, vertical, and outline border lines. You configure the font type, font size, and font color in the Font tab of this dialog box.

Trying It Out in the Real World

Andrew Fuller, the Vice President of Northwind Traders, is opening another office in Mexico. He's planning to promote one of his sales representatives to a sales manager. Andrew has asked that you prepare a report that graphically depicts the sales each year for all the sales representatives to see which sales representatives are continuing to increase sales.

Andrew has contacted the company's database administrator to prepare the SQL query shown here to use for your PivotChart report:

```
SELECT emp.LastName                        AS [Employee],
       DATEPART(YEAR,OrderDate)            AS [Year],
       SUM(dtl.UnitPrice*dtl.Quantity)  AS [Sales Amount]
FROM "Order Details" dtl
INNER JOIN Orders ord ON ord.OrderID = dtl.OrderID
INNER JOIN Employees emp ON emp.EmployeeID = ord.EmployeeID
WHERE emp.Title = 'Sales Representative'
GROUP BY emp.LastName,
         DATEPART(YEAR,OrderDate)
```

> **ON THE WEB** You can download the ch09_rwe.txt query file to
> your computer from the companion website at www.wiley.com/go/
> excelreporting.

You've been asked to create a PivotChart that graphically displays the annual sales for each sales representative. Because this is an important decision, Andrew also suggested that you include numerical support for the annual sales figures.

Getting Down to Business

Complete these steps to create the PivotChart report:

1. From Excel, choose Data ⇨ PivotTable And PivotChart Report to bring up the PivotTable And PivotChart Wizard Step 1 of 3 dialog box.

2. Select External Data Source from the top of the dialog box, select PivotChart Report (With PivotTable Report) at the bottom of the dialog box, and then click Next to continue to the next step.

3. When the PivotTable And PivotChart Wizard Step 2 of 3 dialog box appears, click Get Data to bring up the Choose Data Source dialog box.

4. When the Choose Data Source dialog box appears, verify that Use The Query Wizard To Create/Edit Queries is unchecked, select the NorthwindCS Database data source, and then click OK.

5. When the Microsoft Query program is launched, you are presented with the Add Tables dialog box. Close this dialog box and click the SQL button.

6. Paste or type the query in the SQL dialog box and click OK.

7. Click the Return Data To Microsoft Excel button to return the data to Excel and continue.

8. Click Finish when the PivotTable And PivotChart Wizard Step 2 of 3 dialog box appears to create the PivotTable and the PivotChart.

9. Verify that you see a blank PivotChart in the Chart1 worksheet tab (refer to Figure 9.2).

10. Drag Employee to the Category Axis area, Year to the Series Axis area, and Sales Amount to the Data area.

11. Right-click in the Chart area, and then select Chart Options from the pop-up menu to bring up the Chart Options dialog box.

12. Click the Legends tab of the Chart Options dialog box and uncheck the Show Legend option.

13. Click the Data Table tab of the Chart Options dialog box and check Show Data Table And Show Legend Key.

14. Click OK to close the Chart Options dialog box.

15. Right-click the Chart area and select Chart Type to bring up the Chart Type dialog box.

16. Click Cylinder in the Standard Types pane, and then select the 3-D Column with a cylindrical shape chart sub-type in the bottom left of the Chart Sub-type section.

17. Click OK to use the new chart type and to close the Chart Table dialog box.

18. Double-click Sum Of Sales Amount to bring up the PivotTable Field dialog box. Click Number, and then select Accounting with 0 (zero) decimal places and the $ symbol in the Format Cells dialog box. Click OK to close the Format Cells dialog box, and then click OK again to close the PivotTable Field dialog box and apply the format changes to the data table.

19. Click the PivotChart button in the PivotChart toolbar; and then choose Hide PivotChart Field Buttons to suppress the display of Field Buttons.

20. Verify that your PivotChart looks like Figure 9.19.

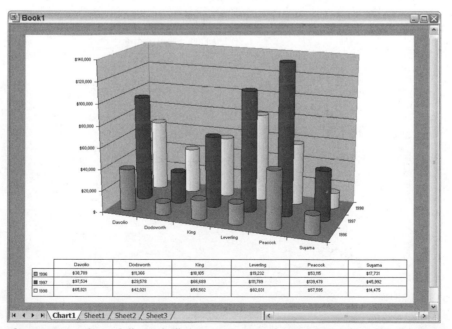

Figure 9.19 If you followed all the steps correctly, your PivotChart should now look like this.

WATCH THE VIDEO You can watch the video ch0901_video.avi to see how this PivotChart is created at www.wiley.com/go/excelreporting.

Reviewing What You Did

This real-world example demonstrated how you can use a PivotChart to illustrate trends in data. Looking at this chart, you can easily see that only Ms. Dodsworth has continued to increase her sales each year. However, her sales amount is much less than those of Ms. Leverling and Mrs. Peacock. Because the chart may not provide all of the necessary information for Andrew Fuller to make such an important decision as promoting a sales representative to a sales manager, the data table is also included at the bottom of the Chart Area to provide further numerical support. An alternative method to using a data table is to place both the PivotTable and the PivotChart on the same worksheet tab.

Chapter Review

This chapter outlined the similarities and differences between a PivotChart report and a PivotTable report. It covered the terminology and described the various components displayed in a PivotChart. It also provided information and examples on the various types of formatting functions and options available in a PivotChart report. This included chart type selection, 3-D functionality, and data table display.

CHAPTER 10

Working with OLAP Cubes

Earlier chapters mainly used the NorthwindCS database, an OLTP data source. This chapter focuses on OLAP — online analytical processing — data sources. If you have ever run into memory or performance problems with trying to analyze very large datasets, an OLAP data cube can be a great alternative. Excel also delivers three client-based OLAP solutions that provide a very innovative and automated method for easily building data cubes. This is an ideal stepping stone for small businesses that do not have the resources and expertise for a more robust server-based solution.

This chapter starts by providing an overview of OLAP, including terminology, concepts, and processing options. Next, it outlines the differences between client and server-based OLAP processing, describing the process flow and key considerations of each method. After that, this chapter covers both of these OLAP processing methods in more depth. This includes information on how to create offline data cubes from an Analysis Server cube, and a comprehensive review of each client-based OLAP processing option. Before you start the real-world example at the end of the chapter, you're shown how these OLAP cubes actually look and function in a PivotTable report, including some of the key differences in features, functionality, and display.

Introducing OLAP

The reason I've used the NorthwindCS database for my examples up to this point is because it is widely available and can be updated from the graphical user interface in Access. However, as you start to develop PivotTable reports that run against enterprise-level databases with extremely large datasets, you may encounter some limitations with the amount of data that can be loaded into Excel. Although the number of rows that can be imported into a Pivot-Table report is restricted only by your computer's memory, you can run into performance issues and memory problems as the dataset gets very large. That's where OLAP comes into the picture.

With OLAP, you connect to a *data cube* where only the necessary information to support a particular view is imported into the PivotTable report. The data in the cube has already been aggregated and computed for various row and column report combinations, often resulting in much faster PivotTable performance and less memory consumption than what would be required for the same report with OLTP (online transactional processing) source data. Thus, this technology enables you to analyze and report on much larger datasets using fewer processor and memory resources than what is required when the data is not aggregated.

> **NOTE** So how many rows can you insert into an Excel PivotTable using an OLTP data source? Despite popular belief, you're not limited to 65,536 rows. You can load in as many rows as your computer's memory can handle. I've imported over 300,000 rows into numerous PivotTable reports and experienced acceptable performance using my laptop computer that has a 2.4 GHz processor and 1MB of RAM memory.

In a very broad and general sense, the primary advantages of using OLAP over OLTP include the following:

- Capability to organize dimensions into a hierarchy and drill through dimension levels (explained in later sections)
- Capability to analyze very large datasets
- Ultra-fast performance with large datasets

Conversely, the primary advantages of using OLTP over OLAP include the following:

- Capability to drill down to the underlying data
- Capability to analyze data in real time
- Capability to modify how Data area items are summarized

NOTE This is a very simplified list of the differences between OLTP and OLAP data sources. In reality, this topic is much more complex in the enterprise. IT professionals typically evaluate and assess how this technology impacts their organization. For example, although you can analyze data in real time from an OLTP database, this can result in an adverse impact on users who are accessing the transactional database through the enterprise software system.

The following sections provide a brief synopsis of OLAP and how it fits into the bigger picture of data warehousing. Keep in mind that this is just an overview to help you better understand the technology and available options. If you would like to develop a more comprehensive understanding of OLAP, I suggest you check out the following books from Wiley: *Microsoft SQL Server OLAP Developer's Guide* by William C. Amo (ISBN: 0-7645-4643-0) and *Professional SQL Server 2000 Programming* by Robert Vieira (ISBN: 0-7645-4379-2).

Understanding OLAP Cubes and Data Warehouses

OLAP cubes are often just one part of a larger data warehousing solution. A *data warehouse* stores stable data — data that has been fully processed and isn't likely to change — as opposed to volatile data — data that hasn't been fully processed and is likely to change or be deleted — stored in an OLTP *(transactional)* database. The transactional database is also designed for real-time data entry and processing, whereas an OLAP database is designed for reporting and interrogation.

In a transactional database, several data elements are used to support the daily operations of an organization. This is true even for a small transactional database, such as NorthwindCS. Whereas a human resources manager, a buyer, or a sales representative might consider fields such as employee picture, customer phone number, or supplier homepage important in the daily operation of the database, a manager who needs to assess employee-selling aptitude, customer-buying patterns, or supplier contributions would not find that these fields provide the information they need to make important business decisions. Instead, the manager would seek information in fields such as Product Name, Quantity Sold, Order Amount, Supplier Name, Customer Name, and Employee Name to formulate judgments on what salesperson to promote, what customers to discount, and what suppliers to squeeze.

NOTE The process of deciding which fields to include in an OLAP database is similar to the process of choosing which fields to include in a PivotTable report. The main difference is that an OLAP database is designed to store all the data that is important in the organization instead of extracting the data for a single report using an SQL query.

It's also possible for an OLAP database to include data from several transactional databases. These transactional databases might be tied to different enterprise software systems, different corporate divisions, or both. If multiple divisions are used, a field might be added to some of the OLAP database tables to identify the division number from which each transaction originated. If the data is taken from multiple transactional databases, the data may be changed so that everything is displayed in a consistent format within the single OLAP database. For example, the Discontinued field in the Product table of the NorthwindCS database uses a 0 and 1 to represent whether the product is available (0) or discontinued (1). Other transactional databases might use True and False or Yes and No to represent product availability. It doesn't matter which convention is used, but it should be consistent once the data is in the OLAP database. Imagine how confusing it would be to see Yes, No, True, False, 0, and 1 all in the same drop-down list of a PivotTable report field.

After the data is in the OLAP database and is in a consistent format, the OLAP cubes can be created. These cubes are multidimensional structures that store the numerically aggregated data — or *measures* (the fields used in the Data area of a PivotTable) — against the alphanumeric fields — or *dimensions* (the fields used in the Row, Column, and Page areas of a PivotTable). The amount of data, the number of dimensions, and the number of measures directly affect how long it takes to build an OLAP cube. Of course, the processing capabilities of the computer building the cube also factors into this processing period, which can take seconds, minutes, hours, or even days. However, once the cube has been created, one or more computers running Excel can connect to it. And since the data in the cube is already aggregated, the report performance is generally much quicker than it is with an OLTP data source, because the client computer does not have to import all the data into the report and calculate the aggregate totals each time the PivotTable report view is modified.

> **NOTE** Server-based OLAP solutions such as Oracle OLAP or Microsoft Analysis Services include tools for creating different types of cubes and selecting the level of aggregation within the cube. The higher the level of aggregation, the faster the cube performance.

Figure 10.1 shows one possible model for how data from multiple transactional databases are loaded into an OLAP database. Once in the OLAP database, the data is aggregated into OLAP cubes where one or more clients can connect to the cubes using an Excel PivotTable.

Key OLAP Concepts and Terminology

With OLAP, you deal primarily with measures and dimensions. *Measures* are numeric fields that are aggregated. These are the fields that you drop in the Data area of a PivotTable. *Dimensions* are non-numeric fields that you can drag to the

Row, Column, or Page area of a PivotTable. Dimensions provide some meaning or context to measures. This is analogous to what you've seen in the earlier OLTP PivotTable report examples in this book. The main difference is that fields are categorized as either measures or as dimensions in the OLAP cube, rather than left as unclassified fields that can dropped into any area of the PivotTable.

NOTE Unlike OLTP, a measure can be dropped only in the Data area, and a Dimension can be dropped only in a Page, Row, or Column area of an OLAP PivotTable report.

Understanding Measures and Dimensions

Using the NorthwindCS database, an example of a measure might be Quantity Sold in the Order Details table. An example of a dimension might be Product Category in the Categories table. Looking at Quantity Sold on its own provides little value. However, looking at Quantity Sold against a dimension such as Product Category or Shipping Company provides some additional meaning or context to the measure, Quantity Sold. Instead of just a single quantity sold figure, you can examine the quantity sold by product category, the quantity sold and transported by shipping company, and even the quantity sold by multiple combinations of product category and shipping company.

The following SQL query depicts how measures and dimensions can be conceptually organized in an OLAP cube:

```
SELECT cat.CategoryName AS [Product Category],
       dtl.Quantity     AS [Quantity Sold],
       pro.Discontinued AS [Status],
       shp.CompanyName  AS [Shipping Company]
FROM "Order Details" dtl
INNER JOIN Products pro ON dtl.ProductID = pro.ProductID
INNER JOIN Categories cat ON pro.CategoryID = cat.CategoryID
INNER JOIN Orders ord ON dtl.OrderID = ord.OrderID
INNER JOIN Shippers shp ON ord.ShipVia = shp.ShipperID
```

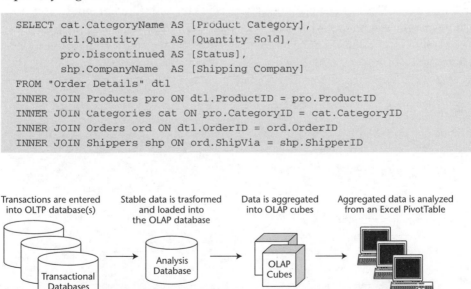

Transactions are entered into OLTP database(s)

Transactional Databases

Stable data is trasformed and loaded into the OLAP database

Analysis Database

Data is aggregated into OLAP cubes

OLAP Cubes

Aggregated data is analyzed from an Excel PivotTable

Clients using an Excel PivotTable

Figure 10.1 In this diagram, the OLAP database is populated from several transactional databases.

In this query, the dimensions are Product Category, Shipping Company, and Status. The only measure, Quantity Sold, is a numeric field summarized across these various dimensions, as shown in Figure 10.2.

As you can see in Figure 10.2, the OLAP cube structure comprises several individual cubes — in this case, 48 of them. Each cube stores the total Quantity Sold for each intersection of Shipper, Product Category, and Status. At the front of the cube structure, the total Quantity Sold is shown for all of the orders shipped by Federal Shipping. The cubes on the bottom level represent products that have been discontinued, while the cubes at the top represent products that are currently available. The product categories are represented from left to right.

NOTE OLAP data is often referred to as *multidimensional data* because it stores the calculated aggregations for multiple dimensions (fields that can be used in the Row, Column, or Page area of a PivotTable).

The cubes are analogous to what you've seen in earlier chapters of this book with PivotTable reports. However, instead of waiting for Excel to interactively calculate totals for different arrangements of Row and Column area fields, it simply loads in the already calculated totals from an OLAP cube. Consequently, a PivotTable report connected to an OLAP data source generally runs much quicker than it would if it were connected to an OLTP data source.

NOTE With Analysis Server cubes, it's possible to control the amount or level of aggregation in an OLAP cube. Higher levels of aggregation result in faster PivotTable report performance but require more storage space and processing time.

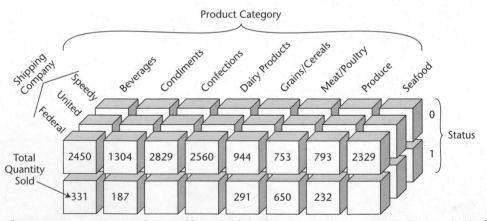

Figure 10.2   A conceptual view of how fields in the SQL query are organized into individual cubes that make up the larger OLAP cube structure.

Arranging Dimensions into a Hierarchy

Dimensions can be organized into a hierarchal order within the OLAP cube. This hierarchy is also transported to the PivotTable report where users can drill-through the various dimension levels. The position in which a specific dimension is ordered in the hierarchy refers to its level. For example, if Product Name is added to the earlier SQL query, the hierarchy might be arranged in the order of Product Category ➪ Status ➪ Product Name. An example of how this might look is shown in Figure 10.3.

Using this technology, you can organize fields into an intuitive hierarchy. This might translate to common relationships, such as Country ➪ State/Province ➪ City, to more sophisticated relationships unique to your organization. Various sections in this chapter include a few dimension-hierarchy examples that you can review for additional perspective.

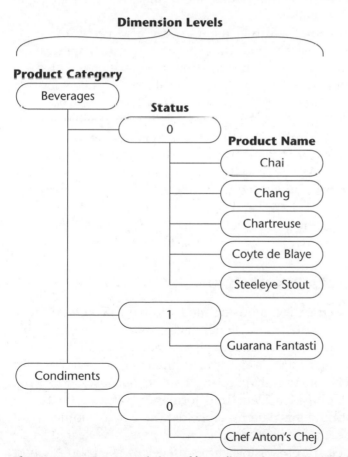

Figure 10.3 Conceptual view of how dimensions are organized into a hierarchy.

WARNING After dimensions are organized into a hierarchy, they cannot be rearranged in the PivotTable report. For example, in Figure 10.3, Product Category cannot be displayed as an inner row of Status in a PivotTable.

Client- and Server-Based OLAP Processing

Two OLAP cube-processing methods are outlined in this chapter. The first method, Server-Based OLAP, uses the more powerful resources commonly associated with a server. This typically includes multiple processors, substantially increased memory, and sophisticated OLAP-processing software. The second method, Client-Based OLAP, uses only the memory and processor resources available on the personal computer running Excel. Therefore, it generally takes much longer to create a cube using this method than it takes using server-based OLAP.

The software programs for these two methods are also vastly different. Server-based OLAP uses software applications such as Microsoft Analysis Services or Oracle OLAP. These programs include tools for processing incremental cube updates, designing cube storage, and controlling the cube's level of aggregation. Client-based OLAP, on the other hand, uses the Offline Cube Wizard included as part of Microsoft Excel. This program doesn't include any of the bells and whistles that I mentioned with Analysis Services, but it does provide three innovative options for creating OLAP cubes. And, unlike with server-based OLAP, client-based OLAP lets you refresh the cubes with the most current data from the OLTP database by simply using the Refresh Data function in Excel.

This section provides a high-level overview of each OLAP processing method, describing some of the key concepts and the process flow.

Understanding Server-Based OLAP

Many enterprises utilize a data-warehousing model in which an OLAP database is created from one or more transactional databases, as shown in Figure 10.1. Information in the transactional database that is not useful for analysis is excluded. Some of the extracted data is also transformed as it is loaded into the OLAP database for consistency and report-formatting purposes. Microsoft SQL Server includes a tool, called Data Transformation Services (DTS), for transferring and transforming this data from one data source to another.

After the data is in the OLAP database, the OLAP cubes are created by an Analysis Server running OLAP-processing software, such as Microsoft Analysis Services. This software includes options for processing only the incremental updates that are added to the OLAP database, thereby decreasing the amount of time it takes to ensure that the cube remains current. The software includes numerous other functions for designing the cube storage, partitioning data, creating virtual cubes, configuring security, and even controlling the level of aggregation in the cube.

After the cubes are created, they can then be accessed from a Microsoft Excel PivotTable report using an OLAP data driver. A sample diagram of how this might look is shown in Figure 10.4.

NOTE The diagram in Figure 10.4 shows only one of many possible ways that server-based OLAP processing might work. For example, many organizations run both SQL Server and Analysis Services on a single server.

Using a PivotTable with Server-Based OLAP Cubes

Using server-based OLAP, the PivotTable report must be able to connect to the Analysis Server cube in order to process changes to the report view or to the Page, Column, or Row filters. And unlike OLTP, where all the data is stored in the PivotTable report, Excel queries and returns only the pertinent and aggregated data from the Analysis Server cube to support a particular report view.

Although a connection to the cube is required for changing the report view or refreshing the cube data, Excel includes tools for saving a portion of the OLAP cube to an offline cube file. Using this feature, you can even toggle the connection between the Analysis Server and the offline cube file, enabling you to send cube files to remote personnel who do not have access to the Analysis Server. (You learn about creating offline cube files from an OLAP on an Analysis Server in the section "Creating and Working with Offline Cube Files" later in this chapter.)

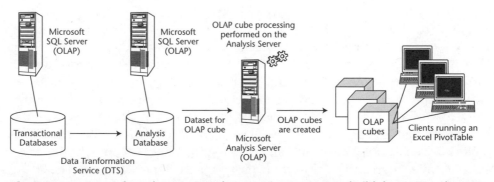

Figure 10.4 Server-based OLAP uses the server's resources to build the OLAP cube. Once the cube is created, Excel can connect to it using an OLAP data driver.

Reviewing the Key Considerations and Concepts

If you choose to use server-based OLAP, keep in mind that the PivotTable report is only as current as the Analysis Server cube. Unlike client-based OLAP, there aren't any native tools included in Excel for refreshing an Analysis Server cube with the most current data in the transactional database. This function can be performed only from the Analysis Server or from running a DTS job.

The key concepts associated with this OLAP processing method include the following:

- It is an enterprise-level solution that generally requires data warehousing expertise.

- The cubes are created by the Analysis Server and are accessed in a typical client-server paradigm.

- No native tools are included in Microsoft Excel for refreshing the OLAP cubes with the most current data in the OLTP database.

Understanding Client-Based OLAP

Client-based OLAP uses the processor and memory resources of the local computer to build the OLAP cubes from an OLTP data source. Like server-based OLAP, the number of rows, the number of dimensions, and the number of measures directly impact the amount of time it takes to create the OLAP cube. However, unlike server-based OLAP, client-based OLAP typically has much less powerful resources for calculating the various aggregations required to build an OLAP cube. Moreover, there aren't any options for controlling the level of aggregation in the cube as there are with server-based OLAP.

TIP Carefully evaluate what fields are required in the OLAP cube, as each new dimension and measure noticeably increases the total processing period.

Although client-based OLAP is not an enterprise-level solution, it does provide a powerful and innovative means for analyzing large datasets. Often, it is also the most appropriate solution when the report is needed only for a temporary period of time, and an organization does not have the expertise to set up and configure an Analysis Server. This method may even be a natural steppingstone to the more versatile and powerful server-based OLAP processing model.

Client-based OLAP is delivered through the Offline Cube Wizard that is included as part of Microsoft Excel. This program enables you to build OLAP cubes from an SQL query that runs against a transactional database. The OLAP cube can also be reprocessed with the most current data in the transactional database by simply using the Refresh Data function in an Excel PivotTable report. A sample diagram of how this might look is shown in Figure 10.5.

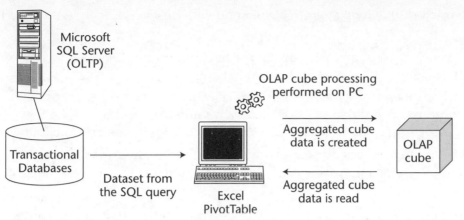

Figure 10.5 Client-based OLAP uses the personal computer's resources to build the OLAP cube.

As you can probably surmise from the diagram shown in Figure 10.5, the client-based OLAP option requires more time than just importing the rows directly into the Excel PivotTable report from an OLTP data source. However, in return for the extra processing time, you are able to analyze and report on much larger datasets than what's possible with OLTP.

Using a PivotTable with Client-Based OLAP Cubes

If you choose to build an offline data cube from Excel, the OLAP cube is created by first querying the OLTP data source and then creating a data cube from the dataset returned from the query. Excel then connects to the data cube and brings back only the necessary and aggregated information required for the report.

TIP There are three very different options for how client-based OLAP cubes can be created and read by an Excel PivotTable report. The "Working with Client-Based OLAP" section covers each option in comprehensive detail a little later in this chapter.

Reviewing the Key Considerations and Concepts

Client-based OLAP is not intended to be an enterprise-level solution. The more robust and powerful features that are included with the Analysis Services program are not available with client-based OLAP. There are no tools for performing incremental cube updates, configuring cube security, or controlling the level of aggregation in an offline cube file. If you choose to use client-based OLAP, you are also constrained to the processing capabilities of the local computer building the cube.

Keep the following key concepts in mind with this model:

■ This is not an enterprise-level solution. It can take a long time to process cubes, and there aren't any functions for partitioning data, designing storage, or configuring security.

■ The cubes are created by the personal computer running Excel. Although multiple users can access the offline cube files, file-sharing errors can sometimes result, as this is not a true client-server model.

■ You can reprocess the cube with the most current information in the OLTP database by using the Refresh Data function in Excel.

Working with Server-Based Cubes

Analysis Services provides an enterprise-level solution for creating, managing, and processing OLAP cubes using a true client-server model. This software program, included with Microsoft SQL Server, can be installed on the same server as the SQL Server or on a separate server. Using Analysis Services, you can create OLAP cubes from numerous types of data sources, including Access, SQL, and Oracle databases. There are also powerful tools for designing the cube storage, partitioning data, creating virtual cubes, configuring security, and even controlling the level of aggregation in the cube.

Accessing an OLAP Cube on the Analysis Server

In order to connect to an OLAP cube on an Analysis Server, you must specify the Analysis Server, database, and OLAP cube. This information is saved in the DSN file that you can access on the OLAP Cubes tab of the Choose Data Source dialog box shown in Figure 10.6.

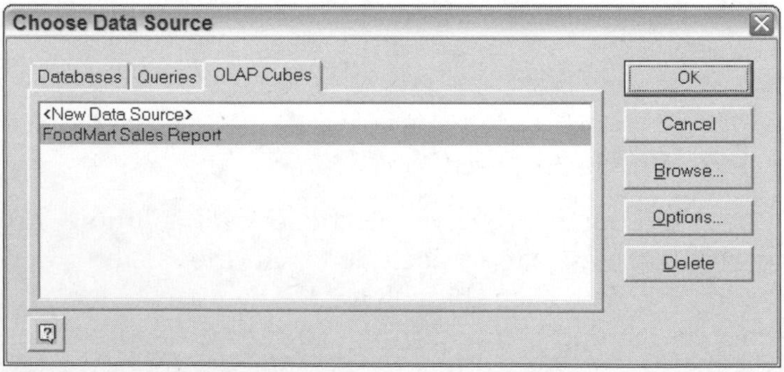

Figure 10.6   Click the OLAP Cubes tab of the Choose Data Source dialog box to connect to an OLAP cube on an Analysis Server.

CROSS-REFERENCE Chapter 3 provides a detailed, step-by-step example of how to create a data source for the Sales cube in the Foodmart 2000 database. It references the Foodmart Sales Report DSN file example that was created in Chapter 3 for the various steps in this section.

For more information about how to connect to an OLAP cube on an Analysis Server, refer to Chapter 3.

Creating and Working with Offline Cube Files

You can use the Create Cube File Wizard included with Microsoft Excel to create an offline cube file from an OLAP cube on an Analysis Server. This tool allows you to analyze and report on data in the PivotTable without having to maintain a connection to the Analysis Server. Figure 10.7 illustrates how this might work.

You can use an offline cube file when the Analysis Server is unavailable. You can also send this offline cube to other users who do not have access to the Analysis Server, or you can save it to your laptop for offsite analysis and reporting. Once the cube is created, it's easy to toggle the PivotTable report connection between the Analysis Server and the offline cube. You can even add or remove measures and dimensions after the cube has been created by reconnecting to the Analysis Server and launching the Create Cube File Wizard.

Creating an Offline Cube File from an Analysis Server Cube

This section outlines the various steps required to create an offline cube file from an OLAP cube on an Analysis Server. It demonstrates how you create the offline cube file by using the Sales cube in the Foodmart 2000 database that is included as part of a default installation of Microsoft Analysis Services.

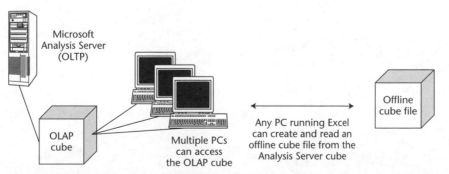

Figure 10.7 Server-based cubes created from Analysis Services can be saved as an offline cube file.

CROSS-REFERENCE Refer to Chapter 3 for help if you have not already set up a DSN connection to the Analysis Server.

To create an offline cube file from an OLAP cube on the Analysis Server, follow these steps:

1. Ensure that the PivotTable report is selected, and then choose Offline OLAP from the PivotTable toolbar menu to bring up the Offline OLAP Settings dialog box shown in Figure 10.8.

NOTE The Offline OLAP menu item is only enabled when the PivotTable report is selected and there is at least one field in the PivotTable.

2. Click the Create Offline Data File button to bring up the Create Cube File — Step 1 of 4 dialog box.

3. Click Next to continue to the second view of the Create Cube File Wizard.

4. Expand Customers, and then check the Country, State Province, and City levels. (Note that the higher-level dimension Customers is automatically selected when you check a level that is lower in the dimension hierarchy.)

5. Check the dimensions Education Level, Gender, and Marital Status. (As you check each dimension, the dimension labels change to a bold font, to indicate that all levels in the dimension have been selected, as shown in Figure 10.9.)

NOTE The Time dimension is checked by default in Step 2 Of 4. Leave this dimension checked if you are following along with this example. (You need to use the scroll bar on right in Figure 10.9 to see this field in the Step 2 of 4 dialog box.)

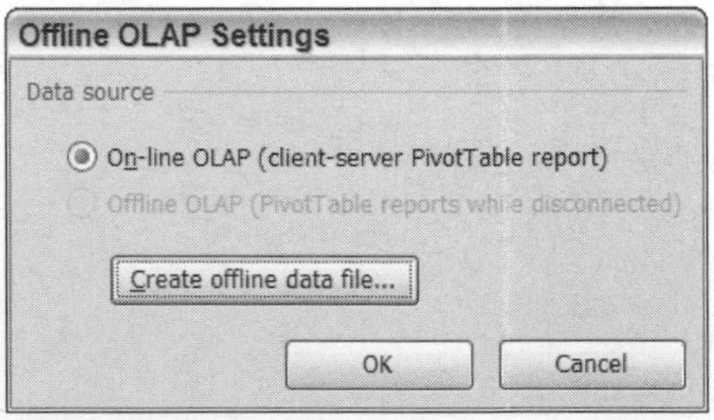

Figure 10.8 You can create an offline data cube file from this dialog box.

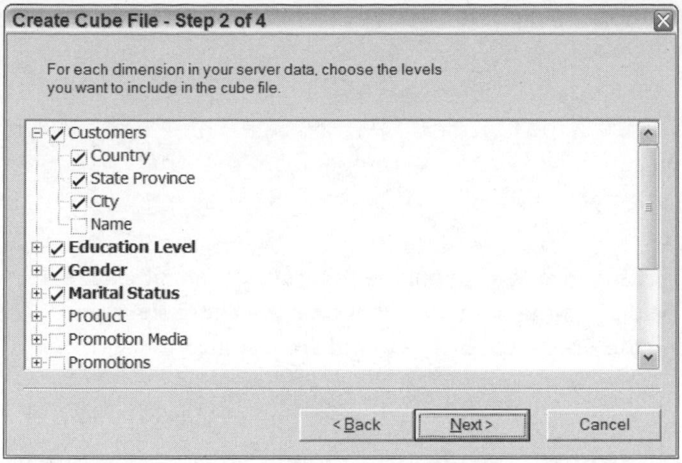

Figure 10.9 In this second step of the Wizard, select the dimensions and levels for the offline cube file.

6. Verify that your dialog box looks like Figure 10.10, and then click Next to bring up Step 3 of the Wizard.

7. Check Measure, Country, Gender, and Marital Status. Expand Education Level and check Bachelors Degree, Graduate Degree, and High School Degree.

8. Verify that your dialog box looks like Figure 10.10, and then click Next to continue to the last view of the Create Cube File dialog box.

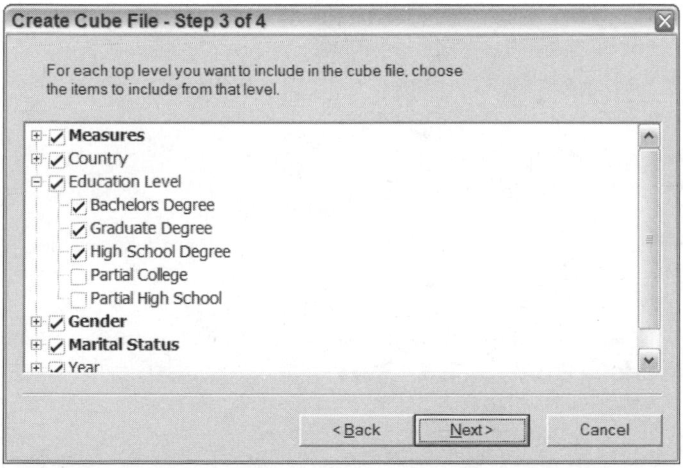

Figure 10.10 Choose the items included in each top-level dimension of this dialog box.

9. Select a directory to save the offline cube file or leave it as the default My Documents folder; and then click Finish to create and save the offline cube file.

10. When you are returned to the Offline OLAP Settings dialog box, shown in Figure 10.11, you can click OK to disconnect from the Analysis Server and start working from the offline OLAP cube file.

TIP After you disconnect the PivotTable from the Analysis Server cube, take a look at the PivotTable Field List window. Notice that only the dimensions and measures you selected in the Create Cube File Wizard are displayed.

Reconnecting to the Analysis Server

You can toggle the PivotTable report connection between the offline cube file and the Analysis Server by choosing Offline OLAP from the PivotTable toolbar menu. Selecting this function brings up the Offline OLAP Settings dialog box you saw earlier in Figure 10.11.

Clicking the On-Line OLAP option disconnects the PivotTable report from the offline cube file and reconnects the PivotTable to the Analysis Server. Once connected, you'll notice that the PivotTable Field List displays all the available fields in the Analysis Server cube instead of just the ones selected in the offline cube.

Clicking the Edit Offline Data File button launches the Create Cube File Wizard, where you can change what dimensions and measures are selected for the offline cube file.

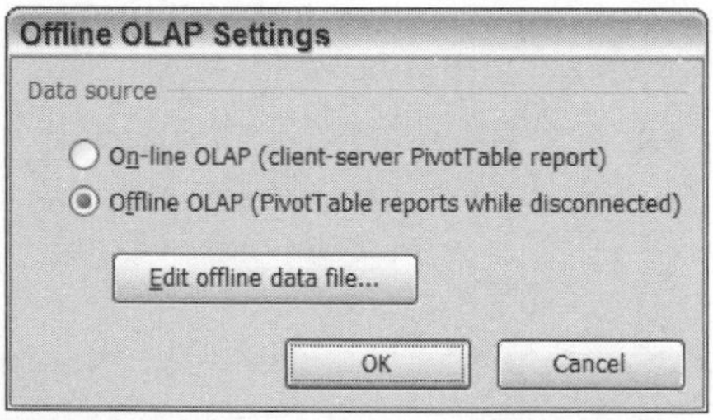

Figure 10.11 You can toggle whether the PivotTable report is connected to the offline cube file or the Analysis Server from this dialog box.

Working with Client-Based OLAP

The OLAP Cube Wizard included with Microsoft Excel delivers a client-based OLAP solution, meaning that the OLAP cube is created using just the memory and processor resources of the local computer running Excel. The Wizard is accessed through the Microsoft Query program and includes three options for creating OLAP cubes. All three options enable you to refresh the OLAP cube with the most current data from the OLTP data source by simply using the Refresh Data function that is accessible from the PivotTable toolbar and from the PivotTable pop-up menu in Excel.

Table 10.1 provides some general information on resource usage and the cube design for each of the three options available in the OLAP Cube Wizard.

The following sections offer more comprehensive information about each option listed in the table and include a process flow diagram and some additional guidelines about when to use each option.

WARNING It's best to start with a new report if you are using any of these three options. The OLAP Cube Wizard frequently skips the process of actually building a cube if a PivotTable report has already been created with the OLTP source data (a known software bug that is loosely documented in the Online Help).

Table 10.1 Resources and Cube Design Options Available in OLAP Cube Wizard

CUBE OPTION	RESOURCE USAGE	CUBE DESIGN
Option #1 Retrieve Data on Demand	Memory and temporary disk space resources are minimized, but changes to the report view require the OLAP data to be calculated for the new report view.	Temporary cube that includes only the data necessary to support a particular report view. The initial cube is processed much faster than the other two options.
Option #2 Retrieve All Data At Once	Requires enough memory and disk space to store the temporary cube that includes all the data necessary to support any report view. Changes to the report view are processed much faster than the first option.	Temporary cube that includes all the data necessary to support any report view.
Option #3 Save the Cube File	Memory resources are minimized, but permanent disk storage is required for the offline cube file. Changes to the report view are processed much faster than the first option.	Permanent cube that includes all the data necessary to support any report view.

Option 1 — Retrieving Data on Demand

The first option, shown in Figure 10.12, generates a temporary data cube that is generally just large enough to support a single PivotTable report view. You should use this option when the PivotTable report view will not be frequently changed and the dataset is too large for direct OLTP access.

Using this option, the PivotTable report relies heavily on the OLTP data source for its data. Changing the report view or applying a filter in the PivotTable frequently triggers a query to the OLTP data source in order to retrieve the required data.

WARNING Even though the OLTP data source is regularly queried when the report view is modified, problems can arise if the data in the OLTP data source falls out of synch with the temporary OLAP cube. This happens because the aggregated measures and the dimension values are calculated only when the PivotTable is first opened or refreshed. You can simply refresh the PivotTable report to correct any problems related to the data not being synchronized.

The cube created with this first option is going to be much smaller than the same cube that would be processed using either of the next two options because only the data necessary to support a single report view is generally aggregated and returned to the PivotTable. As a result, the initial cube is also processed more quickly, allowing you to obtain the data for the selected report view in a shorter period of time.

TIP If you are accessing an SQL database with this first option, and you are planning to make several changes to the report view, try to use Trusted Security instead of an SQL login to access the database. Otherwise, you'll continually be prompted to enter the password each time the report view is modified (even if the Save Password option is checked).

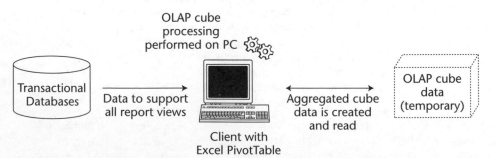

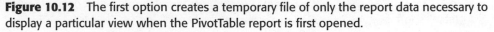

Figure 10.12 The first option creates a temporary file of only the report data necessary to display a particular view when the PivotTable report is first opened.

Select Option 1 when

- Only one user must access the cube
- Only a single view of the PivotTable report is used
- Memory and disk space resources must be minimized

Do not select Option 1 when

- Multiple users must access the cube
- The PivotTable report view is frequently changed

Option 2 — Retrieving All Data at Once

The second option, shown in Figure 10.13, generates a temporary data cube that contains all the data necessary to support any PivotTable report view. You should choose this option when the PivotTable report view will be changed frequently and there is sufficient available memory and temporary disk space for this larger cube.

Using this option, the PivotTable report relies on the temporary OLAP cube for its data. All the data necessary to display any report view is retrieved into a temporary cube when the report is first opened or any time the report is refreshed. Depending on the size of the cube, it can take much longer to open or refresh the report than it would take using the first option. However, once the data is in the PivotTable, you are able to make various changes to the report view without having to continually access the OLTP data source.

Select Option 2 when

- Only one user must access the cube
- Multiple views of the PivotTable report are used
- Permanent disk space resources must be minimized

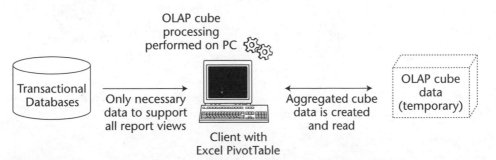

Figure 10.13 The second option creates a temporary file of all the report data when the PivotTable report is first opened.

Do not select Option 2 when

- Multiple users must access the cube
- You encounter memory problems
- Temporary disk space is unavailable

WARNING I think Microsoft has a few bugs to work out with this second option. With Excel 2003/Service Pack A, I've found that the OLTP data source is regularly queried when changes to the report view are made, even though the cube has supposedly been processed with all the data required to display any report view. And worse, the entire cube is reprocessed each time the OLTP data source is queried. As a result, this option actually takes much longer than the first option when it comes to making changes to the report view.

Option 3 — Saving a Cube File

The third option, shown in Figure 10.14, creates a permanent offline cube file. Like the second option, the entire cube must be processed before it can be used in a PivotTable report. However, unlike the second option, this cube is saved to permanent storage.

Using this option, the PivotTable report relies on the offline OLAP cube for its data. All the data necessary to display any report view is retrieved into this permanent cube when the report is first opened or any time the report is refreshed. Depending on the size of the cube, it can take much longer to open or refresh the report than it would take using the first option. However, once the data is in the PivotTable, you are able to make various changes to the report view without having to continually access the OLTP data source.

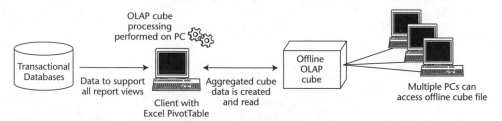

Figure 10.14 The third option creates a permanent file of all of the report data when the PivotTable report is first opened. Multiple PC's can open this cube file.

In most cases, this is the best option to use because the cube data is stored in an offline file that multiple clients can access. And because only the necessary cube data is loaded into the report, memory resources are conserved. Furthermore, a connection to the OLTP data source is not required to analyze and report on the data, yet when the OLTP data source is accessible, the cube can automatically be refreshed with the most current data by simply using the Refresh Data function in Excel.

WARNING Unlike Analysis Server cubes, this is not a true client-server model, so file-sharing errors may occasionally result when multiple clients concurrently access the same cube file.

Select Option 3 when

- Multiple users must access the cube
- Multiple views of the PivotTable report are used
- There is sufficient disk space to store a permanent offline cube file

Do not select Option 3 when

- Permanent disk space is not available to store the offline cube file

Security Options Related to Offline Cubes

Now that I've explained the three options you have for creating OLAP Cubes, I need to explain a security setting that Microsoft fixed by allowing connections only to trusted resources. This security fix disables the first two options from working by presenting the user with the Data Source Initialization error box shown in Figure 10.15.

This security fix also disables the offline cube to be refreshed when the third option is selected, presenting the user with the dialog box message shown in Figure 10.16.

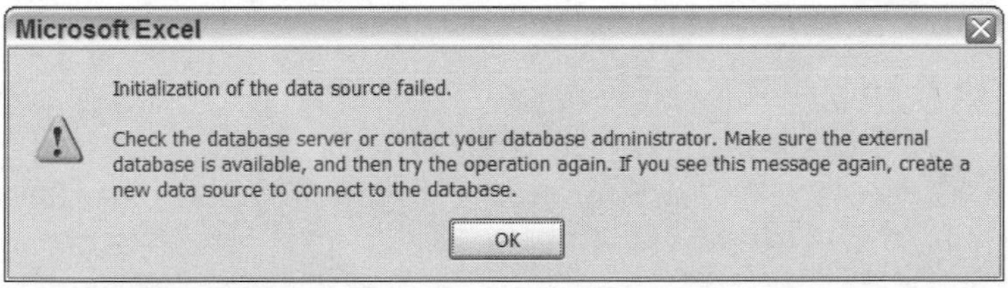

Figure 10.15 This dialog box warning is displayed when either of the first two options in the OLAP Cube Wizard is selected.

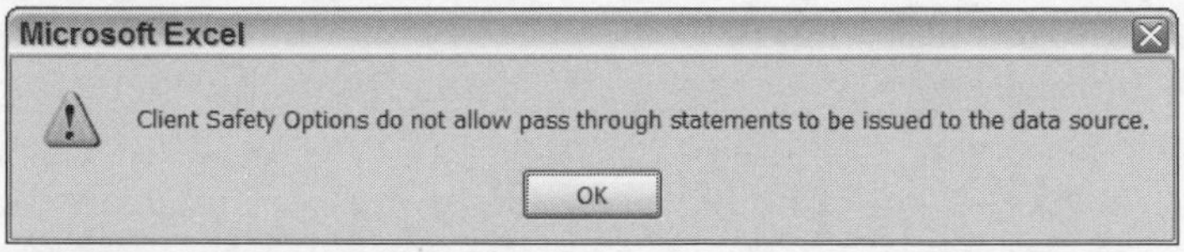

Figure 10.16 This dialog box warning is displayed when the third option is selected, and you attempt to refresh the offline OLAP cube.

As of this writing, there aren't any methods for configuring a resource to be trusted. The only available workaround is to modify the registry, which may result in your computer being more vulnerable to attack by malicious users or by malicious software, such as viruses. I recommend that you check the Microsoft web site to determine whether a more permanent solution is available before applying this workaround. You should also consult with a knowledgeable system administrator in your organization, and back up your registry before making any changes to it.

Follow these steps to apply the OLAP access security workaround:

1. Choose Start ➪ Run to open the Run dialog box.

2. Type **REGEDIT** in the Run dialog box and press Enter to open the Registry Editor program.

3. Choose HKEY_CURRENT_USER ➪ SOFTWARE ➪ Microsoft ➪ Office ➪ 11.0 ➪ Excel ➪ Options.

4. Click the Options key (displayed as a Folder under Excel in the Registry Editor), and then choose Edit ➪ New ➪ DWord Value.

5. Type **OLAPUDFSecurity**, and press Enter to add the new registry entry under the Options key.

6. Double-click OLAPUDFSecurity to open the Edit DWord Value dialog box, and type **1** in the Value Data field, as shown in Figure 10.17.

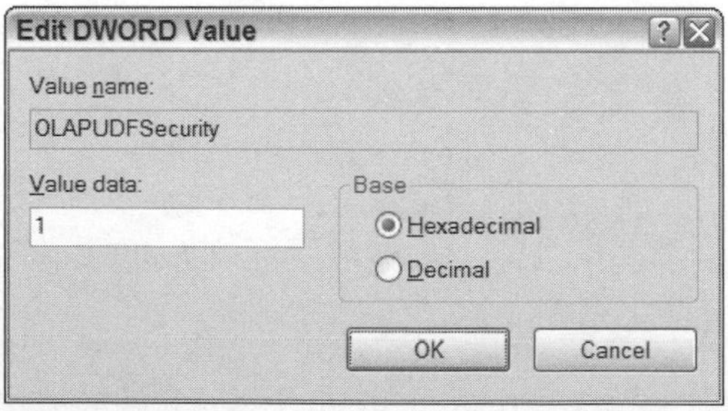

Figure 10.17 Enter 1 in Value Data for the new OLAPUDFSecurity entry.

7. Verify that the Edit DWORD Value dialog box looks like Figure 10.17; and then Click OK to assign the registry entry value and to close the dialog box.

8. Choose File ⇨ Exit to save the changes and quit the Registry Editor program.

After you have applied the OLAP Access workaround by adding the OLAPUDFSecurity key, you are prompted with the dialog box shown in Figure 10.18 each time you attempt to refresh the OLAP cube.

Using the OLAP Cube Wizard

This section provides an example of how you can create an OLAP cube from Excel using an SQL query that runs against the NorthwindCS database. It demonstrates how you can use the OLAP Cube Wizard to choose measures, select and organize dimensions into a hierarchy, and build an offline OLAP cube that can be saved to permanent storage.

Complete these steps to use the OLAP Cube Wizard to create an OLAP cube and follow along with this example:

1. From Excel, choose Data ⇨ PivotTable and PivotChart Report to bring up the PivotTable And PivotChart — Wizard Step 1 of 3 dialog box.

2. Select External Data Source and click Next to continue.

3. Click Get Data in the PivotTable And PivotChart Wizard — Step 2 of 3 dialog box to bring up the Choose Data Source dialog box.

4. When the Choose Data Source dialog box appears, verify that Use The Query Wizard To Create/Edit Queries is unchecked, select the NorthwindCS Database data source, and then click OK to continue.

5. When the Microsoft Query program is launched, you are presented with the Add Tables dialog box. Close this dialog box and click the View SQL button.

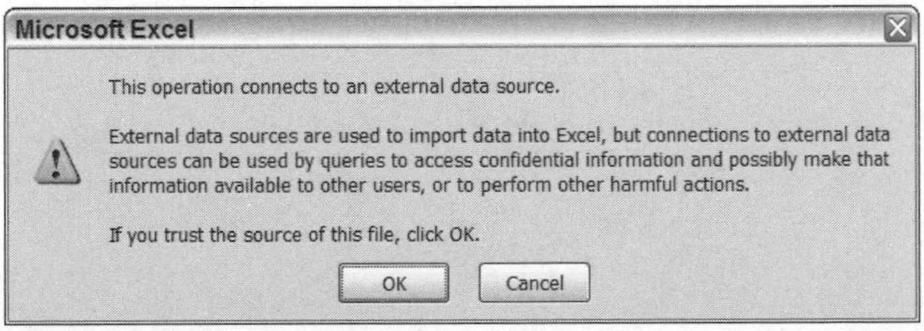

Figure 10.18 After the workaround has been applied, you are prompted to confirm that you trust the data source each time the OLAP cube is refreshed.

6. Paste or type the query shown here into the SQL dialog box and click OK:

```
SELECT  ord.OrderDate                 AS [Order Date],
        ord.ShipCountry               AS [Country],
        CASE
            WHEN ord.ShipRegion IS NULL
                THEN '*N/A'
                ELSE ord.ShipRegion
                END                   AS [State-Province],
        ord.ShipCity                  AS [City],
        ord.ShipName                  AS [Company],
        dtl.Quantity                  AS [Quantity],
        (dtl.UnitPrice *
         dtl.Quantity  *
         (1 - Discount))              AS [Total Order],
        cat.CategoryName              AS [Category],
        pro.ProductName               AS [Product],
        CASE
            WHEN pro.Discontinued = '0'
                THEN 'Available'
                ELSE 'Discontinued'
                END                   AS [Status],
        sup.CompanyName               AS [Supplier],
        emp.LastName                  AS [Employee]
FROM Orders ord
INNER JOIN "Order Details" dtl ON ord.OrderID = dtl.OrderID
INNER JOIN Products pro ON dtl.ProductID = pro.ProductID
INNER JOIN Categories cat ON pro.CategoryID = cat.CategoryID
INNER JOIN Suppliers sup ON pro.SupplierID = sup.SupplierID
INNER JOIN Employees emp ON ord.EmployeeID = emp.EmployeeID
```

ON THE WEB You can download the ch10_example.txt query to your computer from the companion website at www.wiley.com/go/excelreporting. Look for this document in either the Chap10.zip file or Chap10 directory, depending on which .zip file you download.

7. Click OK to acknowledge the dialog box warning that the query cannot be displayed graphically.

8. Choose File ➪ Create OLAP Cube to start the OLAP Cube Wizard program.

9. Click Next when the OLAP Cube Wizard startup screen appears.

10. When the OLAP Cube Wizard Step 1 of 3 dialog box shown in Figure 10.19 appears, click Next to continue — both Quantity and Total Order have been automatically selected as summarized data fields.

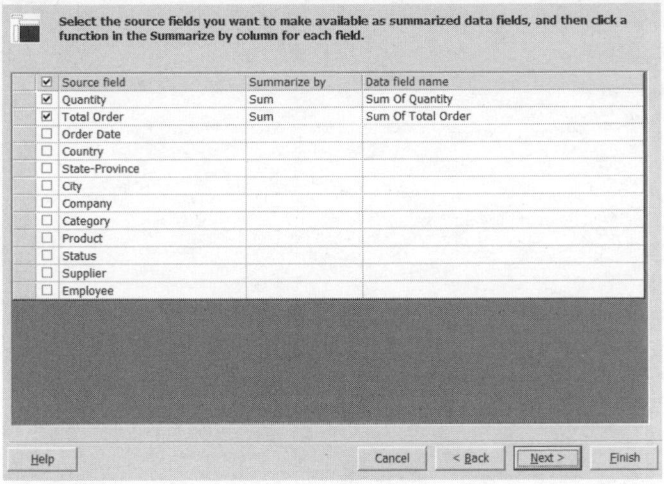

Figure 10.19 Select the fields that should be summarized for the data cube in the first step of the OLAP Cube Wizard.

NOTE The default handling of the OLAP Cube Wizard is to automatically select all numerical fields for summarization.

In this dialog box, you can choose Sum, Count, Minimum, or Maximum as the aggregate function in the Summarize By column. You can also change the field heading names for any summarized field in the Data Field Name column. Review the summary and field heading names here before clicking Next.

11. When the OLAP Cube Wizard Step 2 of 3 dialog box appears, click the box with the double right arrow to move all the fields in the Source Fields pane to the Dimensions pane, as shown in Figure 10.20.

12. Uncheck Quarter in the Order Date hierarchy.

13. Drag Status under Category and Product under Status; and then drag State-Province under Country and City under State-Province, as shown in Figure 10.21.

14. Click Next to continue to the OLAP Cube Wizard Step 3 of 3 dialog box shown in Figure 10.22.

15. The third option, Save A Cube File Containing All Data For The Cube, is the default. Click Finish to choose this third option that creates an offline OLAP cube from the dataset returned by the SQL query.

16. When the Save As dialog box shown in Figure 10.23 appears, click Save to save the cube definition file and the cube data file in the Queries directory.

Figure 10.20   In this step, you select the dimensions for the OLAP cube.

Figure 10.21   Organize the dimension hierarchies as shown here.

NOTE The offline OLAP cube file is saved in the same location as the OLAP cube definition file.

17. When the Microsoft Query dialog box appears, click Yes to create the offline OLAP cube file and return it to Excel.

18. Click Finish when the PivotTable And PivotChart Wizard — Step 2 of 3 dialog box appears.

19. Drag Category to the Row area, Order Date to the Column area, Country to the Page area, and Sum of Quantity to the Data area.

20. Verify that your PivotTable report looks like Figure 10.24.

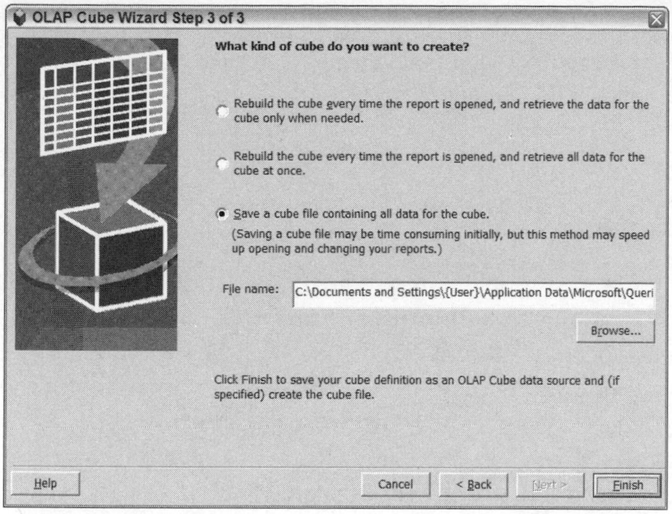

Figure 10.22 Select this third option to create an offline OLAP cube that is permanently saved to disk.

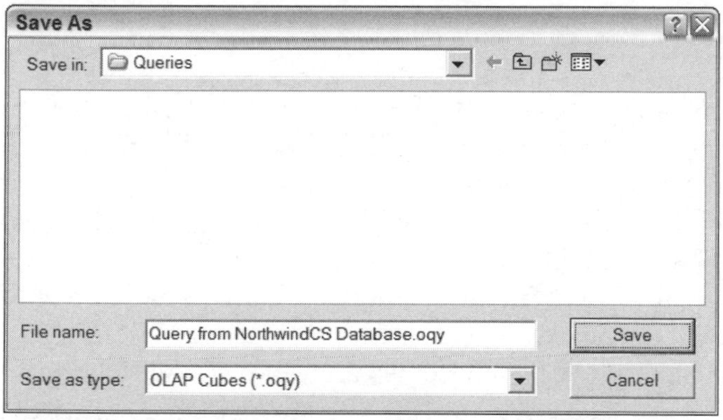

Figure 10.23 Both the query definition file and the offline cube file are saved here.

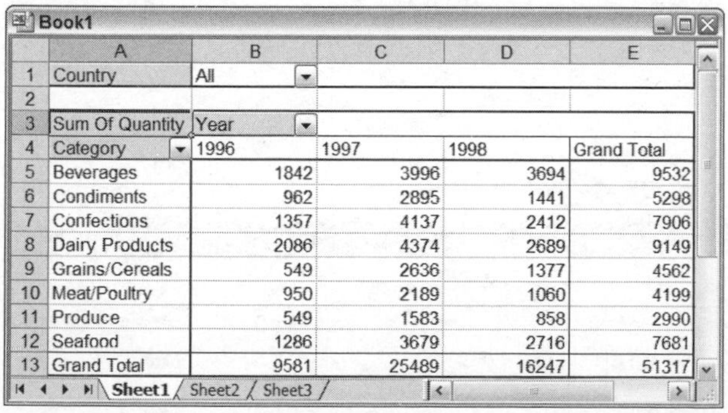

	A	B	C	D	E
1	Country	All			
2					
3	Sum Of Quantity	Year			
4	Category	1996	1997	1998	Grand Total
5	Beverages	1842	3996	3694	9532
6	Condiments	962	2895	1441	5298
7	Confections	1357	4137	2412	7906
8	Dairy Products	2086	4374	2689	9149
9	Grains/Cereals	549	2636	1377	4562
10	Meat/Poultry	950	2189	1060	4199
11	Produce	549	1583	858	2990
12	Seafood	1286	3679	2716	7681
13	Grand Total	9581	25489	16247	51317

Figure 10.24 If you did everything right, your PivotTable report should look like this.

WATCH THE VIDEO To see how to create the OLAP cube from Excel, click the ch1001_video.avi file at this book's companion website at www.wiley.com/go/excelreporting and watch the video.

Working with OLAP Data in a PivotTable

Excel works with OLAP data in a much different way than it does with OLTP data. There are many subtle and not-so-subtle differences in the handling, the display, and the available report functions between these two types of data sources in a PivotTable. This section highlights these differences and covers many of the features available only when a PivotTable is connected to a data cube.

This section compares how OLAP and OLTP data sources are handled in a PivotTable report and discusses some of the report display changes, including the PivotTable Field List window and the field drop-down filters. The section concludes with a review of how dimensions and measures are uniquely handled when the PivotTable report uses an OLAP cube.

Comparing OLAP and OLTP

There are several differences in how an Excel PivotTable report handles an OLAP data source versus how it handles an OLTP data source. First, with OLAP, you may not be able to obtain your data in real-time. And, while you do have the capability to drill through dimension levels, you lose the capability to drill down to the underlying dataset because the data has already been aggregated in the cube. Additionally, some functions that are readily available with OLTP are disabled for OLAP. For example, the Show Pages function is disabled, and the summary type of Data area items cannot be changed because the aggregations in the OLAP cube have already been calculated when the cube was processed. In other words, if Quantity Sold was summed in the data cube, the summary type cannot be changed to an Average, a Minimum, or a Maximum in the PivotTable report, as it can with OLTP.

Table 10.2 provides a more complete list of the differences between these two data source types.

Table 10.2 OLAP and OLTP Differences

FUNCTION	OLAP	OLTP
Analyzes very large datasets	Yes	No
Provides ultra-fast performance for large data sets	Yes	No
Offers hierarchal relationships of dimensions	Yes	No
Includes hidden items in totals	Yes	No

Table 10.2

FUNCTION	OLAP	OLTP
Offers drill through capability on Column and Row area fields	Yes	Yes*
Analyzes data in real-time	Yes†	Yes
Renames report fields	Yes‡	Yes
Uses Show Pages in the PivotTable toolbar	No	Yes
Offers drill down capability on Data area items	No	Yes
Modifies how Data area items are summarized	No	Yes
Moves fields to any area of the PivotTable	No	Yes
Provides full use of the Layout Manager	No	Yes
Creates calculated fields and formulas	No	Yes

* You can drill through Column and Row area fields using OLTP, but fields cannot be organized into an intuitive hierarchy as they can with OLAP.

† There are some client-based OLAP options where data can be fetched from the OLTP data source in near real –time, such as the first option in the OLAP Cube Wizard.

‡ OLAP doesn't remember the updated field name when the field is dragged off the PivotTable report.

Understanding the Display of OLAP Report Fields

A PivotTable report that is connected to an OLAP data source looks a little different from one that is connected to an OLTP data source. For example, in the PivotTable Field List window shown in Figure 10.25, two types of buttons are used instead of just the single one used with an OLTP data source.

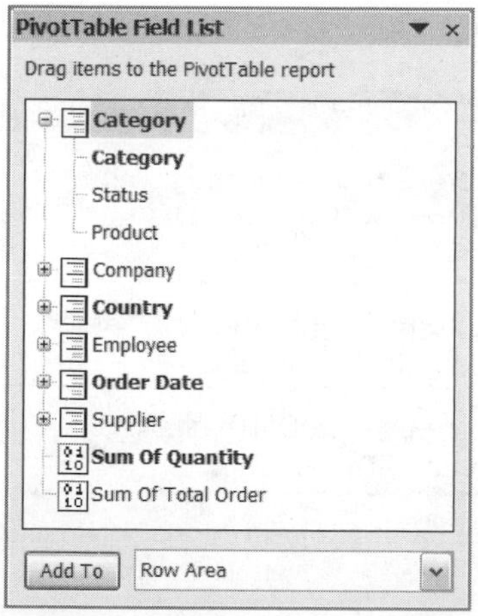

Figure 10.25 You can toggle the various levels of the dimension hierarchy by using the plus (+) and minus (–) signs in the tree.

Table 10.3 describes the icons used in the PivotTable Field List window. Notice that the Dimension icon looks very similar to the Data Field icon you've seen in earlier chapters of this book.

In addition to the new icons, notice that not all fields are initially displayed in the PivotTable Field List — only the top-level dimensions are shown. Clicking the plus (+) and minus (–) signs toggles whether the various levels in the dimension hierarchy are shown. Keep in mind that all dimensions are considered to have at least a top level, even if they were not organized into a multi-level hierarchy. For example, clicking the plus sign of fields that have only a single level, such as Company, Country, or Employee, displays the same field name again; but this time, it displays the field as a level in the dimension.

Working with Dimensions

Dimensions can only be dragged to the Page, Column, or Row area of a Pivot-Table report. If a dimension has several levels, only the top-level is initially displayed when it is dragged to the PivotTable. This is true even if you expand the dimension hierarchy and attempt to drag a lower-level dimension to the report.

TIP The Add To button in the PivotTable Field List window is enabled only when the top-level dimension is selected.

Although you can also use the Layout Manager to move fields to the Pivot-Table report, it is not designed to handle many of the features that are unique to OLAP. As a result, you cannot launch the PivotTable Field List window by double-clicking a field in the Layout Manager as you can with an OLTP data source. Additionally, you can only view and work with the top-level dimensions in this dialog box.

Table 10.3 Explanation of PivotTable Field List Icons

ICON	NAME	DESCRIPTION
≡|	Dimension	Fields marked with this icon are dimensions and can be dropped only in the Row, Column, or Page area of the PivotTable.
01 10	Measure	Fields marked with this icon are measures and can be dropped only in the Data area of the PivotTable.
▤	Data Field	Fields marked with this icon are used in OLTP data sources and can be dropped in any area of the PivotTable.

All fields of an OLTP PivotTable report use the Data Field icon because the fields can be dropped in any area of the PivotTable.

Drilling through the Levels of a Dimension

You can drill through dimension levels of a PivotTable report using four different methods:

- Double-clicking an item in the dimension to reveal or hide the items below it.
- Selecting items in one or more levels in the tree of a top-level dimension.
- Selecting a dimension field heading or a dimension field item and then choosing Group and Show Detail ⇨ Show Detail from the PivotTable toolbar or from the PivotTable pop-up menu.
- Selecting a dimension field heading and then choosing Show Levels from the PivotTable toolbar or from the PivotTable pop-up menu.

Although you can double-click a specific item in the dimension to reveal the items below it, you cannot double-click the field heading to reveal all items in the next lower level. If you want to reveal all items in the next lower level, you should select the dimension field heading and then either choose Group and Show Detail ⇨ Show Detail, or choose Show Levels from the PivotTable toolbar or from the PivotTable pop-up menu.

TIP The PivotTable toolbar includes both menu items and toolbar button shortcuts for drilling through dimension levels.

Hiding Levels above a Selected Dimension

If you want to hide levels above a selected dimension, click on the dimension field heading and choose Hide Levels from the PivotTable toolbar or from the PivotTable pop-up menu. Keep in mind that this function hides both the selected dimension level and all the levels above it (note that levels above are displayed to the left of the dimension field in the PivotTable).

Hiding Levels below a Selected Dimension

If you want to hide levels below a selected dimension, click the dimension field heading and choose Group And Show Detail ⇨ Hide Detail. Keep in mind that this function hides all the levels below (to the right of) the selected dimension, but not the selected dimension, itself.

TIP Try hiding the dimension levels Category and Product while keeping the dimension level, Status displayed. This exercise will help ensure you understand how to drill through the dimension hierarchy.

Using Dimension Filters

The drop-down filters in the PivotTable report for an OLAP data source look much different than they do for an OLTP data source. First, you can choose to display multiple items in any area of the PivotTable. (You might recall that the drop-down list for a Page area field only supports a single value or all values to be displayed when using an OLTP data source.) Next, the drop-down field list is shown only for the top-level dimensions in the report. For example, in Figures 10.26 and 10.27, the drop-down arrow is displayed only for Category and not for Status or Product. The drop-down list of a dimension field is also organized into a tree, where you can choose to display items from one or more levels of a dimension hierarchy.

The tree can show a blank, a check mark, or a double check mark in the check box next to the dimension items, as shown in Figure 10.26. A blank check box indicates that the dimension item and all the items below it are not selected. A single check mark indicates that the dimension item and all the items below it are selected. A double check mark indicates that the dimension item and one or more items below it are selected.

Figure 10.26 A double check mark means that one or more levels below the dimension are selected.

	A	B	C	D	E
1	Country	All			
2					
3	Sum Of Quantity	Year			
4	Category	1996	1997	1998	Grand Total *
5	Beverages	1842	3996	3694	9532
6	Confections	1357	4137	2412	7906
7	Dairy Products	2086	4374	2689	9149
8	Grains/Cereals	549	2636	1377	4562
9	Meat/Poultry	950	2189	1060	4199
10	Seafood	1286	3679	2716	7681
11	Grand Total *	9581	25489	16247	51317

Sheet1 / Sheet2 / Sheet3

Figure 10.27 An asterisk is displayed next to the Grand Total fields to indicate that hidden fields are included in the totals.

Configuring the Grand Totals Display

With OLAP data sources, you can choose to display the Grand Totals for all Row and Column area fields, even if some of the items are hidden. The Pivot-Table toolbar includes an Include Hidden Items in Totals button for toggling whether the Grand Totals include hidden items. You can also use the Mark Totals With * in the PivotTable Options dialog box to display an asterisk next to the Grand Totals when the Display Hidden Items toolbar button is enabled.

Complete these steps to hide a dimension item and display the report Grand Totals for all the items:

1. Starting with the PivotTable report view in Figure 10.24, click the Category drop-down list, and then uncheck Condiments and Produce by clicking the check box next to each dimension item twice.

2. Click the Include Hidden Items in Totals button to display the grand totals for hidden and displayed items in the PivotTable report.

3. Right-click the PivotTable report, choose Table Options from the pop-up menu, check Mark Totals With *, and then click OK to add an asterisk next to the Grand Totals labels and close the Table Options dialog box.

4. Verify that your PivotTable report looks like Figure 10.27.

NOTE Because of the way the data is organized and aggregated in a cube, this feature is available only with OLAP data sources.

Working with Measures

Measures are numerical data fields that have been aggregated for all the dimensions in the OLAP cube. They appear as a unique icon in the PivotTable Field List window and can be dragged only to the Data area of the PivotTable report.

Drilling Down on Data

You cannot drill down to the underlying data of an OLAP PivotTable report because the data has already been aggregated and the detail just isn't there to display. If you do attempt to drill down on the data by double-clicking a numerical value — or measure — in the Data area of the PivotTable, a dialog box warning appears, stating that Microsoft Excel cannot show detail for the selection.

Changing the Way Data Area Items Are Aggregated

Unlike with OLTP, you cannot change the summary type of measures simply by double-clicking the Data area field to bring up the Field Settings dialog box. If you try this, you'll notice that the various summary types are disabled. This is because the data has already been aggregated into the OLAP cube. There simply isn't enough information in the cube for Excel to calculate a different summary type. If you want to modify the aggregate function, you have to re-create the PivotTable report using a new data cube (client-based OLAP), or just redesign the cube and refresh the report (server-based OLAP).

WARNING Client-based OLAP does not support the Average aggregate function. This is available only with server-based OLAP (as a calculated measure).

Although the summary types of measures cannot be changed in the Pivot-Table report, you can still use the custom calculation functions that are available by double-clicking the Data area field to bring up the PivotTable Field dialog box. Clicking Options in this dialog box reveals the Show Data As drop-down field list where you can apply a custom calculation to a measure.

CROSS-REFERENCE Refer to Chapter 7 to learn more about custom calculation functions.

Trying It Out in the Real World

Northwind Trader's management has been very pleased with your remarkable success in helping them out on earlier reporting projects. As a result, they have asked you to help them implement a client-based OLAP solution. Andrew Fuller, the company's Vice President, has asked that you create a presentation that shows how their data can be organized into a hierarchy. Andrew has communicated that many of the salespersons are not technology-savvy and will likely use only a single report view. He's also asked that the OLAP report meet the following requirements:

- Client computer memory is minimized and permanent cube files are not stored to disk.
- The PivotTable is automatically refreshed when the report is first opened and every five minutes while the report remains open.
- The Date Ordered hierarchy is ordered as Year ⇨ Quarter ⇨ Month.
- The customer hierarchy is ordered as Country ⇨ Region ⇨ City ⇨ Company ⇨ Position ⇨ Contact.

Andrew has asked that you use the following SQL query for the OLAP cube and PivotTable report:

```
SELECT ctm.Country        AS [Country],
       ctm.Region         AS [Region],
       ctm.City           AS [City],
       ctm.CompanyName    AS [Company],
       ctm.ContactName    AS [Contact],
       ctm.ContactTitle   AS [Position],
       ord.OrderDate      AS [Date Ordered],
       1                  AS [Orders],
       (UnitPrice *
       Quantity  *
       Discount)          AS [Order Amount]
FROM Customers ctm
INNER JOIN Orders ord on ctm.CustomerID = ord.CustomerID
INNER JOIN "Order Details" dtl on ord.OrderID = dtl.OrderID
```

ON THE WEB You can download the ch10_rwe.txt query file to your computer from the companion website at www.wiley.com/go/ excelreporting. Look in the Chap10.zip file or the Chap10 directory.

Getting Down to Business

Complete these steps to create the PivotTable report for the Northwind presentation:

1. From Excel, choose Data ⇨ PivotTable And PivotChart Report to bring up the PivotTable And PivotChart Wizard — Step 1 of 3 dialog box.

2. Select External Data Source, and then click Next to continue.

3. Click Get Data in the PivotTable And PivotChart Wizard — Step 2 of 3 dialog box to bring up the Choose Data Source Dialog box.

4. When the Choose Data Source dialog box appears, verify that Use The Query Wizard To Create/Edit queries is unchecked, select the NorthwindCS Database data source, and then click OK to continue.

5. When the Microsoft Query program is launched, you are presented with the Add Tables dialog box. Close this dialog box, and then click the View SQL button to bring up the SQL window.

6. Paste or type Andrew's query into the SQL dialog box and click OK.

7. Click OK to acknowledge the dialog box warning that the query cannot be displayed graphically.

8. Choose File ➪ Create OLAP Cube to start the OLAP Cube Wizard.

9. Click Next when the OLAP Cube Wizard startup screen appears.

10. When the OLAP Cube Wizard Step 1 of 3 dialog box appears, change the value in Summarize By from Count to Sum for Orders, as shown in Figure 10.28; and then click Next to continue.

11. When the OLAP Cube Wizard Step 2 of 3 dialog box appears, click the box with the double right arrow to move all the fields in the Source Fields pane to the Dimensions pane.

12. Modify the hierarchy for Date Ordered to use Year ➪ Quarter ➪ Month, and then organize the customer dimensions into the hierarchy Country ➪ Region ➪ City ➪ Company ➪ Position ➪ Contact, as shown in Figure 10.29.

13. Verify that the dimensions are ordered as shown in Figure 10.29, and then click Next to continue to the OLAP Cube Wizard — Step 3 of 3 dialog box.

14. Select the first option: Rebuild The Cube Every Time The Report Is Opened And Retrieve The Data For The Cube Only When Needed. Click Finish to create a temporary OLAP cube from the dataset returned by the SQL query.

Source field	Summarize by	Data field name
☑ Orders	Count	Count Of Orders
☑ Order Amount	Sum	Sum Of Order Amount
☐ Country		
☐ Region		
☐ City		
☐ Company		
☐ Contact		
☐ Position		
☐ Date Ordered		

Figure 10.28   Summarize Orders by a Count instead of a Sum.

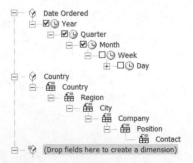

Figure 10.29   Organize the dimensions fields into the hierarchy shown here.

15. When the Save As dialog box appears, click Save to save the cube definition file in the Queries directory.

16. Click Yes when the Microsoft Query dialog box appears and asks if you want to create the OLAP cube and return to Microsoft Excel.

17. Click Finish when the PivotTable And PivotChart Wizard — Step 2 of 3 dialog box appears.

18. Drag Country to the Row area, Date Ordered to the Column area, and Count of Orders to the Data area.

19. In the Row area, double-click Brazil to display the regions RP and SP, and then double-click SP to display the cities in that region.

20. Verify that your PivotTable report looks like Figure 10.30.

21. Right-click the PivotTable report and choose Table Options from the pop-up menu to bring up the Table Options dialog box.

22. Check the Refresh On Open option to configure the PivotTable report to automatically refresh whenever the report is opened.

23. Check the Refresh Every option and type **5** in the Minutes field to configure the PivotTable report to automatically refresh every five minutes.

24. Click OK to close the Table Options dialog box and return to the Pivot-Table report.

WATCH THE VIDEO To see how to create this PivotTable report, you can click the file **ch1002_video.avi** at www.wilcy.com/go/excelreporting **to** watch the video.

	A	B	C	D	E	F	G
1			Drop Page Fields Here				
2							
3	Count Of Orders			Year			
4	Country	Region	City	1996	1997	1998	Grand Total
5	Argentina				12	22	34
6	Austria			27	60	38	125
7	Belgium			6	19	31	56
8	Brazil	RJ		19	35	29	83
9		SP	Campinas		16	3	19
10			Resende	2	11	6	19
11			São Paulo	15	44	23	82
12		SP Total		17	71	32	120
13	Brazil Total			36	106	61	203

Figure 10.30 Your PivotTable report should look like this if you did everything right.

Reviewing What You Did

This example demonstrated how a client-based OLAP solution might be used in the enterprise to organize a company's data into a hierarchal structure for reporting and analysis in a PivotTable report. This example assumed that the report users were not familiar with the technology, requiring you to enable automatic refreshes and configure an OLAP solution optimized for a single report view. In addition, you were asked to use only a minimal amount of the computer's memory, processing, and disk resources.

Chapter Review

This chapter provided a basic overview of OLAP technology and how it fits into the bigger picture of data warehousing. You learned about client-based and server-based OLAP processing methods, the process flow, and the key concepts of each of these methods. The chapter provided in-depth coverage of each OLAP processing method and described how OLAP data looks and functions in a PivotTable report.

CHAPTER 11

Creating and Using Spreadsheet Reports

This chapter shows you how to create professional-looking Spreadsheet reports using the powerful tools and functions that are included in Excel 2003. It assumes you have already read over the PivotTable report chapters and have a basic understanding of this technology, as it makes some comparisons between these two types of reporting tools.

This chapter provides some perspective on why you might use a Spreadsheet report in place of a PivotTable report. It starts out by covering the terminology and concepts of Spreadsheet reports, and then shows you how to use the numerous functions and tools included with Spreadsheet reports to manage your report data. The chapter also discusses using a web query to import web page data into a Spreadsheet report, and it explains how you can integrate parameters into SQL queries and stored procedures to accept user-input values that are mapped to variables in a SQL query or stored procedure. When you have finished working through the chapter, try the real-world example at the end to put into practice what you have learned.

Introducing Spreadsheet Reports

You can use Spreadsheet reports to organize data into the traditional columnar-format, as opposed to the cross-tabular format of a PivotTable report. And despite its traditional roots, a columnar report is still quite powerful. You've probably heard about or used report development programs such as Business Objects (formerly Crystal Reports), Oracle Forms, or Microsoft Access Reports. You can use any of these software applications to create cutting-edge reports and business forms from external data sources. Although Excel provides much more powerful functionality in the area of cross-tabular functionality with its PivotTable reports, it does not match the columnar report features available in these other software programs. Nevertheless, Spreadsheet reports include several innovative features and tools that cover the basics and offer some advanced functionality quite well.

Looking at Some Features of Spreadsheet Reports

Spreadsheet reports let you access data from numerous types of external data sources, including databases, text files, and even web pages. With the exception of web page data sources, Spreadsheet reports use the Microsoft Query program to access external data. Thus, you can create a simple SQL query using the graphical tools included in the Query Wizard (covered in Chapter 4), build a more advanced SQL query in the Microsoft Query program (covered in chapters 5 and 6), or just paste an SQL query created from a query development software application, such as Query Analyzer, SQL Server Management Studio, Toad, or SQL Plus. And, by using the Web Query dialog box (covered later in this chapter), you can import specific text and table data into the Spreadsheet report from an Internet or intranet web page.

Spreadsheet reports also support parameters that enable the report user to specify values that are mapped to conditions in the `Where` part of an SQL query or to variables in a stored procedure. The parameters can store default values or reference particular cell values in the Excel workbook. If worksheet cells are used, the report can even be configured to automatically refresh whenever the value in a referenced cell is modified.

Other innovative features of Spreadsheet reports include fill-down formulas, conditional formatting, and auto-refreshing. All these functions are covered in greater detail in the coming sections.

Comparing Spreadsheet Reports to PivotTable Reports

Consider using a Spreadsheet report in place of a PivotTable report when one or more of the following conditions are met:

- The report data should not be aggregated
- The report has no numeric fields to summarize
- The report data needs to be displayed in a columnar format

Figure 11.1 shows an example of a Spreadsheet report that extracts product information from the NorthwindCS database. (Note that the SQL query for this report is shown a little later in the "Before You Begin" section.) This report includes the product status, the product category, the quantity of the product in stock, the quantity of the product currently on order, and the product's reorder level. The quantity in stock and the quantity on order for each product are subtotaled for each category group.

As you can see in Figure 11.1, the Spreadsheet report displays the data set in a columnar layout, similar to how the data set is presented in the Microsoft Query program. Notice that the Beverages item in Category Name and the Available item in Status are shown multiple times in the report, rather than as a single unique item as they would be in a PivotTable report. Now, look at Figure 11.2, which shows how this same data might appear in a PivotTable.

	A	B	C	D	E	F
1	Category Name	Product Name	Status	In Stock	On Order	RO Level
2	Beverages	Chai	Available	39	0	10
3	Beverages	Chang	Available	17	40	25
4	Beverages	Chartreuse verte	Available	69	0	5
5	Beverages	Côte de Blaye	Available	17	0	15
6	Beverages	Guaraná Fantástica	Discontinued	20	0	0
7	Beverages	Ipoh Coffee	Available	17	10	25
8	Beverages	Lakkalikööri	Available	57	0	20
9	Beverages	Laughing Lumberjack Lager	Available	52	0	10
10	Beverages	Outback Lager	Available	15	10	30
11	Beverages	Rhönbräu Klosterbier	Available	125	0	25
12	Beverages	Sasquatch Ale	Available	111	0	15
13	Beverages	Steeleye Stout	Available	20	0	15
14	**Beverages Total**			559	60	
15	Condiments	Aniseed Syrup	Discontinued	13	70	25
16	Condiments	Chef Anton's Cajun Seasoning	Available	53	0	0

Sheet1 / Sheet2 / Sheet3 /

Figure 11.1 A typical Spreadsheet report displays data in a columnar format without any aggregation.

	A	B	C	D	E	F
1			Drop Page Fields Here			
2						
3	Category Name ▼	Product Name ▼	Status ▼	RO Level ▼	Data ▼	Total
4	Beverages	Chai	Available	10	Sum of In Stock	39
5					Sum of On Order	0
6		Chang	Available	25	Sum of In Stock	17
7					Sum of On Order	40
8		Chartreuse verte	Available	5	Sum of In Stock	69
9					Sum of On Order	0
10		Côte de Blaye	Available	15	Sum of In Stock	17
11					Sum of On Order	0
12		Guaraná Fantástica	Discontinued	0	Sum of In Stock	20
13					Sum of On Order	0
14		Ipoh Coffee	Available	25	Sum of In Stock	17
15					Sum of On Order	10

Sheet1 / Sheet2 / Sheet3 /

Figure 11.2 A PivotTable report displays the information in a cross-tabular format.

Notice how the PivotTable report shows only the unique category names. Additionally, the Data area items (In Stock, On Order) are displayed in rows moving downward, rather than in columns moving across the report.

Although it is possible to change the orientation of the Data area items to display them as columns (as shown in Figure 11.3), it isn't possible to display a non-numeric field after the Data area items, for example, RO Level after In Stock and On Order. Additionally, Excel runs into limitations with the number of fields that can be simultaneously dropped into the Row area and the Data area of the PivotTable report for large datasets.

In a Spreadsheet report, numeric fields are optional. In contrast, at least one field must be dropped in the Data area of a PivotTable report. Although there are some ways to work around this requirement (by not using the Layout Manager, for example), the report appears incomplete, as the Drop Data Area Items Here background message is displayed until a field is dropped into the Data area of the PivotTable.

Spreadsheet reports and PivotTable reports have many differences besides just the way the data is organized. Table 11.1 lists some of these differences.

Don't worry if you don't understand all these differences. The features that pertain to Spreadsheet reports are explained in greater detail throughout the appropriate sections of this chapter.

CROSS-REFERENCE Refer to Chapters 7 and 8 if you need more information on the features included with PivotTable reports.

	A	B	C	D	E	F
1			Drop Page Fields Here			
2						
3					Data ▾	
4	Category Name ▾	Product Name ▾	Status ▾	RO Level ▾	In Stock	On Order
5	Beverages	Chai	Available	10	39	0
6		Chang	Available	25	17	40
7		Chartreuse verte	Available	5	69	0
8		Côte de Blaye	Available	15	17	0
9		Guaraná Fantástica	Discontinued	0	20	0
10		Ipoh Coffee	Available	25	17	10
11		Lakkalikööri	Available	20	57	0
12		Laughing Lumberjack La	Available	10	52	0
13		Outback Lager	Available	30	15	10
14		Rhönbräu Klosterbier	Available	25	125	0
15		Sasquatch Ale	Available	15	111	0
16		Steeleye Stout	Available	15	20	0
17	Beverages Total				559	60
18	Condiments	Aniseed Syrup	Discontinued	25	13	70

Figure 11.3 PivotTable reports are not suited for a columnar format, but it is possible to show Data area fields across columns rather than down rows.

Table 11.1: Differences between Spreadsheet and PivotTable Reports

SPREADSHEET REPORT	PIVOTTABLE REPORT
Organizes data into a columnar format.	Organizes data into a cross-tabular format.
Works with OLTP data sources.	Works with OLTP and OLAP data sources.
Limited to 65,536 rows.	Only limited by the client computer's available memory.
Numeric data not required.	Numeric data required.
Supports parameters that can be mapped to conditions in the `Where` part of an SQL query.	Does not support parameters.
Supports web queries.	Does not support web queries.
Includes Fill Down fields for adding formulas to report data.	Includes Calculated Field and Calculated Items for adding formulas and items to the report.
The data set is sorted by specifying a sort order in the SQL query or a sort order in the Spreadsheet report.	Individual fields are sorted, not the entire dataset
Subtotals can be applied to individual fields.	Subtotals are applied to all of the fields in the Data area.
Conditional formatting works well since columns are not shifted.	Conditional formatting does not work well because the report shape can change as new items are added or fields are dragged on or off the report.

A Review of Spreadsheet Report Components

This section covers the basic features and tools of a Spreadsheet report, including the Spreadsheet report toolbar. It starts by providing a basic SQL query used as an example throughout this chapter. If you plan to follow along with the examples, be sure to complete the steps in the following "Before You Begin" section first.

Before You Begin

Following these steps:

1. From Excel, choose Data ➪ Import External Data ➪ New Database Query to bring up the Choose Data Source dialog box shown in Figure 11.4.

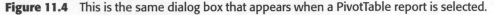

Figure 11.4 This is the same dialog box that appears when a PivotTable report is selected.

2. In the Choose Data Source dialog box, verify that Use The Query Wizard To Create/Edit Queries is unchecked, select the NorthwindCS Database data source, and click OK to continue.

3. When the Microsoft Query program is launched, you are presented with the Add Tables dialog box. Close this dialog box, and then click the View SQL button to bring up the SQL window.

4. Paste or type the following query into the SQL dialog box, and then click OK:

```
SELECT cat.CategoryName              AS [Category Name],
       pro.ProductName               AS [Product Name],
       CASE
           WHEN pro.Discontinued = '0'
               THEN 'Available'
               ELSE 'Discontinued'
               END                   AS [Status],
       pro.UnitsInStock              AS [In Stock],
       pro.UnitsOnOrder              AS [On Order],
       pro.ReorderLevel              AS [RO Level]
FROM Products pro
INNER JOIN Categories cat on pro.CategoryID = cat.CategoryID
```

ON THE WEB You can download the ch11_example01.txt query file to your computer from this book's companion website at www.wiley.com/go/ excelreporting. Look for this document in either the Chap11.zip file or Chap11 directory, depending on which .zip file you download.

5. Click OK to acknowledge the dialog box warning that the query cannot be displayed graphically.

6. Click the Return Data button to return the data to Excel and continue.

7. When the Import Data dialog box shown in Figure 11.5 appears, click OK to create the Spreadsheet report in the existing worksheet tab.

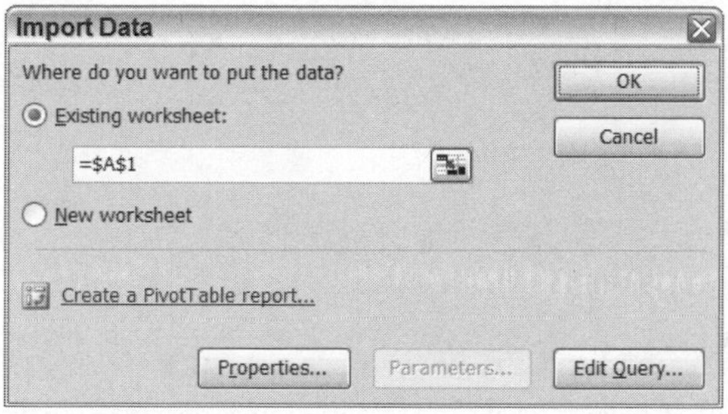

Figure 11.5 Click OK to create the Spreadsheet report from the SQL query.

TIP Clicking the Create a PivotTable Report hyperlink in Figure 11.5 creates a PivotTable report instead of a Spreadsheet report.

8. Verify that your Spreadsheet report looks like Figure 11.6.

	A	B	C	D	E	F
1	Category Name	Product Name	Status	In Stock	On Order	RO Level
2	Beverages	Chai	Available	39	0	10
3	Beverages	Chang	Available	17	40	25
4	Condiments	Aniseed Syrup	Discontinued	13	70	25
5	Condiments	Chef Anton's Cajun Seasoning	Available	53	0	0
6	Condiments	Chef Anton's Gumbo Mix	Discontinued	0	0	0
7	Condiments	Grandma's Boysenberry Spread	Available	120	0	25
8	Produce	Uncle Bob's Organic Dried Pears	Available	15	0	10
9	Condiments	Northwoods Cranberry Sauce	Available	6	0	0
10	Meat/Poultry	Mishi Kobe Niku	Discontinued	29	0	0
11	Seafood	Ikura	Available	31	0	0
12	Dairy Products	Queso Cabrales	Available	22	30	30
13	Dairy Products	Queso Manchego La Pastora	Available	86	0	0
14	Seafood	Konbu	Available	24	0	5

Sheet1 / Sheet2 / Sheet3 /

Figure 11.6 If you did everything right, the Spreadsheet report should look like this.

Using the Spreadsheet Report Toolbar

You can access many of the tools and functions of a Spreadsheet report from the External Data toolbar shown in Figure 11.7. You toggle the display of this toolbar by choosing View ➪ Toolbars ➪ External Data.

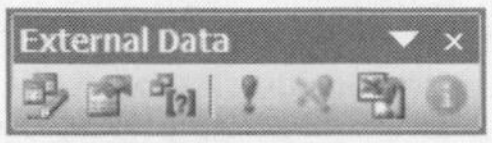

Figure 11.7   You can use the External Data toolbar to manage many of the Spreadsheet report functions.

Clicking the down arrow next to the Close box (X) in the top-right corner of the External Data toolbar brings up the Add or Remove menu item where you can customize what buttons are displayed.

NOTE Unlike the PivotTable toolbar, all available buttons are shown by default in the External Data toolbar.

Table 11.2 provides an explanation of the various graphical buttons available on the External Data toolbar.

Table 11.2   External Data Toolbar Buttons and Descriptions

BUTTON	NAME	DESCRIPTION
ma033	Edit Query	Opens the Microsoft Query program where the SQL query can be modified.
ma034	Data Range Properties	Opens the External Data Range Properties dialog box.
ma035	Query Parameters	Opens the Parameters dialog box.
ma036	Refresh Data	Refreshes the Spreadsheet report using the current query in the Edit Query dialog box.
ma037	Cancel Refresh	Cancels the currently executing query (enabled only when a query is running).
ma038	Refresh All	Refreshes all of the Spreadsheet and PivotTable reports in the current Excel workbook.
ma039	Refresh Status	Displays the Refresh Status of the currently running query (enabled only when a query is running).

These buttons and functions are explained in greater detail throughout the appropriate sections of this chapter.

Managing the Spreadsheet Report

After the data is imported into the Spreadsheet report, you can use numerous functions and tools to analyze, format, and manage the report data. Additionally, all the functions included in Excel are still available, enabling you to edit, delete, and insert new data, add formulas, apply conditional formatting, create PivotTable or PivotChart reports, and group and subtotal data. There are also some tools and functions specially designed to help you manage and format the data in the Spreadsheet report. This section covers the following topics:

- Configuring Spreadsheet report formatting options
- Changing column location
- Using filters
- Sorting data
- Calculating subtotals
- Using fill-down formulas
- Applying conditional formats
- Configuring Spreadsheet report data options

Configuring Spreadsheet Report Formatting Options

You access formatting options in the External Data Range Properties dialog box. Here, you can toggle the field heading and row number display and whether the report formatting changes are maintained each time the Spreadsheet report is refreshed.

You access the formatting options by right-clicking the Spreadsheet report and choosing Data Range Properties from the pop-up menu. Alternatively, you can just click the Data Range Properties button on the External Data toolbar to bring up the External Data Range Properties dialog box, as shown in Figure 11.8.

The options in the bottom of this dialog box control how some of the formatting features are handled in the Spreadsheet report. Table 11.3 provides a description of each option in this dialog box.

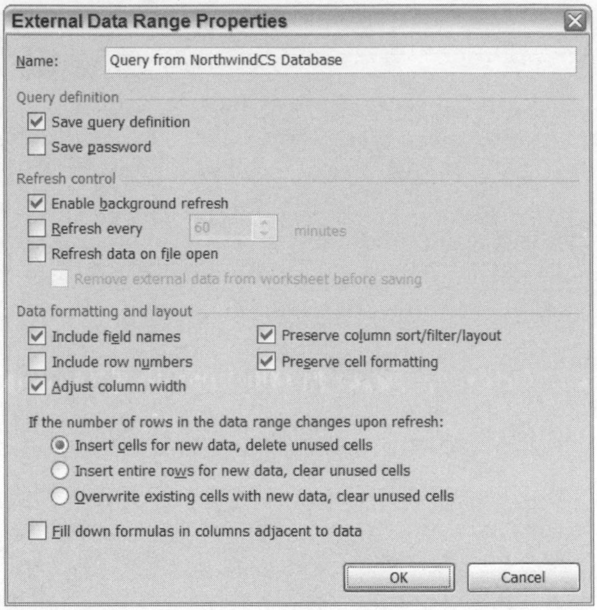

Figure 11.8 The bottom part of the External Data Range Properties dialog box, shown here, is used to manage the formatting functions of the Spreadsheet report.

Table 11.3 Formatting Options in the External Data Range Properties Dialog Box

OPTION NAME	DESCRIPTION
Include Field Names	Toggles whether field headings are displayed in the first row of the report.
Include Row Numbers	Toggles whether row numbers are included as a column in the report. (Note that the row number starts at 0, instead of 1.)
Adjust Column Width	Toggles whether the column widths are automatically adjusted (each time the report is refreshed) to display the best fit for the returned dataset.
Preserve Column Sort/Filter/Layout	Toggles whether the sort, filter, and layout are preserved when the Spreadsheet report is refreshed.
Preserve Cell Formatting	Toggles whether formatting changes are preserved each time the report is refreshed. Use this option in conjunction with Adjust Column Width.
Insert Cells For New Data, Delete Unused Cells	Enables you to insert cells for new data and delete unused cells.
Insert Entire Rows For New Data, Clear Unused Cells	Enables you to insert entire rows for new data and clear unused cells.

Table 11-3 *(continued)*

OPTION NAME	DESCRIPTION
Overwrite Existing Cells With New Data, Clear Unused Cells	Enables you to overwrite existing cells with new data and clear unused cells.
Fill Down Formulas In Columns Adjacent To Data	Automatically fills down column formulas adjacent to the Spreadsheet report when the report data is refreshed.

The next few sections provide additional information about some of these formatting options.

Including Field Headings in the Spreadsheet Report

The Include Field Names option toggles whether the report headings are displayed. When this option is checked, the same headings shown in the Microsoft Query program also appear in the first row of the Spreadsheet report. The default handling is to display field headings in a bold font. You can change the font style, but keep in mind that the Preserve Cell Formatting option determines whether the formatting changes are maintained when the report is refreshed.

Including Row Numbers

If the Include Row Numbers option is checked, a row number column is added to the Spreadsheet report. This column appears as the left-most column in the report and by default does not include a field heading. I find this option deficient in that the row numbers start at 0, instead of 1.

Adjusting the Column Width

When the Adjust Column Width option is checked, the Spreadsheet report automatically adjusts each column width for a best fit. These column width settings are automatically applied each time the report is refreshed. Thus, the column widths can change based on the length of the data in each column of the report. This option is generally used in conjunction with Preserve Cell Formatting, as both of these options toggle whether the Spreadsheet report is automatically formatted each time a refresh operation is performed.

Preserving Column Sort/Filter/Layout

The Preserve Column Sort/Filter/Layout option controls three settings in the Spreadsheet report:

- **Sort Order:** The specified sort instructions
- **Filter Settings:** The specified filter settings
- **Layout:** The order of columns (left to right)

If this option is unchecked, any changes made to the sort, filter, or layout in the Spreadsheet report are removed when the Spreadsheet report is refreshed.

> **NOTE** The sort, filter, and layout settings apply only to the changes specified in the Spreadsheet report. The sorting, filtering, and column order used in the SQL query are not controlled by this option unless you consider that the settings in the Spreadsheet report are actually overriding the sort order, the number of rows displayed, or the order of columns (left to right) specified in the SQL query.

Preserving Formatting Changes

The Preserve Cell Formatting option toggles whether formatting changes made in the Spreadsheet report are saved each time the Spreadsheet report is refreshed. This option applies to both the field headings and the report data. This option is generally used in conjunction with Adjust Column Width, as both of them impact whether the Spreadsheet report is automatically formatted each time a refresh operation is performed.

Changing Column Location

When you first create a Spreadsheet report, the columns are displayed in the same order in which they are listed in the SQL query. Although it's possible to modify the query to change the column location, this only works when the Preserve Column Sort/Filter/Layout option is unchecked. And because this option also includes the sort and filter settings, you may not want to uncheck it.

When the Preserve Column Sort/Filter/Layout option is checked, the best method for changing the column location is to cut-and-insert the report column. If you do not have any logos or report titles in the Spreadsheet report, just select the entire column, right-click it, and choose Cut from the pop-up menu, and then right-click on the column where you want to paste the cut column and choose Insert Cut Cells from the pop-up menu. This inserts the cut column into the selected column.

> **WARNING** If the AutoFilter setting is toggled on, the cut column cannot be inserted using this cut-and-insert method. If that's the case, you can temporarily toggle the AutoFilter settings off to complete this operation.

Complete these steps to move RO Level before In Stock and On Order in the Spreadsheet report and follow along with the example:

1. Click the F cell to select the entire RO Level column, right-click the highlighted area, and then choose Cut from the pop-up menu.

2. Right-click the D cell to select the entire In Stock column to bring up the pop-up menu. Choose Insert Cut to move RO Level before In Stock and On Order.

3. Verify that your Spreadsheet report looks like Figure 11.9.

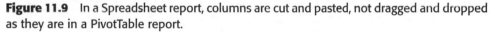

	A	B	C	D	E	F
1	**Category Name**	**Product Name**	**Status**	**RO Level**	**In Stock**	**On Order**
2	Beverages	Chai	Available	10	39	0
3	Beverages	Chang	Available	25	17	40
4	Condiments	Aniseed Syrup	Discontinued	25	13	70
5	Condiments	Chef Anton's Cajun Seasoning	Available	0	53	0
6	Condiments	Chef Anton's Gumbo Mix	Discontinued	0	0	0
7	Condiments	Grandma's Boysenberry Spread	Available	25	120	0
8	Produce	Uncle Bob's Organic Dried Pears	Available	10	15	0
9	Condiments	Northwoods Cranberry Sauce	Available	0	6	0
10	Meat/Poultry	Mishi Kobe Niku	Discontinued	0	29	0
11	Seafood	Ikura	Available	0	31	0
12	Dairy Products	Queso Cabrales	Available	30	22	30
13	Dairy Products	Queso Manchego La Pastora	Available	0	86	0
14	Seafood	Konbu	Available	5	24	0
15	Produce	Tofu	Available	0	35	0
16	Condiments	Genen Shouyu	Available	5	39	0

H ◄ ► H \ **Sheet1** / Sheet2 / Sheet3 /

Figure 11.9 In a Spreadsheet report, columns are cut and pasted, not dragged and dropped as they are in a PivotTable report.

Using Filters

You can apply an Auto Filter by clicking any cell in the Spreadsheet report and choosing Data ➪ Auto Filter. After Auto Filter is enabled, a drop-down arrow is displayed next to all the column headings in the report. Clicking the drop-down arrow in a field heading brings up the drop-down box shown in Figure 11.10.

Figure 11.10 The Auto Filter drop-down list includes sort order functions at the top and filters at the bottom.

The filter drop-down box shown in Figure 11.10 is separated into two sections. The top section has functions for specifying an ascending or a descending sort order to the Spreadsheet report data based on values in the selected column of the report. The bottom section lists the unique values in the selected column. At the top of the list are functions for removing the filter (All), showing the top ten values (Top 10), and specifying a custom filter (Custom).

WARNING If the Preserve Column Sort/Filter/Layout option is unchecked in the External Data Range Properties dialog box, the filter settings are removed when the Spreadsheet report is refreshed.

Choosing Custom from the pop-up menu brings up the Custom AutoFilter dialog box shown in Figure 11.11. Here, you can specify up to two conditions for the filter. These conditions include a drop-down list of mathematical and string operators on the left side of the dialog box, and a filter value on the right side of the dialog box. The conditions can be joined by an And or Or operator.

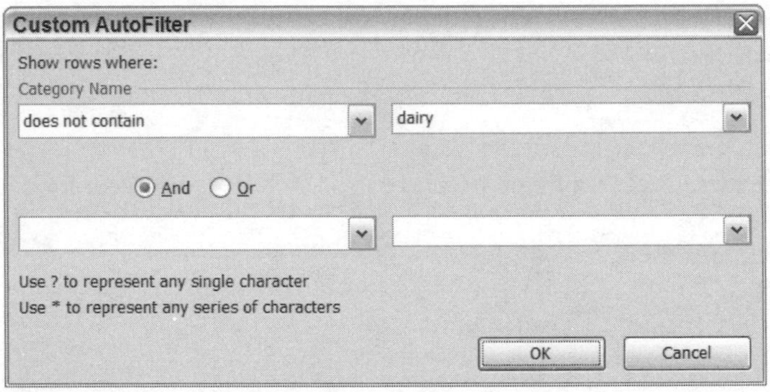

Figure 11.11 You can specify up to two conditions in the Custom AutoFilter drop-down box.

CROSS-REFERENCE The mathematical and string operators are described in more detail in Chapter 4.

To apply a filter and continue working along with the example, follow these steps:

1. Click the Spreadsheet reporting heading Category Name in cell A1 of the Spreadsheet report. Choose Data ⇨ Filter ⇨ AutoFilter to add filter drop-down arrows to all the field headings in the Spreadsheet report.

2. Click the Category Name field heading in cell A1 to select it, and then choose Custom from the drop-down list to bring up the Custom AutoFilter dialog box.

3. Select Does Not Contain from the Category Name field, press Tab to move to the Data field on the right, type **Dairy**, and then click OK to apply the filter.

4. Verify that Dairy Products has been removed in the report and that your Spreadsheet report now looks like Figure 11.12.

	A	B	C	D	E	F
1	Category Nan ▼	Product Name ▼	Status ▼	RO Lev ▼	In Sto ▼	On Ord ▼
2	Beverages	Chai	Available	10	39	0
3	Beverages	Chang	Available	25	17	40
4	Condiments	Aniseed Syrup	Discontinued	25	13	70
5	Condiments	Chef Anton's Cajun Seasoning	Available	0	53	0
6	Condiments	Chef Anton's Gumbo Mix	Discontinued	0	0	0
7	Condiments	Grandma's Boysenberry Spread	Available	25	120	0
8	Produce	Uncle Bob's Organic Dried Pears	Available	10	15	0
9	Condiments	Northwoods Cranberry Sauce	Available	0	6	0
10	Meat/Poultry	Mishi Kobe Niku	Discontinued	0	29	0
11	Seafood	Ikura	Available	0	31	0
14	Seafood	Konbu	Available	5	24	0
15	Produce	Tofu	Available	0	35	0
16	Condiments	Genen Shouyu	Available	5	39	0
17	Confections	Pavlova	Available	10	29	0
18	Meat/Poultry	Alice Mutton	Discontinued	0	0	0

Sheet1 / Sheet2 / Sheet3 /

Figure 11.12 After you enable the AutoFilter feature, drop-down filters are added next to each report heading field.

TIP Excel displays the filter column headings with a blue drop-down arrow to signify that the column is being filtered. The row numbers in the report are also shown in a blue font to signify that not all the rows in the report are being displayed due to a filter setting.

You can create more advanced filters by customizing the Where part of the SQL query. If the filters need to be interactive, you can use a parameter query to map user-input values to variables in the Where part of a SQL query or stored procedure. This topic is covered in more detail in the "Using a Parameter Query" section later in this chapter.

Sorting Data

In a Spreadsheet report, you can either specify the sort order in the SQL query (before the data set is returned to Excel), or you can specify the sort order in the Spreadsheet report (after the data set is returned to Excel). Specifying the sort order in the SQL query increases the time it takes to run the query, but results in faster overall processing time than sorting the data on the client computer running Excel. I recommend sorting the dataset in the query for a standard Spreadsheet report view, and then using the Sort features in Excel to apply additional interactive sorts as necessary.

After the data is in Excel, you can sort the data by selecting a field heading and clicking the A ⇨ Z or Z ⇨ A sort buttons in the Standard toolbar. Alternatively, you can choose Data ⇨ Sort to bring up the Sort dialog box shown in Figure 11.13.

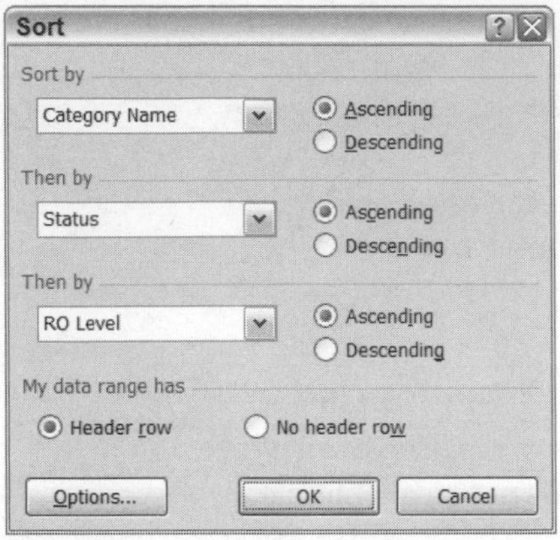

Figure 11.13   You can sort up to three fields from this dialog box.

You can select up to three fields to sort in the Sort Order dialog box. Clicking the Options button enables you to sort on fields with date information (for example, days of the week or months of the year).

WARNING If the Preserve Column Sort/Filter/Layout option is not checked in the External Data Range Properties dialog box, the sort order settings are removed when the Spreadsheet report is refreshed.

To apply a sort order and continue working along with the example, follow these steps:

1. Click the Spreadsheet reporting heading Category Name in cell A1 of the Spreadsheet report, and then choose Data ⇨ Sort to bring up the Sort dialog box.

2. Sort by Category Name, next by Status, and finally by RO Level. Verify that all the sort orders are in ascending order.

3. Click OK to apply the sort order, and then verify that your report looks like Figure 11.14.

	A	B	C	D	E	F
1	Category Nan ▼	Product Name ▼	Status ▼	RO Lev ▼	In Sto ▼	On Ord ▼
2	Beverages	Chartreuse verte	Available	5	69	0
3	Beverages	Chai	Available	10	39	0
4	Beverages	Laughing Lumberjack Lager	Available	10	52	0
5	Beverages	Sasquatch Ale	Available	15	111	0
6	Beverages	Steeleye Stout	Available	15	20	0
7	Beverages	Côte de Blaye	Available	15	17	0
8	Beverages	Lakkalikööri	Available	20	57	0
9	Beverages	Chang	Available	25	17	40
10	Beverages	Ipoh Coffee	Available	25	17	10
11	Beverages	Rhönbräu Klosterbier	Available	25	125	0
14	Beverages	Outback Lager	Available	30	15	10
15	Beverages	Guaraná Fantástica	Discontinued	0	20	0
16	Condiments	Chef Anton's Cajun Seasoning	Available	0	53	0

ᴵⁿ ◀ ▶ ᴹ \ **Sheet1** / Sheet2 / Sheet3 /

Figure 11.14 The Spreadsheet report is now sorted in ascending order, first by Category Name, next by Status, and then by RO Level.

> **TIP** You can sort a maximum of three columns in the Sort dialog box, as opposed to 1,024 columns in the Order By part of an SQL query. An SQL query also supports Case logic in the Order By section, enabling you to programmatically assign a sort order on conditions that are specified in the query.

Calculating Subtotals

You can apply subtotals to the Spreadsheet report that are based on changes in values of a particular column. Unlike PivotTable reports, where all the fields in the Data area are subtotaled, you can choose which columns to subtotal. The subtotal calculation supports many functions, such as Count, Average, Min, Max, Sum, Product, Standard Deviation, and Variance. There are also options for adding page breaks between groups and displaying the subtotal at the bottom or the top of each group.

> **TIP** Before you apply a subtotal, you should verify that the data in the Spreadsheet report is properly grouped by sorting the data in the appropriate order. I also recommend that you arrange the report so that all the numeric columns are displayed on the right-most side of the report.

Complete these steps to subtotal In Stock and On Order for each product category group and continue following along with the example:

1. Verify that your Spreadsheet report looks like Figure 11.14; and then click on a cell in the Spreadsheet report and choose Data ➪ Auto Filter to toggle the auto filter settings off.

2. Right-click the report and choose Refresh Data to re-sort the previously filtered rows.

3. Click on the field heading Category Name in cell A1, and then choose Data ⇨ Subtotals to bring up the Subtotal dialog box shown in Figure 11.15.

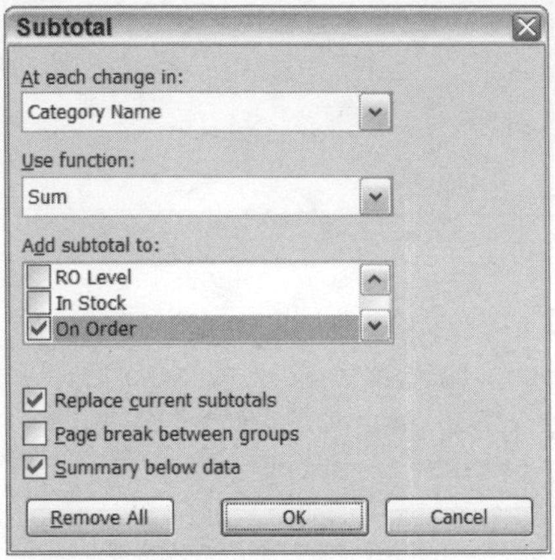

Figure 11.15   Use this dialog box to subtotal grouped data in a Spreadsheet report.

NOTE When the Subtotal dialog box is launched, the right-most numeric column in the Spreadsheet report is automatically checked for subtotaling.

4. Verify that your dialog box looks like Figure 11.15, add a check mark next to In Stock in the Add Subtotal To pane, and then click OK to subtotal On Order and In Stock for each Category Name group.

In Figure 11.15, the check mark next to Replace Current Subtotals removes any current group subtotals and replaces them with the ones specified in this dialog box. You can check the Page Break Between Groups option to automatically insert page breaks after each group. Checking the Summary Below Data option toggles the display of subtotals at the end of each group). If this option is unchecked, subtotals are displayed at the start of each new group. Clicking the Remove All button removes all subtotal calculations for the group.

5. Verify that your Spreadsheet report looks like Figure 11.16.

1 2 3		A	B	C	D	E	F
	1	Category Name	Product Name	Status	RO Level	In Stock	On Order
	2	Beverages	Chartreuse verte	Available	5	69	0
	3	Beverages	Chai	Available	10	39	0
	4	Beverages	Laughing Lumberjack Lager	Available	10	52	0
	5	Beverages	Sasquatch Ale	Available	15	111	0
	6	Beverages	Steeleye Stout	Available	15	20	0
	7	Beverages	Côte de Blaye	Available	15	17	0
	8	Beverages	Lakkalikööri	Available	20	57	0
	9	Beverages	Chang	Available	25	17	40
	10	Beverages	Ipoh Coffee	Available	25	17	10
	11	Beverages	Rhönbräu Klosterbier	Available	25	125	0
	12	Beverages	Outback Lager	Available	30	15	10
	13	Beverages	Guaraná Fantástica	Discontinued	0	20	0
	14	**Beverages Total**				559	60
	15	Condiments	Chef Anton's Cajun Seasoning	Available	0	53	0

Sheet1 / Sheet2 / Sheet3 /

Figure 11.16 Adding a subtotal automatically groups the items and calculates the subtotal function (or functions) selected in the Subtotal dialog box.

After a subtotal is applied, the data is automatically grouped. The group tree appears in the Group pane (left-most section) of the Spreadsheet report, and includes nodes to show (+) or hide (–) the data in each group. If you uncheck the Summary Below Data option (refer to Figure 11.15), the nodes appear at the top of each group instead of at the bottom of each group, as shown in Figure 11.16. Clicking the 1, 2, or 3 icon displayed at the top of the Group pane shows just the report grand totals (1), the report subtotals and grand totals (2), or all of the detail in the Spreadsheet report (3).

Using Fill-Down Formulas

Spreadsheet reports can use formula fields just like any Excel worksheet. The difference with Spreadsheet reports is that the formula can also be automatically filled down when the report is refreshed. This is akin to adding a calculated field in a PivotTable report. Essentially, the new formula field is automatically filled-down and looks like it is part of the Spreadsheet report.

The Fill Down Formulas In Columns Adjacent To Data option in the External Data Range Properties dialog box must be enabled for fill-down formula fields to work. By default, this option is unchecked.

Complete these steps to add a Fill Down formula and continue following along with the example:

1. Verify that your Spreadsheet report looks like Figure 11.16, right-click on a cell in the Spreadsheet report, and then choose Data ⇨ Data Range Properties to bring up the Data Range Properties dialog box.

2. Check the Fill Down Formulas In Columns Adjacent To Data option to enable the formulas to be filled down. Click OK to close the Data Range Properties dialog box.

3. Click cell G1 (to the right of On Order), type **Difference**, and press Return or Enter to enter the new column heading into the Spreadsheet report.

4. Click Cell G2, type **=E2+F2-D2**, and press Return or Enter to enter the new report formula into the report.

5. Right-click the report (note that Column G is not considered part of the Spreadsheet report), and choose Refresh Data.

6. Verify that your Spreadsheet report looks like Figure 11.17.

	A	B	C	D	E	F	G
1	Category Name	Product Name	Status	RO Level	In Stock	On Order	Difference
2	Beverages	Chartreuse verte	Available	5	69	0	64
3	Beverages	Chai	Available	10	39	0	29
4	Beverages	Laughing Lumberjack Lager	Available	10	52	0	42
5	Beverages	Sasquatch Ale	Available	15	111	0	96
6	Beverages	Steeleye Stout	Available	15	20	0	5
7	Beverages	Côte de Blaye	Available	15	17	0	2
8	Beverages	Lakkalikööri	Available	20	57	0	37
9	Beverages	Chang	Available	25	17	40	32
10	Beverages	Ipoh Coffee	Available	25	17	10	2
11	Beverages	Rhönbräu Klosterbier	Available	25	125	0	100
12	Beverages	Outback Lager	Available	30	15	10	-5

I ◀ ▶ ▶I \ **Sheet1** / Sheet2 / Sheet3 /

Figure 11.17 After the Spreadsheet report is refreshed, the formula for Difference is automatically filled-down for all cells in the column.

Notice that the formula in cell G2 has been automatically applied to the entire column. This feature is useful when the report user is not able to modify the underlying SQL query or when calculating the formula in the SQL query is not practical. An example of this situation is when the referenced column values are derived from complex, high-cost (that is, extensive CPU processing time) fields in the SQL query.

Conditional Formatting

Conditional formatting enables you to format cells in the report based on particular cell values or cell formulas in a referenced column. This feature is useful for highlighting particular data conditions in the report, such as a low inventory level, a net loss, or an abnormal variance.

Conditional formatting includes functions that allow you to customize these cell attributes:

- Font style (bold, italics, regular)
- Font color
- Borders
- Cell patterns and colors

Conditional formatting can evaluate either formulas or values in a work-sheet cell. These conditions are specified in the Conditional Formatting dialog box (see Figure 11.18), which you bring up by choosing Format ➪ Conditional Formatting.

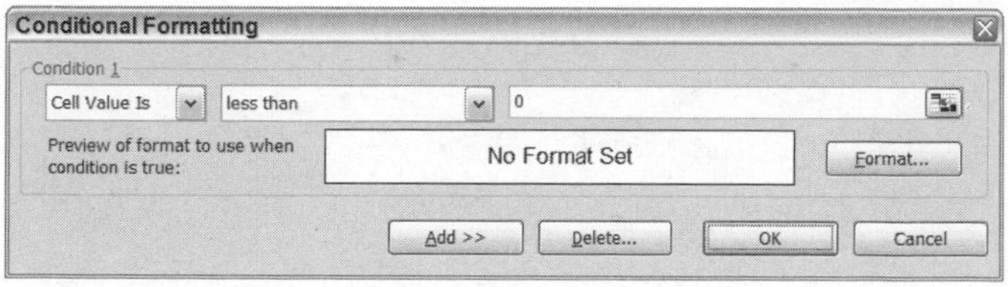

Figure 11.18 Formula and cell values can be identified in this dialog box.

TIP You can program multiple conditions into the Conditional Formatting dialog box by clicking the Add button to open another condition pane in the dialog box.

To apply a conditional format to the Spreadsheet report, follow these steps:

1. Click the G cell to select the entire Difference column, and then choose Format ➪ Conditional Formatting to bring up the Conditional Formatting dialog box.

2. Choose Cell Value Is in the Condition 1 field, choose Less Than in the Operator drop-down field, and then type **0**.

3. Click the Format button to open the Format Cells dialog box.

4. Select the color Red on the Color drop-down box in the Fonts tab and then click OK to close the Font dialog box. Click OK again to close the Conditional Formatting dialog box and apply the conditional formatting to the Difference column.

On your screen, notice that the cells in the Difference column appear in red when the stock on order plus the stock on hand is less than the reorder level point for that product. Using this conditional formatting feature, you can quickly hone in on products where additional stock needs to be procured.

Configuring Spreadsheet Report Data Options

Spreadsheet report data options are configured in the External Data Range Properties dialog box. Right-click the Spreadsheet report and then choose Data Range Properties from the pop-up menu to open the dialog box (see Figure 11.19). Alternatively, click the Data Range Properties button to open the dialog box.

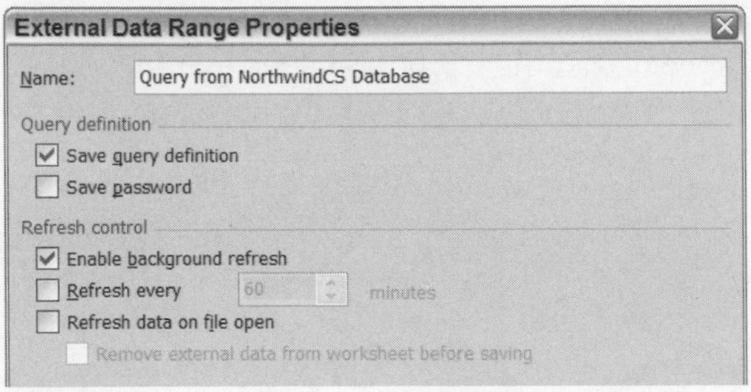

Figure 11.19 You manage the data features of the Spreadsheet report in the top portion (shown here) of the External Data Range Properties dialog box.

The options in the top half of the External Data Range Properties dialog box are separated into two sections: Query Definition and Refresh Control. You use the options in the Query Definition section to toggle whether the underlying SQL query and the password (SQL authentication method) are stored when the report is saved and closed. You use the options in the Refresh Control section to manage refresh operations. Table 11.4 provides a description of each option in this dialog box.

Table 11.4 Data Options in the External Data Range Properties Dialog Box

OPTION NAME	DESCRIPTION
Name	Sets the name of the Spreadsheet report (optional). This can usually be ignored unless you plan to incorporate Visual Basic for Application code that references the Spreadsheet report.
Save Query Definition	Saves the underlying SQL query with the Spreadsheet report.
Save Password	Toggles whether the password used to access the external data source is saved with the Spreadsheet report.
Enable Background Refresh	Toggles whether the report refresh halts all operations in the Excel worksheet until the refresh is completed (unchecked) or whether the user can continue working in Excel while the refresh query runs in the background (checked).
Refresh Every	Refreshes the report every *n* minutes.
Refresh Data on File Open	Toggles whether the report is immediately refreshed when it is first opened.
Remove External Data from Worksheet before Saving	Toggles whether the underlying data set is saved with the report.

Many of the options identified in this dialog box are fundamentally the same as the options available in the Table Options dialog box for a PivotTable report. More comprehensive examples and information on how these options can be used to customize your report are available in Chapter 8.

Refreshing Data

A Spreadsheet report is refreshed in much the same way as a PivotTable report. Clicking the Refresh Data button triggers a refresh data operation that updates the report with most current information from the data source. There are also options for refreshing the report when it is first opened (Refresh Data on File Open), and for refreshing the report at predefined intervals (Refresh Every). You can configure both of these options in the Data Section of the External Data Range Properties dialog box.

Checking the Refresh Status

During a refresh operation, you can view the refresh status by clicking the Refresh Status button in the External Data toolbar. Clicking this button brings up the External Data Refresh Status dialog box, as shown in Figure 11.20. From this box, you can monitor the number of rows fetched and the elapsed time it has taken for the query to run.

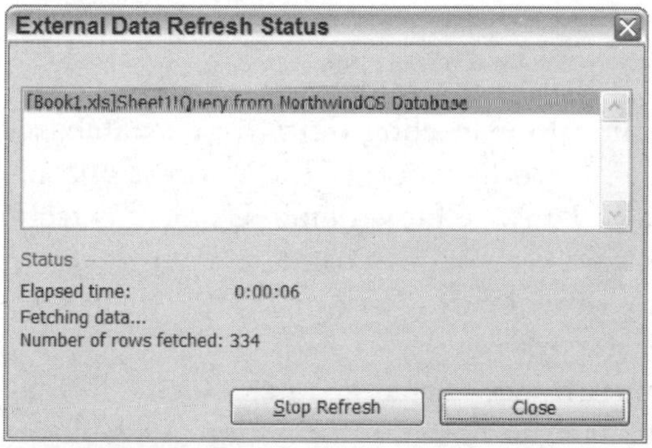

Figure 11.20 This dialog box shows the current status, elapsed time, and number of rows fetched from the Spreadsheet's report external data source.

Using Refresh All

You can refresh all Spreadsheet reports in a workbook by clicking the Refresh All button in the External Data toolbar. This feature is useful when there are several reports in the same workbook, as clicking this button refreshes them all.

TIP This button is included by default on the External Data toolbar. It is optionally available with PivotTable reports.

Canceling a Refresh

If a refresh operation is taking too long, you can click the Cancel Refresh button in the External Data toolbar. This function immediately cancels any currently running query and returns you to the current report view.

Removing External Data

Checking the Remove External Data from Worksheet Before Saving option removes all external data retrieved by the Spreadsheet report when the Excel workbook is saved and closed. This option can be useful if you need to email the report to a programmer for troubleshooting or to another user who can refresh it. Rather than trying to send a huge file, you can send just the Spreadsheet report shell with the saved SQL query.

Modifying the Spreadsheet Report Query

You can modify the SQL query for the Spreadsheet report by right-clicking the Spreadsheet report and choosing Edit Query from the pop-up menu. This function brings up the Microsoft Query program where you can modify the SQL query used in the report.

Using a Web Query

Spreadsheet reports include a *web query* feature that enables you to extract data from a web page. The process is similar to extracting data from a database, except that you specify a Uniform Resource Location (URL) address and an HTML table instead of a database and database table name. Using this technology, you can extract information from web pages posted to an intranet or Internet site. There are also options for downloading information in plain text, rich text, or HTML format, including hyperlinks.

Using a web query, you can retrieve currency exchange rates, stock information, mortgage interest rates, financial data, and other information available on the web. You can even configure your Spreadsheet report to automatically extract the website data at scheduled intervals by using the data options in the top part of the External Data Range Properties dialog box, or on demand by using the Refresh Data function, just as you can with any Spreadsheet report.

Trying a Web Query

To try a web query, follow these steps:

1. From Excel, choose Data ➪ Import External Data ➪ New Web Query to bring up the New Web Query dialog box.

2. Type **www.wiley.com/go/excelreporting/sample_web_table** in the Address field, and then click Go to open the sample website that shows the first six months of 2004 stock performance for Wiley Publishing, Inc.

3. Click the Prices table to select it (the icon changes from a yellow arrow to a green checkmark).

4. Verify that your New Web Query dialog box looks like Figure 11.21, and then click the Import button to import the financial data into Excel.

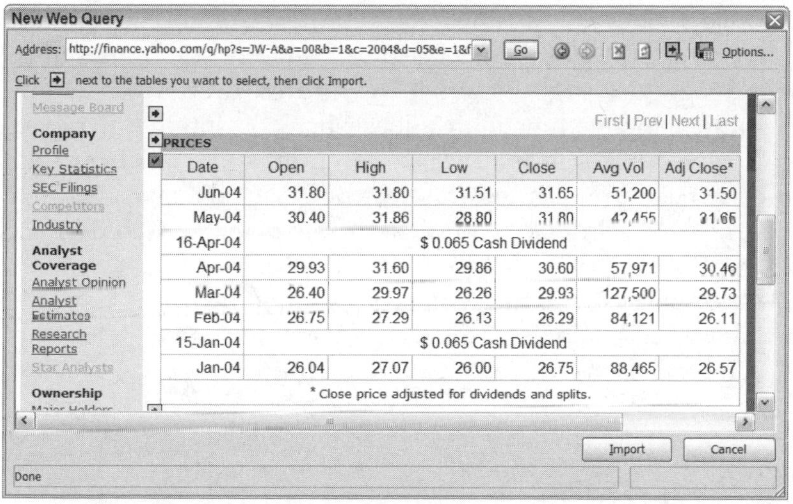

Figure 11.21 Select tables and frames in a web query by clicking a yellow arrow icon; once selected, the icon appears as a green checkmark.

5. Click OK when the Import Data dialog box appears.

6. Verify that your Spreadsheet report looks like Figure 11.22.

WATCH THE VIDEO To see how a web query is accomplished, click the **ch1101_video.avi file at** www.wiley.com/go/excelreporting **and watch the video.**

TIP The web data in this Spreadsheet Report can be refreshed by simply right-clicking anywhere on the report and selecting Refresh Data from the pop-up menu.

	A	B	C	D	E	F	G
1	Date	Open	High	Low	Close	Avg Vol	Adj Close*
2	4-Jun	31.8	31.8	31.51	31.65	51,200	31.5
3	4-May	30.4	31.86	28.8	31.8	42,455	31.65
4	16-Apr-04	$ 0.065 Cash Dividend					
5	4-Apr	29.93	31.6	29.86	30.6	57,971	30.46
6	4-Mar	26.4	29.97	26.26	29.93	127,500	29.73
7	4-Feb	26.75	27.29	26.13	26.29	84,121	26.11
8	15-Jan-04	$ 0.065 Cash Dividend					
9	4-Jan	26.04	27.07	26	26.75	88,465	26.57
10	* Close price adjusted for dividends and splits.						

Sheet1 / Sheet2 / Sheet3

Figure 11.22 The website data in a Spreadsheet report.

Working in the Web Query Dialog Box

The Web Query dialog box works just like a web browser, although you may notice that the performance is a little slow because the tables and frames must be identified as each new web page is loaded. The Address drop-down feature does not use the auto-complete function as does Microsoft Internet Explorer. However, all your saved URLs in Internet Explorer are still available in the Address drop-down field. You can either select a previously saved URL or type in a new one, and then click Go or press Return to open the web page for the specified address.

Keep in mind a web query can extract data from a single URL only, meaning that you access the final URL address. This means that you cannot access data protected by a login and password. You also cannot import graphics, icons, or pictures.

Using the Web Query Toolbar

The Web Query toolbar shown in Figure 11.23 is similar to the Internet toolbar. It includes functions for moving back and forward to previously viewed web pages, refreshing the currently viewed web page, and stopping the current web page from loading. There are also options for toggling the display of the table/frame icon, saving the web query, and setting query options.

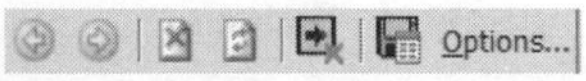

Figure 11.23 The Web Query toolbar includes functions for navigating the web, saving queries, and setting query options.

Table 11.5 provides an explanation of the toolbar buttons available in the Web Query toolbar.

Table 11-5 Web Query Toolbar Buttons and Descriptions

NUMBER	BUTTON	DESCRIPTION
	Back	Loads the web page of the next previously viewed URL address in memory.
	Forward	Loads the web page of the last previously viewed URL address in memory.
	Stop	Stops the current web page from loading.
	Refresh	Refreshes the web page for the selected URL address in the Address field.
	Hide Icons	Toggles the display of icons for frames and tables.
	Save Query	Saves the current URL as a web query using an .iqy file extension. The query can be accessed from the Select Data Source dialog box by choosing Data ⇨ Import External Data ⇨ Import Data.
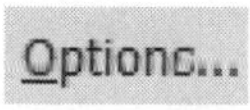 Options...	Options	Launches the Web Query options dialog box for customizing how the web page information is loaded into Excel.

Customizing Web Query Options

You can open the Web Query Options dialog box (see Figure 11.24) by clicking the Options button on the Web Query toolbar. In this dialog box, you configure how data is imported and formatted in the Spreadsheet report.

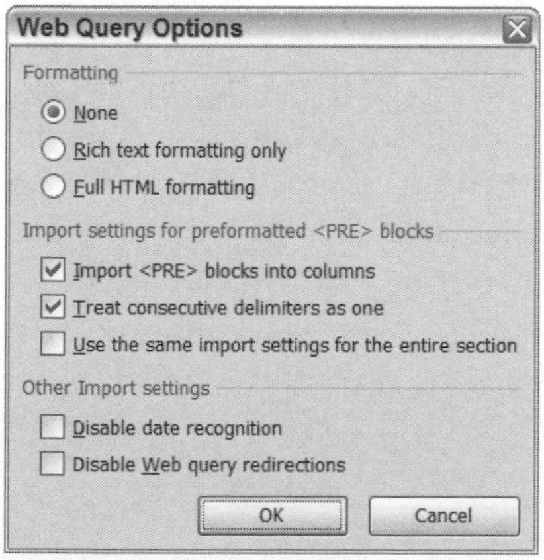

Figure 11.24 Formatting and import options for web queries are configured in this dialog box.

Table 11.6 provides a description of each option in the Web Query Options dialog box.

Table 11.6 Web Query Options Dialog Box

OPTION NAME	DESCRIPTION
Formatting	Imports the website text as plain text, rich text, or HTML. Selecting Plain Text Formatting removes all formatting for the imported text. Selecting Rich Text Formatting maintains the formatting, but discards hyperlinks. The Full HTML Formatting option maintains the formatting and the hyperlinks.
Import <PRE> Blocks into Columns	Separates the data in the preformatted sections into columns. Uncheck this option to load the data into a single cell.
Treat Consecutive Delimiters as One	Ignores additional delimiters between data fields. Only available when the Import <PRE> Blocks into Columns option is checked.
Use the Same Import Settings for the Entire Selection	Imports preformatted sections using the same settings for all selections. Uncheck this option to have Excel determine the best settings. Only available when the Import <PRE> Blocks into Columns option is checked.
Disable Date Recognition	Disables date or text data from being formatted as a Date field in the Spreadsheet report.
Disable Web Query Redirections	Disables automatic web query redirections within the Web Query dialog box.

Using a Parameter Query

A parameter query enables the user to input parameter values into Excel for the Spreadsheet report. These values are mapped to variables in the `Where` part of an SQL query or a stored procedure. The parameter values are evaluated each time the report is refreshed, working at the server level and filtering data before it is even imported into the Spreadsheet report. This typically results in a reduced dataset size and faster query processing time, allowing the user to focus on a concentrated range of data, such as a particular period of time, a specific business segment, or any other data element (or elements) that can be specified in a stored procedure or SQL query.

A few things to keep in mind with this technology:

- Parameters can be used only in a Spreadsheet report. (This technology does not currently work in a PivotTable or a PivotChart report.)
- Parameters can be used only in an SQL query where the query can be graphically displayed.
- Parameters can be integrated with stored procedures (even if the stored procedure query cannot be graphically displayed).

Although parameters cannot be used in a PivotTable report, you can create a PivotTable report from the data once it is in Excel. However, since the data must be imported using a Spreadsheet report, you are limited to a maximum of 65,536 rows.

Understanding Parameters

On the surface, a parameter might appear similar to the AutoFilter function in the Spreadsheet report. However, while both filter data, they do it at different points in the process. With filters, you specify the criteria *after* the dataset is returned to Excel. In contrast, a parameter is mapped to a variable in the Where part of a SQL query. Therefore, the dataset is filtered *before* it is returned to Excel. This usually results in much faster query processing time and a reduced dataset size.

Parameters can be integrated into an SQL query or into a stored procedure. Keep in mind that parameters work only with a SQL query that can be graphically displayed. (Read Chapter 5 if you are unfamiliar with this concept.) However, it's easy to work around this restriction by transforming the query into a view or a stored procedure.

TIP When the stored procedure or view is created, the query plan (that is, the instructions for how the database server calculates the most efficient path for obtaining the data) is also created and saved with the object. This results in the query running faster than it would as a regular SQL query because the query plan does not have to be created at runtime.

Integrating a Parameter into an SQL Query

You can specify a parameter in a query by using a question mark (?) in the Where part of an SQL query. For example, try entering the following query into the SQL window of the Microsoft Query program of a Spreadsheet report:

```
SELECT * FROM Categories WHERE CategoryID = ?
```

The Enter Parameter Value dialog box shown in Figure 11.25 comes up asking for a Parameter value. Entering **1** in this box causes only a single row to appear for the Beverages category.

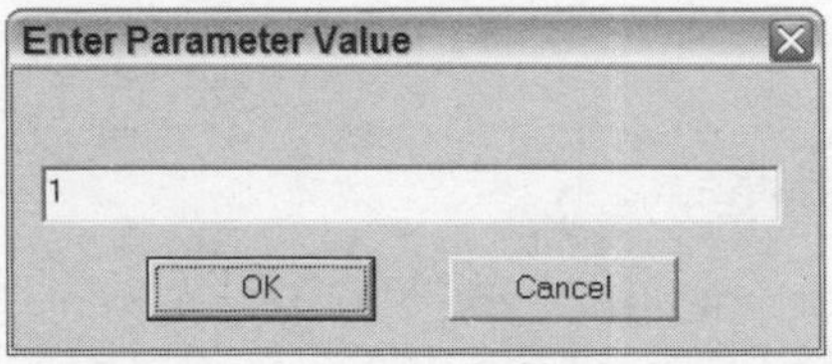

Figure 11.25 This dialog box appears for each Parameter field.

Queries that cannot be displayed graphically do not allow parameter values to be accepted. For example, try using the query from earlier in this chapter with a parameter for Category Name, as shown here:

```
SELECT cat.CategoryName              AS [Category Name],
       pro.ProductName               AS [Product Name],
       CASE
           WHEN pro.Discontinued = '0'
               THEN 'Available'
               ELSE 'Discontinued'
               END                   AS [Status],
       pro.UnitsInStock              AS [In Stock],
       pro.UnitsOnOrder              AS [On Order],
       pro.ReorderLevel              AS [RO Level]
FROM Products pro
INNER JOIN Categories cat on pro.CategoryID = cat.CategoryID
WHERE cat.CategoryName = ?
```

When you attempt to execute this query, you see the dialog box shown in Figure 11.26.

Figure 11.26 Parameter queries cannot be used in queries that cannot be graphically displayed.

Despite this restriction, it's not all that difficult to work around. You can either create a stored procedure or a view for the query. Once either of these objects is created on the database server, you can just pass in the parameter values.

Integrating a Parameter into a View

A view is just like a virtual table, except that is doesn't contain any records like a regular database table. Instead, the view is simply an optimized SQL query that is stored on the database server. The query can comprise particular fields in a single table or fields in multiple tables. The field names can also be renamed with more descriptive and easily understandable names.

NOTE There's much more to the topic of views, but it is a bit outside the scope of this book. If you are not familiar with how a view works, I suggest you read up on this topic in the SQL books online.

Creating a View

Creating a view from an existing SQL query is simple. All you need to do is add one line before the SQL query:

```
CREATE VIEW {ViewName} AS
```

To create a view in the NorthwindCS database from the earlier SQL query, follow these steps:

1. Choose Data ⇨ Import External Data ⇨ New Database Query.

2. When the Choose Data Source dialog box appears, select the NorthwindCS Database data source and click OK to open the Microsoft Query program.

3. Close the Add Tables dialog box and choose File ⇨ Execute SQL to bring up the Execute SQL dialog box.

4. Paste the following SQL query into the Execute SQL dialog box:

```
CREATE VIEW ProductLevel AS
SELECT cat.CategoryName                 AS [Category Name],
       pro.ProductName                  AS [Product Name],
       CASE
           WHEN pro.Discontinued = '0'
                THEN 'Available'
                ELSE 'Discontinued'
```

```
              END                     AS [Status],
      pro.UnitsInStock               AS [In Stock],
      pro.UnitsOnOrder               AS [On Order],
      pro.ReorderLevel               AS [RO Level]
FROM Products pro
INNER JOIN Categories cat on pro.CategoryID = cat.CategoryID
```

ON THE WEB You can download the ch11_example02.txt query file
to your computer from the companion website at www.wiley.com/go/
excelreporting. **Look in the Chap11.zip file or Chap11 directory.**

5. Verify that the NorthwindCS database is selected in the database drop-
    down field (at the bottom of the Execute SQL dialog box), and then
    click the Execute button to run the query and create the view.

6. Click OK to acknowledge that the query was successfully executed.

7. Click Cancel to close the Execute SQL dialog box.

NOTE The column names in the view are created from the names specified
for each column in the AS part of the SQL query. For example, Discontinued
becomes Status, and UnitsInStock becomes In Stock.

Executing a Parameter Query against the View

After the view is created on the SQL server, just paste this query into the SQL
dialog box:

```
SELECT * FROM ProductLevel Where "Category Name" = ?
```

After you execute this query, the Enter Parameter Value dialog box appears,
where you can enter a category name. Try entering **Beverages** or **Produce** to
see how this works.

TIP When working with parameters, I prefer using a stored procedure to using
an SQL query. It is difficult (if not impossible) to program conditional logic into
a query that can be graphically displayed in the Microsoft Query program. It's
not possible, for example, to modify the query to show all the categories when
the parameter value is set to a <blank> or some other value, like it is with a
stored procedure.

Integrating a Parameter into a Stored Procedure

A stored procedure can perform several complex tasks. However, for the purposes of Spreadsheet reporting, think of a stored procedure as an SQL query that can accept variables. And like a view, a stored procedure is stored in the database and optimized for fast performance. Additionally, you obtain a couple of other benefits with a stored procedure, including

- Changes to the stored procedure query are automatically reflected in the Spreadsheet report when the report is refreshed.

- The stored procedure can accept numerous input parameters, and logic can be programmed into the report to handle default values and potential errors.

Any changes to the stored procedure are automatically applied to the Spreadsheet and PivotTable reports. Fields added or removed in the stored procedure are automatically reflected in the Excel report when it is refreshed. This enables you to modify the stored procedure in one place instead of modifying the queries in every Excel report.

In the stored procedure example (ch11_example03.txt, which is provided on the website) used in the next section, I demonstrate one method for how a special value, such as 'All', can be used to pull the entire dataset instead of just the data for a particular value.

Creating a Stored Procedure

Creating a stored procedure from an existing SQL query is simple. All you need to do is add one line before the SQL query:

```
CREATE PROCEDURE {ProcedureName} AS
```

I've transformed the earlier query in this chapter into a stored procedure. I also added variables for the product status and for the product category. These variables are used in the Where part of the stored procedure query and are mapped to parameters in the Spreadsheet report.

To create a stored procedure that has variables for Status and Category in the NorthwindCS database, and that you will use in future examples in this section, follow these steps:

1. Choose Data ⇨ Import External Data ⇨ New Database Query.

2. When the Choose Data Source dialog box appears, select the NorthwindCS Database data source and click OK to open the Microsoft Query program.

3. Close the Add Tables dialog box and choose File ⇨ Execute SQL to bring up the Execute SQL dialog box.

4. Paste the following SQL query into the Execute SQL dialog box:

```
CREATE PROCEDURE NWProductLevel
(@Status CHAR(1),
 @Category VARCHAR(14))
AS
SELECT cat.CategoryName                   AS [Category Name],
       pro.ProductName                    AS [Product Name],
       CASE
            WHEN pro.Discontinued = '0'
                 THEN 'Available'
                 ELSE 'Discontinued'
                 END                       AS [Status],
       pro.UnitsInStock                   AS [In Stock],
       pro.UnitsOnOrder                   AS [On Order],
       pro.ReorderLevel                   AS [RO Level]
FROM Products pro
INNER JOIN Categories cat on pro.CategoryID = cat.CategoryID
WHERE pro.Discontinued = @Status
  AND cat.CategoryID
      BETWEEN CASE
                WHEN @Category = 'All'
                THEN 0
                ELSE (SELECT ctx.CategoryID
                        FROM Categories ctx
                       WHERE @Category = ctx.CategoryName)
                END
          AND
             CASE
                WHEN @Category = 'All'
                THEN 8
                ELSE (SELECT ctx.CategoryID
                        FROM Categories ctx
                       WHERE @Category = ctx.CategoryName)
                END
ORDER BY 1, 2
```

ON THE WEB You can download the ch11_example03.txt query file to your computer from the companion website at www.wiley.com/go/ excelreporting. **Look in the Chap11.zip file or the Chap11 directory.**

5. Verify that the NorthwindCS database is selected in the database drop-down field (at the bottom of the Execute SQL dialog box), and then click the Execute button to run the query and create the stored procedure.

6. Click OK to acknowledge that the query was successfully executed (meaning that the stored procedure was successfully created).

7. Click Cancel to close the Execute SQL dialog box.

Executing a Parameter Query against the Stored Procedure

You can enter a stored procedure without variables into the SQL dialog box by simply typing the stored procedure name into the SQL window. However, if the stored procedure has variables, you must also enter the values for each variable. If the variable is defined as text, enter the variables in single quotes as shown here:

```
NWProductLevel '0', 'Beverages'
```

This query shows only the rows for products that are available and have a Category Name of Beverages. Now, if you want the user to interactively specify the values for these variables using report parameters, you should use the following *exact* format in the SQL window of the Microsoft Query program:

```
{Call NWProductLevel (?,?)}
```

WARNING There are many ways to run a stored procedure (for example, Exec ProcedureName, Call ProcedureName, ProcedureName, and Execute ProcedureName), but you must use the *exact* format {Call NWProductLevel (?,?)} if parameters are specified.

Customizing the Parameters

The parameters are initially named as Parameter n, where n represents the number in which the variable is first defined in the stored procedure. You can rename the parameters to use more meaningful names by editing the parameter in the Microsoft Query program.

Choose View ➪ Parameters to bring up the Edit Parameter dialog box, shown in Figure 11.27, where you can rename the parameter.

NOTE Parameter names can be customized only in the Parameters dialog box, and this dialog box is accessible only from the Microsoft Query program.

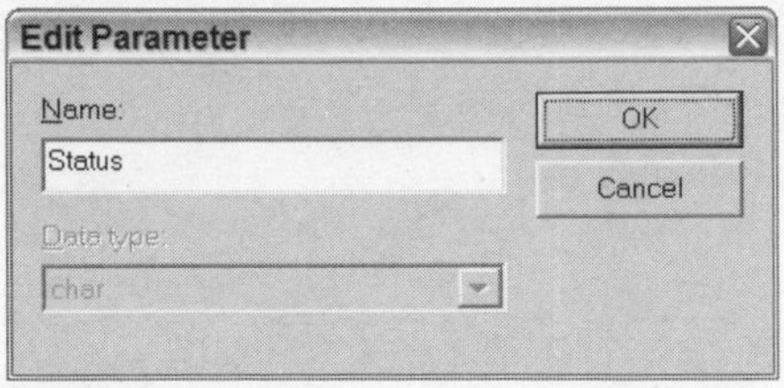

Figure 11.27 The Edit Parameter dialog box enables you to rename Parameter 1 to a more meaningful name.

In Figure 11.28, you can see how I renamed Parameter 1 to Status and Parameter 2 to Product Category.

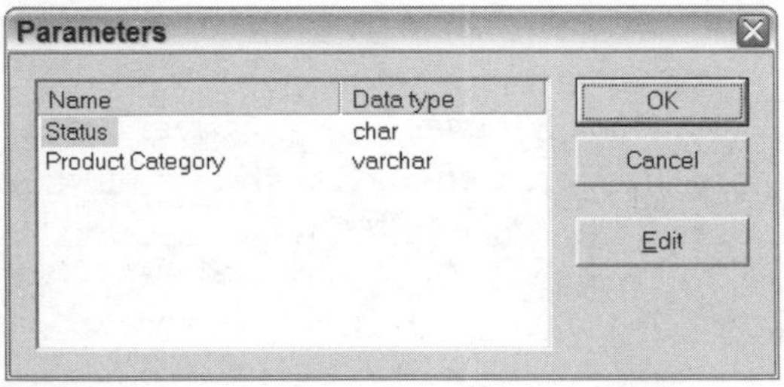

Figure 11.28 You can rename parameters in this dialog box.

Using Parameters in the Report

After the parameters are successfully integrated into an SQL query or a stored procedure, you have three options for determining how to use the parameters in a Spreadsheet report:

- Prompt the user with a value each time the report is refreshed.
- Use a default value specified by the user.
- Fetch the data from a cell in the Excel workbook.

If you prefer to prompt the user for the values, you can customize the prompt that is presented to the user for report refreshes. If you choose to configure a default value, the default value is used as the parameter value each time the report is refreshed. If you choose to fetch the data from a particular cell value in the Excel workbook, you have the option to configure the Spreadsheet to automatically refresh whenever the cell value is changed.

TIP Each parameter can be customized to use a specific option; they do not all have to use the same one. For example, one parameter can use a default value, while another could fetch values from a particular worksheet cell. It's also easy to configure the parameter to use a different method.

These options are all controlled in the Parameters dialog box that you access from the Spreadsheet report. You can access this dialog box by using any of the following methods:

- Clicking the Parameters button
- Right-clicking the Spreadsheet report and choosing Parameters from the pop-up menu
- Choosing Data ⇨ Import External Data ⇨ Parameters

Prompting the User for the Parameter Value

You can configure a parameter to prompt the user for the parameter value each time the report is refreshed. If you are using an SQL query, you can configure this prompt in the Microsoft Query program or in the Parameters dialog box. If you are using a stored procedure, you can configure the prompt only in the Parameters dialog box. This is because the changes are made in the Criteria pane, and that pane is not available for stored procedures because they cannot be graphically displayed in the Microsoft Query program.

Customizing the Prompt from the Microsoft Query Program

You can customize the prompt for a parameter in the Microsoft Query program by entering a prompt string in brackets in the Value field of the Criteria pane. For example, try pasting this SQL query into the SQL dialog box:

```
SELECT *
FROM Categories
WHERE CategoryID = ?
```

After you click OK in the SQL dialog box to run the query, the Microsoft Query program adds closed brackets ([ ]) in Value in the Criteria section. Now, all you need to do is replace the closed brackets in Value with the string [**Enter a Category ID**], as shown in Figure 11.29.

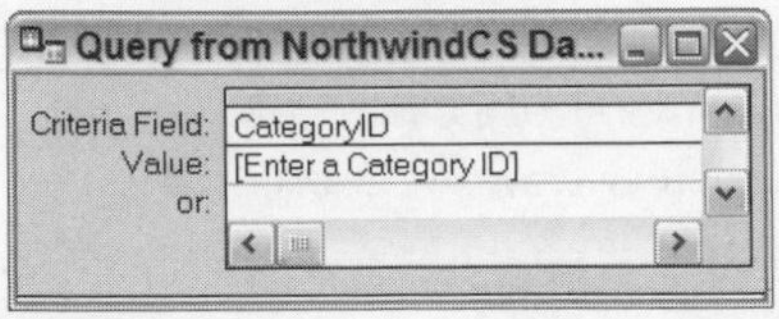

Figure 11.29 The prompt can be customized for a parameter in the Microsoft Query program by adding brackets around the prompt string in the Value cell.

TIP This prompt can be customized only for parameters in an SQL query. Prompts for a stored procedure must be configured in the Parameters dialog box.

After you press the Tab key in Value (see Figure 11.29), the dialog box in Figure 11.30 appears with the prompt you just added.

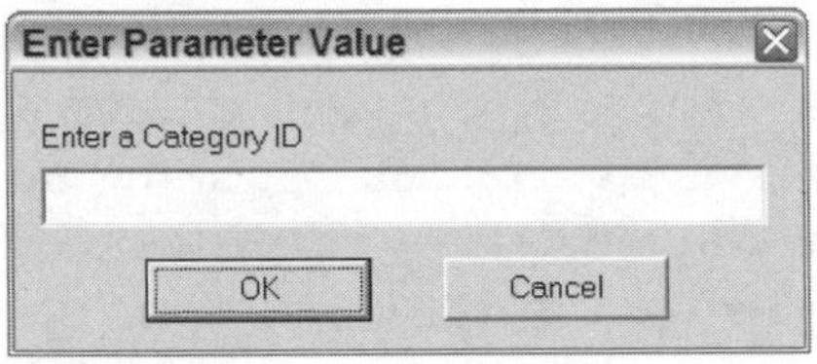

Figure 11.30 A customized prompt for the parameter.

Customizing the Prompt from the Spreadsheet Report

You can configure the prompt for a parameter in the Spreadsheet Report by accessing the Parameters dialog box. This method works well for parameters in both queries and stored procedures.

Complete these steps to customize the prompt for a parameter field in the earlier stored procedure query and to follow along with the example in this section:

1. Right-click the report and choose Parameters from the pop-up menu to bring up the Parameters dialog box shown in Figure 11.31.

2. Click Status in the Parameter Field pane (on the left side of the Parameters dialog box), click the Prompt for Value Using The Following String button, and then type **Enter in the Status Code (0 = Available, 1 = Discontinued)** into the string prompt field, as shown in Figure 11.31.

3. Click OK to add the prompt for the Status parameter and to close the Parameters dialog box.

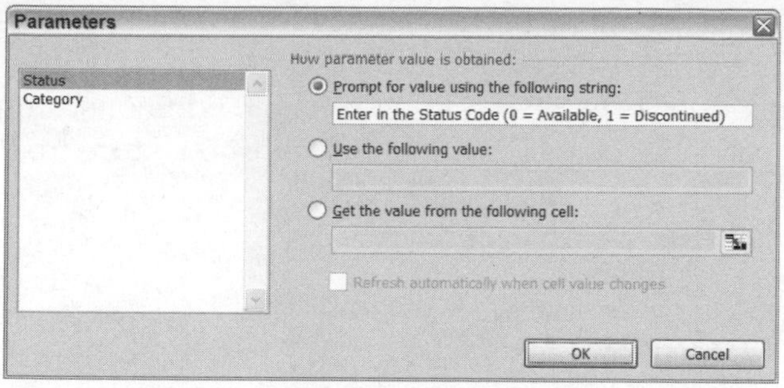

Figure 11.31   A prompt can be customized in the Parameters dialog box for parameters in a stored procedure or in an SQL query.

Now, when you refresh the report, the Enter Parameter Value dialog box with the newly added prompt string appears for the Status parameter field, as shown in Figure 11.32.

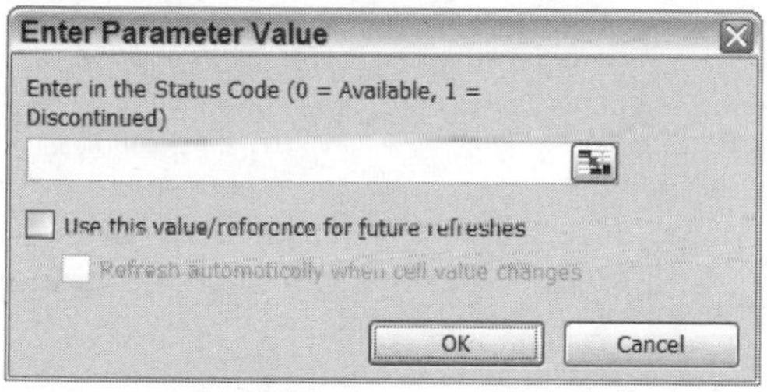

Figure 11.32   The prompt string appears for the Status field whenever the report is refreshed.

Setting a Default for the Parameter Value

A default value is useful when you want the flexibility of specifying a parameter value, but you don't want to be bothered with having to enter a value each time the Spreadsheet report is refreshed.

You can set a default value for a parameter in the Parameters dialog box by clicking the Use The Following Value button and then typing the default value. By checking the Use This Value/Reference For Future Refreshes option when the value is entered into the Enter Parameter Value dialog box (refer to Figure 11.32), you can also specify a default value when the report is refreshed.

Obtaining the Value from a Cell

A parameter can be configured to fetch its value from a cell in the Excel workbook. (Note that this cell can be in the same worksheet or a different worksheet of the workbook.) This method provides an ideal way to build an impressive reporting solution in which the user can just select values from a drop-down list. You can even configure the Spreadsheet report to trigger a refresh operation whenever the referenced value is changed. In Figure 11.33, I demonstrate how this might look in a Spreadsheet report, using the stored procedure that was included earlier in this section (ch11_example03.txt).

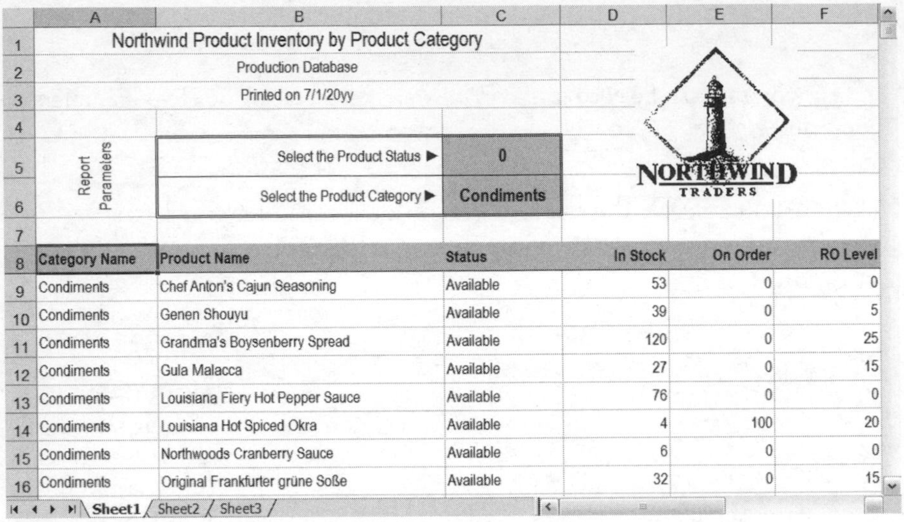

Figure 11.33 The parameter values for Status and Product Category are obtained in the worksheet cells C5 and C6, respectively.

ON THE WEB You can download the ch11_ReportExample.xls Spreadsheet report to your computer from the companion website at www.wiley.com/go/ excelreporting. Look in the Chap11.zip file or the Chap11 directory.

I've configured the Spreadsheet report shown in Figure 11.33 to obtain the Status parameter value from cell C5 and the Category value from cell C6. I've also created a drop-down list for the product category field and configured both cells to accept only valid values that I've specified by using the Validation features included in Excel (explained in the next section).

You can configure the parameter to use a worksheet cell in the Parameters dialog box by clicking the Get The Value From The Following Cell button and then typing the cell reference as shown in Figure 11.34. Check the Refresh Automatically When Cell Value Changes option to configure the Spreadsheet report to automatically refresh whenever the value is changed in the referenced cell.

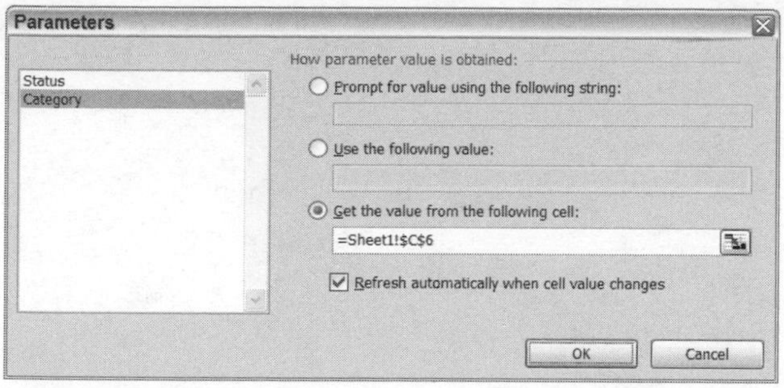

Figure 11.34 You can configure parameters to fetch data from any worksheet cell in the Excel workbook and to automatically refresh the Spreadsheet report whenever the cell value is changed.

Validating the Parameter Values

Setting a validation for a parameter field works well when there are only a limited number of acceptable text values or when a specific numeric or date range is required. It also creates a professional edge to the report and helps prevent errors that might confuse the report user.

You can define the validation for a particular worksheet cell by clicking a cell and choosing Data ➪ Validation to bring up the Data Validation dialog box shown in Figure 11.35.

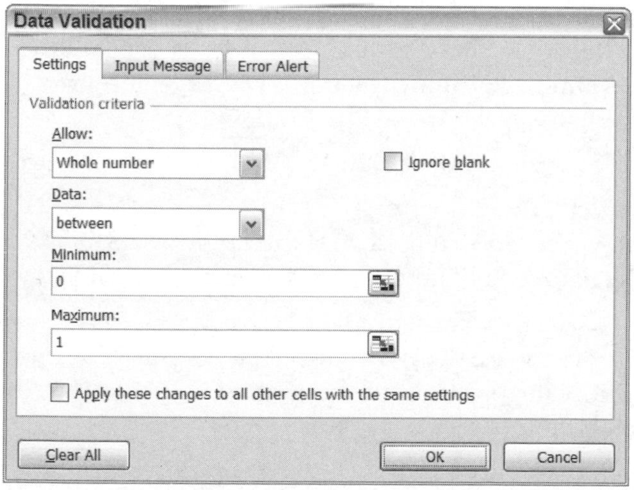

Figure 11.35 You can validate parameters from this dialog box.

From the Data Validation dialog box, you can configure a cell to accept only a

- Whole number in a particular range
- Decimal value in a particular range
- List of items in a range that can be defined in the worksheet
- Date value in a particular range
- Particular text length or text length range
- Custom formula

Using this Data Validation dialog box, you can create an input message when the cell is selected, and you can also customize an informational, warning, or error message when the validation conditions you've set are not satisfied.

Complete these steps to customize the parameter values for Status and for Category and to follow along with the example in this section:

1. Click cell C5 to select it, and then choose Data ⇨ Validation to bring up the Data Validation dialog box.

2. Select Whole Number from the Allow drop-down list, select Between from the Data drop-down list, type **0** in the Minimum field, type **1** in the Maximum field, and uncheck the Ignore Blank option.

3. Verify that your dialog box looks like Figure 11.35, and then click the Error Alert tab.

4. Select Stop from the Style drop-down field list, type **Invalid Product Status** in the Title field, and then type **Select 0 for Available or 1 for Discontinued** in the Error Message field.

5. Verify that your dialog box looks like Figure 11.36, and then click OK to add the validation rules and to configure the Input Message and Error Message dialog boxes.

6. Click cell C6 to select it, and then choose Data ⇨ Validation to bring up the Data Validation dialog box.

7. Select List from the Allow drop-down field, and then type **=$K$1:$K$9** in the Source field. (The Source field appears only after you select List from the Allow field.)

8. Click the Input Message tab, type Select a Product Category in Title, and then type Select a product category from the drop-down list. Choose All to select all product categories.

9. Click the Error Alert tab, select Stop from the Style drop-down list, type **Invalid Product Category** in the Title field, type **You did not select a valid product category. Please try again.** in the Error Message field, and then click OK to add the validation rules and configure the Error Message dialog box.

10. Click the Spreadsheet report and choose Data ⇨ Import External Data ⇨ Parameters to bring up the Parameters dialog box.

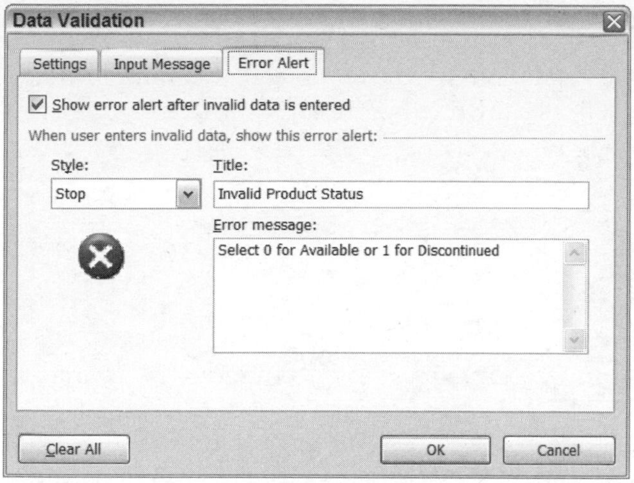

Figure 11.36 You can configure informational, warning, and error message dialog boxes on this tab of the Data Validation dialog box.

11. Select the Status parameter, click the Get the Value From the Following Cell button, select worksheet cell C5, and then click on the Refresh Automatically When Cell Value Changes option.

12. Select the Category parameter, click the Get the Value From The Following Cell button, select worksheet cell C6, and then click the Refresh Automatically When Cell Value Changes option.

13. Click OK to configure the new parameters options and to close the Parameters dialog box.

14. Type the valid values for category in the worksheet range K1:K9 as shown in Figure 11.37.

15. Click Column K to select it, and then choose Format ⇨ Column ⇨ Hide to hide the column in the Excel worksheet.

Figure 11.37 Enter the valid values for the Category field in the report range that you defined in step 7.

Working with Validated Parameter Fields in the Report

After you have configured the validations for the report cell, the input message appears once the cell is selected, as shown in Figure 11.38.

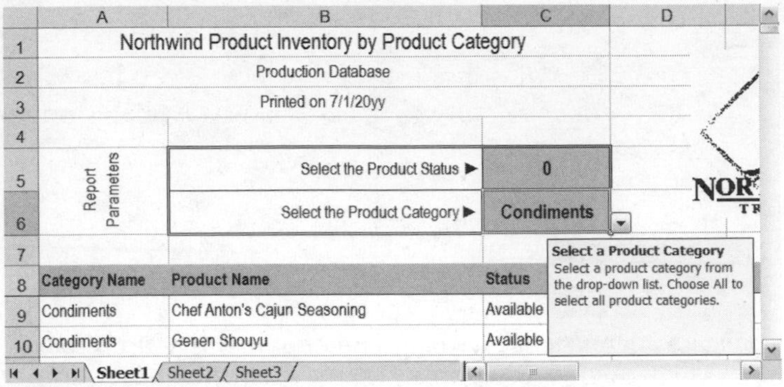

Figure 11.38 Selecting the cell shows the message that you entered.

Clicking the drop-down field list, as shown in Figure 11.39, reveals all of the values that were entered into the K1:K7 range. Additionally, each time the value in the list is changed, the report is automatically refreshed with the most current data in the data source.

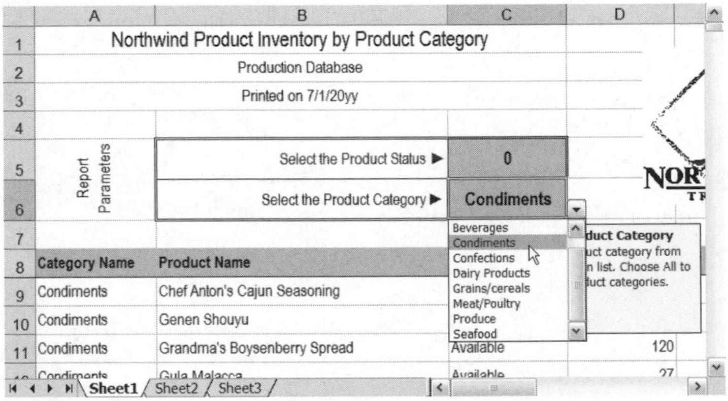

Figure 11.39 The drop-down list shows all values that were entered in the validation list.

If the report user tries to enter an invalid value into the field, the error message that you defined in step 9 is displayed, as shown in Figure 11.40. Thus, the value is not accepted until it conforms to the validation rules that are defined in the Data Validation dialog box.

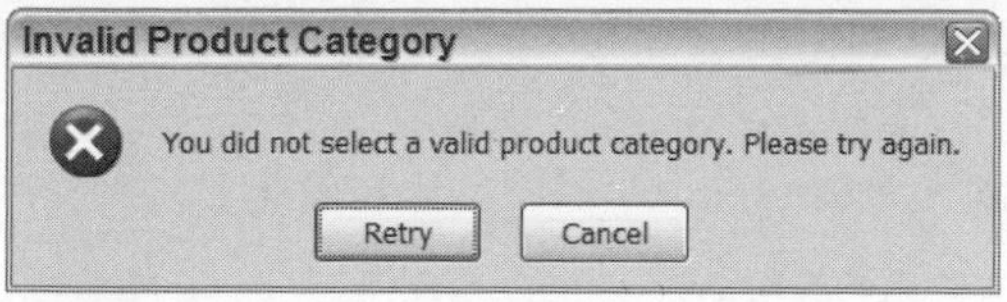

Invalid Product Category

You did not select a valid product category. Please try again.

Retry   Cancel

Figure 11.40   Selecting an invalid value displays the error message.

As you can see with this example, validations and parameters can help you build innovative and powerful reporting solutions using readily available functions that are included in Microsoft Excel.

Trying It Out in the Real World

Margaret Peacock, a Sales Representative in the Northwind Trader's office in Redmond, Washington, has asked you to provide her with a list of all of Northwind's customers. She has requested this information be provided as an Excel Spreadsheet report. The report should include all the columns in the Customers database table and use a parameter for country name so that Margaret can select customers for just a particular country.

Getting Down to Business

Follow these steps to complete this exercise:

1. Choose Data ➪ Import External Data ➪ New Database Query.

2. When the Choose Data Source dialog box appears, verify that Use The Query Wizard To Create/Edit Queries is unchecked, select the NorthwindCS Database data source, and then click OK to continue.

3. When the Microsoft Query program is launched, you are presented with the Add Tables dialog box. Close this dialog box, and then click the View SQL button to bring up the Execute SQL window.

4. Paste or type the following query into the SQL dialog box, and then click OK:

```
SELECT * FROM Customers WHERE Country = ?
```

5. When the Enter Parameter Value dialog box appears, type **USA;** and then click OK to input the parameter value and to execute the SQL query.

6. Click the Return Data to Excel button to return the data to Microsoft Excel.

7. When the Import Data dialog box appears, click OK to create the Spreadsheet report.

8. Click the Parameters button on the External Data toolbar to bring up the Parameters dialog box.

9. Click the Prompt For Value Using The Following String button and type **Enter Country Name** into the prompt field.

10. Click the Refresh Data button on the External Data toolbar to refresh the Spreadsheet report and bring up the Enter Parameter Value dialog box.

11. Type **Italy** for the Country Name, and then click OK to refresh the Spreadsheet report with only the customers in Italy.

12. Verify that your Spreadsheet report looks like Figure 11.41.

	A	B	C	D	A
1	CustomerID	CompanyName	ContactName	ContactTitle	A
2	FRANS	Franchi S.p.A.	Paolo Accorti	Sales Representative	Vi
3	MAGAA	Magazzini Alimentari Riuniti	Giovanni Rovelli	Marketing Manager	Vi
4	REGGC	Reggiani Caseifici	Maurizio Moroni	Sales Associate	St
5					
6					
7					
8					

Sheet1 / Sheet2 / Sheet3 /

Figure 11.41 If you did everything right, your Spreadsheet report should look like this.

WATCH THE VIDEO To see how this exercise works, click the ch1102_video.avi file from www.wiley.com/go/excelreporting and watch the video.

Reviewing What You Did

This example provides a simple demonstration of how a parameter is integrated into an SQL query. Additionally, you can see that this type of report is not suited for a PivotTable because there aren't any numeric fields to aggregate. In the real world, you may need to include logic that enables the report user to extract all of the customers, instead of just the customers in a particular country.

Chapter Review

This chapter covered a lot of ground. It introduced you to Spreadsheet reports, web queries, and parameters. It provided a perspective on how Spreadsheet reports are used in the enterprise and helped you compare this reporting technology to PivotTable reports. It reviewed the functions and tools included with Spreadsheet reports, including subtotaling, formula fields, sorting, and conditional formatting. You learned how to integrate a web query into a Spreadsheet report to extract data from Internet and intranet websites. You also examined how to use parameter queries with SQL queries and stored procedures to restrict the size of the returned dataset and accept user-input values that are mapped to variables in a stored procedure or a SQL query. Finally, the chapter explained how you can use various parameters in the report and how you can integrate those parameters with data validation.

CHAPTER 12

Using Excel Reports on the Web

For this chapter, I make a couple of assumptions about what you know at this point. I assume you have read through the earlier chapters on PivotTable and Spreadsheet reports and that you are familiar with some of the technologies covered there — specifically, parameter queries, web queries, and OLAP. You need that background to fully understand what's covered here. This chapter introduces PivotTable lists and demonstrates how you can create them from an Excel report.

The chapter starts with the basics of publishing Excel reports to the web, including an overview of PivotTable lists and a discussion of how this technology provides interactive, web-enabled report access over Internet and intranet web pages. It provides a brief example of how a PivotTable report is converted to a PivotTable list using native Microsoft Excel tools. Then the chapter outlines the basic tools and terminology of PivotTable lists, which includes a review of the PivotTable list areas, toolbar, and Field List window.

Following these introductory sections, this chapter is broken into three more sections. The first of these focuses on PivotTable list management and includes information on how to aggregate and group data, apply filters, sort data, create calculated fields, and export a PivotTable list to Excel as a PivotTable report. The next section discusses the formatting tools and options available for customizing the display and behavior of the PivotTable list. Finally, the chapter provides another real-world example that you can use to practice what you learned in the chapter.

The Basics of Publishing Excel Reports to the Web

Microsoft Excel includes tools that enable you to convert Excel PivotTable and Spreadsheet reports into web-enabled PivotTable lists. You save the PivotTable list as a web page that can be published to an Internet or intranet website where report users can access it using a web browser. Most of the report functions available in the various Excel report types are also available in this web page. In fact, a PivotTable list actually combines many of the best features of PivotTable and Spreadsheet reports. There are even tools for exporting the PivotTable list, with all the data and the DSN connection information, back to Excel as a PivotTable report.

Using PivotTable list technology, you can accomplish the following:

- Centralize all your PivotTable and Spreadsheet reports to an Internet or intranet website

- Provide report users with a web-enabled reporting solution that includes interactive report design tools and instantaneous access to source data

- Present a default report view that is made available to all users who access the PivotTable list

- Incorporate parameters that enable the user to interactively specify values that are mapped to variables in a stored procedure or SQL query for improving query runtime and reducing the size of the dataset

- Access numerous types of data sources such as OLAP cubes, OLTP databases, web tables, and text files

- Provide users with the capability to transfer the PivotTable list to Excel as a PivotTable report

- Configure numerous options that toggle whether the user can change the PivotTable layout, apply filters, display detail rows, and access advanced options

PUBLISHING PIVOTTABLE REPORTS TO THE WEB

If you plan to implement PivotTable lists, be sure to do complete and comprehensive security analysis to prevent unauthorized access or attack by malicious users or by malicious software, such as viruses. Keep in mind that the DSN information is also readily available, for example, when you download the PivotTable list to the web or edit the web page with Microsoft FrontPage 2003.

You may also want to back up the IIS metabase file before installing any of the web components. If you are already running production applications on IIS, this backup will help enable you to quickly revert back to the IIS configuration, should the need arise.

> **NOTE** In order to use the PivotTable list in a browser, you must have installed the Microsoft Office Web Components. You also must have a valid Microsoft Office 2003 license and use Microsoft Internet Explorer 5.01 with Service Pack 2 (SP2) or later.

Before You Begin

First, this chapter shows you how to convert an Excel PivotTable report to a PivotTable list, which is then accessed through the Internet Explorer browser. This PivotTable list is referenced in many examples throughout this chapter. You can download the Excel PivotTable report from the web, although you must update the DSN connection information in order to access the NorthwindCS database on your own SQL Server.

> **ON THE WEB** You can download the NorthwindWebReport.xls Excel workbook to your computer from this book's companion website at www.wiley.com/go/excelreporting. Depending on which file you download, look in either the Chap12.zip file or the Chap12 directory (from within Excel Reporting.zip).

Complete these steps to start this chapter and follow along with the examples:

1. Download the NorthwindWebReport.xls PivotTable report from www.wiley.com/go/excelreporting.

2. Open the PivotTable report and verify that it looks like Figure 12.1.

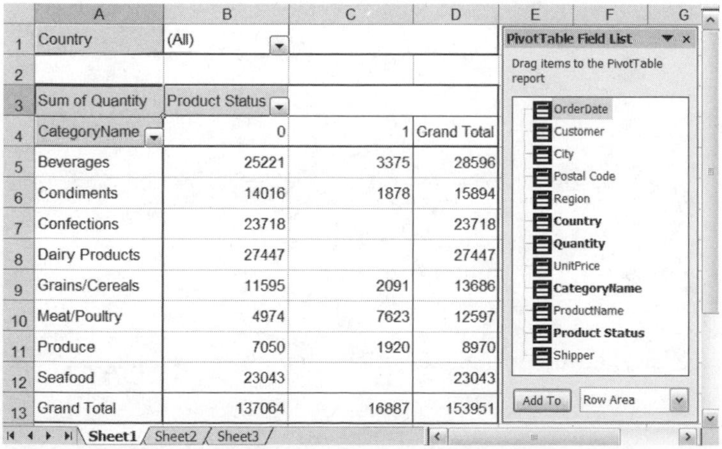

Figure 12.1 The PivotTable report that you download from the Wiley website should look like this.

3. Right-click the report and choose Refresh Data from the pop-up menu to bring up the SQL Server Login dialog box.

4. Enter your login credentials, click Options, and then select NorthwindCS from the database drop-down list to connect to the database on your SQL Server and refresh the report data.

5. Choose File ⇨ Save As Web Page to bring up the Save As dialog box.

6. Click the Selection: Sheet button, check the Add Interactivity option, and click the Change Title button to bring up the Set Title dialog box. Type **Northwind Order Analysis Report** in the Title field, and thenclick OK to add the report title and close the Set Title dialog box.

7. Type **NorthwindWebReport.htm** in the File Name field. Verify that your dialog box looks like Figure 12.2, and then click Publish to bring up the Publish As Web Page dialog box.

8. Click PivotTable in the Choose pane and select PivotTable Functionality from the Add Interactivity With drop-down box. Verify that your dialog box looks like Figure 12.3, and then click Publish to convert the PivotTable to a web page and open the web page in the Internet Explorer browser.

9. If the Internet Security Bar warning message appears, click Allow Block Content from the Internet Security toolbar to enable the PivotTable report to be opened from your web browser.

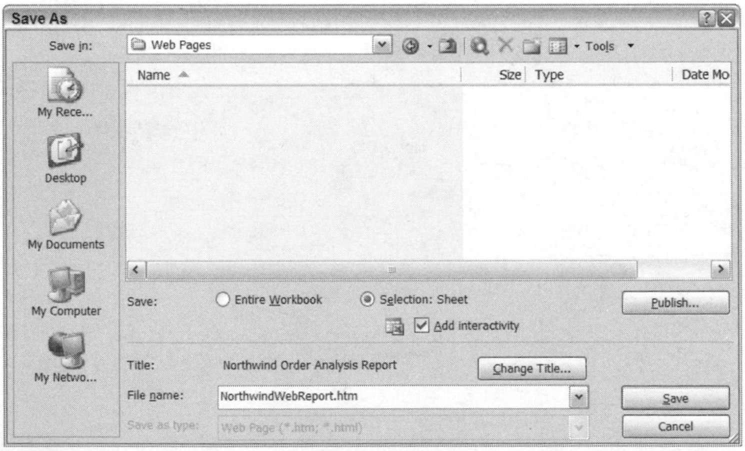

Figure 12.2 You can save Excel documents and PivotTable reports as web pages in this dialog box.

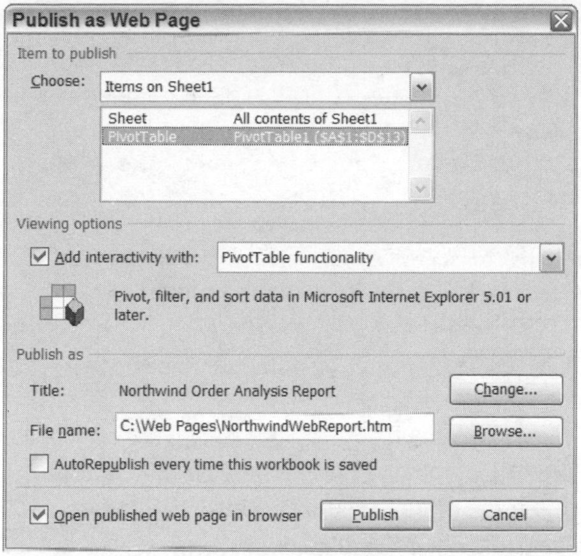

Figure 12.3 Publish the PivotTable report as a web page from this dialog box.

If you're using an SQL authentication type, the Data Source Logon box appears when the PivotTable list is initially displayed, regardless of whether you checked the Save Password option before the Excel report was converted to a PivotTable list. Keep in mind that the SQL Login ID displayed in the User Name field of Figure 12.4 is the same one that was stored in the PivotTable report.

TIP Microsoft FrontPage 2003 includes tools for setting and saving data source logon passwords for an SQL authentication method. Saving the password prevents this prompt from appearing each time the PivotTable list is initially accessed by a user. Alternatively, you can leave it blank to add another layer of security.

Figure 12.4 If you are using SQL Authentication instead of Trusted Security, the user must specify a User Name and Login to access the PivotTable list.

CONFIGURING SECURITY FOR A PIVOTTABLE LIST

There are two security items that you may need to configure in order to view and work with a PivotTable list. The first is an Internet Explorer option setting for accessing data across domains. By default, this option is disabled. If it's not enabled, the PivotTable List can't connect to an external data source. The second security item simply involves adding the applicable web page to the list of Trusted Sites.

In order to enable the PivotTable list to access an external data source, you must configure Internet Explorer security to access data across domains.

To configure Internet Explorer security, follow these steps:

1. From Internet Explorer, choose Tools ➪ Internet Options to open the Internet Options dialog box.

2. Click the Security tab, select the content zone in which you will access the PivotTable list (this will be the Internet Zone unless otherwise specified), and then click Custom Level to bring up the Security Settings dialog box.

3. Scroll down to Access Data Sources Across Domains under the Miscellaneous node, and then click the Enable button to allow a PivotTable list to access data from an external data source.

4. Click OK to change the security settings for this content zone and to close the Security Settings dialog box.

5. When the Warning dialog box appears, click Yes to acknowledge that you want to change the security setting.

6. Repeat this step for all content zones where you might access this PivotTable list.

In order to prevent the Internet Security Bar warning from appearing, you need to add the web page with the PivotTable list to the Trusted Sites content zone. Once this site is added to the list of Trusted Sites, don't forget that you also have to enable the Access Data Across Domains option for the Trusted Sites content zone, since this web site is now assigned to the Trusted Sites content zone.

10. Verify that your PivotTable list is now open and looks like Figure 12.5.

WARNING You will not be able to view this PivotTable list if you don't have the Microsoft Internet Explorer security option Access Data Across Domains enabled. Read the sidebar "Configuring Security for a PivotTable List" in this chapter for more information about setting security options.

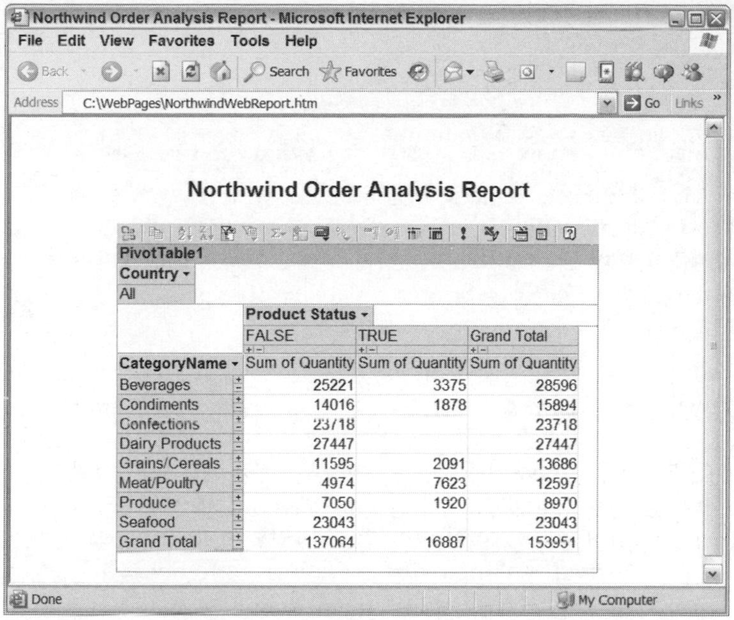

Figure 12.5 The PivotTable report you saw in Figure 12.1 now appears as a PivotTable list.

TIP I use this PivotTable list in several examples throughout this chapter. You can reset its display back to this initial view by clicking in the address field of the Internet Explorer program and pressing Enter to reload the web page. Clicking the Refresh button won't reset the PivotTable to the initial display.

WATCH THE VIDEO To see how to convert a PivotTable report to a PivotTable list, click the ch1201_video.avi file at www.wiley.com/go/ excelreporting to watch the video.

Reviewing the Converted PivotTable List

As demonstrated in the preceding section, Excel includes tools for converting reports to a web-based PivotTable list. However, this conversion method is best suited to a starting point. If you are using complex queries or advanced report features — or if you plan to pursue a web-based reporting strategy — you will most likely want to create or modify the PivotTable list using Front-Page 2003. This web editor program includes powerful tools for designing and formatting PivotTable lists, allowing you to customize the initial layout and disable functions.

If you are using an OLTP data source, and you converted the PivotTable report to a PivotTable list from Excel (as described in the "Before You Begin" section), all the report fields appear as Data fields in the PivotTable list.

WARNING If the PivotTable report uses an SQL query that can't be graphically displayed in the Microsoft Query program, the field list names will be converted as Field 1 . . . Field *n* in the PivotTable List. If you want the correct field name to be used, you must edit the field names using Microsoft FrontPage 2003.

Introducing PivotTable Lists

PivotTable lists incorporate many of the best elements of PivotTable reports, OLAP data display, and Spreadsheet reports. They include the cross-tabular reporting features of a PivotTable but retain the capability to display data in a tabular form, either as part of the PivotTable or on its own. Date fields are organized into a dimension level hierarchy for OLTP data, and expansion nodes are included for expanding and collapsing items in Inner and Outer Row or Column area fields. Parameter and web query capabilities are also enabled for PivotTable lists, regardless of whether data is organized in a tabular or cross-tabular format. All this — and the PivotTable list is accessible over an Internet or intranet web page that can be downloaded as a PivotTable report to the user's local computer running Excel. And the PivotTable report comes complete with the report dataset, format/sort/filter settings, and the connection string. Sound exciting? You bet!

NOTE Although this is cutting-edge technology, there are some inherent design limitations that you cannot avoid. For example, if you choose to use an OLAP cube, the Detail area (the tabular section of the PivotTable list) is disabled because that level of detail is simply not stored in the data cube.

Just like with an Excel PivotTable report, a PivotTable list works with several types of data sources, including OLTP databases, OLAP cubes, and web queries. Additionally, the PivotTable list works with PivotCharts reports, PivotTable reports, and Spreadsheet reports.

Most functions available in Excel reports are retained in a PivotTable list. However, the execution of these functions works differently — and that can require some adjustments on your part, especially if you are used to working with Excel PivotTable reports. There is also a new Detail area for displaying data in a tabular form. This area is shared with the Data area of the PivotTable list. The handling and display of this shared area can change as fields are dragged on or off the PivotTable.

> **NOTE** I suspect that the function you will miss most in a PivotTable list is probably Undo. This is especially true if you are accustomed to working with Excel reports, where you are prone to working with the PivotTable list as if it were a PivotTable report. Although a PivotTable list looks very similar to a PivotTable report, you'll soon discover that there are numerous differences in the handling of many basic operations in these two types of reports.

Looking at the Detail Area of a PivotTable List

If you look back to Figure 12.5, you can see that all the fields in the PivotTable Field List window are bold, except OrderDate By Week and OrderDate By Month. You may remember from reading earlier chapters that a bold font style indicates the field is in the PivotTable. But where is it? Click the plus (+) node next to any of the Row or Column area items to reveal the Detail area with all the hidden fields, as shown in Figure 12.6.

> **TIP** Any field not in the Excel PivotTable report is automatically placed in the Detail area when it is converted to a PivotTable list (for OLTP data sources).

You can choose to display the tabular data for a particular cell (for example, where the items Beverages and False intersect), or for the entire PivotTable list. This is explained in more detail in the "Showing and Hiding the Detail" section of this chapter.

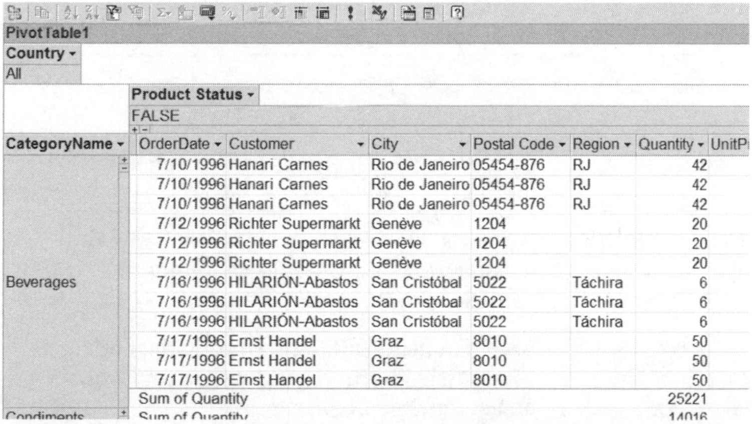

Figure 12.6   Clicking the plus (+) node of Beverages reveals the Detail area fields and items.

Looking at Date Fields

Date fields are treated as if they were organized into an OLAP dimension hierarchy. Notice that the OrderDate field is listed three times in the PivotTable Field List window:

- **OrderDate:** This instance works just like a regular OLTP date field; the components of the data are not broken apart or arranged in a dimension-level hierarchy.

- **OrderDate By Week:** This instance breaks the components of the Order Date apart and organizes them into the hierarchy Year ⇨ Week ⇨ Day ⇨ Hour ⇨ Minute ⇨ Second.

- **OrderDate By Month:** This instance breaks the components of the Order Date apart and organizes them into the hierarchy Year ⇨ Quarter ⇨ Month ⇨ Day ⇨ Hour ⇨ Minute ⇨ Second.

These last two fields are added automatically when Excel converts the PivotTable report to a PivotTable list. Of course, these fields are also automatically removed if the PivotTable list is exported back to Excel because a PivotTable report is not set up to display OLTP data in a hierarchal format.

Comparing PivotTable Lists to PivotTable Reports

There are many other distinctions between PivotTable reports and PivotTable lists. Table 12.1 includes a list of some of these differences.

Table 12.1   PivotTable Report and PivotTable List Differences

PIVOTTABLE REPORT	PIVOTTABLE LIST
Includes Page, Column, Row, and Data areas for report fields	Includes Page, Column, Row, Data, and Detail areas for report fields
Works with OLTP and OLAP data sources	Works with OLTP, OLAP, and web data sources
Cannot display OLTP data in a hierarchal format	Displays OLTP date fields in a hierarchal format
Does not support parameters	Supports parameters that can be mapped to variables in a stored procedure or to conditions in the `Where` part of an SQL query
Doesn't include any tools to disable functions for report formatting or management (unless VBA programming is used)	Several functions (filtering, grouping, adding calculate fields, modifying the report layout, and so on) can be disabled

Table 12.1   *(continued)*

PIVOTTABLE REPORT	PIVOTTABLE LIST
Decentralized model where users access their own copy of a PivotTable report	Centralized model where users access a shared web page that stores a default view of the PivotTable list
Double-clicking a Data area item reveals the underlying dataset	Double-clicking a Data area item reveals the fields in the Detail area
The Page area drop-down list supports filtering of only one item (no items, one item, or all items)	The Page area drop-down list (referred to as a Filter field) supports filtering of multiple items (no items, one item, multiple items, or all items)
Any field can be dropped into the Data area	Only Total fields can be dropped into the Data area

If you are reading this chapter for the first time, you may not understand all these differences between PivotTable reports and PivotTable lists. If that's the case, don't worry; the features that pertain to PivotTable lists are explained in greater detail throughout the appropriate sections of this chapter.

Basic Components and Terminology

This section covers the basic terminology and components of a PivotTable list. It assumes that you are already experienced with and knowledgeable about PivotTable reports as it draws upon references to earlier chapters that provided more comprehensive information on this topic.

CROSS-REFERENCE Read Chapters 7 and 8 for more information on PivotTable reports, Chapter 10 for more information on OLAP data, and Chapter 11 for more information on Spreadsheet reports.

Using the PivotTable List Toolbar

You can perform many functions of a PivotTable list from the PivotTable list toolbar shown in Figure 12.7. This toolbar is displayed at the top of the PivotTable list. Its display can be toggled by right-clicking the report and choosing Toolbar from the pop-up menu.

Figure 12.7 The PivotTable list toolbar is used to manage many of the functions of the PivotTable list.

TIP You can edit the PivotTable list in Microsoft FrontPage to configure whether the toolbar will be available to report users who access it.

Table 12.2 provides explanations for the various buttons available in the PivotTable list toolbar.

Table 12.2 PivotTable List Toolbar Buttons

BUTTON	NAME	DESCRIPTION
	Web Components	Brings up the About Microsoft Office 2003 Web Components dialog box, where you can view the installed version number and access technical support.
	Copy	Copies selected cells in the PivotTable report into your clipboard. Once you've copied them, you can paste the copied cells into Microsoft Word or Microsoft Excel.
	Sort Ascending	Sorts the selected Row, Column, or Detail data in alphanumeric order. You can also click this button to apply an ascending sort based on a selected Data area item.
	Sort Descending	Sorts the selected Row, Column, or Detail data in reverse alphanumeric order. You can also click this button to apply a descending sort based on a selected Data area item.
	AutoFilter	Toggles the current filter settings on and off.
	Show Top/ Bottom Items	Brings up a pop-up menu where you can apply a filter that shows only the Top or Bottom n values or Top or Bottom n%.
	AutoCalc	Applies an aggregate function against the items in a selected Column, Row, or Page field.
	Subtotals	Toggles the display of subtotals and grand totals for a selected Column or Row area field.
	Calculated Totals and Fields	Brings up the Calculation tab of the Commands and Options dialog box where you can create a Calculated Total field or a Calculated Detail field.
	Show As	Displays a selected Data area item as a percent of a row, column, or grand total.

Table 12.2 *(continued)*

BUTTON	NAME	DESCRIPTION
	Collapse	Collapses the display of Inner Row or Inner Column area fields.
	Expand	Expands the display of Inner Row or Inner Column area fields.
	Hide Details	Hides fields in the Detail area.
	Show Details	Shows fields in the Detail area.
	Refresh	Refreshes the report data.
	Export to Microsoft Excel	Exports the PivotTable list to a PivotTable report in Excel.
	Commands and Options	Opens the Commands and Options dialog box.
	PivotTable Field List	Toggles the display of the PivotTable Field List window.
	Help	Opens the Microsoft Office 2003 PivotTable Component Help dialog box.

These buttons and functions are explained in greater detail throughout the appropriate sections of this chapter.

Accessing the PivotTable List Menus

There are four different types of pop-up menus that can appear when you right-click on the PivotTable list:

- **PivotTable list menu:** Appears when you click the PivotTable list, but not on a particular field or item

- **PivotTable Data menu:** Appears when you click a Filter, Row, or Column area field or item

- **PivotTable Total menu:** Appears when you click a Total field or item in the Data area

- **PivotTable Detail menu:** Appears when you click a Detail area field or item

The type of pop-up menu that you see depends on where you are clicking in the PivotTable list. If you right-click on the PivotTable, but not on a particular field, you bring up the PivotTable list pop-up menu for accessing general functions that apply to the PivotTable list, such as refreshing data, toggling the display of the PivotTable toolbar, and exporting the PivotTable list to Excel.

Clicking a Total field in the Data area brings up the PivotTable Total pop-up menu for showing only Top/Bottom *n* values, sorting data, and showing data in a custom format. Likewise, clicking a Row, Column, or Filter area field brings up the PivotTable Data pop-up menu for grouping data, expanding and collapsing items, copying data, and filtering by selection. The pop-up menu for the Detail area includes functions for filtering data, creating Total fields, and sorting data.

NOTE Clicking in the browser window, but not anywhere on the PivotTable list, brings up the pop-up menu for the Microsoft Internet Explorer program, which is outside the scope of this book.

The available menu functions are covered throughout the rest of this chapter where they are most relevant.

Understanding the Terminology and Display of a PivotTable List

The layout of a PivotTable list is similar to that of a PivotTable report, except that the Detail and Data areas share the same drop zone, as shown in Figure 12.8.

Looking at Figure 12.8, you can also see that Page fields are referred to as Filter fields. The most notable adjustment for first-time users of a PivotTable list is getting used to working with the tabular data in the Detail area. And since both the Data and Detail areas share the same drop zone, there are some important considerations to keep in mind when dragging fields on or off the PivotTable list. This is covered in more detail in the "Dragging Fields to the PivotTable List" section of this chapter.

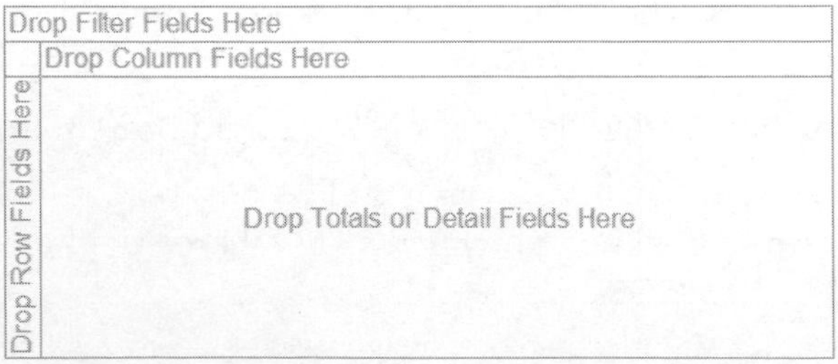

Figure 12.8 A shared drop zone is used for Detail and Data area fields.

The Areas

The areas in a PivotTable list are basically the same as the areas in a PivotTable report. The principal difference is the new Detail area for displaying tabular data in a columnar format. Table 12.3 provides a more complete description of each PivotTable list area.

The Field Types

Two types of fields are used in a PivotTable list: Data fields and Total fields. Data fields can be displayed in any area of the PivotTable list except the Data area. Total fields are aggregated and can be displayed only in the Data area. If you are using an OLAP data source, the measures and dimensions will look the same as they look in an Excel PivotTable report.

> **WARNING** If you are accustomed to using an Excel PivotTable report, this new terminology can be confusing. One of the most important things to keep in mind is that *Data* fields are NOT *Data area* fields. Only Total fields can be displayed in the Data area of a PivotTable list.

Table 12.3   PivotTable List Areas

AREA	DESCRIPTION
Filter area	Drag fields to this area to display data as if it were on separate pages. This area works just like the Page area in a PivotTable report, except that you can select multiple items to filter from the field drop-down list.
Row area	Drag fields to the Row area to vertically display unique fields, one item per row. This area can display dimension levels, and there are options for toggling whether expansion nodes are displayed for expanding and collapsing the display of Inner fields (OLTP) or dimension levels (OLAP).
Column area	Drag fields to the Column area to horizontally display unique fields, one item per column. This area can display dimension levels, and there are options for toggling whether expansion nodes are displayed for expanding and collapsing the display of Inner fields (OLTP) or dimension levels (OLAP).
Detail area	Drag fields to this area to show non-aggregated data in a tabular form. You can configure this area to automatically display data, or to display data when the nodes on the right of the inner-most Row area field or the nodes at the bottom of a Column area field are expanded. This area is disabled for OLAP data sources.
Data area	Drag fields to this area to perform some type of aggregation. Here you can choose to calculate a count, an average, a sum, a minimum, a maximum, a standard deviation, or a variance.

Table 12.4 shows the icons for each type of field, along with a brief description.

> **NOTE** If the PivotTable list uses an OLAP data source, you cannot drag the Data fields to the Detail area. This is because the OLAP storage method doesn't have the necessary level of detail to display information in a non-aggregated, tabular form.

Dragging Fields to the PivotTable List

Now that you know some of the terminology and a little about the PivotTable list display features, you're ready to start working with the PivotTable list you created earlier in the "Before You Begin" section of this chapter. The following sections review how various display configurations affect how fields can be dropped into the various areas of the PivotTable list. If this material is new to you, I suggest you follow the exercises included in this section to obtain a better understanding of drop indicators and how the shared Data and Detail area drop zone works.

The Drop Icon Indicators

There are two types of drop indicators for a PivotTable list: drop icons and drop bars. The *drop icon* is displayed when fields are dragged over a particular area of the PivotTable. This icon appears only when the field is being dragged from one area of the PivotTable list to another. It does not appear when the field is being dragged to a PivotTable area from the PivotTable Field List window.

> **WARNING** It's a mystery to me why Microsoft decided to display the drop icons only when a field is being dragged from one area on the PivotTable list to another area. As I have gained experience with Excel PivotTable reports, I find that I keep looking for the drop indicator when dragging fields from the PivotTable Field List window. So I know from firsthand experience that this display difference can take some adjustment. The new Detail area in the PivotTable list also doesn't help make this adjustment any easier. I recommend that you carefully review the material in this section to better understand how fields are dragged and dropped onto the PivotTable list.

Table 12.4 PivotTable List Field Type Icons

FIELD TYPE	ICON	DESCRIPTION
Data field	☰	These fields can be dragged to any area of the PivotTable list, except the Data area.
Total field	01 10	These fields can be dragged only to the Data area of the PivotTable list.

The second type of drop indicator is the *drop bar* that appears alongside the drop icon as fields are dragged over different areas of the PivotTable list. Unlike the drop icon, the drop bar is always displayed, regardless of whether the selected field is being dragged from the PivotTable Field List window or from another area in the PivotTable. I recommend that you become familiar with both types of drop indicators if you are just learning this technology. The next section provides several examples that should help you better understand where fields will be dropped in the PivotTable list.

To increase your understanding, start by reviewing the drop icons displayed when fields are dragged from one area on the PivotTable list to another area. Table 12.5 shows these drop icons, along with a brief description of each.

Dragging a Field to the Detail Area

As you drag fields over various areas of a PivotTable list, the drop bar indicates where the selected field will be dropped when it's released. Additionally, if you are dragging a selected field to the shared Data and Detail areas, the drop bar is especially helpful for signifying the area where the field will be dropped, as drop icons are not displayed when fields are dragged from the PivotTable Field List window to the PivotTable.

Table 12.5   PivotTable List Drop Icons

ICON	EXPLANATION
	Field will be dropped in the Filter area
	Field will be dropped in the Row area
	Field will be dropped in the Column area
	Field will be dropped in the Detail area
	Field will be dropped in the Data area
	Field will be removed from the PivotTable
	Field drop will be canceled as the drop location is not valid

Drop icons appear only when fields are being dragged from one area of the PivotTable list to another area on the PivotTable list.

To try dragging a field to the Detail area of the PivotTable list, follow these steps:

1. Starting with the PivotTable list shown earlier in Figure 12.5, click the Show Details button to display the Detail area.

2. Drag all the fields out of the Detail area, except Quantity.

3. Drag Product Status in the Column area off the PivotTable list.

TIP Did you notice what happened when you dragged Product Status off the report? Because Product Status was the only field in the Column area of the PivotTable list, the Data area was automatically hidden when this field was removed (indicated by the column heading, Sum of Quantity, no longer being displayed). This is because a PivotTable list can only simultaneously display the Detail and Data areas when there is at least one field in both the Row and the Column areas of the PivotTable list.

4. Click the PivotTable Field List button to bring up the PivotTable Field List window.

5. Drag Unit Price from the PivotTable Field List window to the Detail area of the PivotTable list, before Quantity. Notice that the drop icon is center-filled and the drop bar turns inward, as shown in Figure 12.9.

TIP You might be surprised that the field was not automatically aggregated as it would have been in an Excel PivotTable report. Actually, it is not possible to automatically aggregate a Data field when the Data area is not displayed.

6. Verify that your PivotTable list looks like Figure 12.10.

Dragging a Field to the Row Area

You can drag fields to the Row area of the PivotTable list using a procedure that is similar to dragging a field to the Detail area. Just drag the field a little more to the left so that the drop icon is left-filled and the direction of the drop-bar turns outward as shown in Figure 12.11.

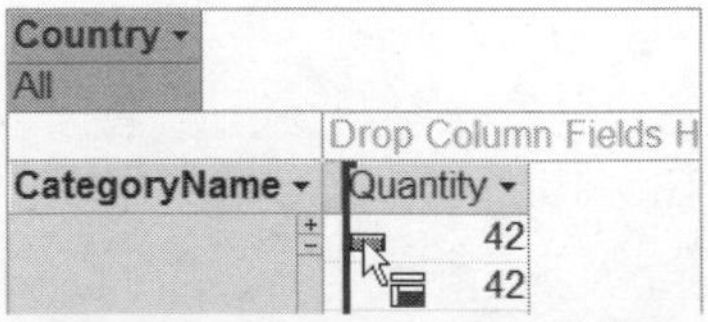

Figure 12.9 The drop bar turns inward and the pointer icon shows the filled Detail area to indicate that the selected field will be dropped in the Detail area of the PivotTable list.

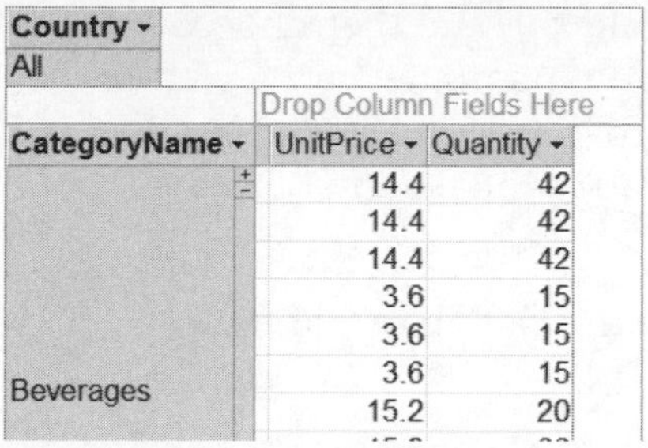

Figure 12.10   You cannot drop UnitPrice in the Data area of the PivotTable list unless there is at least one field in both the Row and Column areas.

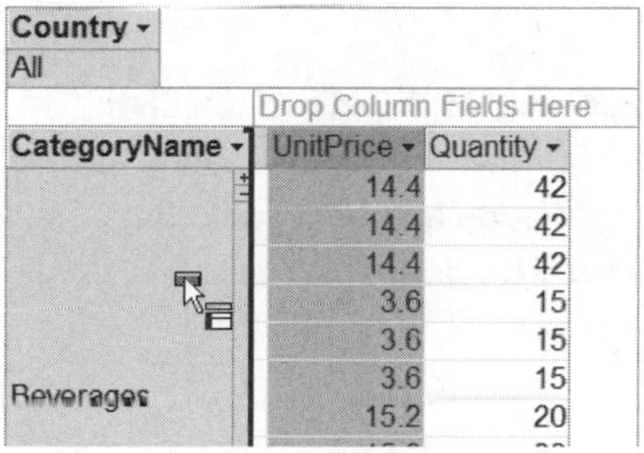

Figure 12.11   The drop bar turns outward and the pointer icon shows the filled Row area to indicate that the selected field will be dropped in the Row area of the PivotTable list.

Try dragging UnitPrice to the Row area of the PivotTable list as both an Inner Row area field and an Outer Row area field. Notice how the drop bar changes when the selected field is moved into the Row area, as an Inner field and an Outer field. When you are finished, drag UnitPrice back to the Detail area.

Dragging a Total Field to the Data Area

Only a Total field can be dragged to the Data area of a PivotTable when the Data area is hidden. If you are accustomed to working with PivotTable reports in Excel, this may seem counterintuitive. However, once you understand the handling and options, it's not that difficult, with some practice, to make the adjustment.

Here are a few ways you can move fields into the hidden Data area:

- Click the Hide Details icon to show the Data area while hiding the Detail area, and then drag the field to the Data area.

- Click the field to select it in the PivotTable list, select Data area in the Add To drop-down list, and then click the Add To button.

- Drag the field to the Details area, right-click it, and then choose Auto-Calc ⇨ *Aggregate Function* from the pop-up menu, where *Aggregate Function* is the type of function you want to perform (for example, Count, Sum, or Average). This method adds the field to both the Details and the Data area of the PivotTable.

To aggregate a Data field that is already in the Detail area of the PivotTable list, follow these steps:

1. Starting with the PivotTable list shown in Figure 12.10, right-click Unit-Price to select it (the column becomes highlighted), and then choose AutoCalc ⇨ Average to calculate the average unit price and add it as a Total field in the Data area of the PivotTable list.

> **NOTE** Notice that nothing appears to have happened in the PivotTable list itself. However, if you look at the PivotTable Field List window, you should see the new field Average of UnitPrice under the Totals node in a bold font. The bold indicates that the field has been added to the PivotTable list (in this case, to the hidden Data area).

2. Click the Hide Details button to hide the Detail area and display the Data area.
3. Verify that your PivotTable list looks like Figure 12.12.

In Figure 12.12, the Data area is displayed and the Detail area is hidden. In this display configuration, you can drag Data fields to either the Data area or the Detail area of the PivotTable list.

Country ▾		
All		
	Drop Column Fields Here	
CategoryName ▾	Sum of Quantity	Average of UnitPrice
Beverages	28596	29.23675743
Condiments	15894	21.32083333
Confections	23718	22.60269461
Dairy Products	27447	26.98306011
Grains/Cereals	13686	21.24642857
Meat/Poultry	12597	42.87473988
Produce	8970	35.19448529
Seafood	23043	19.0629697
Grand Total	153951	26.21851972

Figure 12.12 The new Total field, Average of UnitPrice, appears in the PivotTable list when the Data area is shown.

WARNING Understanding which fields can be dropped into the shared Data and Detail area for different display configurations can be confusing. Although Microsoft could have done a better job in uniformly handling how fields can be placed in the PivotTable areas, I recommend that you pay attention to which fields can be dropped into each area to avoid mistakes that you can't reverse using Undo. (Remember, there is no Undo function in a PivotTable list.)

To practice dropping fields into the PivotTable list using this new display configuration, follow these steps:

1. Drag UnitPrice between Sum of Quantity and Average of Unit Price, but don't drop it in the PivotTable. Notice that the drop icon does not change to the Data area indicator.

2. Drag UnitPrice to the Filter area of the PivotTable list, and drop it to the right of Country.

3. Click the Show Details button to show the Detail area of the PivotTable list. Notice that UnitPrice no longer appears in the Detail area.

NOTE As with Excel PivotTable reports, a field can be in only one area of the PivotTable list unless it is in the Data area (where it is actually considered a separate, aggregated field).

4. Click the Hide Details button to show the Data area of the PivotTable list.

5. Drag UnitPrice (currently in the Filter area) between Sum of Quantity and Average of Unit Price. Notice that the drop icon changes to the Data area indicator, as shown in Figure 12.13.

NOTE The Data area drop icon is displayed only when the selected field is being dragged to the Data area from another area of the PivotTable list. This drop icon does not appear when you are dragging a field from the PivotTable Field List window.

Country ▾	UnitPrice ▾	
All	All	
	Drop Column Fields Here	
CategoryName ▾	Sum of Quantity	Average of UnitPrice
Beverages	28596	29.23675743
Condiments	15894	21.32083333
Confections	23718	22.60269461
Dairy Products	27447	26.98306011
Grains/Cereals	13686	21.24642857

Figure 12.13 This time, the drop icon indicates that the selected field will be dropped in the Data area of the PivotTable list.

6. Drop UnitPrice between Sum Of Quantity and Average Of UnitPrice. Notice that UnitPrice still appears in the Filter area of the PivotTable list, but it is now added as a Sum Of UnitPrice in the Data area of the PivotTable and under the Totals node in the PivotTable Field List window.

7. Drag Average of UnitPrice and Sum Of Quantity off the PivotTable list.

8. Drag (but do not drop) UnitPrice between CategoryName and Sum Of UnitPrice. Move the field left and right between these two fields. Notice that the drop icon display toggles between a Row area icon and a Data area icon.

9. Drag UnitPrice to the bottom right of the shared Data and Detail area of the PivotTable list. Drop the field when the area is highlighted in a dark blue outline and the drop-icon is bottom-filled, as shown in Figure 12.14.

Notice that the UnitPrice no longer appears in the Filter area of the Pivot-Table list. You can see it in the Detail area of the PivotTable list by clicking the Show Details button.

Understanding the Shared Data and Detail Areas

As you can see from this last exercise, the dragging and dropping of fields in the shared area of the PivotTable list is performed a little differently than it is with an Excel PivotTable report. If you are new to this topic, keep the following important items in mind; they might help you avoid confusion:

- Detail and Data area fields can be simultaneously displayed only when there are fields in both the Column area and the Row area of the PivotTable list

- Clicking the Hide Details and Show Details buttons toggles the display between the Data area and the Detail area of the PivotTable list

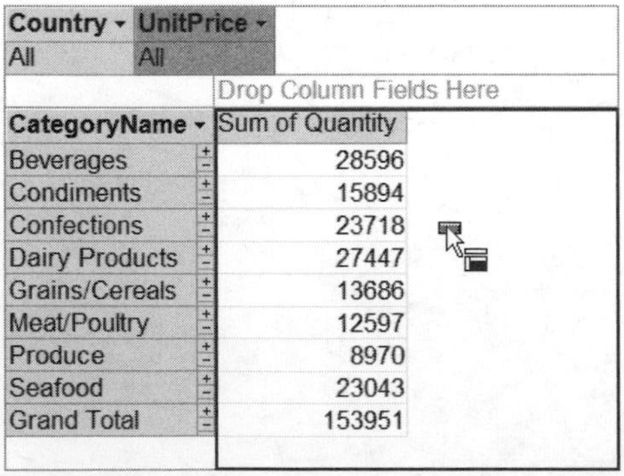

Figure 12.14 When only one Totals field is in the Data area, you can drop a field into the Data area or the Detail area (shown here) of the PivotTable list.

- If there aren't any Data fields in the Detail area, the No Details heading appears when you click the Show Details button. Likewise, if there are no Total fields in the Data area, the No Totals heading appears when you click the Hide Details button.

Using the PivotTable Field List Window

The PivotTable Field List window shown in Figure 12.15 works similarly to the one used with an Excel PivotTable report. All the available fields that can be dragged to the PivotTable are displayed in the PivotTable Field List window; fields already dropped in the PivotTable appear in a bold font. You can also add fields to the PivotTable by selecting an area from the Add To Area drop-down box and clicking the Add To button.

Despite the similarities, there are also some differences between this PivotTable Field List window and the one you saw with the PivotTable report. If you are using an OLTP data source, you may notice some changes in the display and function of the PivotTable Field List window, such as:

- Date fields can be displayed in a dimension-level hierarchy.
- Total fields appear under the Totals node.
- Total fields can be deleted by right-clicking the field under the Totals node and choosing Delete from the pop-up menu.
- A plus (+) node appears next to each Data field.

For OLTP data, the dimension-level hierarchy for date fields is available. However, if you transfer the PivotTable list to Excel by clicking the Export To Microsoft Excel button, these fields are automatically removed because Excel does not have the capability of displaying hierarchal levels for OLTP data.

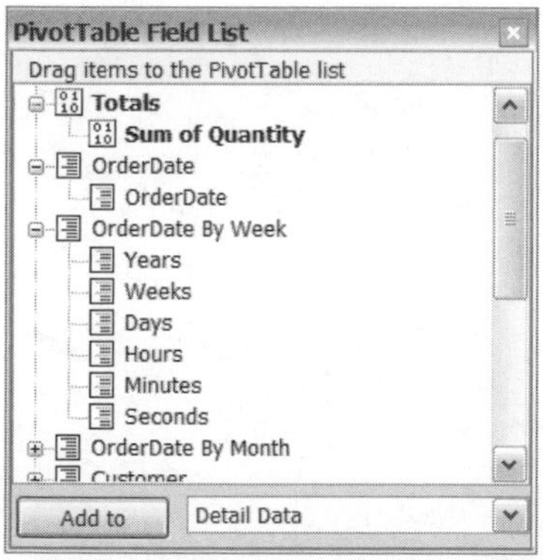

Figure 12.15 The Field List window for a PivotTable list.

Keep in mind that only fields under the Total node can be displayed in the Data area. Each time that you add a new field to the Data area of the PivotTable list, it is added under the Totals node, even if it was already added. You can delete these fields under the Totals node by right-clicking and selecting Delete from the pop-up menu.

TIP You can add all the fields under the Totals node in the PivotTable Field List window to the Data area of the PivotTable list by selecting the node and clicking Add To.

Managing the PivotTable List

Most of the functions available in an Excel PivotTable report remain available in a PivotTable list, although there are often differences in how these functions are accessed and how they work. The following sections highlight the various types of fields and describe the principal available functions. I point out changes in operability compared to that of an Excel PivotTable report.

Working with Total Fields

Total fields, indicated by the 0101 icon in the PivotTable Field List window, are used only in the Data area of a PivotTable list. These fields show the aggregated data for different combinations of Row and Column area fields. This aggregation might be a Count, a Sum, an Average, or a Min or Max. And just like a PivotTable report, you can configure custom calculations, including running totals and difference or percentage-based differences.

This section highlights some of the functions available in a PivotTable list for Total fields, including the following:

- Creating Total fields
- Adding calculated fields
- Applying custom calculations
- Showing the Top n or Bottom n Values
- Deleting and removing Total fields
- Managing subtotals and grand totals

Creating Total Fields

A Total field is simply an aggregated field that can be dropped into the Data area of a PivotTable list. You can only create Total fields for OLTP data. If you are using an OLAP data source, these fields are simply the Measures that were defined in the OLAP cube. You can only add other Total fields by modifying the data cube or creating a Calculated Total field (covered in the "Adding Calculated Fields" section a little later in this chapter).

In an Excel PivotTable report, you create a Total field by simply dragging and dropping a field into the Data area of the PivotTable. With a PivotTable list, this method only works when an existing Data area item is already in the report or there are fields in both the Column and Row areas of the PivotTable list. However, you can also create a Total field using a couple of other methods that are described in the next two sections.

Creating a Total Field from the PivotTable Field List Window

You can add or re-create fields as Total fields by selecting them in the tree of the PivotTable Field List window, selecting Data area from the Area drop-down box, and clicking the Add To button. This adds the field to the Data area of the PivotTable list and as a field under the Totals node in the PivotTable Field List window.

To create a Total field and add it to the Data area of the PivotTable list, follow these steps:

1. Click Customer in the PivotTable Field List window to select it, choose Data Area from the Area drop-down box, and then click the Add To button to add Count of Customer to the Data area of the PivotTable list.

2. Verify that Count of Customer has been added to the Data area of the PivotTable list and as a field under Totals in the PivotTable Field List window.

Creating a Total Field Using AutoCalc

If you are using an OLTP data source, the aggregations are created from a Data field. After the Data field is aggregated, it appears under the Totals node in the PivotTable Field List window. In a PivotTable report, you can simply change the aggregation method from the PivotTable Field dialog box. However, in a PivotTable list, you must create it as a Total field.

To add a new Total field using the AutoCalc function, follow these steps:

1. Drop the field you want to aggregate into the Details area of the PivotTable list.

2. Right-click the field in the Details area that you want to aggregate, and then choose AutoCalc from the pop-up menu.

3. When you click the AutoCalc pop-up menu, several aggregate functions appear. Click the aggregate function you want to use.

4. Notice that the aggregated field now appears in the PivotTable Field List window under the Totals node.

TIP If both the Detail and Data areas are simultaneously displayed, notice that the field is subtotaled in the Detail area as well as totaled in the Data area of the PivotTable list.

Adding Calculated Fields

You can use calculated fields to reference one or more existing Total fields in the PivotTable list. Calculated fields are useful for the following situations:

- The report user does not have the technological skills to modify the SQL query or OLAP cube to include an additional Total field.
- The report user does not have security or access to modify the SQL query or OLAP cube to include an additional Total field.
- The calculated field references other Total fields that have been derived from complex, high-cost (that is, extensive CPU processing time) fields in the SQL query.

I use calculated fields only when they are based on multiple Total fields that are derived from complex subqueries. Instead of writing some convoluted SQL query with multiple subqueries and trying to program the fields into the SQL query, I can reference these fields in the PivotTable list. This can save a lot of processing time because the fields are simply numerical values in the PivotTable list, and I don't have to run numerous subqueries to calculate the totals.

WARNING Using calculated fields spreads the report logic into more locations than just the SQL query, stored procedure, or OLAP cube. This adds an additional burden for managing change and configuration.

Calculated Total Fields

Calculated Total fields are analogous to calculated fields in Excel PivotTable reports. A Calculated Total can be used only in the Data area of a PivotTable list. It can use either a constant value or reference an existing Total field in the PivotTable list.

To create a Calculated Total field, follow these steps:

1. Starting with the PivotTable list shown in Figure 12.5, add UnitPrice to the Data area.

2. Click the Calculated Totals And Fields button in the PivotTable list toolbar. Select Create Calculated Total from the drop-down menu to create a new Total field called New Total and open the Commands And Options dialog box.

NOTE Selecting Create Calculated Total from the Calculated Totals And Fields drop-down menu automatically creates a calculated field called New Total.

3. Select Sum of Unit Price (Total) from the drop-down field list and click the Insert Reference To button.

4. Type an asterisk next to [Measures].[Total1] in the Calculation pane.

5. Select Sum Of Quantity (Total) from the drop-down field list and click the Insert Reference To button.

6. Type **Total Value** in the Calculation Name field.

7. Verify that your Commands And Options dialog box looks like Figure 12.16; and then click the Change button to change the name of the calculated field from New Total to Total Value and add the calculated field to the Data area of the PivotTable list.

8. Click the Close button (X) in the top-right corner of the Commands And Option dialog box to close it.

Notice that the field is added to the Data area of the PivotTable list and the name is changed in the PivotTable Field List window.

WARNING Calculated totals are not exported to an Excel PivotTable report.

Calculated Detail Field

Calculated Detail fields are like new Data fields in a PivotTable list. These fields can be used in the Row, Column, or Detail area. Once created, you can even reference a Calculated Detail field in the formula of a Calculated Total field.

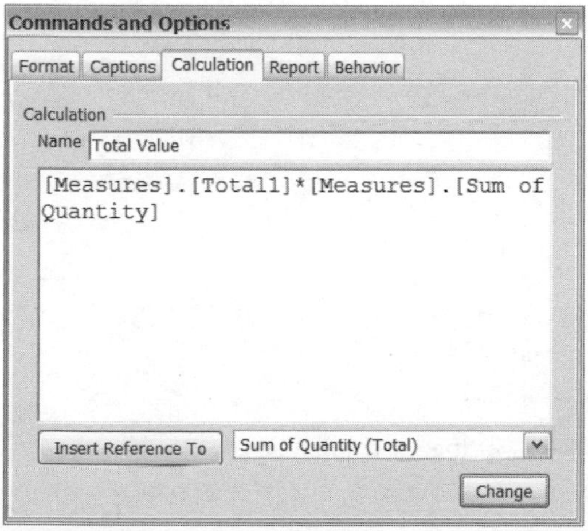

Figure 12.16 You add Calculated Total fields in the Calculation tab of the Commands And Options dialog box.

To try creating a Calculated Detail field, complete these steps:

1. Starting with the PivotTable list shown in Figure 12.5, click the Calculated Totals and Fields button in the PivotTable list toolbar and select Create Calculated Detail Field from the drop-down menu. This creates a new Calculated Detail field called Calculated and opens the Commands And Options dialog box.

   NOTE Selecting Create Calculated Detail Field from the Calculated Totals And Fields drop-down menu automatically creates a Calculated Detail Field called Calculated.

2. Select UnitPrice from the drop-down field list, and then click the Insert Reference To button.

3. Type *** 1.10** next to UnitPrice in the Calculation pane.

4. Type **NextYearUnitPrice** in the Name field.

5. Verify that your Commands And Options dialog box looks like Figure 12.17, and then click Change to change the name of the Calculated Detail Field from Calculated to NextYearUnitPrice and add the calculated detail field to the Detail area of the PivotTable list.

6. Click the Close button to close the Commands And Option dialog box.

Notice that the field is added to the Detail area of the PivotTable list and the name is changed in the PivotTable Field List window.

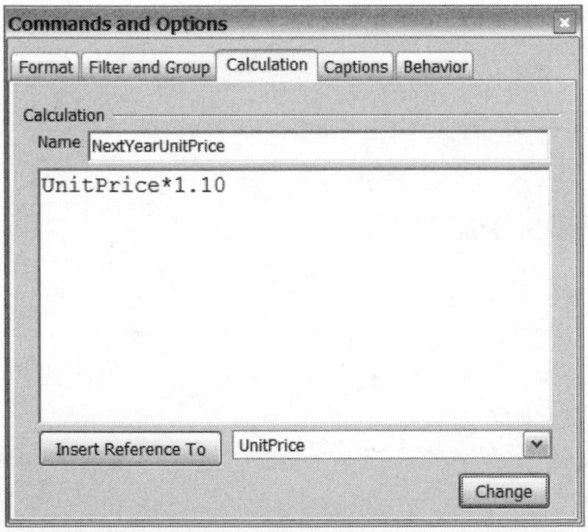

Figure 12.17 You add Calculated Detail fields in the Calculation tab of the Commands And Options dialog box.

Applying Custom Calculations

You can toggle the display of Data area items to show the data as a

- Percent of the row total
- Percent of the column total
- Percent of the parent row item
- Percent of the parent column item
- Percent of the grand total

You can apply a custom calculation by right-clicking a Total field in the Data area of the PivotTable list, and then choosing Show As ➪ *Aggregate Function* from the pop-up menu, where *Aggregate Function* is the type of function you want to perform (for example, Count, Sum, or Average) from the pop-up menu. Alternatively, you can click the Show As button to bring up the Custom Calculation drop-down menu.

Deleting and Removing Total Fields

You can choose to either delete a Total field or temporarily remove it from the Data area of the PivotTable list.

To permanently delete a Total field, you can use either one of these methods:

- Right-click on the field in the PivotTable Field List window and choose Delete from the pop-up menu.
- Right-click on the field in the Data area of the PivotTable and choose Delete from the pop-up menu.

If you just want to remove a Total field (but not delete it) from the Data area of the PivotTable list, you can right-click the field in the Data area and choose Remove Total from the pop-up menu.

Managing Grand Totals and Subtotals

You can toggle the display of subtotals and grand totals by right-clicking the Row or Column area field and choosing Subtotal from the pop-up menu. You can also select the field and click the Subtotals button to toggle the display of subtotals and grand totals. Unlike PivotTable reports in which the subtotals are controlled from the next higher-level field, the subtotal display in PivotTable lists is controlled at the level where the subtotals are actually being calculated. In Figure 12.18, for example, Product Status subtotals by Shipper are toggled by right-clicking Product Status and choosing subtotals from the pop-up menu. The grand total display is toggled by right-clicking Shipper and choosing subtotal from the pop-up menu.

Shipper	Product Status ▾	Sum of Quantity
⊟ Federal Shipping	FALSE	45688
	TRUE	5629
	Total	51317
⊟ Speedy Express	FALSE	45688
	TRUE	5629
	Total	51317
⊟ United Package	FALSE	45688
	TRUE	5629
	Total	51317
Grand Total		153951

Figure 12.18   You control the subtotals by Shipper at the Product Status level.

You can also display totals as column headings instead of row headings from the Report tab of the Commands And Options dialog box. (The Report tab is visible only when the PivotTable list is selected.)

To display totals as row fields instead of column fields, follow these steps:

1. Right-click Sum Of Quantity, and then choose Commands and Options from the pop-up menu to bring up the Commands And Options dialog box.

2. Click the Report tab of the Commands And Options dialog box; and then click the Row Headings button under the Display Totals As option at the top of this dialog box.

3. Click the Close button to close the Commands And Options dialog.

After you have set this option, the totals appear in rows instead of columns, as shown in Figure 12.19.

Shipper	Product Status ▾		
⊟ Federal Shipping	FALSE	Sum of Quantity	45688
	TRUE	Sum of Quantity	5629
	Total	Sum of Quantity	51317
⊟ Speedy Express	FALSE	Sum of Quantity	45688
	TRUE	Sum of Quantity	5629
	Total	Sum of Quantity	51317
⊟ United Package	FALSE	Sum of Quantity	45688
	TRUE	Sum of Quantity	5629
	Total	Sum of Quantity	51317
Grand Total		Sum of Quantity	153951

Figure 12.19   Totals can be displayed in row headings (shown here) rather than as column headings (shown in Figure 12.18).

Showing the Top or Bottom n Values

You can configure the display of the Top *n* or Bottom *n* values from the Filter and Group tab of the Commands and Options dialog box. Alternatively, you can click the Show Top/Bottom Items button. This button provides a drop-down menu where you can choose to show the top or bottom 1, 2, 5, 10, or 25 values or percentages based on a Data value. Selecting Other from the drop-down menu brings up the Commands and Options dialog box where you can type a specific number or percentage for the Top *n* or Bottom *n* group.

If the Top/Bottom *n* filter is applied to an Inner Row field, the filter setting is not repeated for each Outer field, as it is in an Excel PivotTable report. Rather, the filter is applied to the column as a whole. This might be a little confusing, so here's an example to try:

1. Starting with the PivotTable list shown back in Figure 12.5, drag ProductName to the right of CategoryName in the Row area to make it an Inner Row field.

2. Click ProductName to select it (the column becomes highlighted), and then click the Show/Top Bottom Items button and choose Show Only The Top ➪ 2 from the drop-down menu. This causes only the top two products with the highest sum of quantity to be shown.

3. Verify that your PivotTable list now looks like Figure 12.20.

Notice that only the two product names are displayed in the PivotTable list. If you applied this filter in an Excel PivotTable report, the top two product names for each product category would appear.

> **TIP** If you're not sure about how filter settings in a PivotTable list contrast to filter settings in a PivotTable report, click the Export To Microsoft Excel icon to see how this PivotTable list looks as a PivotTable report.

Country ▾				
All				
		Product Status ▾		
		FALSE	Grand Total	
		+|-|	+|-|	
CategoryName ▾	**ProductName** ▽▾	Sum of Quantity	Sum of Quantity	
⊟	Camembert Pierrot	4731	4731	
Dairy Products	Raclette Courdavault	4488	4488	
	Total	9219	9219	
Grand Total		9219	9219	

Figure 12.20 The Top/Bottom *n* values apply only to the selected column and not to each Outer field, as it is with a PivotTable report.

In Figure 12.20, notice that a filter icon is displayed next to ProductName to indicate that a Top/Bottom filter is being applied to that field. Clicking this Filter icon brings up the same drop-down list as the Show/Top Bottom Items button from the second step. It's just that this filter icon applies only to ProductName.

Working with Data Fields

You can drop Data area fields in the Filter, Row, Column, or Detail area of the PivotTable list. These fields are used in much the same way they are used in an Excel PivotTable report. You can use Inner and Outer fields in the Row and Column areas of the PivotTable; filter items in the Row, Column, and Page areas; sort items, and group data. Despite the similarities, however, keep in mind that this is a different type of PivotTable than the one used in Excel. Not only is there a new Detail area, but there are also different procedures for performing functions.

This section reviews some of the differences of how you work with Data fields and describes how many of the functions related to these types of fields are performed. If you plan to follow along in later sections, complete these steps to format the PivotTable list for those examples:

1. Again, starting with the PivotTable list shown in Figure 12.5, drag ProductName from the PivotTable Field List window to the right of CategoryName to make it an Inner Row area field.
2. Drag OrderDate by Month to the Filter area of the PivotTable list.
3. Verify that your PivotTable list looks like Figure 12.21.

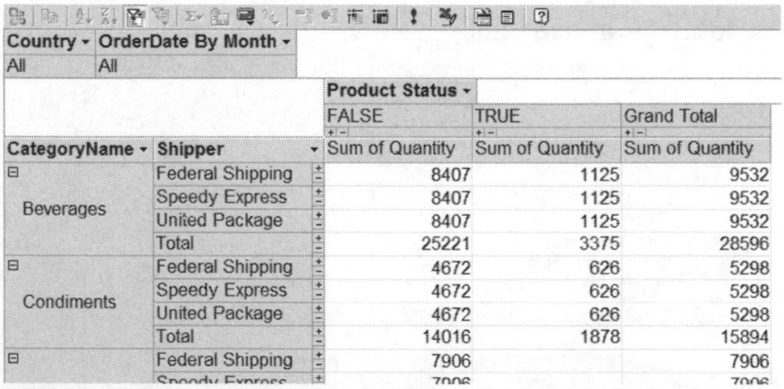

Country: All | OrderDate By Month: All

		Product Status		
		FALSE	TRUE	Grand Total
CategoryName	Shipper	Sum of Quantity	Sum of Quantity	Sum of Quantity
Beverages	Federal Shipping	8407	1125	9532
	Speedy Express	8407	1125	9532
	United Package	8407	1125	9532
	Total	25221	3375	28596
Condiments	Federal Shipping	4672	626	5298
	Speedy Express	4672	626	5298
	United Package	4672	626	5298
	Total	14016	1878	15894
	Federal Shipping	7906		7906

Figure 12.21 Start with this view of the PivotTable list to follow the examples yet to come in this section.

Working with Inner and Outer Fields

If you drag more than one field to a Column or Row field, the field on the right is referred to as an Inner field, while the field on the left is referred to as an Outer field. There can be multiple levels of Inner and Outer fields, a topic covered in depth in Chapter 7. As outlined in that chapter, you should keep the following items in mind when working with Inner and Outer fields:

- Inner fields can be displayed multiple times for each unique value of the Outer field.

- Inner fields are subtotaled for each unique Outer field.

- The default handling is to display only Inner Fields that have a corresponding value for an Outer field

Expanding and Collapsing Items

Notice that there are plus (+) and minus (–) nodes before CateogoryName and after Shipper in Figure 12.21. Clicking the minus (–) node to the left of CategoryName collapses the display of the items in Shipper for that selected category and changes the node to a plus (+). Clicking the plus (+) node expands the values and changes the node to a minus (–). You can also use the right-click pop-up menu or the Expand and Collapse buttons to expand and collapse items.

> **TIP** You can also toggle the display of the Expand Indicator nodes by checking or unchecking the Expand Indictor option in the Behavior tab of the Commands and Options dialog box.

Managing Blank Values

You can opt to show all Inner Row or Inner Column fields, even if there is not a valid combination with an Outer field. Each option is controlled independently through the Always Display Empty Rows and Always Display Empty Columns options in the Report tab of the Commands And Options dialog box shown in Figure 12.22. This tab is visible only when the PivotTable list is selected.

> **TIP** You do not have to close and reopen the Commands And Options dialog box if you launched it from an undesired selected area. Simply click different locations of the PivotTable to display the different tabs of the dialog box.

After the Empty Rows or Empty Columns options are checked, all the Inner items appear, even if there is not a valid combination of the Inner and Outer fields. This can be useful when the combination is expected to take place, but because of latency issues it hasn't happened yet.

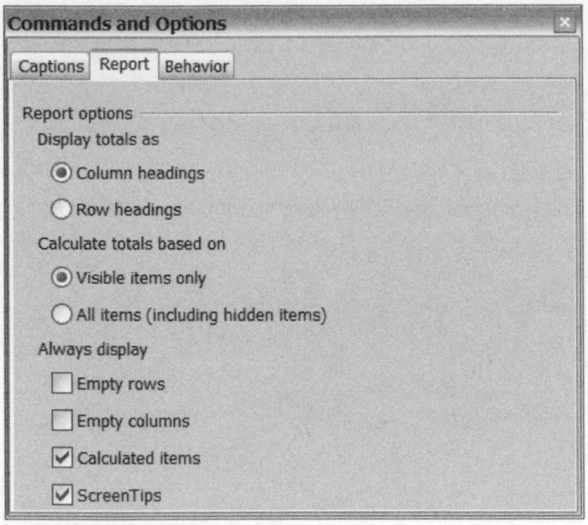

Figure 12.22 The Report tab of the Commands and Options dialog box is visible only when the PivotTable list is selected.

Showing and Hiding the Detail Section

The plus and minus nodes that abut the Data area of the PivotTable list control whether the Detail section is displayed for a particular cell. Unlike the Expand Indictor, you cannot toggle the display of these nodes, even if there are no fields in the Data area of the PivotTable list.

There are three ways to display or show detail in a PivotTable list:

- Use the right-click pop-up menu.
- Use the plus (+) and minus (–) nodes that abut the shared Data/Detail areas of the PivotTable list.
- Use the Hide Detail and Show Detail buttons in the PivotTable list toolbar menu.

WARNING Showing and hiding the Detail area is easy to confuse with Expanding and Collapsing the display of dimensions or Inner fields in the Row and Column areas of a PivotTable list. However, these are separate functions with their own set of pop-up menu items and toolbar icons.

You can choose to display the Detail section for a column, a row, or just a cell in the PivotTable list. To display the Detail section for a column, click the column to select it (or click to select several columns), and then click the plus (+) node or right-click anywhere on the highlighted column and choose Show Detail from the pop-up menu.

You can display the Detail for a single row by clicking the row to select it, and then click the plus (+) node to show the detail. Alternatively, you can right-click anywhere on the highlighted row and choose Show Detail from the pop-up menu. To display the detail for just a particular cell, right-click the cell and choose Show Details from the pop-up menu.

Sorting Data

In the cross-tabular part of the PivotTable list (the Row and Column areas), items are automatically sorted in alphanumeric order. And, as with a PivotTable report, you can sort data in the following ways:

- Ascending alphanumeric sort
- Descending alphanumeric sort
- Based on a value in the Data area
- Custom sort

Sorting in Ascending or Descending Order

You can apply an ascending or a descending sort order to fields in the Row, Column, and Detail areas by first clicking on the field and then clicking the A ⇨ Z or Z ⇨ A button.

Custom Sort Order

You can perform custom sorts in the Column or Row area by simply selecting a field and dragging it to the preferred location in the Column or Row area. The field is ready to be moved when the icon changes from a plus sign to the mouse pointer combined with an arrow that points in four directions.

Grouping Data

You can group items in the Row or Column area into a new field. This function can be useful for grouping particular months into a specific fiscal quarter, sales representatives into a designated territory, or geographic locations into a region. Grouping data can be useful for interactive report analysis, but it may not be a good long-term solution. If these fields are really needed, they usually should be added to the source data.

In order to create a group for the items, highlight the items you want to group, right-click the report, and then choose Group And Show Detail ⇨ Group from the pop-up menu.

Keep in mind that groups do not transfer back to Excel, and they do not appear in the PivotTable field list window. Additionally, if you drag the group off the report, you will permanently lose it.

Exporting Data to Microsoft Excel

You can give report users who access the PivotTable list through the Internet Explorer web browser the capability to download it to Excel as a PivotTable report. In order to perform this task, the user just clicks the Export To Microsoft Excel button on the PivotTable list toolbar menu to transfer the PivotTable list to Excel.

Using the default layout from the "Before You Begin" section of this chapter, complete these steps to transfer the PivotTable list to Excel:

1. Verify that your PivotTable list looks like Figure 12.5, and then click the Export To Excel button to transfer the PivotTable list to Excel.

2. An Excel workbook is created using the convention PivotTable*nnnnn*.HTM and the Query Refresh dialog box appears. You are prompted to click the Enable Automatic Refresh or Disable Automatic Refresh button. Click Enable Automatic Refresh to create the PivotTable report in Excel.

WARNING If you click on Disable Automatic Refresh, the PivotTable report will not be created properly as there is a software bug in the transfer program. You can use the PivotTable Wizard to fix the invalid PivotTable, but it's much easier to just click the Enable Automatic Refresh button.

3. Your PivotTable report should look like Figure 12.1, except that the items in Product Status show True and False, instead of 0 and 1.

NOTE It's interesting that the Product Status shows a True and False instead of a 0 and 1. There isn't any functionality in Excel to convert 0 and 1 to True and False. And there isn't anything in the SQL query, such as a Case statement, to transform the values. Additionally, the query is accessed through the Edit OLE DB Query dialog box instead of the Microsoft Query program, something that cannot be done when the PivotTable report is created in Excel.

You can disable this transfer feature by editing the PivotTable list in Microsoft FrontPage 2003. However, if you are planning to publish numerous Excel reports to the web, this feature can be very useful because users can obtain all their data (even through the use of parameters) and download it back to Excel for analysis.

The tools that convert the PivotTable list to Excel operate similarly to the tools that convert an Excel report to a PivotTable list. This isn't a perfect conversion process for either direction. There are some limitations, and not every object and option setting is handled by these tools. Additionally, keep in mind that there are numerous functions available in a PivotTable list that are simply not available in a PivotTable report. Converting a PivotTable list with functions unsupported by an Excel PivotTable report may result in the data set being copied into a separate tab of the PivotTable report where it is used as the source data for the report (instead of the PivotTable using the embedded data set with the SQL query and DSN connection information).

> **TIP** Depending on your organizational needs and security, you may want to transfer only the data set into a separate worksheet tab, instead of transferring the SQL query, DSN connection information, and embedded data set.

What's Transferred

Here's a brief list of some of the items that are transferred to the Excel PivotTable report:

- Column, Data, Filter, and Row area fields are transferred to the PivotTable report as Column, Data, Page, and Row area fields, respectively.
- Detail area fields (but not as dropped fields in the PivotTable)
- Applied filters in the Column, Row, and Filter areas. (Note that filter settings in the Filter area transfer over as *All* instead of *Multiple Items*, although the filter settings are maintained.)
- Font colors, font styles, and font sizes for field headings and items
- Advanced sorting and Top/Bottom n filter settings
- The underlying SQL query and the DSN connection information

What's Not Transferred

Here's a brief list of some of the items that are not transferred to the Excel PivotTable report:

- Web query connection information — The web query data is transferred, but the connection information is not included in the PivotTable report.
- Parameters — PivotTable reports do not support parameters. The PivotTable report is created with a copy of the dataset in a separate tab of the PivotTable report as the data source.

- Total fields not dropped in the Data area of the PivotTable list
- Dimensional date fields (this is OrderDate by Month and OrderDate by Week for the example in the "Before You Begin" section of this chapter)
- Fields created by grouping items
- Calculated Total and Calculated Detail fields

Formatting the PivotTable List

There are several tools and functions you can use to format a PivotTable list. In this section, I cover the display and formatting settings configured in the Format and Captions tabs of the Commands and Options dialog box. You can bring up this dialog box using any of the following methods:

- Right-click anywhere on the PivotTable list and choose Commands And Options from the pop-up menu.
- Click the Commands and Options button.
- Press the ALT+Enter keys.

The tabs displayed in the Commands And Options dialog box change as you click different areas of the PivotTable list. Keep in mind that you do not have to close the Commands And Options dialog box; you can carry out other activities or click different areas of the PivotTable list while this modeless dialog box remains open.

Numerous functions and options for formatting a PivotTable list are covered in this section. Keep in mind that if these changes are made in the web browser, they are not saved when you close the browser or even when you save the web page from Internet Explorer. This is by design, as one of the benefits of providing the PivotTable lists on the web is that there aren't multiple copies of the PivotTable to maintain. This makes configuration management much easier to handle. Additionally, changes made by one user do not affect another user. Of course, if users do want to save their changes, they can download the PivotTable list to Excel as a PivotTable report.

TIP The PivotTable list can be refreshed to the initial view by clicking in the Address bar of Internet Explorer and pressing Return.

If you want to permanently change the PivotTable list, you must edit the web page in FrontPage 2003. If this program is installed on your computer, you can choose File ➪ Edit With Microsoft Office FrontPage from the Internet

Explorer program menu to open the PivotTable list in the Microsoft FrontPage editor.

Configuring Display Behavior Options

You use the display behavior options to control which objects are displayed in the PivotTable list (expansion indicators, toolbars, and drop areas), how items and details are displayed when Data fields are dropped into the PivotTable list, and how the PivotTable list size can grow or shrink. This section covers the following display behavior options:

- Toggling the display of PivotTable objects
- Setting expansion options
- Limiting the size of the PivotTable list

You configure these options in the Behavior tab of the Commands And Options dialog box. You can bring this dialog box up by right-clicking the PivotTable list (but not on any particular field) and choosing Commands and Options from the pop-up menu. After the dialog box appears, click the Behavior tab to show the dialog box in Figure 12.23.

Toggling the Display of PivotTable Objects

The Hide/Show section of the Behavior tab includes four check boxes for toggling control of the following:

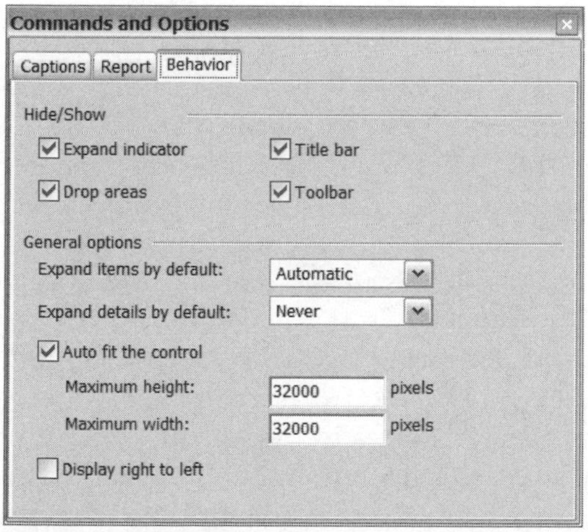

Figure 12.23   You use the Behavior tab to configure display options and default handling features of the PivotTable list.

- **Expand Indicator:** Check this box to display the expansion nodes to the left of Inner fields in the Row And Column area of the PivotTable list.

- **Drop Areas:** Check this box to display the drop zones in the PivotTable list. If this option is unchecked, you can drop fields only in the Detail area and where fields exist in other areas of the PivotTable list.

- **Title Bar:** The default caption display for the Title Bar is PivotTable 1. You can modify the caption (explained later) or you can hide it by unchecking this box.

- **Toolbar:** The PivotTable list toolbar displayed above the PivotTable can be toggled from this option box.

Clicking the Display Right To Left option box at the bottom of the Behavior tab toggles whether the Row and Filter areas appear on the left side (unchecked) or the right side (checked) of the PivotTable area. Checking this option is almost like displaying a mirror image of the PivotTable list, as the objects move from the right to the left, instead of from the left to the right.

Setting Expansion Options

The General Options section of the Behavior tab of the Commands And Options dialog box includes two drop-down fields for controlling the default display of items and details:

- **Expand Items By Default:** Applies to Inner Row and Inner Column fields and controls whether the items are always displayed, never displayed, or displayed automatically by default

- **Expand Details By Default:** Applies to the Detail section and controls whether the Detail area is always displayed, never displayed, or displayed automatically by default

Limiting the Size of the PivotTable List

PivotTable lists automatically fit to the default size of 250 pixels by 500 pixels unless specified to be larger or smaller. To specify a particular size, check the Auto Fit The Control option on the Behavior tab of the Commands And Options dialog box. Here, you can indicate how much larger or smaller you want to make the PivotTable list by specifying the pixel sizes in the Maximum Height and Maximum Width fields. Note that scroll bars are automatically added when a PivotTable list is larger than what can be displayed in the PivotTable window. Additionally, the PivotTable list automatically shrinks to the default size and grows to the maximum specified size as long as the Auto Fit The Control option remains checked.

Formatting and Renaming Captions and Fields

You can rename and format captions and fields in the Captions and Format tabs of the Commands And Options dialog box. On these tabs, you can

- Set caption titles
- Rename field headings
- Format Data and Total fields

Setting Caption Titles

You can set captions for objects in the PivotTable list, field headings, and field-sets (note that a *fieldset* is the top-level of a dimension field). The text used in the drop areas of the PivotTable list (for example, "Drop Filter Fields Here") and the PivotTable title bar comprise the objects where captions can be defined. Field headings include any fields in the PivotTable list. Fieldsets are used only to rename top-level dimension fields. I provide an example of how you do this for OrderDate By Month since it is organized into a hierarchal form.

Setting PivotTable Captions

The PivotTable Captions tab appears when you click the PivotTable list but not on a specific field. Here you can set the captions for the drop area fields and the Title Bar.

To see how to set a PivotTable caption, follow these steps:

1. Starting with the PivotTable list in Figure 12.5, drag Country out of the Filter area of the PivotTable.

2. Right-click the PivotTable list, but not on a specific field, and choose Commands and Options from the pop-up menu to bring up the Commands And Options dialog box.

3. Verify that the Captions tab is displayed and Report Title Bar appears in the Select Caption drop-down list.

4. Type **Category Analysis Report** in the Caption field, and then change the font size from 10 to 14.

5. Select Filter Drop Down area from the Select Caption drop-down list, type **Filter Area** in the Caption field, and click the Bold format.

6. Click the Close box (X) in the top corner of the Commands And Options dialog box to close it.

7. Verify that your PivotTable list looks like Figure 12.24.

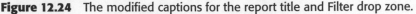

Category Analysis Report

Filter Area

		Product Status ▾		
		FALSE	TRUE	Grand Total
		+|−	+|−	+|−
CategoryName ▾		Sum of Quantity	Sum of Quantity	Sum of Quantity
Beverages	±	25221	3375	28596
Condiments	±	14016	1878	15894
Confections	±	23718		23718
Dairy Products	±	27447		27447

Figure 12.24   The modified captions for the report title and Filter drop zone.

Setting Field Headings and Fieldset Captions

The Captions tab for field headings and fieldsets appear when you click any field heading in the PivotTable list. Here you can set the captions for field headings in the Row, Column, Filter, Detail, and Data areas. You can also apply font style, font color, and font size settings in this tab of the Commands And Options dialog box.

To see how to set field headings and fieldset captions, follow these steps:

1. Starting with the PivotTable list in Figure 12.5, drag OrderDate By Month to the right of Country in the Filter area of the PivotTable.

2. Right-click on OrderDate By Month in the Filter area and choose Commands and Options from the pop-up menu to bring up the Commands And Options dialog box.

3. Click the Captions tab if it is not displayed, choose Fieldset from the Select Caption drop-down field list, and type **Order Date (Month)** in the Captions field. Notice that the field heading has changed in the Filter area and in the PivotTable Field List window.

4. With the Commands And Options dialog box still open, click Category-Name in the Row area to select it.

5. Select Field in the Select Caption drop-down field, and then type **Product Category** in the Caption field. Notice that the field heading has changed in the Row area but not in the PivotTable Field List window.

NOTE If you expand CategoryName in the PivotTable Field List window, you will see Product Category under CategoryName. This option is really intended for OLAP data, where fields can be organized into a dimension-level hierarchy.

6. Click the Close box to close the Commands And Options dialog box.

Formatting Total Fields

The Total fields in the Data area of a PivotTable list are formatted in the Commands and Options dialog box. This dialog box includes tools for formatting the field heading and the data for the field.

In order to change the display format, complete these steps:

1. Right-click the Total field in the Data area and choose Commands And Options from the pop-up menu to bring up the Commands And Options dialog box shown in Figure 12.25.

2. Select a font type, font size, and number format in the Text Format section of the Commands And Options dialog box.

3. Choose a number format in the Number drop-down box.

4. Click the Close box to close the Commands And Options dialog box, apply the formatting changes, and return to the PivotTable list.

Table 12.6 lists the number formats supported in a PivotTable list. Note that the Accounting and Fraction formats available in a PivotTable report are not available in a PivotTable list.

NOTE If you are using Visual Basic programming, you can customize the number object. However, there are no graphical tools to select or customize a format for the PivotTable list menus.

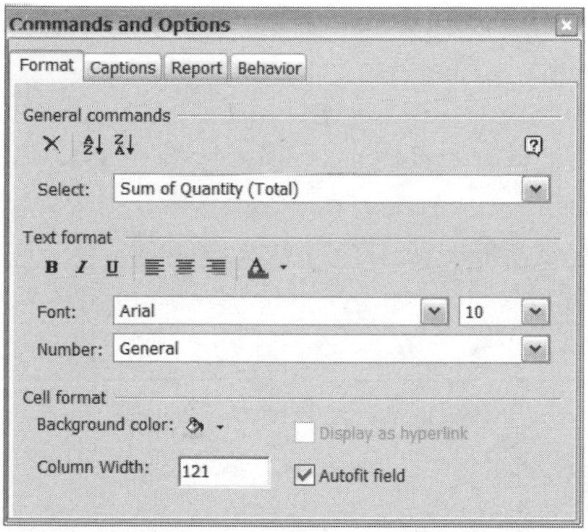

Figure 12.25 You manage the text format, font style, and number format for Data area numbers in the Format tab of the Commands And Options dialog box.

Table 12.6 Available Number Formats for Data Area Numbers

FORMAT	DESCRIPTION
General	Displays numbers without a thousandths separator. If the number is negative, it is preceded by a minus sign. This format can display up to 11 digits, or 10 digits with a decimal point.
General Date	Displays the number as a date. This format can also display the time information (if it is included in the number).
Long Date	Displays the date using the Windows regional setting for the long date format.
Medium Date	Displays the date in the format MMM-DD-YYYY (for example, JUL-15-2005).
Short Date	Displays the date using the Windows regional setting for the short date format.
Long Time	Displays the time using the Windows regional setting for the long time format.
Medium Time	Displays the time in the format HH:MM PM or AM (for example, 12:15 PM).
Short Time	Displays the time using the Windows regional setting for the short time format.
Currency	Displays the number according to the Windows regional setting for currency.
Euro Currency	Displays the number using the Euro currency code (€).
Fixed	Displays the number with two decimal points.
Standard	Displays the number using the Windows regional setting for numbers.
Percent	Displays the number as a percentage. Note that the number is multiplied by 100.
Scientific	Displays the number in exponential notation.
Yes/No	Displays No for 0's and Yes for 1's.
True/False	Displays False for 0's and True for 1's.

Note: The Windows regional settings for date, time, and number formats are configured in the Regional Options tab of the Regional and Language Options dialog box. You can access this dialog box from the Windows Control Panel.

Trying It Out in the Real World

In just a short time, you have been able to impress your colleagues and managers with your skills in developing cutting-edge Excel PivotTable reports. Margaret Peacock has talked to her supervisor, Andrew Fuller, and demanded that you be hired as a consultant, making beaucoup bucks. Andrew fondly remembers hiring you as a financial analyst not that long ago, and he has agreed to provide work for you as a consultant on the company's new web-enabled reporting project.

Andrew has asked that you start by showing them how to convert Margaret's customer report (from Chapter 11) to a web-based PivotTable list. The PivotTable list should look just like the Spreadsheet report and provide the capability for report users to specify parameter values.

Getting Down to Business

Follow these steps to complete this exercise:

1. Start with the Spreadsheet report you created in Chapter 11 or download it from the book's companion web site, and choose File ⇨ Save As Web Page.

ON THE WEB You can download the CH11_rwe.xls Excel spreadsheet report from www.wiley.com/go/excelreporting. **If you choose to download the file from the web site, don't forget to update the DSN connection information. The "Before You Begin" section earlier in this chapter explains how to do this update.**

2. Click the Selection: Sheet button, check the Add Interactivity option, click Change Title to bring up the Set Title dialog box, type **Country Analysis Report** in the Title field, and click OK to add the report title and close the Set Title dialog box.

3. Type **CountryAnalysisReport.htm** in the File Name field, and then click Publish to bring up the Publish As Web Page dialog box.

4. Click Query in the Choose pane, choose PivotTable Functionality from the Add Interactivity With drop-down box, and then click Publish to convert the Spreadsheet report to a web page and to open the web page in the Internet Explorer browser program.

5. Verify that your PivotTable list properly opens.

6. Enter USA for the Param1 field in the Enter Parameters dialog box, and then click OK to continue.

7. Verify that your PivotTable list appears as shown in Figure 12.26.

WATCH THE VIDEO To see how a Spreadsheet report with parameters is converted to a PivotTable list, click the ch1201_video.avi file at www.wiley.com/go/excelreporting to watch the video.

Reviewing What You Did

This example provides you with some additional practice on how to convert an Excel report to a PivotTable list. The "Before You Begin" section of this chapter demonstrated how a PivotTable report could be converted to a PivotTable list. This real-world example increases the level of complexity by using a Spreadsheet report that had only tabular data and included a parameter in the query. This was a relatively straightforward conversion, but it did include some features you might not have seen in a PivotTable list. I recommend that you drag the fields in the Detail area into the Column, Row, and Data areas of the PivotTable to see how this works in a cross-tabular format. After that, try transferring the PivotTable list back to Excel as a PivotTable report and watch what happens.

TIP After you have read over this chapter and completed the real-world example, I recommend that you convert previous Excel reports to PivotTable lists to get an idea of how the report is converted to a web page format and how the various functions, data sources, and features translate from an Excel report to a PivotTable list.

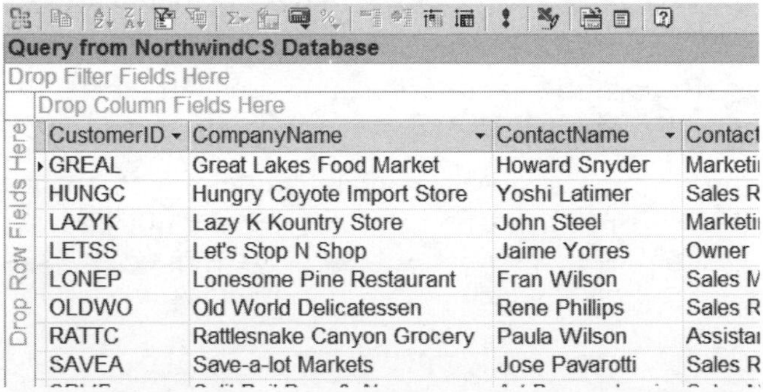

Figure 12.26 If you did everything right, your PivotTable list should look like this.

Chapter Review

This chapter covered PivotTable lists and demonstrated how you can create them from Excel reports. You learned how PivotTable lists are used and how this technology compares to Excel's reporting tools. You were introduced to the basic tools and terminology associated with PivotTable lists, such as the PivotTable list toolbar and Field List window. The chapter also covered PivotTable list functions, including information on how to aggregate and group data, apply filters and sort instructions, and work with the various field types. Finally, you examined some of the formatting features and options available for customizing the display of your PivotTable list.

Closing Thoughts

This is the final chapter of the book. I hope you have found the organization of this book and the real-world examples useful. As you worked through the various chapters in PivotTable reports, Spreadsheet reports, client and server OLAP data cubes, parameter queries, and PivotTable lists, you probably picked up on the importance of understanding SQL programming. This is a key requirement in being able to develop powerful reports because the report is only as good as the data. After you obtain the data, you can decide on what type of report to use and how the data should be accessed: directly from the OLTP database, from a corporate intranet web page, or from an OLAP cube.

In Chapters 2 and 7, you learned that PivotTable reports provide a report shell from which several report views can be created. I recommend using this type of report when the user needs to work interactively with the report and drill down on data. This solution is also ideal when it's hard to nail down the user's requirements, as PivotTables enable the user to customize the layout, summarization, totaling, and formatting of their report.

If the data needs to be represented graphically, consider using a PivotChart report, covered in Chapter 9. If there isn't any numerical data to summarize, or if report data does not fit into a cross-tabular format, consider using the Spreadsheet report solutions covered in Chapter 11. More technology-savvy companies might be interested in publishing their reports to the web, as a PivotTable list. Chapter 12 described how a PivotTable list is probably the most powerful type of report, combining the cross-tabular capabilities of PivotTables with the columnar features of Spreadsheet reports. Moreover, you can even use parameters and web queries for accessing the source data.

And on the topic of source data, keep in mind the options described in Chapter 10. If the data set is very large, you may want to use server- or client-based

OLAP. This storage model works for PivotTable reports, PivotChart reports, and PivotTable lists. Excel even includes tools for taking a slice of a server OLAP cube as an offline data cube file.

As you have discovered throughout this book, Excel reports offer a multitude of options and features. I tried to cover them from my own experience. I wish you the best of luck in your own report development endeavors, and I welcome any comments or suggestions for improvement. Please feel free to send me email at excelreports@earthlink.net.

PART

III

Appendixes

Configuring Your System

This appendix shows you how to configure your Windows operating system to display file extensions for known file types. It also outlines the steps for installing the NorthwindCS database on your SQL Server from the Microsoft Access program. In addition, this appendix discusses the importance of displaying file extensions and provides examples of how to import files into Excel.

I use the NorthwindCS database for examples in this book because it enables users without much SQL programming experience to enter and modify data in a SQL database using the Microsoft Access graphical user interface (GUI). For advanced SQL users, you can still follow along with most of the examples in this book by simply using the Northwind database included in a default installation of SQL Server 2000.

Displaying File Extensions

Displaying file extensions for known file types, such as comma-delimited files with a .csv extension, enables you easily change the file extension from Windows. If you are importing files with a .csv extension into Microsoft Excel, the Import Wizard is skipped. Changing the file extension to .txt or some other extension enables you to specify what columns are imported and assign data types to the imported columns. Chapter 3 provided some examples of how data type mismatches can cause problems, such as rounding or conversion of text data to numeric data.

To display file extensions for known file types, follow these steps:

1. Right-click the Windows Start button and choose Explore to bring up the Windows Explorer program.

2. Choose Tools ➪ Folder Options to bring up the Folder Options dialog box.

3. In the Folders Options dialog box, click the View tab, uncheck the Hide Extensions For Known File Types option, and click OK (see Figure A.1).

With this option set, you can readily modify file extensions for files that are already assigned to an installed program (for example, .xls is assigned to Microsoft Excel and .doc is assigned to Microsoft Word). With this capability, you can change the .csv file extension for comma-delimited files to .txt or some other extension to ensure that the Import Wizard is used when importing the file into Microsoft Excel.

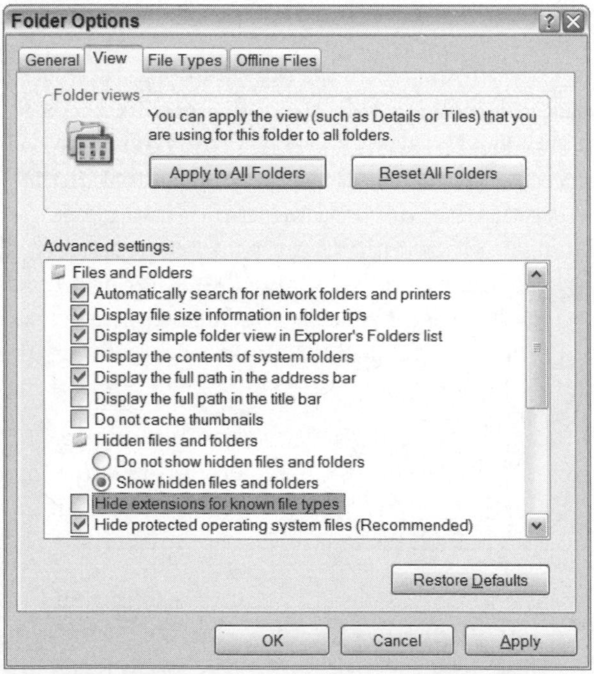

Figure A.1   Uncheck Hide Extensions For Known File Types to display the file extensions for known file types.

Creating the NorthwindCS SQL Database

Many examples in this book reference the NorthwindCS SQL database that is created from Microsoft Access. Although this database uses an Access GUI, the data is actually stored in the NorthwindCS database on an SQL Server. If you are new to SQL programming and you want to modify existing data to see how it works with various types of Excel reports and Excel report options, you can simply change the data right from the Access screen. More advanced users of SQL can simply use the Northwind database to follow along with the examples in this book.

Follow these steps to create the Northwind database:

1. From Access 2003, choose Help ➪ Sample Databases ➪ Northwind Sample Access Project.

2. A dialog box prompting for confirmation appears, as shown in Figure A.2. Click Yes to perform the installation.

3. If the Security Warning dialog box appears, as shown in Figure A.3, click Open to enable the Northwind install program to run. The display of this dialog box appears when the Macro Security level is set to the default level of Medium.

> **NOTE** If the Macro Security level is set to High, the program cannot be opened. You can change the security level from the Security dialog box. Open the Security dialog box by choosing Tools ➪ Macro ➪ Security. On the Security Level tab, click the Medium button.

4. The program attempts to create the NorthwindCS database on your local computer. If you have SQL Server installed on your computer, click Yes, as shown in Figure A.4.

   If you do not have an SQL Server instance installed on your computer, the Data Link Properties dialog box is launched, as shown in Figure A.5. Here, you can specify the SQL Server and login credentials to install the database as a remote SQL server. Check with an experienced SQL database administrator or click Help if you are not familiar with how to configure a connection to the remote server.

Figure A.2   Click Yes to confirm the installation of the SQL Northwind database.

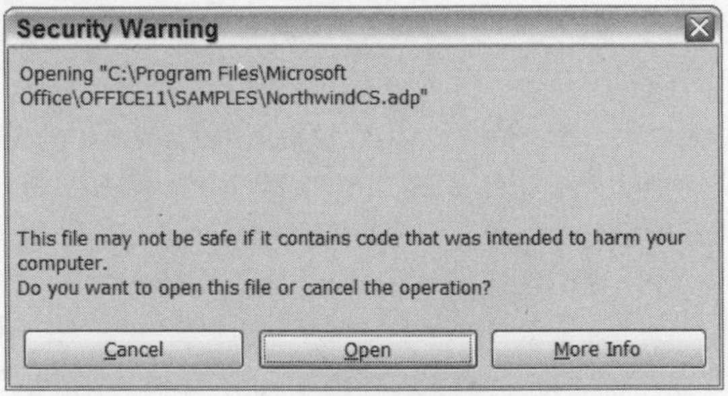

Figure A.3 A Macro Security level of Medium requires user confirmation to open a file. Click Open to run the installation program.

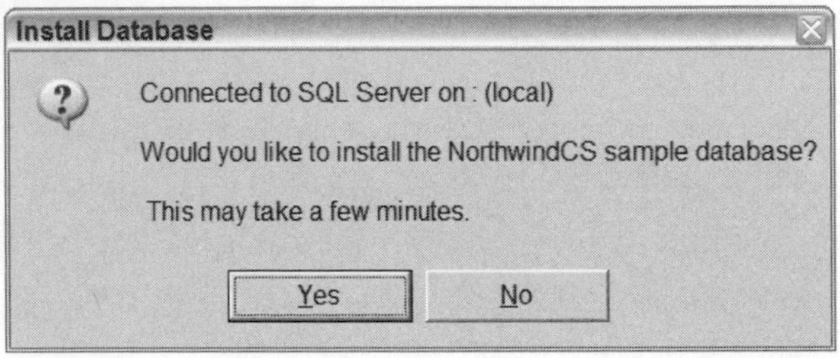

Figure A.4 Click Yes to install the NorthwindCS database on your local computer running SQL Server.

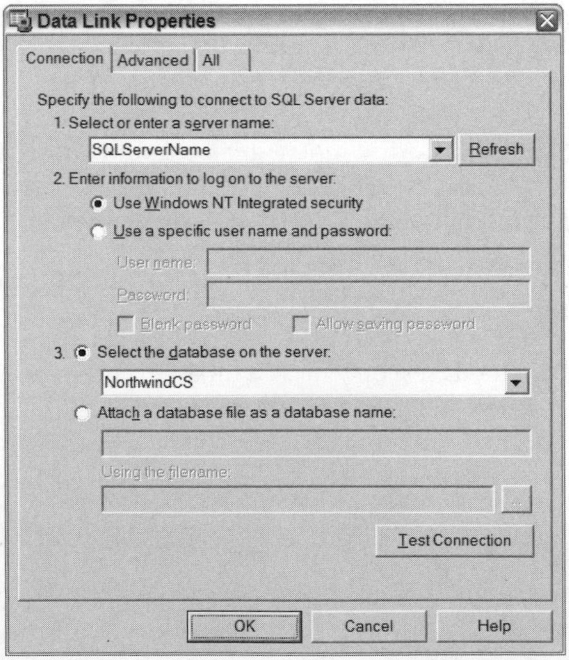

Figure A.5 If you don't have SQL Server installed on your computer, you need to supply the name and login credentials for a remote SQL Server.

5. Click OK to acknowledge the successful installation of the NorthwindCS database, as shown in Figure A.6.

Congratulations! You have successfully installed the NorthwindCS database on an SQL Server. You're now ready to complete the SQL practice exercises throughout this book.

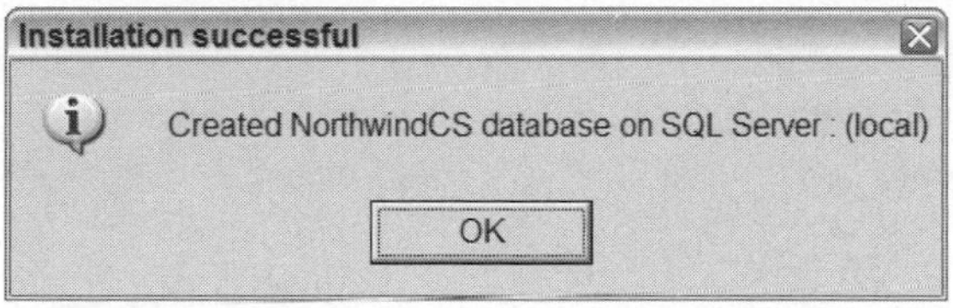

Figure A.6   The last step is to confirm the installation of the NorthwindCS database.

SQL Reference

Understanding how to use SQL is important for developing powerful and innovative reports from external data sources Although there are several functions available in the Microsoft Query program and numerous tools included with Excel's reports, you must hone your SQL programming skills to really take your report development capabilities to the next level. I've included this brief appendix to help get you started. I provide instructions, examples, and guidelines to help you understand and immediately begin using SQL in your Excel reports. It is not meant to be a comprehensive manual, but rather a basic instructional guide and reference.

This appendix starts by outlining how a basic query is structured and shows you the fundamental elements of the Select, From, and Where parts of a query. It also provides an example of a more sophisticated query, breaking apart each section of the query into separate components that are then covered in more detail. Here, string functions, case logic, aggregate functions, table joins, operators, and sorts are all reviewed.

The queries in this appendix, like the queries throughout this book, use the NorthwindCS database and are designed so that you can adjust various lines of the code to see how changes affect the resulting dataset. You can use the information in this appendix, along with the code and examples provided throughout the various chapters, to start writing your own SQL queries.

Dissecting a Basic SQL Query

If you are just learning SQL, it's important that you first learn about the basic structure of a SQL query, as outlined here:

```
SELECT <Column Name>
FROM   <Object Name>
WHERE  <Conditions>
```

You can select one or more fields (also called *columns*) in the Select part of the SQL query. If you are selecting from multiple tables, I recommend that you specify the table name or the table alias before each field. In the From part of the SQL query, the object name is typically a database table name or a database view name. The conditions in the Where statement are used to restrict the number of rows that are returned from the data source.

Working in the Select

If you put in an asterisk (*) after the Select statement, you will pull all the columns from the database table or the database view identified in the From part of the query. If you want only a specific column, type the column name after the Select.

The following query pulls from the NorthwindCS database all the rows from the Shippers table.

```
SELECT * FROM Shippers

ShipperID CompanyName                                    Phone
--------- -------------------------------------- --------------------
1         Speedy Express                          (503) 555-9831
2         United Package                          (503) 555-3199
3         Federal Shipping                        (503) 555-9931
```

In order to select just one field, say ShipperID, use this query:

```
SELECT ShipperID FROM Shippers

ShipperID
-----------
1
2
3
```

If you want to label ShipperID as something different, say ID, add AS [New Name] after the column, like this:

```
SELECT ShipperID AS [ID #] FROM Shippers

ID #
-----------
1
2
3
```

If you want to select multiple columns from the table, just separate each column with a comma, as shown here:

```
SELECT ShipperID AS [ID #], CompanyName AS [COMPANY] FROM Shippers

ID #            COMPANY
-----------     --------------------    --------------------
1               Speedy Express
2               United Package
3               Federal Shipping
```

TIP If you are new to SQL programming, watch out for missing or extra commas after column names. This is one of the most frequent problems that users new to SQL seem to experience.

You can also add text in the SQL query by placing it within single quotation marks (' '). For example, I could further describe the shipping method by adding the text 'Ground', as shown here:

```
SELECT ShipperID    AS [ID #],
       CompanyName AS [COMPANY],
       'Ground'    AS [METHOD]
FROM   Shippers

ID #            COMPANY                                   METHOD
-----------     -------------------------------------     ------
1               Speedy Express                            Ground
2               United Package                            Ground
3               Federal Shipping                          Ground
```

In this example, I labeled the new column as Method, but it could be anything you choose. I also put each field in the query on its own line. The extra lines make the query easier for me to read and understand and should be a help to others who might have to read or adjust it.

Working in the From

A table name or a view name is used after the `From` in an SQL query. In the last section, the table name was Suppliers. If you are selecting from multiple tables, you must assign the table name to any fields that have the same name in the `Select` part of the query. For example, the following query does not work because the database server doesn't know which table to pull SupplierID from:

```
SELECT EmployeeID FROM Employees, Orders

Server: Msg 209, Level 16, State 1, Line 1
Ambiguous column name 'EmployeeID'.
```

If the table name is specified before the field name (in the format `tablename.field name`), the database server is able to run the query because it now knows which table to pull SupplierID from:

```
SELECT Employees.EmployeeID FROM Employees, Orders
```

Of course, putting the table name before each field seems like a lot of work. So you could simply put an alias after the table name and then use that alias before each field name, as shown here:

```
SELECT emp.EmployeeID FROM Employees emp, Orders
```

CROSS-REFERENCE In this example, the tables are Cross joined, producing a Cartesian product from the records of each table. Read Chapter 6 for more information about using table joins.

Working in the Where

The results returned from a query can be restricted by specifying the filter conditions in the `Where` part of an SQL query. For example, to limit the rows returned from the Shippers table to just the records with a ShipperID of 2, simply add that condition to the query as shown here.

```
SELECT * FROM Shippers WHERE ShipperID = 2

ShipperID   CompanyName                                Phone
----------- ------------------------------------------ ------------------
2           United Package                             (503) 555-3199
```

> **NOTE** Filters based on aggregated data must be put in the `Having` part of the SQL query.

Working with More Sophisticated SQL Queries

The basic SQL query described in the preceding section shows you how to extract data from a single database table or database view. However, it does not provide any instruction on how to extract data from multiple database sources, use aggregate functions, program case logic, or incorporate string functions. This section provides a concise reference on these topics that you can use as a guide or a reference.

Dissecting a Sophisticated SQL Query

This section provides an example of a more sophisticated SQL query. I recommend that you retype the query into your SQL development software program to get a better idea of how it works. In order to help you with some of the functions, I break the query apart into more easily understandable components that are covered in detail throughout the remaining sections of this appendix. Here's the query:

```
SELECT UPPER(pro.ProductName)              AS [Product Name],
       CASE
            WHEN pro.Discontinued = '0'
                 THEN 'AVAILABLE'
                 ELSE 'UNAVAILABLE'
                 END                        AS [Status],
         SUM(dtl.Quantity)                  AS [Units Sold]
FROM Products pro
INNER JOIN "Order Details" dtl ON pro.ProductID = dtl.ProductID
WHERE pro.SupplierID IN ('2','10','20')
GROUP BY pro.ProductName,
         pro.Discontinued
HAVING SUM(dtl.Quantity) > 600
ORDER BY 2,3


Product Name                              Status        Units Sold
----------------------------------------- ------------  -----------
GULA MALACCA                              AVAILABLE     601
LOUISIANA FIERY HOT PEPPER SAUCE          AVAILABLE     745
SINGAPOREAN HOKKIEN FRIED MEE             UNAVAILABLE   697
GUARANÁ FANTÁSTICA                        UNAVAILABLE   1125
```

You may not always need to use all the parts listed in this query. However, if you do need to use all of them, you must specify them in this order: `Select`, `From`, `Join`, `Where`, `Group By`, `Having`, and then `Order By`.

You should specify the fields and conditions common to both tables in the `Join` (tables) and `On` (conditions) parts of the query. Although `Join...On` are not required, it is the ANSI programming standard, and I recommend that you follow it.

Specify the conditions that should be used to restrict the rows returned in the `Where` part of the SQL query. If the filter conditions are based on aggregated data, such as a Sum or Count, the conditions must be specified in the `Having` part of the SQL query.

If you are using an Aggregate function, you must include all non-aggregated fields in the `Group By` part of the SQL query. Otherwise, the following error message is produced:

```
Server: Msg 8120, Level 16, State 1, Line 1
Column 'pro.ProductName' is invalid in the select list because it is not
contained in either an aggregate function or the GROUP BY clause.
```

The `Order By` part of the SQL query is used to sort the data. You can either specify the column number or the column name. If you specify a column number instead of a column name, be careful to remember that any change to the field order (left to right) or to the number of fields included in the `Select` part of the SQL query, could impact the `Order By` instructions.

TIP If you are just learning SQL programming, try to start with a basic query that you can understand and successfully execute. After that, introduce only one new step at a time and verify that each new component works before moving to the next. It's much easier to diagnose a problem when you know where it exists in the SQL query. Adding multiple components at one time can quickly lead to confusion and frustration for beginner-level SQL programmers.

Using String Functions

String functions are typically used in the `Select` part of an SQL query to format the results in a particular way. Table B-1 lists some of the String functions available in SQL and the results they produce. You can see how these functions work by replacing the text `UPPER(pro.ProductName)` (used in the query shown earlier in this section) with the function listed in the first column of this table.

Table B-1   String Functions

FUNCTION	RESULT	EXPLANATION
LOWER(ProductName)	ipoh coffee	Displays the field in lowercase
UPPER(ProductName)	IPOH COFFEE	Displays the field in uppercase
LEFT(ProductName,3)	Ipo	Displays the first three positions of the field
RIGHT(ProductName,3)	Fee	Displays the last three positions of the field
SUBSTRING(ProductName,7,3)	Off	Displays three positions of the field, starting at position seven
REVERSE(ProductName)	eeffoC hopI	Displays the field in reverse order
LEN(ProductName)	11	Displays the length of the field
STUFF(ProductName, 2, 3, 'ced')	Iced Coffee	Deletes three positions of the current field, starting at position two, and replaces it with 'ced'
REPLICATE('*',8)	********	Displays eight asterisks
SPACE(8)		Displays eight spaces
LTRIM(Field)		Removes the leading spaces from a field
RTRIM(Field)		Removes the trailing space from a field

You can also combine multiple String functions to achieve a particular format, and use the + operator to concatenate fields and expressions. Here's a query that uses multiple string functions and concatenates fields. Try experimenting with this query and the functions in Table B-1 to get a better idea of how String functions can be used in your own queries:

```
SELECT 'I am ' +
       REVERSE(UPPER('ytsriht')) +
       REPLICATE('!',6) +
       ' I would like 11 ' +
```

```
        STUFF(ProductName, 2, 3, 'ced') +
        's.'                                 AS [MESSAGE]
FROM Products WHERE ProductID = '43'

MESSAGE
--------------------------------------------------
I am THIRSTY!!!!!! I would like 11 Iced Coffees.
```

Using Case Logic

Case logic adds a powerful dimension to your reports. Using this function, you can create new fields and new values in the field name. Here's the Case statement that was used in the SQL query shown earlier in this appendix:

```
CASE
      WHEN pro.Discontinued = '0'
            THEN 'AVAILABLE'
            ELSE 'UNAVAILABLE'
            END                     AS [Status],
```

The logic used in this Case statement was simple enough. I only evaluated whether the Discontinued field was set to 0. If it was, I assigned the value Available. Otherwise, the value was set to Unavailable.

With a Case statement, I have the capability to evaluate multiple conditions, tables, and fields. For example, if the status was not available, I could have chosen to select the supplier name and contact information for the suppliers in the Midwest or the number of units sold for suppliers in the Northeast. The possibilities are only limited by your imagination.

When working with Case logic, it's important for you to keep in mind that the first True condition is always used. Be sure to arrange the order of the When statements with this understanding in mind.

Try experimenting with this query to get a better idea of how Case logic can be used in your own queries.

```
SELECT TitleOfCourtesy + ' ' + LastName              AS [NAME],
      CASE
          WHEN TitleOfCourtesy = 'Mrs.' THEN 'Female'
          WHEN TitleOfCourtesy = 'Ms.'  THEN 'Female'
          WHEN TitleOfCourtesy = 'Mr.'  THEN 'Male'
                                        ELSE 'Unknown'
                                        END            AS [GENDER]
FROM Employees
```

```
NAME                                              GENDER
------------------------------------------------- -------
Ms. Davolio                                       Female
Dr. Fuller                                        Unknown
Ms. Leverling                                     Female
Mrs. Peacock                                      Female
Mr. Buchanan                                      Male
Mr. Suyama                                        Male
Mr. King                                          Male
Ms. Callahan                                      Female
Ms. Dodsworth                                     Female
```

In this example, I created a new field called Gender and used multiple When statements to determine whether employees were male or female. The Case logic was not written well, as there were unnecessary lines and I was not able to identify the gender for one employee. Here's another example that is more suitable for the NorthwindCS database:

```
SELECT TitleOfCourtesy + ' ' + LastName                     AS [NAME],
       CASE
          WHEN TitleOfCourtesy
               IN ('Miss.','Ms.','Mrs.') THEN 'Female'
          WHEN TitleOfCourtesy
               = 'Mr.'                    THEN 'Male'
          WHEN Notes
             LIKE '%his%'                 THEN 'Male'
          WHEN Notes
             LIKE '%her%'                 THEN 'Female'

                                          ELSE 'Unknown'
                                                       END AS [GENDER]
FROM Employees
```

Notice that I first tested on TitleOfCourtesy. If the query encounters a gender-neutral title, it searches the Notes field to see if a reference to "his" or "her" can be found to identify the employee's gender.

Using Aggregate Functions

Aggregate functions compute a single value result for a particular column (or columns). In the query used earlier in this section, I summed the quantity of units sold as shown here.

```
    SUM(dtl.Quantity) AS [Units Sold]
```

If you decide to use an aggregate function in your query, keep the following items in mind:

■ All non-aggregated fields must be included in a `Group By` statement of the SQL query.

■ If filters are based on aggregated data, the filter must be specified in the `Having` part of the SQL query, not the `Where` part.

In this example, there were two non-aggregated fields in the SQL query, so I had to include them both in the `Group By` statement as shown here:

```
GROUP BY pro.ProductName,
         pro.Discontinued
```

In order to filter the dataset to only the rows with a total quantity sold greater than 600, I specified the criteria in the `Having` part of the SQL query, as shown here:

```
SHAVING SUM(dtl.Quantity) > 600
```

Try modifying the query by placing the filter instructions in the `Where` part of the SQL query. The query still runs, but the quantity is evaluated *before* the data is aggregated (`Where` clause), giving you much different results than it does when the quantity is evaluated *after* the data is aggregated (`Having` clause).

Joining Tables

Tables are joined to one another using fields or conditions common to both tables. If you are just beginning to learn SQL programming, I recommend that you start with the Microsoft Query program to join tables because this is one of the most difficult topics for beginner-level SQL users to understand. You can use the program's graphical tools to build the table joins while the SQL query with the table joins are automatically created in the background.

NOTE Microsoft Query does not create the table joins using the ANSI standard, it applies its own style (explained in Chapter 6). However, it does work, and you can use it as a template or starting point for your SQL query.

There are several types of table joins that are available. Read Chapter 6 for more information about the meaning of each type of table join and the effect each one has on the resulting dataset.

In the query shown earlier, I created an Inner join between the Products table and the Order Details table using the ProductID field that is common to both tables, as shown here:

```
FROM Products pro
INNER JOIN "Order Details" dtl ON pro.ProductID = dtl.ProductID
```

It does not matter if you use pro.ProductID = dtl.ProductID or dtl.ProductID = pro.ProductID in the ON part of the Join. However, I do recommend that you be consistent in whatever method you decide to use. Also, keep in mind that the field names do not necessarily have to be the same on each table, and that you might have to specify multiple conditions for the join to work properly.

Using Operators

Several operators are available for you to use in the Where or Having parts of your SQL query to filter data. This section covers the ones you are most likely to use, including the following:

- Mathematical operators
- Comparison operators
- Logical operators

You can read the SQL Books Online (accessed from the Query Analyzer program by choosing Help ➪ Transact SQL Help) if you need more information or examples for other available operators.

Mathematical Operators

Table B-2 provides a list of the mathematical operators. These operators perform mathematical functions on numeric data and are typically used in the Select part of the SQL query to compute some type of value, or in the Where or Having parts to build an appropriate filter.

Table B-2 SQL Mathematical Operators

SQL OPERATOR	EXPLANATION
+	For addition
–	For subtraction
*	For multiplication
/	For division
%	For a modulus (remainder value)

Comparison Operators

Table B-3 provides a list of the comparison operators. You use these operators in the Where or Having parts of a SQL query to filter data.

TIP You can use the operators in Table B-2 only to evaluate a single condition. You cannot use these operators to evaluate multiple values like you can with a logical operator, such as IN.

Logical Operators

Logical operators evaluate whether a particular condition is true. Some logical operators such as IN and NOT IN are not limited to a single value, as comparison operators are. In the Where part of the SQL query shown earlier, I used the logical operator IN to select the products with a SupplierID of 2, 10, or 20, as shown here:

```
WHERE pro.SupplierID IN ('2','10','20')
```

You cannot use a comparison operator for multiple values. In other words, the following query does not work because multiple values are attempting to be evaluated:

```
WHERE pro.SupplierID = ('2','10','20')

Server: Msg 102, Level 15, State 1, Line 10
Incorrect syntax near ','.
```

Table B-3 SQL Comparison Operators

SQL OPERATOR	EXPLANATION
=	Equals the specified value
<>, !=	Does not equal the specified value
>	Is greater than the specified value
>=	Is greater than or equal to the specified value
<	Is less than the specified value
<=	Is less than or equal to the specified value
!>	Is not greater than the specified value
!<	Is not less than the specified value

Table B-4 provides a list of logical operators that you can use in the Where or Having parts of your SQL query. Keep in mind that any of these operators accept a preceding NOT to reverse the specified conditions (for example, NOT IN or NOT LIKE).

Sorting the Result Set

You can sort one or more columns of the result set by specifying the column name or column number reference in the Order By part of the SQL query. By the column number, I mean the order in which it appears in the Select part of the SQL query. For example, in the Order By part of the SQL query shown earlier, I used the column numbers 2, and then 3, as shown here:

```
ORDER BY 2,3
```

If you decide to use the column number, instead of the column name, keep a close eye on the Order By statement whenever fields are ever added, moved, or rearranged in the query. Inserting a new field between Product Name and Status requires that you adjust the Order By to maintain the original sort order. Alternatively, if field names are used instead of field numbers, you no longer have to remain concerned if fields are added or removed. This is what the Order By statement looks like with column names instead of column numbers:

```
ORDER BY pro.Discontinued, SUM(dtl.Quantity)
```

Table B-4 SQL Logical Operators

SQL OPERATOR	EXPLANATION	EXAMPLE
IN	Contains one of the specified values.	IN ('A','B','C')
LIKE	Used in conjunction with the % wildcard to evaluate whether a text string starts, contains or ends with the specified text.	Starts with an A: LIKE 'A%' Contains the text Red: LIKE '%RED%' Ends with the text eld: LIKE '%eld'
BETWEEN	Between two values.	BETWEEN 10 and 20
NULL	Has a null value. Fields with a data type of Datetime either have a specific date or a null value.	IS NULL

An ascending or descending sort order can also be specified after the field name. If no sort order is specified, the database server assumes an ascending sort order. Here's the `Order By` statement with a descending sort on Quantity and an ascending sort order on Discontinued.

```
ORDER BY pro.Discontinued ASC, SUM(dtl.Quantity) DESC
```

Appendix Review

This appendix covered the basics of SQL programming. It started with a review of the basic query structure (`Select`, `From` and `Where`). After that, I showed you a more sophisticated SQL query and reviewed each part in detail. Keep in mind that this appendix was meant only as a reference or starting point for readers new to SQL programming. As you know if you have some experience with SQL, there are often several ways to accomplish a particular task, and there are many more advanced topics that I simply could not cover in these few pages. Nonetheless, I hope you found this appendix a useful reference and that it inspires you to learn more about SQL.

Index

Index